The English Seaside Resort: A Social History 1750-1914

The English Seaside Resort
A Social History 1750-1914

John K. Walton

Leicester University Press 1983
St Martin's Press, New York

First published in 1983 by Leicester University Press
First published in the United States of America
by St. Martin's Press, Inc.
For information write: St. Martin's Press Inc.,
175 Fifth Avenue, New York, N.Y. 10010

Designed by Douglas Martin
Text set in 10/11 pt Linotron 202 Garamond, printed and bound
in Great Britain at The Pitman Press, Bath

British Library Cataloguing in Publication Data
Walton, John K.
The English seaside resort.
1. Seaside resorts – England – History – 18th century
2. Seaside resorts – England – History – 19th century
3. Seaside resorts – England – History – 20th century
4. England – Social life and customs – 18th century
5. England – Social life and customs – 19th century
6. England – Social life and customs – 20th century
I. Title
942   DA665
ISBN 0–7185–1217–0

Library of Congress Cataloging in Publication Data
Walton, John K.
The English seaside resort.
Includes index.
1. Seaside resorts – England – History.   2. Seaside
resorts – England – Social aspects.   I. Title.
DA665.W34   1983   306′.0942   82-23121
ISBN 0-312-25527-6 (St. Martin's Press)

Contents

List of tables

List of illustrations

Preface

This book has been in the making since 1971, and it is a great pleasure to be able to thank the large number of people and institutions who have helped it on its way. Harold Perkin and John Marshall helped to put the show on the road when my research began as a University of Lancaster Ph.D. thesis, and my colleagues in Lancaster's excellent Department of History have provided endless stimulation. Mike Winstanley's help on all fronts has been especially valuable, as has Bob Bliss' bottomless coffee jar. The contribution of my postgraduate students will be apparent from a glance at the notes. Graham Rogers and John Liddle forced me to think through and reconsider my ideas about the rôle of large landowners in resort development, and Robert Poole's sharp critical intelligence has been a beneficial influence on my writing for several years, to a greater extent than he probably suspects. The University of Lancaster M.A. degree in Modern Social History has made its contribution through seminar discussions and research dissertations, and many undergraduates have helped to crystallize and redefine my interpretations by asking awkward questions and supplying unexpected answers. A full list would be intolerably long, but special thanks go to Cliff O'Neill, Brian Jones, John Easton, Bruce Hanson, Isabel Thompson, Lynne Crockett, Lyn Murfin and Su Lowy. Apart from providing a stimulating environment for teaching and research, the University of Lancaster also supplied a staff research grant to help with the final stages of the research, and two terms' study leave during which most of the writing was done. Lancaster has been good to me.

Outside Lancaster, the most important influence was the late Professor Dyos, who first urged me to break out from my original bridgehead in Blackpool and to try to survey the whole range of seaside activity in a single work. As usual, he was right, although it took him a year or two to convince me. Peter Boulton of Leicester University Press bore with my vacillations patiently. Many colleagues have kindly provided typescripts of work in progress or in advance of publication: John Liddle, Graham Rogers, Richard Roberts, Doug Reid, Sue Farrant and John Whyman have all been conspicuously generous in this respect. John Travis of the University of Exeter and the excellent Seawood Hotel, Lynton, put me on to the useful cache of manuscript material in the Public Record Office series MT.10; and I have incurred many similar academic debts, too numerous to mention here. Periods of exile in London have been made easier for me (as a dedicated provincial with an ingrained distrust of the metropolis) by the hospitality of friends, especially Michael and Pat Mulcay and Paul McGloin. The Public Record Office at Kew has been a haven of friendliness and efficiency, against all the odds, since its opening, and the House of Lords Record Office has also been a particularly congenial place in which to work.

I owe most of all to my family. My parents and in-laws have always been supportive and interested, and my wife has tolerated peculiar working hours and long absences with stoicism and understanding. The book is dedicated to her; but I must not forget to mention Helen and Samantha, who arrived on the scene just in time to enliven and disrupt the writing of the last few chapters.

None of these people (least of all Helen and Samantha) deserve to be blamed for any shortcomings in this book. They remain, in the conventional phrase, the sole responsibility of the author.

Lancaster, 23 March 1982.

For Bernice, who was there at the beginning, and stayed

1 The seaside and the historians

The rise of the seaside holiday industry sometimes receives a passing mention in textbooks on British history in the nineteenth and twentieth centuries. Often these references are wildly inaccurate, and invariably they fail to do justice to the importance of the subject.[1] By 1881 the aggregate population of 106 seaside resorts in England and Wales was about one million, and by 1911, 145 resorts accounted for over 1.6 million people, nearly 4½ per cent of the national total.[2] These figures omit many of the smallest resorts; but more to the point, they take no account of the wider influence of the seaside on the population at large. Resort populations were highly volatile, with rapid growth in many places fuelled by net in-migration rather than natural increase; and population turnover could also be very swift, with high levels of out-migration to set against the inward flows.[3] A Lancashire example provides a good illustration of the drawing power of the seaside in late Victorian and Edwardian times. At the 1911 census over 5 per cent of all those who had been born in Blackburn and had since migrated elsewhere, were enumerated in Blackpool and Southport. For Burnley the figure was nearly 5 per cent, for Rochdale over 4 per cent, and even for Manchester over 3 per cent.[4] If we added in the other leading resorts, especially in northern England, these figures would be still more impressive; but they account for only a small proportion of those who experienced seaside residence at some stage of the life cycle, especially in the middle and later years; for the census offers only a one-off snapshot of population composition. If we were able to reconstruct the life-histories of our Blackburn migrants, the proportion experiencing a period of residence in Blackpool or Southport would be multiplied severalfold. The seasonal comings and goings of entertainers, hawkers, servants and even lodging-house keepers increased the volatility of resort populations still further, for the early spring censuses of 1851–1911 can take no account of the numerous temporary residents who were regularly drawn in by the opportunities offered by the summer season.[5]

Lancashire was a special case; but a very substantial minority of late Victorians and Edwardians, and in some areas perhaps even a majority, experienced residence in a seaside resort at some time in their lives. On top of this, of course, there were the holidaymakers and seasonal migrant workers, some of whom stayed for several weeks or even months at a time. By the early nineteenth century a summer or early autumn seaside visit was almost *de rigueur* for the aristocracy and gentry, and for affluent merchants, professional men, manufacturers and even farmers, with their families and servants. Already, too, shorter visits were becoming commonplace among the better-off London tradesmen, and by the 1850s the annual seaside holiday was spreading through the growing ranks of shopkeepers and white-collar workers. The last quarter of the nineteenth century saw the holiday habit spread to the better-off skilled workers, and in some parts of the country, especially the Lancashire textile district, it had become almost universal by the turn of the century.[6] By this time, of course, the seaside day-trip had long been familiar to most industrial workers, if only as an occasional adventure under the patronage of employers or voluntary organizations.

The sheer scale of seaside resort growth and popularity, especially after 1850, could hardly fail to have important and revealing causes and consequences; but few historians have paid much attention to them. There are two main exceptions. Pimlott's splendid pioneering work, *The English-man's Holiday*, written by a busy and successful civil servant in his spare time and still remarkable for its wide coverage in time and space and its anticipation of many of the concerns of subsequent economic and social historians, is still the best general work on the seaside, while James Walvin's *Beside the Seaside* provides a follow-up study which uses the general historiographical advances of the intervening thirty years, but otherwise breaks little new ground.[7] The other general books on the history of the seaside are journalistic in tone and of little scholarly merit.[8] Pimlott and Walvin concentrate on the nature and causes of changing holiday patterns, and say very little about their possible implications for the wider economy and society; this may help to explain the limited extent to which their findings on the seaside have been fed back into the mainstream of historical discussion.

Local case studies have proliferated since Pimlott's time, especially in thesis form. Most of the earlier works were contributions to the descriptive school of historical geography which flourished particularly strongly in the 1950s. They concentrated on urban form, spatial relationships, settlement patterns and morphology, and their themes were pulled together in a general survey and taxonomy of resorts by J. A. Barrett in 1958.[9] Of the local studies, Gilbert's work on Brighton was the most ambitious and has remained the best-known, ranging as it does beyond the narrower concerns of historical geography to attempt a full-scale urban biography.[10] The historical geographers have been particularly concerned with the influence of transport, landownership and estate development policy, and in these respects they have contributed significantly to our understanding of the evolution of the seaside resort.[11]

At the level of the individual town or holiday region, social and economic historians have also tended to approach the seaside resort through transport innovation, landownership and building patterns. This need not impose an unduly restrictive angle of vision, as is shown by Cannadine's work on the Devonshire estate and Eastbourne, or by Perkin's attempt to explain the differences between the seaside resorts of the Lancashire coast; but I shall suggest that it has given undue emphasis to these admittedly important formative influences on resort development.[12] A balanced account will have to pay just as much attention to patterns of demand and investment, the provision of entertainment, the rôle of local government and the maintenance of public order. Moreover, the social structure of the seaside holiday town itself has yet to be properly investigated.[13]

This book is an attempt to repair some of the deficiencies in the historiography of the seaside. I have tried to analyse the whole range of forces at work on the rise of the English seaside holiday habit, and to elucidate the relationship between the seaside holiday and urban development. I shall begin by describing and explaining the all-important changes in demand which fuelled the rapid rise of the resorts, and by examining the pace and pattern of resort growth, and the peculiarities and problems of seaside social structure. I shall then try to explain the wide variety of resort experiences in terms of several key influences on growth and 'social tone', especially landownership, local government and entertainment provision. In the penultimate chapter, I shall argue that the Victorian and Edwardian seaside resort was important not only as a repository for investment, consumer spending and social emulation, but also as a crucible of conflict between classes and lifestyles, as wealthy and status-conscious visitors and residents competed with plebeian locals and roistering excursionists for access to and enjoyment of amenities. The seaside brought mutually incompatible modes of recreation and enjoyment into close proximity in ways which seldom happened inland, and gave an added edge to the perennial Victorian debate about the proper relationship between leisure, class, religion and morality.

Some aspects of these themes will be covered in greater depth than others. The analysis depends heavily on case-studies of certain selected resorts, and I am grateful to the authors of the many unpublished theses whose work I have quarried for information, as well as conducting my own research in primary sources. Even so, some important topics have had to remain underdeveloped for want of accessible material. The building industry, religion and education are obvious, if disparate, cases in point. This book will certainly not be the last word on the seaside; indeed, I suspect that it will raise at least as many questions as it answers. But I hope that it will at least draw attention to the importance of the subject, and bring it into the mainstream of the rising tide of research into the economic, social and indeed political history of this period.

The final chapter is especially relevant here. Various contemporaries and historians have drawn stray conclusions about particular aspects of the wider significance of the rise of the seaside; but no-one has ever attempted to assess the impact of the seaside holiday and the seaside resort on English society as a whole. The flight of capital to the seaside, as well as overseas, has been seen as a contributor to the allegedly low rates of investment and return in British industry in the late nineteenth century; and seaside residence added its genteel allure to the forces attracting businessmen away from full identification with and involvement in the industries in which their money was made.[14] The impact of resort development on the building cycle has been examined, as have the implications of resort promotion for the finances of aristocratic landowners.[15] Resort local authorities have been displayed at the forefront of innovation in the extension of municipal activity, and resort entrepreneurs were in the vanguard of the mid- and late-Victorian commercialization of leisure.[16] The seaside has been seen as an influence for public order and social stability, as the popular resorts and their amenities provided counter-attractions which lured the working classes away from the pub, the beerhouse and the racecourse. It might even be argued that the seaside holiday took its place in late Victorian and Edwardian times among a glittering if sometimes tawdry array of new consumer goods and services which distracted the masses from the reality of their economic exploitation and political subservience. Social mixing at the resorts generated conflict between the classes, but contemporaries thought that it also encouraged the diffusion of more 'civilized' and 'refined' modes of behaviour, and awakened the sensibilities of working-class visitors to an appreciation of the desirability of beautiful and orderly surroundings.[17] These and other possible implications of the rise of the seaside need to be tackled directly, and in the concluding chapter I shall look at the significance of the seaside for the general development of English society over this long period of rapid and accelerating change. The conclusions will inevitably be tentative, but at least this final chapter will pull together some of the fragments and show that the importance of the seaside was more than just a matter of ephemeral amusement and placid retirement. Seaside resorts, with their notorious preponderance of elderly spinsters and small businesses, have not been attractive hunting-grounds for a generation of social historians weaned on the study of working-class structure, consciousness and organization; but the growing interest in the lower middle class is one of several pointers which suggest that the time is ripe for an extension of the field of vision.[18] If we are to understand the processes of change in English society, we must try to study it as a whole; and if we are to study the history of English towns, we must try to find ways of generalizing about them. A study encompassing all classes, and covering a distinctive and important 'family' of English towns, can hardly fail to make a contribution to our understanding of the general processes of urban development and social change.

2 The demand for seaside holidays

Seaside resorts, like the spas before them, owed their initial expansion to the demand for accommodation and services generated by transitory seekers after health and pleasure in a congenial setting. The residential element in resort economies, in the form of business commuters and people of independent means, was growing significantly in many places from an early stage, as we shall see; but even at the end of the nineteenth century, most seaside resorts still owed their continuing growth mainly to the needs of a visiting public which was still rapidly increasing in numbers and spending power. As the seaside holiday habit percolated downwards through the increasingly complex social strata of the first industrial nation, moreover, its changing manifestations came to influence the development of individual resorts in varying and often divergent ways, as the holiday expectations of a widening range of social and cultural groupings sought expression and satisfaction in styles which were not always mutually compatible. Resorts often had to come to terms with competing claims for access to and use of their amenities, and although leading citizens and local government institutions were usually able to exert a considerable and sometimes a controlling influence on the evolution of the character of their resort, the range of policies open to them was limited by the developing pattern of demand in the areas from which the visitors were drawn. We shall explore these themes more thoroughly in subsequent chapters; what matters for present purposes is that the changing structure of demand for seaside holidays was an essential influence not only on the growth-rate of resorts, but also on their social characteristics. The pattern and style of resort growth was in large part determined by the number of holidaymakers and by their social background and cultural expectations. To understand the evolution of the English seaside holiday town, we must first try to come to terms with the changes which took place in the visiting public over time, and with the significant variations in the generation of demand which emerged in resort hinterlands with differing economies, social structures and holiday traditions. Even when the affluent residential or less-affluent retired or white-collar sectors of resort economies came to the fore in some areas by the later nineteenth century, their development was strongly influenced by the pre-existing reputations of resorts as holiday centres; and this reinforces the obligation to begin an examination of change and growth in the English seaside holiday town with an analysis of the visiting public.

The fashion for sea-bathing grew up among the aristocracy and gentry during the middle years of the eighteenth century. The early development of the seaside resort formed part of a pattern of increasing conspicuous consumption and competitive display which was already becoming apparent in the later seventeenth century. By this time the provincial capitals and county towns, which brought together gentry from a wide area on legal and administrative business, were beginning to follow London's established example in offering entertainment, services and luxury consumer goods to persons of rank and leisure.[1] The pursuit of health and enjoyment were becoming ends in themselves, and it was during the century after 1660 that the spa towns, and especially Bath, became firmly established as highly-specialized centres providing accommodation and commercialized recreations for polite society.[2] This was also the period in which increasing wealth among the upper ranks of society began to express itself in a wide range of educational, cultural and sporting interests.[3] Nor was this activity confined to the leading lights of landed society. The middle ranks of merchants and professional men continued to grow rapidly in numbers and wealth during this period, and their assimilation into polite society was often made easier by existing blood relationships with landed families.[4] Professional men, broadly defined, may have increased their numbers by 70 per cent to as many as 60,000 between 1680 and 1730, and this period saw the emergence of the half-pay army officer and the superannuated civil servant, important groups for resort growth.[5] But the fashion cycle was already making its influence felt lower down the social scale than this, even in the provinces, as aspiring craftsmen and tradesmen jockeyed for position with prospering substantial farmers; and in the relative anonymity of a large or cosmopolitan urban setting, the pressure to express status tangibly in ostentation and display became particularly strong.[6] Under these circumstances, the social graces and accomplishments which came with the right kind of upbringing became especially valuable; but as the leisure towns developed into marriage markets, strong motives remained for social mixing, under controlled conditions, between old families and the newly wealthy.[7]

The widening ripples of prosperity in the relatively open English society of the first half of the eighteenth century ensured that the most fashionable of the spas soon came to attract an occupationally heterogeneous visiting public. Already in the later seventeenth century Bath and Tunbridge Wells were being frequented by merchants, tradesmen and professional men, especially from London.[8] In practice, however, the high charges for travel, accommodation and entertainment acted as an efficient social filter well into the eighteenth century. At a time when high premiums were levied on aspiring entrants into the most lucrative trades and professions, and abrasively rapid advancement from obscurity to prosperity was still unusual, most visitors even to Bath, with its national catchment area, could be presumed to share a consensus of expectation about the proper modes of public behaviour, whether they came from the aristocracy, the gentry or those groups within the middle ranks whose members were closely connected to landed society by birth, upbringing and lifestyle.[9] By the second quarter of the eighteenth century, the spas could be perceived as socially neutral ground, as behaviour was firmly regulated by a Master of Ceremonies whose task was to maintain harmony among the company by insisting on the observance of due public formality, civility and order. In practice, his strictures were probably most in demand to regulate gambling and banish prostitutes, to curb excesses of aristocratic *hauteur* or to detach the more bucolic of the squires from their riding-boots and dogs, at least on ceremonial occasions, rather than to put down the pretensions of a small minority of *nouveaux riches*; but in any case the rule of the Master of Ceremonies depended on the existence of a consensus among the visitors about what constituted proper behaviour.[10] This perception of a common culture uniting the company, in spite of considerable inequalities of wealth, was no doubt strengthened by the spread of metropolitan manners and attitudes through the provinces after the Restoration, as travel became easier, private schools and itinerant teachers of dancing and deportment proliferated, and the publishing and engraving industries developed.[11]

It was not until the later eighteenth century that this consensus came to be undermined at Bath by an influx of less-polished middle-class visitors, all too obviously drawn from the *nouveaux riches*. They were lampooned by Smollett and others, and their advent presaged the decline of the fashionable season.[12] Visitor numbers probably continued to increase into the nineteenth century, but the office of Master of Ceremonies lost its significance as the visiting public broke up into private parties, and by the early nineteenth century, as the residential function began to predominate over the visiting season and the pursuit of health reasserted itself at the expense of pleasure and diversion, Bath could be described as 'a sort of great convent . . . peopled by superannuated celibates of both sexes, but especially women.'[13] Tunbridge Wells underwent a similar evolution, with an invasion of retired planters and East India Company men, half-pay officers, tradesmen and manufacturers threatening the solidarity of the more genteel company, and an eventual shift to a predominance of aged visitors and retired residents.[14] The old clientèle of the most fashionable spas was increasingly being lured away to the seaside and, in peacetime at least, the continental watering-places, although new centres of fashion at Cheltenham and Leamington enjoyed a brief spell of élite popularity in the 1820s and 1830s before following, over a much shorter period, the same evolutionary process as their predecessors. Significantly, however, Cheltenham in particular took special pains to retain its aristocratic exclusiveness in the 1820s and after.[15]

Long before the invasion of Bath and Tunbridge Wells by the *parvenu* middle class which began to grow in numbers, disposable wealth and self-confidence during the second half of the eighteenth century, the spa habit had spread to the less polished of the gentry and urban middle ranks, and even to the more prosperous farmers, as London and the provinces spawned more accessible and less pretentious spas of their own. Epsom was already catering mainly for London businessmen in the later seventeenth century, and Pepys remarked on the presence of people who 'are there (almost) without knowing what to do, but only in the morning to drink waters.'[16] The company at weekends was particularly mixed, and drew the censure of Celia Fiennes for the prevailing 'noise, vulgarity and loose morals'; and the many spas closer to London were 'principally places of evening or week-end resort.' Their place in the social scale was expressed tersely by Defoe in 1724: 'As the Nobility and Gentry go to *Tunsbridge*, the Merchants and Rich Citizens to *Epsome*; so the Common People go chiefly to *Dullwich* and *Stretham*.'[17] These London spas were already proving vulnerable to the rapid shifts of popular fashion by the mid-eighteenth century.

The provinces developed their own hierarchy of spas. At the top, catering for mainly northern gentry and a sprinkling of aristocrats without quite aspiring to the opulent cosmopolitanism of Bath or Tunbridge Wells, came Scarborough, Harrogate and perhaps Buxton, although the last of these was much the smallest of the three. Each was already flourishing by the later seventeenth century, and Scarborough by 1705 was said to attract in the summer season 'the most of the gentry of the north of England and of Scotland.' By the 1750s the new turnpike roads from York and the West Riding were bringing clergy, professional men and substantial merchants, and cloth manufacturers were well in evidence by the end of the century.[18] Harrogate and Buxton developed in a similar manner, as, no doubt, did Clifton, though here metropolitan influences were at least as strong as those of the West Country.[19]

Below this level in the hierarchy of inland resorts, a large number of provincial spas saw their prosperity ebb and flow, with an essentially local catchment area and a clientèle of lesser gentry, farmers, and attorneys, shopkeepers and tradesmen from the nearby towns. Matlock, in Derbyshire, retained this level of patronage from the Restoration to the railway age, although it secured brief visits from more fashionable travellers as the cult of romantic scenery increased its attractions in the later eighteenth century; Carey, indeed, believed that, 'This place . . . is visited more from the romantic pictures of nature which it displays, than from the efficacy of its springs.' Long before this, indeed, Matlock had gained from its position as a convenient base from which to view Charles Cotton's 'Seven Wonders of the Peak'.[20] But most of the lesser spas lacked this kind of additional distinction, and many never developed beyond the basic provision of a pump-room, baths and a single hotel, perhaps supplemented by the odd lodging-house. Many of those which displayed a modest prosperity in the seventeenth century declined in the eighteenth, to be replaced by a new burst of speculative initiatives designed to tap the new urban wealth of the Industrial Revolution, or to exploit the rising prosperity of substantial farmers, in the early nineteenth.[21] By 1840 Woodhall Spa, a recent speculation in Lincolnshire, was prospering quietly by catering for 'farmers and people belonging to the industrious classes', while Ilkley was the height of fashion among 'the higher grades of *factory* society' in the West Riding and even Manchester.[22] These snap judgments are based on the hasty and often snobbish impressions of Dr Granville, the compiler of a lively and often outspoken early Victorian guide to the *Spas of England, and Principal Sea-Bathing Places*. With all their limitations as reliable evidence,[23] his comments should remind us of the continuing existence of a limited but significant local demand for the medical, social and recreational amenities of spas in an accessible and inexpensive form. Moreover, there was sufficient elasticity of demand at this unpretentious provincial level for new spas to be successfully founded by entrepreneurs, especially in the remoter areas of northern England, in the early railway age and beyond. On this lowest rung of the inland resort hierarchy, the emphasis clearly shifted over the years from gentry to tradesmen and farmers, as the wealthiest local families began to aspire to regional or even national resorts; but the small local spas continued to hold their own, and even to proliferate, well into the second quarter of the nineteenth century.

We have dealt with the spas at some length because in many ways the changing social structure of their visiting public, expressed as it was partly through the evolution of a hierarchy of resorts, anticipated developments at the seaside. It is important to remember that for most of the eighteenth century, at least, the seaside resorts lagged behind the spas in fashionable favour and social development, and that the older watering-places retained a distinctive vitality of their own as health and pleasure centres even beyond the mid-nineteenth century. The fashionable seaside holiday began, in some respects, as an adjunct to the spa season, and it took several generations for the seaside to supersede the spa in the affections of the growing number of affluent seekers after health, pleasure and status in attractive surroundings.

Not all spa visitors were affluent, however. In several places, the reputation of holy wells lived on among the common people long after the Reformation. At Copgrove, near Harrogate, St Mungo's Well continued to be frequented by poor people in the eighteenth century, although medical practitioners had long before dismissed its springs as being composed of 'pure and simple waters only'. At Holywell in Flintshire, St Winifred's Well was as heavily used until at least the mid-eighteenth century, and its reputation survived into the railway age, with excursion trains regularly bringing Roman Catholic pilgrims in mid-Victorian times. At Axwell, in Northumberland, 'sundry holiday people' could be found in 1840 'quaffing the limpid stream' of a mineral spring which 'in former times, enjoyed great repute.'[24] Bath, Buxton and other spas were visited by poor people in search of cure during Elizabeth's reign, and Poor Law authorities were sending invalids to take the waters at their local spas 200 years later.[25] By that time, of course, it had become impossible to disentangle the influences of custom, magic, emulation and the transmission of medical opinion as explanations for the visits of the poor to take the waters, especially where there was no apparent tradition attached to a particular site, or where an old well had been laid aside and rediscovered. What are we to make of Slaithwaite, Lockwood and Askerne, in the West Riding, where 'the dense population of manufacturers, and other mechanics' accounted for most of the visitors in 1840; or of Shotley Bridge in Northumberland, where a landowner followed up a tradition that a holy well had existed in his grounds, and found the people of the country villages flocking to his rediscovered mineral spring?[26] In many places, tradition clearly played a greater part than medical expertise in attracting the lower orders to mineral springs for whose use their betters increasingly required a more sophisticated justification.[27]

Much the same is true of the popular tradition of therapeutic sea-bathing which can be shown to have existed at various points along the coastline, especially in Lancashire and parts of Wales. It was certainly being practised in south Lancashire at the beginning of the eighteenth century, when Nicholas Blundell of Crosby had his daughters dipped in the sea to cure a skin eruption. Blundell was closely identified with the folk customs of his area, and it is most unlikely that the new medical ideas about sea-bathing, which were only just beginning to stir, would have reached or influenced him; when the sea-bathing was unsuccessful he had recourse to wise women and a variety of popular remedies.[28] Early, and probably traditional, belief in the curative power of sea-water was not confined to Lancashire; at least two innkeepers 'dipped' diseased men and beasts in the Severn estuary in the 1730s.[29] It is not until the late eighteenth and early nineteenth century that improved sources enable us to build on these tantalizing hints; and by then, as in the case of the spas, it might be argued that popular sea-bathing was motivated by emulation and the percolation downwards of the new medical ideas. In fact, however, the evidence is more consistent with the survival of sea-bathing traditions which had hitherto gone unrecorded. In Lancashire, at least, the sea-bathing habit at this time was prophylactic as well as therapeutic in intent, with quasi-magical overtones. At various points along the Lancashire coast, from the Mersey to Morecambe Bay, hundreds of artisans and country people bathed and drank sea-water regularly at the August spring tide, which was held to have special powers of purification and regeneration as well as curing all manner of diseases. Bathers told a visitor to Lytham that their motive was to wash away 'all the collected stains and impurities of the year', and Richard Ayton was informed at Blackpool that in August and September, especially at the spring tide, 'There is physic in the sea – physic of a most comprehensive description, combining all the virtues of all the drugs in the doctor's shop, and of course a cure for all varieties of disease.'[30] Popular sea-bathing was also practised in the early nineteenth century on parts of the Welsh coast, in Caernarvonshire and at Aberystwyth, where it was the custom of the country people 'on fine nights to blow horns in order to collect a crowd and to proceed to the beaches to bathe.'[31]

In Lancashire at least, popular sea-bathing was firmly rooted in custom rather than the precepts of orthodox medicine. This is suggested by its attachment to a particular season of the year; by its existence on parts of the coastline which were not frequented by the 'better class' of visitor, such as Hest Bank and even the Ribble estuary as far inland as Preston; and by the inconclusive but suggestive evidence of William Hutton, writing in 1788, to the effect that in the 1760s and before 'the people who then frequented

Blackpool were chiefly of the lower class.'[32] The tradition may have been reinforced or revived by the upper-class sea-bathing fashion, but it had a prior and independent existence. Indeed, it flourished and gained adherents in Lancashire during the first half of the nineteenth century, when Blackpool and Lytham, especially, were inundated with hundreds of artisan bathers at a time in the 1820s and 1830s. In 1836 a *Preston Chronicle* correspondent took a census of the traffic returning from the Fylde Coast on 'Bathing Sunday', as the main festival was called. Between six and eight in the evening he counted eight four-wheeled carriages containing 12 people each, 41 'gigs and cars' with six each, 92 carts with 14 each, 12 shandrays with seven each, and 20 individual riders. This cavalcade of 'rustics', 'new fledged prentices' and artisan families amounted to over 1,700 people, and they were augmented by a similar number of pedestrians.[33] Soon afterwards, the traffic transferred itself to the railways, as excursion trains became available in the early 1840s.

This working-class sea-bathing tradition was to have important implications for the development of the Lancashire holiday industry in the later nineteenth century; but in the meantime it provided little more than an occasional diversion for the affluent visitors who formed the mainstream holiday market at the Lancashire resorts from the late eighteenth century onwards. The 'Padjamers', as they came to be known in Blackpool, required only the most primitive of amenities. They bathed naked, without segregation of the sexes, and drank large quantities of spirits to fortify their stomachs against their enormous consumption of sea-water; their carts had plank seats, and they put their horses out to graze rather than stable them; and they slept, not only several to a bed and several beds to the room, but in shifts, taking it in turns to move out on to the beach. Many used lofts and outhouses. Such economy was not the stuff of which a working-class holiday season might be made, especially as the 'Padjamers' appeared briefly, and only once a year.[34] Even in Lancashire, seaside resort development before the railway, and for a generation afterwards, was fuelled almost entirely by growing demand from the upper and middling strata of society – from the people who already frequented the spas.

Medical writers were already advocating sea-bathing as a cure for a variety of ailments in the later seventeenth century, and Sir John Floyer's *History of Cold Bathing*, first published in 1702, had reached its fifth edition by 1722.[35] As the prestige of the medical profession rose, advice from such sources may well have begun to influence a significant minority of the educated and leisured, and by the 1730s Scarborough, Margate and Brighton, at least, were developing recognizable sea-bathing seasons. At Margate, a sea-water bath was already being provided for visitors in 1736.[36] Some of this early interest may well have been generated by the adoption of existing traditional beliefs rather than by new medical fashions; but the stronger and more certain growth of the cult of sea-bathing and sea-water drinking during the second half of the eighteenth century was clearly based much more securely on an emergent medical orthodoxy. Dr Richard Russell's treatise on the uses of sea-water as a near-panacea, especially for common diseases of leisured town-dwellers, was regularly reissued after the first vernacular edition in

1752; and Russell's colleagues, especially in London, were quick to follow him in prescribing sea-bathing to wealthy clients. Treatises in support of Russell soon multiplied, and sea-water followed spa water from the status of an uncertain fringe medicine to that of a sovereign remedy.[37] The pleasures of the seaside in its own right were soon discovered by the early visitors, and the amenities which were familiar at the spas were reproduced at the seaside with growing confidence as the fashion gathered momentum. As with the spas, pursuers of pleasure, status and fortune followed the health-seekers to the new resorts; and a hierarchy of seaside watering-places grew up to cater for the needs of a widening range of visitor tastes.

In their beginnings, the seaside resorts drew on the same clientèle as the spas of the mid-eighteenth century. They were frequented mainly by the aristocracy and landed gentry, with a leavening of those groups which made up the 'pseudo-gentry' or 'urban gentry' class which has been characterized as a highly significant rising social grouping in pre-industrial England, composed as it was of prosperous and well-connected professional men, merchants and *rentiers* without a country seat, who needed to express their wealth and status through conspicuous consumption and the pursuit of fashion.[38] As with the spas, too, the market widened in the later eighteenth century, as newer and less polished commercial and manufacturing wealth came to the fore, and as farmers, attorneys, and shopkeepers in the provinces prospered and aspired sufficiently to encourage the development of local resorts of limited celebrity and unexacting social pretensions.

The strongest stimuli to early seaside resort development on a large scale came from London, both as political centre and as commercial metropolis. The conversion of George III's court to the joys of sea-bathing brought unexpected prosperity to Weymouth, as aristocratic and other camp-followers flooded into the town during the regular royal visits between 1789 and 1805, which developed out of the establishment of the duke of Gloucester in what was already a rising watering-place.[39] More spectacular and longer-lasting was the influence of the Prince of Wales on Brighton, where from 1783 onwards he and his free-spending courtiers, following the lead given by three of his royal uncles since the mid-1760s, gave the fastest-growing resort of the period a distinctive social tone of its own, combining the aristocratic, the opulent and the raffish. Worthing and Southend also benefited from royal visits in the late eighteenth century, and beyond the confines of the court London's rôle as centre for the transaction of all kinds of political business ensured that it would become more generally a point of departure for influential people in search of health, pleasure and the right kind of company.[40] The continuing development of the London social season during the eighteenth century, which was demonstrated by the building of opulent town houses for aristocratic entertainments, both expressed and reinforced this trend.[41] This helped to ensure that the south coast resorts took the lion's share of the growing volume of aristocratic and genteel demand for seaside amenities, and by the end of the eighteenth century much of this was being channelled into Brighton, conveniently sited as it was at the nearest point to London on the coastline, and Margate, which was conveniently, if not always agreeably, accessible by boat as well as by carriage or stage-coach.

London also generated a rapidly rising demand for seaside visits among its own citizens, and most of the developing resorts in a wide arc from Southend in the east to Southampton and Weymouth in the south-west saw the early appearance of significant numbers of the prospering middle ranks of a metropolis which provided particularly fertile soil for the propagation of that spirit of competitive emulation which was to prove so important to the rise of the seaside.[42] Brighton, despite the very high prices which resulted from its gradual usurpation from Bath of the status of the nation's 'social capital', continued to draw on London's respectable professional and commercial classes, although by 1785 the *Morning Post* could lament the appearance of 'a set of curmudgeonly knaves and dowdies', and by the late eighteenth century the Brighton season was combining elements of the aristocratic, the middling sort and the disreputable to an extent which could only be paralleled at Margate.[43] Here, the corn hoys provided cheap transport from London down the Thames, and even in the 1770s this enabled 'the decent tradesman' and 'people of the middle and inferior classes' to pay regular visits in the summer.[44] By the turn of the century G. S. Carey, commenting on the discomfort likely to be experienced on the hoys by people of sensitivity and refinement, could remark on the way in which they carried 'so many of all descriptions of people at a time, and at so small an expence.' The wealthy sent their servants by the hoys, but many of the less affluent visitors also came that way, with the result that the Pier on a Sunday contained 'a more heterogeneous group than at any place in England', making it a paradise for caricaturists; and Carey was quite confident that most of these people were 'industrious honey-bees from London, who yearly distribute the essence of their winter-labour' among the ungrateful natives.[45]

Elsewhere within London's sphere of influence, the cost of travel still tended to exclude the 'plain and unrefined' tradesmen who were already in evidence at Margate, and London's commercial influence was more likely to be expressed in a politer and more prosperous form.[46] But the most successful aristocratic resorts were also those which were already having to find room, if not actually for the 'lower orders' in the usual sense, at least for the unpretentious lower middle ranks of London traders and shopkeepers. Even in the late eighteenth century, when Brighton and Margate were still well filled with fashionable company throughout the season, the more socially fastidious among the visiting public were already seeking out more exclusive retreats. G. S. Carey's strictures on the recently founded resort of Bognor, a speculation by the London hatter Sir Richard Hotham, illustrate this point at the turn of the century. He commented that, 'It appears at present merely calculated for the superior sort of society', and lamented the desolate air which resulted, even at the height of the season, from the pride and aloofness which prevented the visitors from associating much together.[47] At about the same time Hastings could be praised for its high moral tone, if not for its aristocratic exclusiveness, as a guide-book writer remarked on its lack of 'professional gamblers, unhappy profligates and fashionable swindlers': 'The society at Hastings is gay, without profligacy, and enjoys life, without mingling in its debaucheries.'[48] Quieter resorts of this kind were beginning to multiply in south-eastern England in the late eighteenth century, reflecting the complex pattern of demand for seaside visits which was already being woven by the different visiting publics, aristocratic and commercial, which were centred on the metropolis, and reflecting also the wide range of social attributes, attitudes and expectations which could be subsumed under each label. Aristocrats and gentry could be rackety or aloof, free-spending or in search of retrenchment; citizens could be polished and well-connected, or plain and of uncertain origins. The many shades of religious commitment, from repressive evangelicalism to uncaring hedonism, were also beginning to matter increasingly at this time. The resorts in London's orbit catered for all these groups, but already in the late eighteenth century the volume of demand was such that some could safely specialize.

Even in Kent and Sussex, however, the demand for eighteenth-century resort development was not merely a London-centred phenomenon, important though London was. Those *desiderata* of aspiring resort promoters, 'The very best Company, those regular, steady private families of thorough Gentility and Character',[49] were also to be found among the gentry and urban middle ranks of the south-eastern counties. John Crosier, a 'substantial man of business' as miller and farmer at Maldon in Essex, formed one of the company at Margate and Ramsgate in August 1781, and met several friends there, while a few years later John Savill, a wealthy textile master from Bocking, in the same county, was visiting Weymouth and the Thanet resorts.[50]

These examples illustrate the development of the seaside holiday habit among the prospering provincial middle ranks; and by the late eighteenth century demand from this source was already playing a significant part in resort development in areas where London's direct influence was limited or practically absent. Some of the remoter provincial resorts, admittedly, contrived to establish and maintain a very high social tone. Tenby, in South Wales, succeeded like Weymouth and Ilfracombe in attracting genteel company from Bath, which diffused metropolitan influences into Wales and the West Country and became an important nursery of seaside resorts. In 1803 Tenby's visitors could be described as 'numerous and fashionable', and many brought their own carriages for a long stay.[51] Even Tenby's visitors, however, were 'not so fashionable a set' as those at Aberystwyth, where visitors' lists from the early nineteenth century show large numbers of the titled, with even baronets having to accept a secondary status.[52] Scarborough occupied a similar social niche on the east coast, again reminding us that not all aristocratic demand was channelled through London into the south-eastern resorts; south Devon, too, had its noble and genteel devotees from an early stage.[53]

Increasingly, however, the developing commercial and manufacturing elements in provincial urban society were demanding their place at the seaside, and rural society sent a growing quota as lesser gentry and substantial farmers gained from the Napoleonic Wars. We have seen that Scarborough was already attracting the more affluent northern merchants, as it began to add sea-bathing to its spa facilities in the mid-eighteenth century. In 1806 Catherine Hutton, herself the daughter of a cultivated but self-made

Birmingham bookseller, described the recent additions to the company as 'chiefly cloth-makers and merchants from the West Riding; a set of honest, hearty fellows, who undermine the best constitutions in the world by eating and drinking.'[54] Lancashire manufacturers were also well in evidence by this time, as at Harrogate, and despite the persisting patronage of the nobility and gentry of the North and Midlands, a contemporary guide to the resorts remarked that Scarborough was less fashionable than the major southern bathing-places, if also more morally respectable: 'Except those who are allured by connections and swayed by local considerations, Scarborough contains, among its visitors, more votaries of health than of dissipation.'[55]

Apart from diversifying the company at Scarborough and Harrogate, the Lancashire and West Riding textile districts were already spawning resorts of their own. Blackpool in the 1780s was already beginning to flourish on the custom of merchants and manufacturers from Manchester and the textile district, with a leavening of sometimes unpretentious clergy, Lancashire gentry, Liverpool merchants and a substantial number of lawyers, some of whom provided a congenial audience for Catherine Hutton's amused strictures about the coarseness of manners of the amiable but rough-and-ready 'Boltoners'.[56] On the same coast, Lytham and Southport were beginning to develop under similar auspices. The trading and professional wealth of Norwich and district, too, must have helped to fuel the emergence as a resort of unfashionable Yarmouth, where the early sources of demand seem to have been mainly local.[57] Elsewhere, the urban middle ranks were slower to call their own resorts into being. Bristol merchants were patronizing Weymouth and Lyme Regis, but Weston-super-Mare was a creation of the early nineteenth century rather than the late eighteenth; and the new industrial wealth of the Midlands was, less surprisingly, slow to find cultural expression in seaside visits, perhaps partly because, in Birmingham at least, it was evolving a satisfying and distinctive local urban culture of its own, leaving less need for the emulative borrowing of the aristocratic trappings of the seaside.[58]

Even where the new urban influences were not being strongly felt, the coastline of England was becoming studded with little resorts which inexpensively satisfied an essentially local demand. By 1803 Harwich, in Essex, had acquired an informal Assembly Room to act as social centre for 'a considerable resort of company . . . particularly from the neighbouring districts'; Abergele, Flint and Parkgate, in North Wales and the Wirral, were similarly catering for local bathers by the late eighteenth century; Allonby, a fishing and weaving settlement on the Solway Firth, was the summer meeting-place for the lesser gentry and larger farmers of north Cumberland, while Redcar seems to have served in a similar manner those North Riding families who did not choose to go to Scarborough.[59] The fame of some of these little bathing places was to prove local and transitory, as better-sited or more enterprising rivals captured the market; but every coastal county had at least one embryo resort of this kind by the early nineteenth century, and the universality of the phenomenon reflects the wide geographical and social appeal of the fashion.[60] By the turn of the century, the seaside holiday had become a well-established feature of the social calendar, and its influence was already reaching a long way down the social scale, well beyond the confines of polite society, in parts of the provinces as well as in the London area.

Why did the seaside come to the fore in this way, and how, if at all, did its clientèle differ from that of the inland spas? In the first place, the seaside offered a wider range of health-giving properties than the spa, and this was important to that vast majority of invalids or hypochondriacs who had not been prescribed a specific course of treatment. Several of the larger resorts, and some of the smaller ones, offered mineral springs in their neighbour-hoods: Scarborough was a spa in its own right; Weymouth's mineral spring at Nottington was put forward as almost a universal panacea by a local guide-book at the turn of the century; and Brighton, like several smaller resorts, had its own chalybeate spring, while from 1786 onwards, in a different vein, it could also offer Mahomed's Indian medicated vapour baths.[61] Already, too, the advantages of sea air were being widely appreci-ated, although this aspect of seaside medicine did not become really fashionable until early Victorian times. At Blackpool in 1788 Catherine Hutton's mother benefited less from her stay than expected, and this was ascribed to the prevalence of 'land breezes laden with the smoke of turf' instead of the anticipated sea air.[62]

But there was more to sea-bathing itself than just the pursuit of health. Unlike the consumption of most spa waters, with their often embarrassing after-effects, sea-bathing could be enjoyed in its own right. John Crosier bathed from a machine at Margate in 1781, and described it as 'one of the greatest luxuries I ever experienc'd.'[63] Such reactions should remind us that sea-bathing itself mingled therapy and enjoyment in a way which greatly enhanced the new resorts' attractions.

Bathing apart, the seaside offered a distinctive natural environment which appealed to several kinds of contemporary preoccupation. An interest in natural science, expressed even at a very superficial level by the collection of specimens, often gave an added charm to the foreshore, and at Margate as early as 1763 a local guide-book commented that, 'When the tide is ebbed, many persons go on the sands, to collect pebbles, sea-weed, shells, &c., which although of no great value, are esteemed as matters of curiosity, by those to whom such objects have not been familiar.' Moreover, the visual appeal of such seaside objects could be enhanced by the careful art of tasteful ladies, as the same writer went on to point out: 'Some of these weeds, when spread on writing paper, extended with a needle, and pressed between boards, form an infinite variety of landscapes in beautiful colours.[64]

For those of artistic inclinations, indeed, the seaside landscape could offer satisfactions which were unattainable inland, although the countryside around the resorts was all too often dismissed as uninteresting. Jagged rocks and tumbledown cottages on the shoreline could appeal to the taste for the picturesque which was becoming fashionable in the later eighteenth century, while the devotee of the sublime and the awe-inspiring could achieve his pleasurable *frisson* of horror by contemplating the vasty deep, especially in a storm. The author (wisely anonymous) of *The Isle of Wight, a Poem in Three Cantos*, published in 1782, extolled the virtues of the Undercliff by pointing out that it needed three artists to do it justice; Claude to capture the 'delicate sunshine' over 'cultivated fields, the scattered cots, and hanging coppices', Salvator for 'the horror of the rugged cliffs', and Poussin for 'the majesty of the impending mountains.'[65] By the early nineteenth century the conventional vocabulary of these modes of perception had become a fount of recognizable clichés, and its extravagant abusers were mercilessly lampooned by Jane Austen in her unfinished novel *Sanditon*. For many visitors who had cultivated these fashionable sensibilities, the sea carried a very special emotional charge of its own.[66]

The seaside also offered more practical advantages. Although the formal social institutions of the spas soon appeared at the coastal resorts, the main focus of seaside activity was the open seashore rather than the pump room, and it was easier to economize by leading a quiet and private life, without being completely cut off from the other visitors.[67] The social obligation to participate in expensive assemblies and card parties was not as binding. This was particularly true of some of the smaller resorts. In 1803 Littlehampton, in Sussex, was thought to be a refuge for 'people of moderate condition', seeking to avoid the fashionable extravagance of larger resorts; while Lyme Regis was said to be 'frequented principally by persons in the middle class of life, who go there, not always in search of their lost health, but as frequently perhaps to heal their wounded fortunes, or to replenish their exhausted revenues.'[68] These remarks offer a reminder that the market for seaside holidays did not grow by emulation alone, and that the cramped lodgings of an unpretentious seaside town could offer a haven from the pressures of social competition, or from the demands of creditors at home.[69] On the other hand, the annual seaside visit, like participation in the formal life of the spa and of the London season, was coming to be seen as an almost unavoidable badge of status even when genteel families were in severe financial straits; the Blois family of Suffolk, in spite of money worries, spent £100 on the outward journey alone when they visited Dawlish in 1791.[70] But the overall effect of the greater scope for informality at the seaside was to open out the sea-bathing resorts more readily than the spas to people of little polish and limited means, and as a result they were already becoming more 'popular' than the spas.[71] Moreover, the seashore was sufficiently spacious and accessible to enable a wide range of age-groups to mingle informally, and children could be made welcome to an extent which could not have been countenanced in the more formal and regulated regime of the spa. This mattered increasingly as the upper and middle ranks began to pay more attention to the specific needs of children, and as families began to take more of their pleasures in common. By the turn of the century, the beach was just beginning to take on the rôle of children's playground which was to become such a Victorian commonplace.[72]

A further distinction between seaside resort and spa was that the season in the former was shorter, and the average length of stay probably less. The fashionable season for seaside visits was narrowly constrained into two or three months of a crowded social calendar, and seaside visitors usually stayed for a shorter time than spa-goers.[73] Although seaside resorts could hope to welcome visitors at any time between May and October, the peak periods of demand came in August and September, which were 'the Months' to Jane Austen's hopeful resort promoter Mr Parker.[74] The rhythm of the season at Margate in 1787 was expressed by the rents demanded from visitors to William Stone's lodging house: two guineas per week in May and June, 2½ guineas in July, and three guineas in August, rising to a peak of 3½ guineas in September and early October before falling away again.[75]

By the early nineteenth century, a clear pattern of demand for seaside holidays had emerged; and the great expansion of the visiting public over the next 40 years was largely based on the continuing development of trends which were already apparent in the resorts' formative years. The increase in numbers was especially visible at Brighton and Margate, which continued to set the pace. At Brighton, estimated visitor numbers at the height of the summer season had already increased from 400 in 1760 to over 4,000 in 1794; by 1818 an average of 7,000 could be claimed between June and October, and in 1840 the maximum figure had risen spectacularly to 20,000. By 1818, moreover, winter and spring seasons were developing on a significant scale, as the nobility and gentry retreated from the plebeian invasions of the summer months; and by 1841 the season had become sub-divided to a remarkable extent, as 'the summer months are abandoned to the trading population of London, the early autumn is surrendered to the lawyers; and when November summons them to Westminster, the *beau monde* commence their migration.'[76] Margate experienced the contagion of numbers to an even greater extent in high summer, although its climate made it less attractive than Brighton outside the bathing season, and the thousands of visitors brought by the Thames estuary steamers soon began to crowd out the aristocracy and gentry. Between 1817 and 1835 the steamboat traffic more than quadrupled, and in 1831 the number of visitors was thought to vary between 10,000 and 20,000 in the season.[77] By 1824, Margate's summers were dominated by the unfashionable 'inhabitants of eastern London', and in June 1841 41 per cent of the adult male visitors were drawn from the ranks of trade, commerce and manufacture, and the wealth of most of the 45 per cent who claimed 'independent means' probably had similar origins. Only three titles figured in the list.[78] Nearer to London, the steamboat revolution hit Gravesend even harder, and by the 1820s it was already attracting artisan day-trippers on summer Sundays. During the 1820s the number of passengers landing and embarking at Gravesend increased more than tenfold to nearly 300,000, and by 1840 the million mark had been passed. Only a very small minority indeed can have been staying visitors; but in 1843 Gravesend accounted for over 60 per cent of all steamer passenger traffic out of London.[79] As a result of this accessibility, Gravesend became 'low'. It established the fashion since followed by many other resorts, of sleeping on the beaches, on the piers, or anywhere else.'[80] This was an extreme case of early lower-class colonization, and the solid middle-class invasion of Worthing, which was apparent by the 1820s, was much closer to the norm.[81] But we can identify a general rapid growth in visitor numbers in the south-east during this period, which seems to have been largely fuelled by the London tradesman and, in some cases, the more prosperous artisans.

Beyond the reach of the strongest pull of London middle-class demand, visitor numbers grew less spectacularly. Series of estimates are hard to come by, but Blackpool could claim 400 visitors at a time in 1788, and by 1830 the number had probably only doubled to 800 or 1,000. Five years later the local vicar, an eager publicist, claimed 2,000 visitors at the mid-August peak. Elsewhere in the North-West Southport, Lytham and Douglas all showed broadly comparable figures in the mid-1830s. By this time even these second-rank resorts were outpacing Harrogate, the leading northern spa, in visitor numbers, and it was during the 1830s and 1840s that the balance of patronage generally tipped towards the seaside, after a period in which each kind of resort had followed a similar trajectory of development.[82] The seaside resorts were better able to tap the rapidly expanding sources of demand among the emergent middle classes. Dr Granville's remarks in 1840 suggest that Blackpool's social tone had not improved since Catherine Hutton's time, as he dined at Nickson's among 'a motley of honest-looking people . . . Methinks the highest in rank here might have been an iron-founder, from near Bradford or Halifax, or a retired wine-merchant, from Liverpool'. The 1841 census bears out his impressions, with 30 per cent of the adult male visitors being textile or other manufacturers, and nearly one-quarter in commerce and retailing, while nearly 10 per cent were skilled or semi-skilled labourers.[83] Southport fared little better in Granville's eyes; it was the resort of 'the Manchester factor and artisan – the rich and the "middling comfortable"'. Less socially exacting observers were in broad agreement.[84] At Scarborough, on the other hand, the nobility and gentry were still prominent during the latter part of the season, as at Harrogate; but until mid-August, at least, 'the aristocracy of the farmers from the East and West Ridings figure away in long lists at the hotels and boarding-houses.'[85] The relative importance of the rural and urban middle ranks varied from resort to resort, although the urban influences predominated overall; but these groups provided the main stimulus to the steadily-growing demand for seaside holidays in the provinces.

This pattern of demand encouraged the emergence of new resorts as well as the expansion of existing ones. The opportunities offered by the Bristol middle classes called Weston-super-Mare, Clevedon and Portishead into being during the first two decades of the nineteenth century, and by the 1830s the two first-named resorts could rival Southport in visitor numbers at the height of the season.[86] Similarly, though on a smaller scale, Tynemouth became 'the Brighton of the Newcastle people', and Liverpool merchants and tradesmen stimulated the growth of Crosby, Waterloo and, from the 1830s, the planned resort of New Brighton on the south bank of the Mersey.[87]

During this period, too, the seaside began to compete increasingly effectively with the spas not only for the mainly pleasure-seeking visitors of high summer, but also as places of winter retreat and regular residence for wealthy invalids. As well as adding an extra resource to existing resort economies like those of Southport and Hastings, the search for a mild winter climate, which would be kind to the lung diseases engendered by the polluted atmosphere of large towns, encouraged the growth of seaside resorts whose main stock in trade was climate rather than sea-bathing.[88] Dover was becoming a winter resort of this kind during the second quarter of the nineteenth century, and the climatic virtues of Ventnor, on the Isle of Wight, and Bournemouth were being eagerly advanced by 1840; but the most specialized and successful early example of the residential winter resort was Torquay.[89] Here, an observer as early as 1817 could remark that, 'The town was built to accommodate invalids.' Granville in 1840 noted the presence of a large number of spinsters and a noticeable sprinkling of clergy and medical men, but the wealthy and leisured background of the Torquay visiting public emerges clearly from his comments: 'It is the very nature of the place to have . . . a permanent residentiary set of invalids, who hurry thither at the onset of winter . . . and there remain stationary and ensconced until the warm sun of June again permits them to run up to the metropolis, or return to their country-houses.'[90] Dawlish, Teignmouth and Exmouth, among others in south Devon, were also established winter resorts as well as sea-bathing places at this time, although Torquay captured most of the increased demand which was becoming apparent in the 1820s and 1830s.[91]

The main stimulus to resort growth, however, lay in the expansion of the middle-class visiting public who spent two or three weeks at the seaside in high summer. They were motivated increasingly by the pursuit of status and enjoyment as well as, or instead of, health; and one of the essential attractions of the seaside was that it remained possible at this stage to cater for the lively and the valetudinarian, the serious and the frivolous within the confines of a single resort. The seaside was in itself morally neutral ground; it could be used for health or dissipation, idleness or improvement. Visitors could bathe, walk, ride, botanize, collect shells or visit ancient monuments; or they could save up their energies for dancing and card-parties. This versatility or flexibility was particularly important to the continuing popularity of the seaside in a period of transition from the free-and-easy manners of the Regency aristocracy to the stifling constraints of bourgeois evangelical morality. The seaside resorts could find room for both, while steadily adapting, even in the case of Brighton, to the growing influence of the latter.[92]

The growing numbers of summer visitors came mainly from the ranks of the rapidly expanding propertied, professional and substantial employing classes during the classic period of the Industrial Revolution, with the widespread attainment below the gentry and wealthy merchants of a level of affluence which permitted the enjoyment of a considerable amount of leisure time away from the business routine. The spread of commercial and industrial prosperity coincided with the height of the aristocratic and genteel vogue for sea-bathing, and those who sought to share in some degree the leisured lifestyle of their betters were thus introduced to the joys of the seaside at a time when transport improvements were making the resorts significantly more accessible to those with limited time and money. As with the other trappings of gentility among the middle ranks, the seaside holiday soon became indispensable to the ideal of a leisured and cultivated way of life, and the limited impact of bad trade and agricultural depression on the resorts suggests that it was not lightly discarded.

The continuing growth in demand was made much easier by falling journey times, increasing comfort and convenience of travel, and in some cases by falling transport costs. The spread of turnpikes, coupled with subsequent improvements in road construction and stage-coach technology, cut journey times sharply. The earliest stage-coaches in 1762 took a day between London and Brighton, but by 1791 nine hours was the norm, falling again as competition intensified to six hours in 1811 and between five and six hours in 1833. Fares fluctuated, but the faster journeys must have sharply reduced the additional charges which could be extorted for food, drink and other services by innkeepers along the route.[93] Brighton was unusually well favoured, but increased speeds of a similar order of magnitude were experienced elsewhere, and road improvements, especially in the Macadam era after 1820, made conditions easier for the private carriages which remained important to the upper reaches of the market. Stage-coach services grew enormously in volume between the later eighteenth century and the threshold of the railway age. One calculation suggests, perhaps conservatively, a fifteenfold increase in stage-coach travel between the 1790s, when the system was already well established, and the 1830s.[94] The major resorts shared fully in this expansion of traffic. Scarborough's weekly road passenger links with London alone grew fivefold, from 12 to 60, in the short time between 1781 and 1809, while Weymouth's grew even faster from 12 to 73.[95] Even little Weston-super-Mare, whose career had hardly begun in 1810, saw its summer coaching link with Bristol rise from four weekly return trips in 1818 to 39 in 1831.[96] The improved standard of comfort made possible by the widespread adoption of Obadiah Elliot's elliptical spring by stage-coach builders after 1805 must have been particularly important to the watering-place traffic, with its high proportion of invalids, women and, increasingly, children.[97]

Improved stage-coach services might benefit the seaside resorts, but fares remained high, except during occasional bursts of fierce competition. Many resorts did gain from the falling travel costs which resulted from developments in water transport, especially in the early nineteenth century. From their beginnings in 1815, the Thames steamers brought large numbers of additional visitors to Gravesend and the Thanet resorts, for they were much more capacious and, all expenses considered, much cheaper than the stage-coaches, and faster and more reliable than the hoys. After 1820, moreover, competitive price-cutting brought the fares down from 15s. saloon and 12s. forecabin to 9s. and 7s. in 1831–2 and 4s. and 3s. in 1835, with even lower figures occurring in some subsequent years when competition was particularly fierce.[98] These changes had an immediate impact on the already falling social tone of Margate and Gravesend. This was a uniquely spectacular example, but elsewhere the steamer was also instrumental in expanding the seaside holiday market before the railway age, and in helping to open out new resorts to the provincial middle classes. The early development of Ilfracombe and Rhyl, for example, owed much to the availability of relatively cheap steamer fares from Bristol, South Wales and Liverpool in the 1820s and 1830s.[99] Even the canal revolution was capable of making a localized impact on holiday demand, for Southport's rapid rise after 1820 owed much to the provision of a through passenger service to Scarisbrick Bridge, on the Leeds and Liverpool Canal, from Manchester *via* Wigan.[100] But it was the steamer, where it operated, that alone was really capable of pushing the threshold of demand significantly lower down the social scale.

The first 40 years of the nineteenth century certainly saw a considerable expansion in seaside holiday demand. Although the spas continued to hold their own, and the scenic beauties of the Lake District and North Wales were attracting a few wealthy and discriminating tourists, the seaside was versatile enough to cater for the whole spectrum of rising middle-class demand in a rapidly changing society; among the industrial and commercial groups prosperity was becoming sufficiently widely diffused to ensure a steady flow of recruits to the ranks of the leisured, opulent and status-conscious. The seaside resorts were well enough established, and sufficiently diverse in their visiting publics, to survive the reopening of the Continent after the Napoleonic Wars, and to weather the agricultural problems and the recurrent trade depressions of the years after 1815. Their success, indeed, provides a strong indication of the way in which growing national affluence was being channelled disproportionately into the hands of landowners, employers and their allies.

From the 1830s and 1840s, the railways provided a direct stimulus to the seaside in three ways. They made the journey to the coast easier, faster, cheaper and more comfortable for the existing visiting public, enabling them to stay longer and spend more liberally at the levels where travel costs bulked large in decision-making, and to colonize hitherto inaccessible tracts of coastline. They eased the percolation of the holiday habit down the social scale to the less affluent and more insecure among the middle ranks. Finally, they made the full development of a working-class holiday market possible by providing the facilities for cheap mass transport. All this took many years, especially in the case of the working-class seaside holiday; and although the arrival of the railway made an impressive short-term impact at many resorts, its rôle in the long run must be seen as part of a complex mesh of wider influences. The railways made possible a large-scale expansion of the seaside holiday market, but they did not, in themselves, cause that expansion. They tapped a reservoir of rising demand, but the rise itself was caused by long-term changes in living standards and popular culture which conspired to make the seaside increasingly attractive and attainable.

Even in the largest resorts, the railways showed themselves capable of encouraging the transformation of the scale and quality of the visiting season in a few years. In 1837, the stage coaches brought about 50,000 travellers to Brighton during the whole year; in 1850, the railway carried 73,000 in a single week, although many of these were day excursionists, themselves a phenomenon brought into being by the railways in all but the Thanet resorts.[101] In most places, however, the most significant growth in the railborne visitor traffic came much later, despite the regular provision of cheap fares, covering a variety of periods from a single day to a fortnight and a month, from the 1840s. Blackpool's main railway company, the Lancashire and Yorkshire, enthusiastically took up the excursion-promoting

policy of its precursor, the Preston and Wyre, in the 1840s, and by the early
1850s up to 12,000 trippers might arrive at the Lancashire resort on a
summer week-end; but in the early 1870s the company became more
lukewarm in its attitude, and it took the threat of a competing line to
galvanize it into making a serious effort to keep pace with increasing traffic.
In spite of this, passengers handled at Blackpool stations increased from
135,000 in 1861 to nearly a million in 1879; by 1903 the probable total was
approaching three million, and by the eve of the First World War a further
million had been added.[102] This was, of course, a special case, although the
general trends it illustrates were widespread. Many resorts did not acquire
direct rail links of their own until the mid-Victorian years or even later,
although the railways eased the approaches to them; and indeed, a further
effect of the railway was to make possible the spectacular expansion of tiny
resorts which had hitherto catered for local markets, or even the development of new resorts on virgin sites; and this influence itself helped to expand
the potential holiday market by widening the range of choice and increasing
the number of outlets which could be linked into what was becoming a
national market.[103]

Important though the railways were, they cannot be seen in isolation; and
this point is further emphasized by the evidence that the working-class
seaside holiday was a phenomenon of the last quarter of the nineteenth
century, despite the early emergence of the day-tripper at some resorts near
major population centres. Until the 1870s, and long afterwards in many
places, the main growth sector was still the middle-class market; and we
ought now to examine its development.

The high-class seaside resorts of early and mid-Victorian England continued to attract the patronage of the nobility, gentry and *haute bourgeoisie*,
especially late in the year; but in the mainstream holiday market their
importance was diluted ever faster by the rising tide of visitors drawn from
what R. S. Neale has called the 'middling class', the plain, uncultivated
shopkeeping, trading and sub-professional or clerical groups which combined modest prosperity with economic insecurity and uncertain status.[104]
Brighton in the 1870s continued to attract 'a mob of dukes and duchesses,
marquesses and marchionesses, counts and countesses, and even princes and
princesses', supported by 'sporting men, barristers, men of letters, science,
artists, military men, naval men, doctors and clergymen.' But this was a
winter season, and Brighton was exceptional. Hastings, Folkestone, Lowestoft and Scarborough were prominent among outposts of the fashionable
world in summer at this time, but the middle ranks predominated everywhere.[105] The wealthier among them, who had already figured prominently
at resorts before the 1840s, gained by the way in which the railways began to
cut fares as well as journey times in the early years of the decade, and the
growth of the Victorian middle-class family holiday was also given early
assistance by the acceptance of the principle that children under 12 years of
age travelled half price.[106] Just as the Thanet steamers had anticipated the
way in which the railways opened out the seaside to a widening spectrum of
society, so they pioneered the holiday pattern which the railways made
familiar, whereby wife and children spent several summer weeks at the

seaside while *paterfamilias* commuted at weekends to join them; though the
Victorian upsurge in servant-keeping often resulted in children spending
much of their seaside holiday in the sole charge of a nursemaid or nanny.[107]
The London businessman's mode of holidaymaking was soon copied in the
railway age by the wealthy inhabitants of other major cities.[108] As well as
opening out new patterns of holidaymaking to the substantial mid-Victorian
middle class, moreover, the railways brought new and more distant resorts
within their reach, and the seaside could continue to appeal to an almost
infinite range of tastes and preoccupations. The extremes are well illustrated
by a guide-book's remarks on Bude, which had been made accessible by the
railway system while remaining, in 1876, a long way from the railhead:

> When it is stated that Bude is thirty miles from the nearest railway station,
> the heart of the fashion-hating, German-band-dreading sojourner may be
> at rest. His feminine belongings need not aggravate him by extra luggage,
> containing promenade dresses or fascinating hats . . .

Lyme Regis, with a much longer pedigree as a resort, was also 'eagerly
sought after by quiet families who prefer the beauties of nature to noisy
amusements and dress parades.'[109]

Most middle-class visitors, however, took the demands of a fashionable
watering place in their stride, and the search for the remote, the rustic and
the little-frequented was in its infancy in the 1870s. Meanwhile, the
mainstream holiday market had been greatly augmented. Even when
standard rail fares were still being fixed at a similar level to the stage-coaches,
it was axiomatic by the early 1840s that a new railway would attract
sufficient custom to double the passenger traffic on a given route; and
sometimes the multiplier was much higher. In England and Wales the
number of rail travellers increased twentyfold between 1840 and 1870, and
the resorts accounted for their full share of this traffic.[110] They benefited
particularly from the great increase in the numbers and spending power of
the mid-Victorian middle class. Harold Perkin's calculations from tax
records suggest that the number of businessmen returning profits of more
than £150 per year at 1850 prices increased from 110,000 to well over
150,000 between 1850-1 and 1879-80, while their average profits rose by 60
per cent, comfortably outstripping population growth and inflation. At the
bottom end of the scale, 150,000 new taxpayers crept into the £150 per
annum bracket.[111] Looking at salary-earners through the same sources,
Geoffrey Best, following J. A. Banks, suggests an increase of 95.3 per cent
in the number of incomes over £200 to nearly 40,000 between 1851 and 1871
in Great Britain and Ireland, with a concentration in the lower and middle
ranges between £200 and £900. The census evidence shows that, although
the established professions barely kept pace with overall population growth
between 1851 and 1881, there were marked increases in the representation of
commercial clerks, accountants and bankers (who grew fivefold in number
from 45,000 to 225,000), of wholesale and retail traders (who nearly
doubled), and of such rising professional groups as architects and engineers.
Between 1841 and 1881 white-collar workers in commerce and public

administration rose from 6.3 to 10.3 per cent of the occupied population.[112] These figures present serious problems of definition and interpretation;[113] but their implications for the seaside are clear enough. At these levels, most of the salaried middle classes could dispose of at least a fortnight's paid holiday in the summer. By the late 1860s even ordinary bank clerks could expect at least a week's holiday after only a year's service, and the inspector of the Bankers' Clearing House pointed out that 'they have fewer holidays than any others', as most commercial institutions had their slack seasons when time off could readily be granted.[114] Employers and the self-employed could generally allocate a similar block of free time to themselves, or at least to their families. The growth of the middle classes, and especially the lower middle classes, widened the seaside holiday market very considerably in the mid-Victorian years, especially close to the major population centres, where shop assistants and young white-collar workers without financial responsibilities could augment the ranks of the more prosperous family parties.[115]

The new breed of middle-class visitor, anxiously pursuing gentility on two or three pounds a week, was highly price-sensitive. A representative complaint came in 1872 from 'A poor clerk', who had visited Scarborough every year since 1855 but was now unable to afford a 5s. increase in the rail fare.[116] Despite the occasional setback, however, the trend ran steadily upwards. As befitted the nation's commercial capital, London was the most important generator of this kind of demand. At Great Yarmouth in 1860, the visiting public ranged from 'elderly dowagers and fashionable sets who have nothing to live for in town when everybody is out', through retired merchants, stockbrokers and the habitués of London clubs, to the 'bustling shopkeeper' and the regular occupants of metropolitan office stools.[117] These latter groups typified the main mid-Victorian growth area, in the provinces as well as in London's orbit, as comments from both Scarborough and Blackpool in the early 1870s stressed the local importance of visitors of 'limited means' from Manchester, Leeds and their industrial hinterlands.[118] Even in the mid-1870s, however, many office workers could only manage the occasional day-trip to the coast, to be looked down upon by the *Hastings and St Leonards News* as 'excursionists of a certain office-frequenting, ledger-keeping cast of countenance'.[119] These often ill-paid routine clerical workers were the most obvious beneficiaries of the Bank Holidays Act of 1871 as it came to be more generally observed and extended through the decade.[120]

The same article in the *Hastings and St Leonards News* also commented on the visits of artisans, who were presented in the guise of innocents expressing childlike wonderment at the sea and the flowers. Elsewhere, and subsequently in Hastings itself, they were often depicted in less innocent guise; but their presence reminds us that the railways had long been providing opportunities for working-class excursionists to pay regular visits to the seaside; and in several of the larger resorts the 1870s and 1880s were decades of transition, as ever-growing numbers of trippers began to extend their stay to cover the weekend and even to remain well into the next week. The Scarborough reference at this time to the importance of visitors of 'limited means' certainly covered manual workers as well as members of the burgeoning lower middle class, and it is well known that the groups overlapped in spending power and even in lifestyle, especially at the level of the 'labour aristocracy'.[121] By the 1870s, a significant amount of clearly working-class demand was being generated in London and several of the northern industrial districts, and this was to be built upon spectacularly during the price fall of the last quarter of the nineteenth century.

Apart from the sea-bathing traditions of Lancashire and parts of Wales, working-class visitors appeared at the seaside before the railway age mainly under charitable auspices. Margate acquired a sea-bathing infirmary for 'poor patients afflicted with scrofula', which opened in 1796 and had dealt with 22,000 patients by the end of 1850. In the early nineteenth century Southport, Scarborough and Brighton followed suit; but numbers were always limited, and the patients must have been unobtrusive. At Scarborough, the charity was deliberately sited in the unfashionable part of town close to the old pier, away from the eyes of the 'more affluent visitors'.[122]

All this apart, and with the conspicuous exception of Gravesend, the working-class seaside visitor was a phenomenon of the railway age. The standard fares long remained beyond his reach, but cheap fares on special occasions are as old as passenger railways, and by the mid-1840s a bewildering variety of options existed on many lines, from the day or weekend excursion to the monthly tourist ticket. In Lancashire, the Liverpool and Manchester Railway ran a Sunday School excursion as early as June 1831,[123] and when the Preston and Wyre Railway eased the path from the textile district to the coast in 1840 it put on similar facilities during its first year of operation. In 1844 it began a regular series of cheap Sunday third-class trains between Preston and Fleetwood from June to September for as little as 1s. 6d. return. Regular excursions from the Manchester area, using open wagons, were also operated at very cheap rates, and the opening of the Blackpool branch line in 1846 opened the flood-gates of working-class demand, especially in Whit-week, when a 5s. return fare from Manchester was on offer. The 'Padjamers' became railborne, and where 1,000 was deemed an unusual number of artisan bathers in any individual resort in the days of the horse and cart, this figure could be multiplied twelvefold at Blackpool on busy July and August weekends in the early 1850s.[124] Brighton and Scarborough experienced similar invasions, though on a much smaller scale, at about the same time, and even at Weston-super-Mare fares as low as sevenpence and 1s. 2d. were luring up to 5,000 or 6,000 Whit Monday trippers from working-class districts of Bristol by the mid-1850s.[125] Moreover, the application of the excursion principle to the Severn estuary passenger steamers brought several thousand iron, copper and tinplate workers at a time to Ilfracombe from South Wales in the 1840s.[126]

Cheap fares were provided in several different guises and with varying motives. From the beginning, the railways' own trips were supplemented by those organized by employers, institutions and speculators; and this was especially true of the textile districts of Lancashire and the West Riding, where excursions became very popular at an early stage. Private excursion promoters bought blocks of tickets and undertook to sell them at a discount. Speculators, in Lancashire at least, were allowed up to 10 per cent of the receipts, and societies and institutions were able to sell tickets more cheaply still after covering expenses, though they often took a profit to augment their funds.[127] Sunday schools, the temperance movement and various philanthropic bodies were prominent among pioneering excursion promoters, especially in northern England. Their aim was counter-attractionist, an attempt to provide a healthy, attractive, 'rational' and cheap form of recreation, for adults as well as children, as an alternative to local fairs and races, and to the temptations of public-house-centred entertainment in general. They provided a more effective alternative to 'the seductive allurements of these public attractions, and their contaminating effects', than did the most enterprising local field day and tea meeting; and the presence of clergy and Sunday school teachers often offered some internal restraints on behaviour. As artificial and even fairground attractions came to bulk larger in the popular resorts, however, the cure began to seem worse than the disease. At Blackburn in 1872 it was feared that the trips might become 'hurtful to the minority, as being productive of immoral tendencies'; and subsequently Sunday school excursions declined in numbers and tended to avoid the fleshpots of Blackpool, offering instead long-distance trips to small scenic resorts and historic towns. At Whitsuntide in 1885 Sunday schools accounted for only one-third of Blackburn's excursions, and only one of their 13 trips went to Blackpool, compared with 14 of the 26 others.[128] In most northern towns, the Sunday schools bulked large in excursion provision until the 1870s, but declined in importance thereafter.

Further south, religious bodies were less prominent in excursion organization, although they played a significant part in some of the Midland towns as they began to dispatch growing numbers of trippers to the seaside in the 1870s. At Dudley, for instance, the Wesleyans' annual trip on Tipton Wake Monday was not instituted until 1877, despite the continuing notoriety of the Wake.[129] Most of London's excursion business was channelled through the railway companies from the beginning, although the south coast resorts occasionally experienced such events as the arrival of 5,000 women and children from South London at Ramsgate in 1867, under the auspices of Mrs Carter's evangelical scheme. A few weeks earlier over 1,000 'reputed advocates of total abstinence' had arrived, drawn from six temperance societies, and some Sunday school excursions were also in evidence; but here, as elsewhere, the railway companies' own trips and cheap fares dominated the scene, and for most of the period, in contrast to the North and Midlands, they were concentrated into Sunday and Monday.[130] Opposition from the Lord's Day Observance Society temporarily brought the Sunday excursions to an end on the South Eastern Railway in 1867, but they were soon revived, and their continuing popularity underlined the differences between London and the northern manufacturing towns in the prevailing ethos behind excursion provision in the early railway age.[131] In the south, commercial considerations prevailed much more strongly over motives of paternalism and improvement. Whether that contrast extended from the intentions of the providers to the preoccupations of the participants is another matter, as we shall see.[132]

The North and Midlands also saw a more generous early and mid-

Victorian provision of works excursions. Where they were sponsored by management, a mixture of motives prompted them: the desire to encourage or reward goodwill and loyalty among the labour force, the quest for improved productivity and a reduction in unauthorized absenteeism, and a paternalist wish to offer opportunities for 'rational enjoyment', remoulding the pattern of popular recreations in a desired image, all played their part. Behaviour was often carefully supervised by employers and overlookers, and attempts were sometimes made to use excursions as affirmations of loyalty to constituted authority, at the workplace and beyond it. John Paley's workmen visited Fleetwood in 1845, carrying banners bearing the royal arms, the county arms and the Preston mayoral arms in procession from the station to the sea. Meals were often eaten communally, and rustic sports might be held on the beach, with the presiding management representatives distinctively dressed in 'straw hats . . . gaily adorned with ribbons.'[133] In 1873 Mr Metcalf, a manufacturing chemist of Church, near Accrington, began his works excursion with a church service, complete with a sermon on the duty of the working man 'to make an effort to raise his family to a higher social position'; but this was an unusually explicit piece of moralizing, and a more common approach was to make participation in the excursion conditional on good conduct, which might occasionally be assessed partly by church or chapel attendance.[134] But such overt attempts to use a factory outing as part of a programme of social control or character-building were always the preserve of a minority, and Metcalf's approach was already anachronistic in the 1870s, when the remaining works excursions tended to celebrate goodwill between master and man (especially at the coming of age or marriage of the employer's eldest son) without the explicit early Victorian didactic or moralistic overtones.

The management-sponsored works excursion did not disappear in the late nineteenth century; indeed, the giant trips organized by Lever Brothers, Bass and the Great Western Railway, among others, were taking several thousand people at a time to selected resorts at the turn of the century.[135] Nor was this phenomenon confined to the textile district, for examples from elsewhere are numerous, ranging from Barnsley coalowners and Rotherham brass manufacturers to London candle manufacturers and timber merchants.[136] But its heyday can be identified with the medium-sized family firms of early and mid-Victorian Lancashire and the West Riding, where employer patronage of excursions came to form part of a distinctive political culture based on close relationships between neighbourhood and workplace, work and leisure.[137]

From an early stage, however, organizations of working people began to put on seaside excursions of their own; and again, this was a particularly frequent and successful phenomenon in the northern textile districts. The Oddfellows and Foresters were prominent among the organizers of trips from Leeds to the north-east coast and along the new line to Scarborough in 1846;[138] Bolton's annual August holiday developed in the 1860s out of the trips run by the operative cotton spinners' association;[139] and at Whitehead's mill, Haslingden in 1866 a committee of the workpeople used the 'footings' paid by the 'principal officers' for installation after the mill's reopening to take 400 employees to Blackpool for the day.[140] Such activities continued to grow and diversify in the last quarter of the nineteenth century, when the excursions increasingly took working-class families to the seaside for several days and even a week at a time. As well as temperance societies, friendly societies and the Co-op, there were working men's clubs and sports clubs of all kinds; and the committees at the workplace were supplemented by similar bodies based on streets, neighbourhoods, pubs, churches and chapels. At Blackburn in 1885, the 39 Whit Monday seaside excursions included two organized by temperance societies, three by street committees, three by football clubs, two by friendly societies, one by a cycling club, three described as the 'working men's annual' and two whose organization was based on individual firms, as well as the 13 Sunday schools already mentioned, which were themselves very much part of this pattern.[141]

Such a rich variety of excursion-promoting bodies could only be found in the Lancashire textile towns, and even here Blackburn was unusual in the range of institutions involved. London and Bristol sent out large numbers of 'beanfeasters' from factories and workshops in the summer months, but, like many Sunday schools, they tended to stay closer to home, invading the countryside rather than the seaside. Unlike the Sunday schools, their arrival was more appreciated by publicans than by the community at large, and this sometimes caused problems at Southend and the south coast resorts.

Private excursion agents were also flourishing in many parts of northern England by the mid-nineteenth century, both as promoters and as ticket brokers for the railways. Where Thomas Cook pioneered, others quickly followed, and the early 1850s saw Stanley and Marcus becoming famous trip-promoting names in the Lancashire and Yorkshire and London and North Western lines. Stanley offered four-day and eight-day tickets from Manchester and most Lancashire towns to the coast, the Lake District and Ireland, at an agreed percentage of the value of tickets sold. Marcus dealt with long-distance traffic via the L.N.W.R. line to London, the West Country and the Continent.[142] The trips from Leeds to Scarborough in 1851 were similarly organized by Clapham's, and at a more local level Swinton, in South Yorkshire, had its Mr Audaer, who by 1870 had become known as 'the veteran tripper' for his regular speculations.[143] By this time, however, the railways were handling the organization of a growing proportion of the excursion traffic themselves, even in the north of England, in conjunction with the emergent national travel agencies like Cook's or Frame's. In parts of Lancashire, however, the rush to the sea in the 1870s and 1880s stimulated a new burst of speculation, significantly organized by the beneficiaries of another aspect of rising working-class consumer demand, as grocers and tea dealers took up excursion promotion, offering special concessions to regular customers or purchasers of large quantities. Four of them competed for the favour of Blackburn trippers at Whitsuntide 1885, and at least three at Oldham in 1882, where the Consumers' Tea Company offered a free ticket to the Lancashire coast to purchasers of four pounds of tea. This rush of activity was frenetic but short-lived, and only Altham's of Burnley remained in the excursion market after 1890. They eventually abandoned tea altogether to become specialized travel agents.[144]

By this time, of course, much of the excursion activity went beyond the provision of day-trips, and in many parts of the country working-class people had long been joining their 'betters' at the seaside for several days at a time. By the early 1850s cheap trips departing on Saturday and returning on Monday or Tuesday were commonplace in industrial Lancashire and the West Riding. Some of their patronage came from clerks and tradesmen, admittedly, but many of these were already going further afield and for longer periods. A Leeds solicitor's clerk as early as 1853 could afford to take his wife to Morecambe for a week, with a steamer trip to Belfast thrown in, although he spent little on entertainment, nothing on drink, and quibbled about the odd threepence when seeking refreshments;[145] while in 1854 a Manchester excursion promoter advertised a 16-day trip to North Wales for up to 7s. 6d. return as being for 'families, tradesmen, clerks and the people of Manchester and the surrounding districts'. The 'people' at large, however, are much more likely to have patronized the 3s. Blackpool trips which left on Saturday evenings and allowed passengers to return by any third-class train up to Monday evening, although in 1856 the L. and Y.R. was already issuing eight-day tickets to Blackpool for 'millhands' at the same low fare.[146] Long weekend tickets were available from most northern textile towns at Whitsuntide and the local wakes or feast holidays, and large numbers of working-class visitors were in evidence at the larger northern resorts for two or three days at a time in the early 1850s, especially at Blackpool and Scarborough.[147] Twenty years later, the summer wakes holidays had been lengthened to cover Saturday to Wednesday in most of the textile district, and a growing proportion of the populace used them to enjoy an extended visit to the coast.[148] In the cutlery and metal-working trades of south Yorkshire, too, holidays away from home were common-place among the labour force by the 1870s, when Sheffielders were already famous for taking 'excursions either to town or to the seaside . . . which they are vastly fond of doing', and the Midland Railway was offering four-day trips from south Yorkshire to the coast at every weekend from June to October.[149] London was slower to generate this kind of working-class demand, and although weekend excursions to the coast were well established by the 1860s, the traffic manager of the Brighton line in 1870 aimed his day-trip advertising at the 'Spitalfields operatives', but recommended 'Saturday 'til Monday to overworked clerks'.[150] The distinction between these categories was undermined by the workings of the poverty cycle, and the number of staying visitors from the better-off groups among the working class must have grown rapidly during the 1870s, especially at Southend and the Thanet resorts; but the early hints of swelling demand from London's lower orders did not develop into anything very substantial in mid-Victorian times, and the rest of the country lagged further still. The development of working-class demand beyond the day-trip, and its conversion into a form in which it could act as a stimulus to resort growth in its own right, was pioneered in the northern manufacturing towns, and especially the Lancashire textile district, during the 1850s and 1860s. It was here that the seaside holiday, as opposed to the day excursion, became a mass experience during the last quarter of the nineteenth century. Elsewhere, even in London, the process was slower and patchier. But working-class demand became the most important generator of resort growth in northern England in late Victorian times; and we need to explain the manner and pattern of its development.

Hard figures on this question are difficult to come by, because the quality and content of newspaper reports on holidays varied year by year, and convincing comparisons over time and between places are almost impossible to construct. A few examples from particular towns must suffice to chart the growth of demand for seaside holidays in Lancashire. The number of passengers booked out of Darwen at the July fair rose from 1,400 in 1854 to nearly 7,000 in the mid-1860s, nearly 10,000 in 1872 and nearly 13,000 in 1889. Of these, 500 took four-day tickets in 1854, rising to a peak of 2,328 in 1866 and a second peak of at least 2,850 in 1885; and this tells us nothing about those who went away for longer periods, although it may well provide a reasonable indication of the rise in working-class demand during the 1850s and 1860s. By the 1880s, many working-class Lancastrians were already staying away for a full week. In any case, the really dramatic rise came later than this, although the figures even then rarely distinguish between day excursionists and longer-term holidaymakers. In 1877 nearly 10,000 people left Accrington at the annual fair, excluding day-trippers; and by 1905, 15,000 could afford to stay away for a week, out of a total exodus of 30,000. Most remarkably of all, the Burnley figure, again all-in, shot up from 21,800 in 1889 to between 60,000 and 70,000 in 1899.[151]

These figures are crude, and the sources are riddled with ambiguities; but this level of seaside holiday participation was unique to the cotton district. We must now try to explain the scale and timing of these developments. Five conditions were necessary for the rapid growth of working-class seaside holiday demand.[152] Fast, cheap transport from the population centres was, of course, essential, and so was the availability of a regular surplus income which could be saved to cover the cost of an unpaid holiday away from home. Thirdly, several consecutive days' agreed holiday were required, with the employer's toleration if not his full approval. Fourthly, the accessible resorts needed to be capable of responding to working-class demand, by the adaptation of attitudes, amenities and accommodation to the new opportunities. Finally, a related point: a large proportion of the labour force had to prefer the seaside holiday to alternative ways of allocating free time and surplus income, for the time and money available for leisure remained limited, and there were plenty of more immediate gratifications on offer in the industrial towns.

The Lancashire textile towns had significant advantages on four of these five counts. Their railway service to the coast was cheap and enterprising in early and mid-Victorian times, but less so after the Lancashire and Yorkshire Railway reduced the availability of its cheap fares in 1872; for the price and variety of excursion and tourist tickets was much more important to the working-class holiday market than the quality and cost of ordinary third-class travel, and the innovations made in this respect during the 1870s had little impact at this level. The service was improving again by the 1890s, and in the meantime the lines linking Lancashire with the east coast had provided eager competition; but although the railways were a necessary precondition for the rise of the working-class holiday in Lancashire, their rôle during the crucial years of transition was generally passive.[153] Lancashire had obvious geographical advantages over the Midland population centres, but its railways did little to exploit them during the main growth years, preferring to concentrate on the more lucrative and less inconvenient freight and regular passenger traffic.

The cotton district was strong, however, on surplus working-class incomes and opportunities to save through the year. Wage-rates were relatively high, and the employment structure of the textile industry gave scope for a measure of affluence among the unattached young and families with teenage children who could contribute to the budget. The weaving towns moreover, offered almost the highest female industrial wages in the country. The high family incomes were becoming increasingly reliable during the second half of the nineteenth century, as major strikes and short-time working became unusual even in depression. Friendly societies and savings clubs of all kinds took particularly firm root here, too, and clothing, Christmas and picnic clubs enabled thrift to be harnessed to the pursuit of pleasure as well as security or economic independence. This tradition was readily adapted to the seaside holiday, and 'going-off' clubs proliferated in the cotton towns from the 1880s onwards.[154] Oldham led the way. Here, £23,000 was known to have been paid out in 1882; the total nearly doubled over the next seven years, and doubled again by 1892. By 1906, over 200 clubs paid out £228,000, and many never figured in the returns. Other Lancashire towns lagged behind Oldham's mainly pub-centred clubs, and in Blackburn and Burnley the Sunday schools and Co-op played a more prominent part; but by the turn of the century even late developers like Preston and Bolton were catching up rapidly.

The cotton towns also offered a favourable environment for the extension of consecutive summer holidays. The traditional festivities at Whitsuntide and the local wakes and fairs had survived the early pressures of urban growth and factory discipline, although their extent was reduced during the first half of the nineteenth century. Urban workers clung to local traditions, and holidays were preserved by workforce solidarity in staying away from work on the main popular festivals. Indeed, new holiday traditions were still being created in some areas as late as the 1840s. Factory masters in search of maximum output were increasingly able to restrict casual holidays for most of the year, and the observance of St Monday was in sharp decline among textile workers during the second quarter of the century, as fines, sackings and the occasional prosecution for leaving work without notice were deployed against the unregenerate. Miners and other non-factory groups with established traditions of working remained resistant to change, but the high level of demand for child labour ensured that most of the population came under the influence of factory discipline in their early years, even though most of the men subsequently took other jobs. By the mid-nineteenth century, the Lancashire textile district had the most disciplined labour force in the country.[155]

Employers in the cotton industry were unwilling to tolerate frequent and unpredictable absenteeism, but, as their attitude to excursions illustrates, they were beginning by the 1840s to come to terms with the established customary holidays, and even to allow a few new ones. The total closure of a mill at Whitsuntide or the Wakes was preferable to constant disruption throughout the summer, and there were advantages in channelling holiday observances into agreed periods. Rising living standards from the 1850s on, enabled the labour force in cotton to take advantage of this new tolerance by extending the traditional holidays, sometimes working through the trade unions. By 1850, for example, Burnley had two free days beyond the weekend at the summer fair. An extra day was widely taken by 1870, and in 1899 the textile workers obtained a full week, after securing an additional long weekend in September nine years earlier. The other cotton towns followed a similar pattern with Oldham and Darwen obtaining a week at the Wakes as early as 1889; in the former case this merely legitimized an established custom known as 'running away'. By 1905 only Bolton, which still took several days off at Whitsuntide, and a few of the smaller towns still had less than a week in July or August. Lancashire cotton workers consistently had longer consecutive summer holidays than anywhere else in industrial England, and the benefits rubbed off on their fellow-townspeople. Moreover, the observance of a regular working week for the rest of the year made it easier for them to save and prepare for a seaside holiday, rather than losing time and cash in pursuit of more immediate, local gratifications.

The evolution of this distinctive holiday system enabled several northern resorts to invest on a large scale in accommodation and entertainment for a working-class market, for the survival of traditional holidays meant that different towns took their holidays at different times, and the working-class season came to last from Burnley Fair in early July to Oldham Wakes in early September. In many other areas working-class demand was channelled into August Bank Holiday week as it developed from the 1870s; but in the Lancashire textile district the Bank Holiday was unimportant, and resorts were able to adapt their amenities to working-class tastes, which in turn gave a further stimulus to demand among pleasure-seeking elements of the lower social strata. Indeed, the transformation of Blackpool, Douglas, Rhyl and parts of New Brighton and Scarborough into working-class playgrounds offering unpretentious, cheap accommodation helps to explain the growing Lancashire preference for the seaside holiday over less demanding re-creational choices in the late nineteenth century, although falling prices and stable wages obviously helped by enabling the seaside to supplement other forms of leisure spending rather than competing with them. The well-established Lancashire habit of sea-bathing in August was built upon in the railway age until a seaside visit became the norm in the tightly-knit mill communities, and social pressures began to work in its favour; while the opportunities for organizing cheap fares, and patronizing landladies of local origin, smoothed the path for the novice holidaymaker, and the communal nature of the textile town holidays imposed its own restraints on behaviour and made the working-class presence more acceptable to the established holidaymakers and those who catered for them. Matters were probably helped by the presence of children in large numbers; it was pointed out in

1884 that in Lancashire 'each working man has five or six tickets to pay for.'[156] By the late 1890s whole towns had a deserted air at the Wakes, with shops closed and churches and chapels having to pool their resources to hold services for meagre congregations. The fairgrounds persisted, but many of the showmen had themselves migrated to the coast to follow the holiday crowds. Textile Lancashire pioneered this transformation of the Wakes, and the seaside holiday became a mass experience in the cotton towns a generation before similar developments took place elsewhere.

The West Riding woollen district, with its similar employment structure and working-class institutions, developed on the same pattern as the cotton towns, but its feasts and fairs were slower to extend beyond the middle of the week, and the seaside habit was less pervasive. The woollen district lagged about ten years behind the cotton towns in this respect. Train services to the coast were, if anything, rather better than in Lancashire, and development was probably retarded by lower family incomes, slower factory penetration of the economy, and the lack of a sea-bathing tradition.

Elsewhere, four main patterns of working-class holiday observance can be identified. In the first place, well-paid craftsmen on piecework in workshops where labour discipline was loosely enforced might be able to enjoy seaside visits as part of a persisting pattern of casual holidays throughout the year, supported by spells of sustained hard work. This was true to some extent almost everywhere, but in Sheffield, and to a lesser extent Birmingham, artisan prosperity was sufficiently widespread to enable seaside visits to be commonly enjoyed at an early stage. By the turn of the century Sheffield cutlers and steelworkers had long been patronizing Bridlington and Clee-thorpes, and by 1899 'a large number of Sheffield artisans' could be anticipated at distant Yarmouth, while a local newspaper remarked that, 'There are Sheffield visitors even at Folkestone.'[157] The remarkable level of working-class holiday demand in Sheffield was based on the extension of the St Monday principle; but in Birmingham, where this time-honoured practice was curbed in mid-Victorian times with the widespread adoption of steam-powered machinery, the artisans adopted and extended August Bank Holiday with enthusiasm, and by 1881 many were joining the clerks and shopkeepers on excursions to the coast which were already being prolonged until the Wednesday or Thursday, with further extensions before the turn of the century.

A second pattern of holidaymaking was more common in less prosperous factory and workshop-based economies with relatively lax labour discipline. Here resources were not so readily allocated to extended seaside visits, as the labour force preferred to enjoy traditional holidays in the time-honoured manner, dividing its time between the pub, the fairground and hospitality in the home. Wherever the old wakes and fairs survived along with hand labour and small units of production, this approach to holidays tended to persist. It was best exemplified in the Potteries and Black Country, where the observance of St Monday survived tenaciously (though undermined by the Factory Act extension of 1864 among the potters themselves) alongside a full calendar of spring and summer holidays, as people continued to observe not only Easter and Whitsuntide, but also the wakes of several nearby towns as well as their own. The power of tradition proved too strong for employers in the Stoke and Walsall areas when they tried to consolidate several local wakes into the same week, and the old ways of holidaymaking persisted into the twentieth century, especially in the Black Country. In 1873 the Potteries wakes were alleged to cause 'three days plays (each) on average, and Hanley wakes about eight or nine days', with serious financial loss to working men who might otherwise have afforded seaside visits, as was remarked at the time. As a result, 'the vast majority' still took their holidays locally at the turn of the century, going no further afield than Trentham Gardens or Sutton Park. Holiday clubs were isolated and remarkable phenomena, and remained so until Blackpool advertising agents began to encourage them in the inter-war years.[158] It was not until the turn of the century that the seaside holiday became a widespread working-class expectation in the Potteries, and in the Black Country the breakthrough was delayed until the eve of the First World War. In 1913, for example, Darlaston joined Bloxwich in obtaining a week's holiday at the wakes, and it was thought remarkable that over a thousand factory workers took eight-day tickets to Blackpool alone.[159]

Areas of mining and heavy industry, with little scope for additional income from working wives and children, and widespread observance of St Monday and traditional holiday usages, offered even less encouragement to working-class seaside holidays. The miners of south Lancashire, South Yorkshire, the Potteries and the Black Country were prominent among the exponents of village-centred enjoyments and irregular working habits, and the same applied in the mining and ironworking districts of the north-east, west Cumberland and South Wales, where working-class seaside visits seldom extended beyond the day excursion before the First World War.

In most industrial areas, then, the development of the working-class seaside holiday was retarded by the survival of old locally-based holiday habits and irregular work-rhythms. Over wide areas of the south and east, however, the disappearance of traditional holidays had a still more limiting effect, as holiday expectations were reduced and the pursuit of holiday extension inhibited by the lack of a common focus for absenteeism. Whitsuntide, admittedly, was almost universal, and often became an excursion holiday; but over most of the southern half of England the necessary accepted consecutive holidays were only made possible by the use of August Bank Holiday as the basis for extensions in future years, rather on the Birmingham model. But extensions beyond the Monday were often slow to develop, except among the better-paid artisans; and only where urban populations contained a substantial number of skilled craftsmen, as in London and Bristol, did working-class demand really begin to expand in the late nineteenth century.[160]

The rising level of working-class demand thus varied in timing and impact in different parts of the country; but even where the day-tripper continued to predominate, the working-class presence often posed problems for local authorities and amusement caterers, for the tripper's company was often distasteful to his social superiors. We shall explore these themes further in subsequent chapters; but the frequent conflicts between working-class and

MARGATE

Chatty Visitor. " I like the place. I always come here.
'Worst of it is, it's a little too dressy ! '

Fig. 1 Reproduced from *Mr. Punch at the Seaside.*

'better-class' visitors are important here, because they affected the strength
and direction of seaside holiday demand among the upper and middle classes
in late Victorian and Edwardian England.

In spite of superficially unfavourable economic circumstances, the 'better-
class' holiday market continued to expand rapidly during this period.
Pressure on agricultural rents and on dividends drawn from certain kinds of
well-established industrial investment made retrenchment necessary in some
quarters, as did the growing expense of the 'paraphernalia of gentility', the
servants, accommodation and private education for one's children which
were essential to maintain an accepted place in polite society. But the seaside
holiday was itself one of the essential features of a leisured lifestyle, and it
gained with the rest from the increasingly common practice of family
limitation among the upper reaches of society, just as the working-class
holiday in northern England probably benefited from similar late Victorian
demographic trends in the cotton towns.[161] But the investing classes anyway
still had lucrative outlets overseas, and in the urban land market and
expanding leisure and mass-consumption industries at home; and the ranks

of the middle classes continued to be swelled by the growth in white-collar and supervisory occupations in banking, commerce and government administration. Many of these, admittedly, were ill-paid and increasingly insecure routine clerical jobs, but the solid middle classes continued to recruit new members, although the professions grew much less rapidly than commerce and administration.[162] As in mid-Victorian times, the lower middle classes grew fastest, and in origins, culture and lifestyle many differed little from the upper working class, especially as perceived by their 'betters'. Indeed, complaints about the declining respectability and falling social tone of resorts were still directed as much against the clerk and shopkeeper as against the working-class visitor. *Punch* remarked on the predominance of dropped aitches on Margate's Jetty Extension in 1889, commenting that the most self-consciously respectable of the women present 'must have been the very flowers of the flock of Brixton Rise, or the *crème de la crème* of

Boy (to Brown, who is exceedingly proud of his sporting appearance). "Want a donkey, mister?"

Fig. 2 Common objects of the seashore (reproduced from *Mr. Punch at the Seaside*).

Peckham Rye society.' A list of 'common objects of the seashore' of similar vintage included 'the intensely military young man whose occupation during eleven months of the year is the keeping of ledgers in a small city office', and '(commonest of all) the Cockney who, after a week's experience of the discomforts of the seaside, is weary of them, and wants to go home.'[163] The social embarrassments which might arise from seaside encounters between the pushing but uncultivated lower middle class and their self-consciously genteel and well-connected 'betters', bereft as they were of the usual conventions which regulated social interaction at their own level of 'polite' society, had long been a theme of nineteenth-century humour and fiction, but it becomes particularly obsessive in late Victorian times.[164] It is not surprising that the 'better classes' increasingly sought to avoid the intrusive proximity of their social inferiors, and of those who catered for them. Some retreated to the Continent; others, with more limited resources, sought privacy economically on the remoter parts of the English coastline; but most congregated in expensive and carefully-regulated resorts or parts of resorts which were able to insulate the visitor of wealth, refinement and sensibility from the growing majority of seaside visitors who lacked the essential social graces.

The leisured and genteel had long frequented Provence, whose attractions had become apparent to aristocrats in transit to or from Italy as part of the European Grand Tour in the eighteenth century; and the French and Italian Rivieras were already becoming fashionable winter health resorts before the railways. The continental spas, too, had long had their wealthy devotees. The Romantic love of mountain scenery had also led to the discovery of the Alps by a cultivated élite, and Switzerland was already well-frequented by 1840. In mid-Victorian times English tourist demand really began to make its presence felt, especially on the French Riviera, and devotees of a more orthodox seaside holiday found that resorts on the French side of the Channel offered advantages of economy and social exclusiveness which rendered them desirable to families seeking quiet and seclusion. Already, the Cook's tourist was penetrating the cultural centres of the Continent, as clerks and even 'swart mechanics' took advantage of opportunities for cheap, well-organized travel; but despite the sneers and patronizing jokes, these serious-minded excursionists were readily avoided by those who considered themselves superior, and the European resorts retained their attractions for upper-class winter sojourners, romantic tourists and middle-class family parties.[165] Indeed, the growth of the market for holidays overseas accelerated considerably in late Victorian and Edwardian times. As a *Punch* commentator rightly observed at the turn of the century, 'The most select of seaside places is no longer so select as it was in the pre-railway days, and . . . the wealthier classes, preferring the attractions of Continental resorts, are less in evidence at our own watering-places.'[166] Switzerland began to attract consumptives in search of pure mountain air, and they were soon followed by winter sports enthusiasts and growing numbers of sightseers whose path had been smoothed by the development of the mountain railway system. The new cult of sunbathing transformed the Riviera season in Edwardian times, and middle-class British holidaymakers came to appear in hitherto improbable settings, as Manchester engineers and Cambridge academics pursued energetic pleasures in Norway, Greece or the Black Forest, while the gentler attractions of Egypt and the Near East became accessible to the wealthy sightseer and antiquarian.[167] Nearer home, the competition of the cross-Channel resorts led a patriotic *Punch* to remind its readers, 'That Britons should prefer Ramsgate, Eastbourne, Scarborough and the like, to Dieppe, Dinard and Boulogne.'[168]

This continental competition had only a limited impact on the demand for English seaside holidays. Many of the new overseas holidaymakers had leisure enough to divide their time between several resorts and enjoyments. Torquay's villa residents notoriously spent their summers on the Continent, but sustained the resort's economy by staying for several months in the winter, while Brighton's languishing autumn and winter season was actually revived in late Edwardian times, as renewed royal visits brought a remarkable influx of the titled and influential, for many of whom Brighton was just one staging-post in the annual round of pleasures.[169] The Continental resorts competed directly more with the spas, and with inland resorts whose stock in trade was pure air and picturesque scenery, than with the seaside; and these were much less dynamic elements in the tourist industry at the turn of the century. Upper- and middle-class demand for seaside holidays remained buoyant in this period; it was merely being diverted in new directions.

Almost all large resorts retained some 'better-class' patronage throughout the years of working-class infiltration. Blackpool's North Shore was still attracting leading representatives of Lancashire industry and commerce in Edwardian days, while Margate was still capable of entertaining the occasional aristocrat in the 1890s, as its satellite resorts of Cliftonville (already specializing in wealthy London Jewry) and Westgate provided a measure of seclusion from the lively *bonhomie* of the town centre.[170] Apart from the flourishing condition of such 'marine suburbs', which was brought out most spectacularly by the trebling of Hove's population to well over 30,000 between 1871 and 1901,[171] the buoyant state of the 'better-class' market is well illustrated by the rapid growth of Bournemouth, Folkestone and Eastbourne. Bournemouth's remarkable expansion was fuelled largely by a winter season of wealthy invalids, attracted by its climate and the alleged medicinal properties of the local pine trees, although a summer season of inferior standing was emerging towards the turn of the century; while by 1901 Folkestone and Eastbourne disputed the title of 'most aristocratic seaside resort', as Lord Radnor successfully pursued 'wealth and exclusiveness' at the former place, while T. H. Escott commented on Eastbourne's successful adaptation of 'what is most characteristic in the social exterior of French holiday life', with alfresco meals on the esplanade enjoyed by an ostentatiously prosperous *bourgeoisie*.[172]

In a less concentrated and less assertive way, 'better-class' demand also expressed itself in the colonization by discerning, quiet-seeking visitors of the remoter coasts of west Wales, the West Country and East Anglia. Serious-minded town-dwellers with limited free time were increasingly repelled by conventional resort life and sought simplicity, peace and communion with nature; and at a less rarefied level the Thomas family's preference for a 'nice, damp, inconvenient habitation that was picturesque' and fascinating to the artistic sense, which took them to the obscure (and cheap) North Yorkshire fishing villages of Runswick Bay and Sandsend in 1886, to spend their days in long walks, sketching and earnest argument, was shared by many professional families with artistic tastes.[173] The great success of the Co-operative Holidays Association from small beginnings among Congregationalist ramblers in Colne in 1891 reveals the extent to which such priorities were shared at lower social levels, especially in the idealistic circles where open-minded Nonconformity overlapped with Blatchfordian socialism.[174] But remoteness also meant selectness, and bucolic charms came to hold a fashionable appeal of their own. The fate of Cromer, as chronicled by A. R. H. Moncrieff, illustrates a general trend:

> It is within our own generation that the beauties of Cromer have been discovered, and their praises thus loudly sung by admirers like Mr Clement Scott. Since two railways have made the place more accessible, some of these admirers begin to regret that they did not keep their discovery a secret. Building is going actively on, and the bloom of freshness will soon be lost from this pleasant corner.[175]

The pursuers of rustic retirement as a fashionable vogue, which had its counterparts closer to the population centres in the rise of New Shoreham's self-consciously bohemian 'Bungalow Town' and the rapid spread of the holiday cottage, soon included many who preferred sketching fishermen's cottages to actually staying in them; and by the late 1890s even smallest and quietest of coastal settlements were vulnerable to the incursions of the sort of visitors who insisted on opulent hotels, tennis courts and golf courses, and found entrepreneurs willing to provide them.[176]

By the Edwardian years continuing transport improvements and the persisting quest for novelty and economy were conspiring to spread the mainstream middle-class visiting public to all corners of the English coastline, as speculative builders began to provide accommodation on the fringes of the fishing villages to suit the taste of a more conservative and less adventurous set of visitors. This effect of the fashion cycle was not solely based on metropolitan demand, for even in 1895 Seaton, in Devon, was said to be easily reached from the Midlands, with 'very cheap tickets', and after 1904 the Great Western Railway's 'Cornish Riviera' advertising campaign achieved considerable success in the Birmingham area. By 1913 the *Walsall Observer* was running a regular paragraph of 'Holiday news from Devon and Cornwall'.[177] The cumulative effect of this opening out of new resorts, in which the seekers after charm and local colour were themselves pursued by the larger number who wanted golf, tennis and amusements as well as quaintness, must have been considerable, and the ability of the long and varied English coastline to cater for an infinite range of holidaymaking tastes was itself a strong stimulus to the ever-expanding demand for seaside holidays.

This rapid growth in demand was accompanied by changes in the balance of priorities and expectations among the various visiting publics. Prominent among these was the rise of the middle-class seaside holiday as a family activity, and the increasing child-centredness of many resort attractions. Margate had already become essentially a resort for middle-class families in 1841, if the June census of that year is any guide, for an adaptation of John Whyman's calculations suggests that about two-thirds of the visitors were in family groups containing at least one parent; and children under 15 made up about half this number. Fewer than a quarter of the visitors were single men or women, and only 10 per cent were husband and wife unencumbered by offspring; these couples were mainly at the crests of the wealth cycle, in their twenties or their fifties and sixties. On the less satisfactory evidence of the August visitors' lists, Margate itself had diverged sharply from this picture by 1890, when sample evidence suggests that most of the visitors were unattached and fewer than one-sixth were in family parties.[178] This may reflect the increasing penetration of Margate's economy by working-class visitors from the East End of London, who were unlikely to be able to afford to bring children; but for most middle-class resorts, early Victorian Margate set the standard to which their mid and late Victorian holiday pattern conformed. Some came to specialize in nursemaids and perambulators; Herne Bay was 'Baby Bay' by the turn of the century, while Rhyl in 1899 'as a nursery resort, stands second to none.'[179] A description of Littlehampton by 'Jingle Junior' might stand for many small resorts, and for parts of most large ones: 'Capital place for children – cricket for boys – shrimping for girls – bare legs – picturesque dress – not much caught – salt water good for ankles – excellent bathing'.[180] For most working-class visitors, this kind of family holiday was too expensive, and youthful trippers predominated (outside Lancashire) alongside older couples with grown or growing children; but the seaside holiday, because of its flexibility, was an ideal device for upholding the ideal of the domesticated nuclear family in a healthy and leisured setting, and during the nineteenth century it became an almost universal middle-class norm. Bachelors, single ladies and couples without children could seek their own pleasures, whether cultural, fashionable or energetic, at resorts like Ilfracombe; but perhaps the most important function of the seaside holiday was to display the stability and affluence of the Victorian middle-class family.

The motives for seaside visits changed little in overall identity during the nineteenth century, although there was a continuing change in emphasis from health to pleasure among all social groups. The practice of sea-water drinking declined rapidly in mid-Victorian times, when the seaside spas also lost most of their customers.[181] Sea-bathing, too, began to lose its importance in the working-class resorts towards the turn of the century. The bathing-machine was an infamously uncomfortable invention, and it may be significant that it had already reached the peak of its popularity in Blackpool by the mid-1870s. Numbers in use remained constant between 1876 and 1895, with the five-year averages staying between 108 and 111 during a period of spectacular growth in the working-class holiday season and entertainment industry; and a steady fall ensued, with only 72 being licensed in 1901–5 and 46 in 1911–14.[182] At the other end of the social scale, Richard

Jefferies could comment in 1885 that Brighton's upper-class visitors prom-
enaded endlessly to and fro, but ignored the beach altogether: 'No one
rows, very few sail, the sea is not "the thing" in Brighton, which is the least
nautical of seaside places.'[183] Bathing remained central to the middle-class
family holiday, and as swimming became more widely taught in the public
schools the therapeutic aspects tended to be subsumed by the pursuit of
sheer enjoyment, especially in the remoter fishing hamlets where bathing-
machines (or 'sea-hearses', as A. R. H. Moncrieff called them) were
unknown, and in Edwardian resorts like Bexhill and Littlehampton where
mixed bathing from tents was sanctioned early.[184] But the health-giving
properties of the seaside increasingly resolved themselves into sea air,
sunshine and climate generally, although resorts competed desperately over
subsoils and drainage in mid-Victorian times and long afterwards. For most
late Victorian visitors, the healthiness of the seaside was taken for granted as
a motive for the annual pilgrimage, but other considerations bulked larger in
the actual choice of resort, except for a small minority of invalids who
received detailed and specific medical advice.[185]

The key to the continuing success of the seaside lay, as we have seen, in
the endless variety of social, cultural and recreational facilities the resorts
could offer. Whole families could be catered for much more readily than in

RETURNING HOME FROM THE SEASIDE

All the family have colds, except the under-nurse, who
has a face-ache. Poor materfamilias, who originated the
trip, is in despair at all the money spent for nothing, and
gives way to tears. Paterfamilias endeavours to console her
with the reflection that "*he* knew how it would be, but that,
after all, St. John's Wood, where they live, is such a healthy
place that, with care and doctoring, they *will soon be nearly
as well as if they had never left it!*" [*Two gay bachelors
may be seen contemplating paterfamilias and his little group.
Their interest is totally untinged with envy.*]

Fig. 3 Seaside as 'the fashion' (reproduced from *Mr. Punch at the Seaside*).

the mountains or the countryside; and artificial attractions could be grafted on to natural amenities to cater for the urban lower middle and working classes, who had acquired, by the late Victorian years, a taste for commercial entertainment in the towns from which they came. But botany, conchology, antiquarianism, sport of various kinds (especially golf and tennis) and a very wide range of other pursuits could be enjoyed in the resorts and their surroundings; and it was the flexibility of the seaside in catering for the serious and the hedonistic, the quiet and the noisy, the respectable and the rough, that ensured the scale of its success. We shall take these points further in subsequent chapters. Here, we need only stress the importance of the widening range of seaside pleasures, from the simple to the sophisticated and spectacular, in quickening the continually swelling demand for seaside holidays.

Even so, a seaside holiday could be uncomfortable and expensive. It was a major upheaval in the family calendar, and it could engender a wide range of social disasters and embarrassments. *Punch* listed some of the basic disadvantages: 'In the first place, lodgings are frequently expensive and uncomfortable. Then there is always a chance that the last lodgers may have occupied their rooms as convalescents. Lastly, it is not invariably the case that the climate agrees with himself and family.' Then there was the problem of ensuring the security of the town house during the holiday. In all, 'An expression of heartfelt delight at the termination of the outing and the consequent return home is the customary finish to the, styled by courtesy, holiday.' After all this convoluted phraseology, however, the 'compensating advantage' was rendered quite clearly; it was 'of overwhelming proportions, which completely swallows up and effaces all suggestions of discomfort – it is the fashion.'[186]

These comments were intended for a comfortably-off middle-class readership, but they were equally applicable lower down the social scale, although the working-class visitor must have found it easier to adjust his lifestyle to the cramped space and limited amenities of most seaside lodgings. For some, the tyranny of fashion held sway in the choice of resort as well as for the basic decision to go on holiday, and there were complaints in 1893 that 'better-class' visitors heading for Margate felt the need to hide their luggage-labels and dissemble about their destination.[187] For most people, however, the social burdens of holidaymaking were probably less demanding, and their priorities were not unfairly rendered by A. R. H. Moncrieff:

> The typical paterfamilias, who is the person with most to say in this decision, often asks nothing better than to carry off his olive branches to the bathing-place reached with least trouble, where the children may tumble about in wholesome air without getting into mischief, and materfamilias, released from the cares of housekeeping, will not find time hang too heavy on her hands, while he himself can lie on his back, and read the paper, and enjoy the sea breeze, and smoke his pipe, and generally take things easy till it is time for dinner.[188]

These observations remind us of the importance of the simplest seaside pleasures, and they help to explain the persisting concentration of seaside visits into large resorts close to major population centres, which continued into the early twentieth century despite the centrifugal tendencies of a culturally significant but numerically limited sector of the upper- and middle-class visiting public. The cost and inconvenience of travel, especially with a large family, was also often of major significance even in the railways' heyday. But we have so far discussed the geographical distribution and social characteristics of resorts only incidentally; and before we take our analysis further, we must use the findings of this chapter as the starting point for a brief examination of the changing pattern of resort development in different parts of the country between the mid-eighteenth century and the First World War.

3 The pattern of resort development

The changing volume and character of the demand for seaside holidays was obviously of central importance to the development of the resorts; but they were far from being mere passive receptacles for the demand flows which were generated in their hinterlands. Landowners, entrepreneurs and local politicians all had important parts to play as resorts shaped their own destiny, within a range of options which was limited but not determined by topography, geography, transport and regional demand patterns. We shall now focus our attention on the supply side of the holiday industry, looking at how the infrastructure and amenities of resorts came to be provided, and at the problems and conflicts associated with the responses of interest-groups to their perceptions of actual and potential demand, and of how a resort could and should be developed. Attitudes and policies in the resorts helped in their turn to shape the further development of the holiday market, as visitors' responses to the amenities and atmosphere of resorts affected not only the channelling of demand into particular places and areas, but also the overall popularity of the English seaside holiday as opposed to alternative ways of spending free time and surplus income. Before taking these themes further through studies of landownership, local government, entrepreneurial activity and social control in the resorts, we need to provide a general framework for analysis by describing and explaining the overall chronology and pattern of resort growth. That modest but difficult objective is the aim of this chapter.

Some aspects of the pattern of seaside resort development have already been introduced; but to take the argument further we need to know more about the timing of changes in the rate of growth and scale of operation of holiday towns in different parts of the country. Our starting point must be the printed population figures in the census returns, although their interpretation presents serious problems of organization and definition. In the first place, of course, we lack reliable figures for the formative years of many resorts in the eighteenth century, and the early censuses themselves were inaccurate enough to give pause for thought about their value for precise or elaborate calculations. We also face the familiar problem of how to allow for boundary changes over time, which is exacerbated by the rapid territorial expansion of the larger resorts, built as they were at relatively low housing densities for the time. Two further problems are specific to studies which attempt to focus on a particular kind of local economy, and they are, perhaps, particularly intractable in the case of seaside resorts. Firstly, the printed census normally uses the parish or township as its smallest unit of measurement, and is therefore an unsatisfactory instrument for measuring population change in very small urban centres, which are usually impossible to disentangle from the surrounding rural area, especially in the large parishes of the north and west. Population trends in small resorts with anything up to 2,000 residents are often inaccessible, and at any given time such resorts accounted for a considerable proportion of the whole, in sheer numbers if not in total population. Similar difficulties can arise when a resort was part of a much larger urban area, and was not given separate treatment in the census returns. These problems overlap with an even more intractable question: how should we decide whether the holiday industry was impor-tant enough to a particular town to allow it to qualify as a 'resort' for the purposes of our calculations? The lack of usable occupational and other social statistics at the level of the individual resort, for most places and for most of our period, makes it impossible to classify seaside towns quantita-tively, even if suitable criteria could be established; and in practice such an approach would do serious violence to a complex reality. Although some seaside resorts owed their prosperity, and even their existence, to the influx of holidaymakers, many more combined a variety of functions. Towns which catered for visitors might also be commercial ports, dockyards, fishing ports, residential suburbs or market centres. Significant numbers of their inhabitants might also find employment in agriculture, or in local industries such as linen weaving in north Cumberland, slate quarrying in North Wales or coal mining in Northumberland and Durham. Moreover, the holiday industry itself was highly seasonal, and many people combined catering for visitors with other occupations which often accounted for a considerable proportion of their income. As a final complication, the relative importance of different sectors of the economy in a given town often changed significantly over time, usually but not invariably in the direction of growing specialization in the holiday trades.

A few examples will suffice to suggest the extent and implications of these problems. Until 1851 Southend's population figures were hidden from view, as the census only published the returns from the much larger parish of Prittlewell in which the resort was situated; and the Bognor figures were similarly buried among the returns for South Bersted. In Mid-Wales the parish of Towyn covered over 26,000 acres, including for census purposes 12 other villages and hamlets besides the rival aspiring resorts of Towyn and Aberdovey, which eventually surface as separate entities in the early twentieth century.[1]

Even where it was possible to separate the resort from its surroundings, problems of definition often remain intractable. Contemporary listings of resorts contain many places in which the visiting season was of very limited importance to the economy as a whole. On the smallest scale there were agricultural hamlets like Benllech Bay, which was in 1904 'becoming very much frequented by visitors, who take country lodgings in farmhouses and cottages.'[2] At a less rustic level, fishing continued to dominate the economy in many places which were coming to be known as resorts, even in Edwardian times. In the St Ives of 1908, despite the new villas and 'rows of modern dwelling-houses' away from the harbours, 'everybody and everything spells fish. Nothing else matters in St Ives.'[3] At the upper end of the urban hierarchy some resorts, such as Southsea, Roker and New Brighton, grew up as suburban pleasure and residential centres within the boundaries of much larger towns, and we find such places as Swansea, Southampton and Tynemouth listed among the resorts throughout the nineteenth century, although by early Victorian times their resort functions were fading in relative importance alongside the development of heavy industry and docks. Plymouth, on the other hand, developed late Victorian pretensions as a resort, with a pleasure pier and pavilion, and a steady proliferation of boarding-houses behind the Hoe.[4] The level of provision for the holiday trades in cases like these outstripped many of the smaller specialized resorts in absolute terms, but the inclusion of large industrial and commercial centres in a quantitative study of resort growth would give rise to serious distortion. Even in a popular and well-developed resort, indeed, population trends might be affected more visibly by other sectors of the local economy. At Great Yarmouth in 1851, for example, stagnation was blamed on a decline in shipbuilding and shoe manufacture, and the fishing industry long continued to exert a considerable influence.[5] But Whitby provides the most spectacular warning against reading too much into unrefined population statistics. It was one of the many seaside towns which changed the balance of its economy during the nineteenth century, as the holiday industry flourished while whaling, fishing and the working of jet and alum went sharply into decline. The result was that the town actually declined in population as it grew in the favour of holidaymakers in the late nineteenth century.[6]

This should remind us that not all seaside resorts grew in a rapid, clear-cut manner from negligible origins. In many resorts, indeed most, the holiday industry was grafted on to a pre-existing town or village economy. Under these circumstances, crude population trends often represent a balance between growth induced by the demand for seaside holidays, and decline in older-established sectors of the economy.[7] Comparisons between resorts, and even between regions, are reduced in value because of the impossibility of disentangling the resort influences from the other factors affecting population change.

These problems have made the choice of resorts for the tables of population change somewhat arbitrary, although the few potentially controversial inclusions and omissions will make little difference to the overall picture. The figures which follow must be taken with a pinch of salt, despite the illusion of precision which is always conveyed by percentages. They are useful, however, in providing indications of general trends and orders of magnitude. We shall begin by surveying developments in the eighteenth century from the vantage point of the 1801 census, and we shall examine subsequent changes by taking similar retrospective views from 1851 (when the Census Report first looked at resorts as a separate category, and found them to be growing at a remarkable rate), 1881 (to examine the impact of the mid-Victorian middle-class holiday boom), and 1911 (to assess the extent of the changes brought about by the rise of the working-class seaside holiday and the diversion of much middle-class demand into new channels).

We have already seen that much of the early demand for seaside holidays was generated in or mediated through London. It is therefore no surprise to find a concentration of early resorts on the Kent and Sussex coasts, close to the capital and with direct and relatively easy access from it. Of the 40 or so coastal settlements to show convincing symptoms of a holiday season by the beginning of the nineteenth century, at least 12 were in Kent and Sussex; and among them were the three largest specialized resorts, Brighton, Margate and Ramsgate.[8] Brighton, with a population of over 7,000, was already by far the largest town in Sussex; and already, too, it lived mainly by catering for visitors. Long before the fashion for sea-bathing had begun, Brighton had prospered as a fishing port, and its population had reached a peak of about 3,000 in the mid-seventeenth century; but the decline of the more distant fisheries led to out-migration and urban decay until the early arrival of the holiday industry in the second quarter of the eighteenth century brought renewed prosperity and growth, with new investment in building and amenities marking a turning point in the 1750s and 1760s.[9] The fishing industry was still important at this time, and as late as the 1820s the fishermen were still capable of banding together in forceful opposition to the enclosure of the Steyne and the removal of capstans from the front.[10] Even so, Brighton already depended very heavily on the holiday industry by the late eighteenth century, and despite the survival of older elements in its economy, it was quite clearly the most important seaside resort in England. Its early growth was encouraged by proximity to London, by the ready availability of cheap labour and building in an ailing urban economy, and by the proximity of the county town, Lewes, as a source of capital as well as genteel visitors; but such advantages were not confined to Brighton, and sea-bathing was beginning in at least four other Sussex villages at mid-century. The relative ease of access by road from London to an attractive coastline ensured that Sussex would be an early and a major beneficiary of the sea-bathing fashion, but the reasons for the channelling of demand into Brighton are more fortuitous. The town gained much from the advocacy of Dr Russell, the author of the most influential treatise on sea-bathing, and his successors, especially Dr Relhan, who wrote the first Brighton guide. These advantages ensured that Brighton was already outpacing its Sussex neighbours when the arrival of the Prince of Wales and his circle set the seal on its fashionable success. As a result of these early accidents of fortune, improved travel facilities developed to feed the further growth of Brighton at the expense of its potential competitors.[11]

By 1801 Brighton had long dominated the Sussex holiday industry. Only

Hastings, with a population of just over 3,000, could show a remotely comparable level of development. Like Brighton, it had fallen on hard times as a fishing port, but its decline came somewhat later. A guidebook in 1797 remarked that the fisheries had 'much declined' within the last 30 years; and again, it was as the established economy ebbed that the holiday industry became important. In 1797 there were still between 200 and 300 fishermen, but the impetus to growth now came from the new lodgings which were being built for 'the Nobility and Gentry'.[12] The six other eighteenth-century Sussex resorts,[13] which had a smaller urban base on which to build, saw few visitors and little growth until the 1790s. At Worthing, for example, an observer in 1803 remarked that, 'In a short . . . time, a few miserable fishing-huts and smugglers' dens have been exchanged for buildings sufficiently extensive and elegant to accommodate the first families in the kingdom.'[14] But here, as elsewhere, most visitors came *via* Brighton, choosing the smaller watering-places to avoid the exacting demands of fashion and the moral contagion of raffish frivolity; and in the early nineteenth century the lesser Sussex resorts still counted their populations in hundreds rather than thousands, even at the height of the season.

In Kent as in Sussex, most of the early demand for seaside holidays flowed into a single resort, although the primacy of Margate was being challenged by Ramsgate towards the turn of the century. Margate was a small port specializing in the export of Thanet grain to London. It had fallen on hard times by the 1720s, and the early development of a bathing season, which began in the following decade, rescued the little town from decay. Investment in resort amenities went on apace after mid-century, encouraged by the ease and cheapness of access from London by the hoys which plied the corn trade, and by 1770 new streets of purpose-built lodging-houses were beginning to spread, as Margate attracted a widening cross-section of London's middle ranks.[15] By 1801 the off-season population was approaching 5,000; and although Ramsgate, at 4,178, lagged by fewer than 600, the holiday industry was much less important to its economy. It was an important commercial port which became a harbour of refuge, and a garrison town during the Napoleonic Wars, and the longer sea journey from London round the North Foreland deterred many potential visitors, especially those of limited means.[16] As in Sussex, the most important resorts grew out of existing sea-ports, but the development of a bathing season came earlier and more spectacularly where older economic activities were already in decline, so that investment and participation in resort activities was correspondingly cheaper and more attractive. As in Sussex, too, resort growth in the eighteenth century was very limited in scale and scope outside the two major centres. G. S. Carey described Broadstairs in 1801 as 'another watering-place of little extent and not much note', and Dover and Deal, though more populous than Margate or Ramsgate, were essentially commercial ports and naval stations. The resort function here was still of minimal importance.[17]

Elsewhere, the only marked concentration of resorts was in south Devon, where Exmouth and Teignmouth had been attracting West Country gentry and Exeter merchants since the mid-eighteenth century. In the 1790s the pace of development quickened, as the mild climate, scenic beauties and relatively cheap accommodation of the area became more widely known among the nobility and gentry. Sidmouth, Dawlish and Torquay emerged as resorts during this decade, and many of Sidmouth's visitors stayed on into the winter months. The south Devon coast was already becoming a retirement area for invalids, returned East India Company officials and half-pay officers. But these were small resorts in 1801, remote as they were from London and most of the main centres of the fashionable season. Population figures include the surrounding agricultural areas; even so, Exmouth counted 2,601 inhabitants, Teignmouth 2,012, Dawlish 1,424 and Sidmouth only 1,252. Torquay was still in its infancy as a resort.[18]

By this time a few visitors to south Devon were finding their way from Bath, which stimulated seaside resorts over a wide area of the south-west by bringing together large numbers of wealthy seekers after health, pleasure and novelty. By the turn of the century Minehead, Lyme Regis, Ilfracombe and even Tenby were reaping the benefits of this westward shift in the centre of gravity of fashionable society; and visitor numbers were augmented by the prospering merchants and professional men of Bristol, 'the metropolis of the West'. But these resorts were still relatively unimportant in 1801. Tenby, the most fashionable, had a recorded population of only 844, while Ilfracombe, on paper the largest with 1,838 inhabitants, was still dominated by fishing and agriculture, despite its 'many convenient bathing-machines.'[19] The most conspicuous beneficiary of these regional demand flows was Weymouth, where George III also brought large numbers of London visitors in his wake, although the journey was significantly longer than to Kent or Sussex. Until the mid-eighteenth century Weymouth had prospered as the entrepôt for Dorset and the Channel Islands, as well as trading extensively with France; but its mercantile prosperity began to wane as sea-bathers and sea-water drinkers appeared in the 1750s, and its renewed growth after 1770 was due entirely to the visiting season. The port remained important to the local economy, but already in 1774 merchants' houses were being converted into inns, and in 1800 a directory listed 107 lodging-houses, although most of the proprietors had alternative sources of income. Weymouth's population at the first census was 3,617, and it was clearly one of the two or three most important seaside resorts outside Kent and Sussex.[20]

Elsewhere on the south coast, London demand had as yet made little impact. Southampton was a haven of polite society with a well-established bathing season, but its population of well over 7,000 was sustained by its administrative and general trading functions as well as by numerous visitors. The Isle of Wight was beginning to attract visitors, and the little port of Lymington sustained two baths and occasional assemblies; but there was little else.[21] Outside the orbit of metropolitan fashion, whether its centre was Bath or London itself, provincial England could count only one major seaside resort in the early nineteenth century. This was Scarborough, which could claim a population almost as large as Brighton's, at over 6,000; a greater number of lodging-houses, at about 120, and bathing-machines, at about 40, than were recorded for Weymouth; and, indeed, a far longer roll-call of lodging-houses than the available figures suggest for Margate, although all these sources are decidedly suspect.[22] We must make further qualifications. In 1801 Scarborough was still an important fishing port and shipbuilding centre, a harbour of refuge and a participant in the East Coast coal trade. It was also an established spa, a haunt of Yorkshire gentry and York citizens since the mid-seventeenth century, and more recently a more fashionable spa resort for the nobility and gentry, mainly but not entirely with their roots in northern and midland England. Scarborough was thus, as Pimlott says, a 'hybrid' resort, where sea-bathing began as an additional attraction for spa visitors; but the balance began to tilt away from the spa at mid-century, as its revenues began to fall while the resort as a whole continued to grow. Despite the persisting importance of other economic activities, a feature which it shared with other large resorts at this early stage, Scarborough was, and had long been, by far the most important seaside resort in the provinces at the turn of the century.[23]

Of the score or so of lesser provincial resorts, the vast majority had no more than a local appeal. Great Yarmouth, with nearly 15,000 inhabitants, and Swansea, with over 6,000, were substantial towns, but sea-bathing contributed little to their prosperity, and most of their visitors came from close at hand.[24] Among the smaller places Aberystwyth, with 1,758 residents in 1801, drew fashionable visitors from a wide catchment area, but owed most of its growth in the late eighteenth century to lead mining; while Southend, with a few hundred inhabitants, was the only Essex outpost of London influence, and should really be seen as a relatively inaccessible poor relation of the Kent and Sussex resorts.[25] The rest were mere villages, satisfying an almost completely local demand. This was true even of Bridlington, where the sea-bathing resort and spa of Bridlington Quay was separate and distinct from the old town; and it was certainly true of the Lancashire resorts which were to grow so spectacularly during the ensuing century.

Seaside resorts in 1801 contained a tiny fraction of the total urban population. The 1851 census listed 11 seaside watering-places which were deemed to qualify as towns, and their 1801 populations amounted to 39,447, or just over 1 per cent of British town-dwellers. Moreover, the mixed economies of Scarborough and Dover were recognized even in 1851 by their presence also in the list of ports, and the inclusion of several arguable omissions would have made little overall difference.[26] Only in Sussex were specialized seaside resorts already prominent in the urban hierarchy in 1801, when Brighton and Hastings accounted for 41 per cent of the population living in towns of over 2,000. In more heavily-urbanized Kent, Margate and Ramsgate made far less impact, accounting for only about 10 per cent even if we exclude Kentish London. At national level, the four leading spas still counted nearly as many inhabitants as the eleven seaside resorts.[27] We have seen too, that the largest early resorts (necessarily, in the uncertain early stages of a fashion) grew out of declining seaports, and they were still in a transitional stage at the beginning of the nineteenth century. Specialization was as yet not far advanced, except in Margate, Brighton, Teignmouth and one or two smaller centres. The seaside might be fashionable, but the response in terms of bricks, mortar, jobs and permanent residents was as yet very limited.

The next half-century saw the emergence of many new resorts, and spectacular growth in some established ones; and the 1851 Census Report found that its 11 seaside watering-places had increased in population more than fourfold, far outstripping the manufacturing towns, seaports, mining and hardware towns, county towns and inland watering-places which constituted the Report's other categories of provincial town, and making London's 146 per cent increase look moderate.[28] These figures are deceptive, however. The 11 resorts were arbitrarily chosen, excluding such obvious contenders as Southport, Lowestoft and, as Pimlott points out, Hastings, Folkestone, Teignmouth and Aberystwyth. Pimlott suggests that the inclusion of these and 'the many lesser resorts' in the census calculations would have shown 'the rate of growth to be considerably greater.'[29] In fact, the opposite is true. Table 2 shows that, of 68 seaside resorts whose population changes could be analysed over the period 1801–51, only 12 showed growth-rates higher than the 314 per cent achieved by the 11 analysed in the Census Report. Forty of the 68 grew more slowly than the 177 per cent calculated for the urban population as a whole. In any case, even the relatively large resorts selected by the Census Report were small compared to other types of town, and their percentage growth-rates are inflated by the low base figures from which the calculations begin.[30] The 11 resorts showed an average population of only 3,586 in 1801, compared with over 13,000 for the mining and hardware towns, over 14,000 for the manufacturing towns and over 16,000 for the seaports. In 1851 the resort figure was 14,851, compared with 41,506, 45,917 and 48,740 for the other categories. Only three seaside resorts were among the 70 British towns with over 20,000 inhabitants in 1851, and two of those, Dover and Great Yarmouth, were also important seaports. Brighton was the only specialized seaside resort among the major provincial towns in the mid-nineteenth century; and its growth was on so unique a scale that its inclusion among the resorts examined in the Census Report distorts the overall picture still further. Without Brighton, the other ten seaside resorts grew by 204.6 per cent over the 50 years: still impressive, perhaps, but slower than the manufacturing towns and mining and hardware centres.[31]

All this should set seaside resort growth in perspective. It was considerable, but it was much less spectacular than percentages drawn from the experiences of the largest resorts of 1851 might make it seem. Even if we base our calculations on the seventy or so seaside towns and villages which had some semblance of a visiting season, excluding major ports and manufacturing centres where sea-bathing was relatively unimportant, we find that only just over 2 per cent of the population of England and Wales lived in seaside resorts in 1851. But this was an important period for resort development, formative in some areas, consolidatory in others; and it will repay investigation in greater depth than the 1851 Census Report can provide.

In tables 1 and 2 we try to provide a quantitative framework for a discussion of the pattern and pace of seaside resort growth. As we have seen, the figures must be used with caution. The vagaries of administrative boundaries ensure that some of the larger resorts have alternative population readings, a problem which persists throughout the period; and the problems of detaching small resorts from their agricultural or even industrial[32] surroundings bulk large lower down the list. The tables are not intended as precision instruments, especially as the percentage growth figures are strongly influenced by the size of the 1801 base figure; but they form a useful general guide.

Table 1. Seaside resorts in England and Wales ranked by population size, 1851

1	Brighton	65569	26	Lymington a	4182	50	Rhyl	1563
2	Great Yarmouth a	26880	27	Hove	4104	51	Minehead a	1542
3	Dover a	22244	28	Weston-super-Mare		52	Filey	1511
4	Hastings	17621			4014	53	Cromer	1366
5	Gravesend	16633	29	Ilfracombe	3677	54	Morecambe	1301
6	Ramsgate	14853	30	Dawlish	3546	55	New Brighton	1283
7	Torquay	13767	31	Sidmouth	3441	56	Clacton a	1281
8	Scarborough a	12915	32	Eastbourne a	3433	57	Llandudno a	1131
9	Margate	10099	33	Dartmouth a	3147	63	St Bees a	1084
10	Southport	8694	34	Herne Bay	3094	59	Portishead	1084
11	Weymouth	8230	35	Ventnor	3055	60	Lynton	1059
12	Whitby a	8040	36	Tenby	2982	61	Redcar	1032
13	Folkestone	7549	37	Broadstairs	2975	62	Seaford	997
14	Ryde	7147	38	Lyme Regis	2852	63	St Beesa	951
15	Deal a	7067	39	Paignton	2746	64	Hornsea	945
16	Lowestoft a	6781	40	Lytham	2698	65	Cleethorpes	839
17	Exmouth	5961	41	Bognor a	2694	66	Seaton	766
18	Brixham a	5936	42	Shoreham a	2590	67	Allonby	749
19	Bridlington a	5786	43	Blackpool	2564	68	Walton-on-the-Naze	
20	Worthing	5370	44	Southend a	2461			729
21	Aberystwyth	5189	45	Budleigh Salterton a	2447	69	Bournemouth	695
22	Teignmouth	5149	46	Littlehampton	2436	70	Shanklin	355
23	Cowes	4786	47	Swanage a	2139	71	Skegness	316
24	Bridport a	4655	48	Clevedon	1905			
25	Harwich a	4451	49	Burnham	1701			

a Population considerably inflated by non-resort elements.

Tables 1 and 2 bring out important continuities over the first half of the nineteenth century, especially in the persisting concentration of the seaside holiday industry into Kent and Sussex. Brighton benefited most from rapidly increasing fashionable and metropolitan demand, and it remained prominent among the fastest-growing resorts even in percentage terms, while in absolute terms it far outstripped its rivals. By 1851 it was four times the size of Hastings, its closest competitor among the specialized seaside watering-places. But demand was strong enough to encourage consolidation and even rapid growth elsewhere in Sussex. Hove might be considered an appendage of Brighton, especially at this stage, and Shoreham's prosperity was partly due to the increased coal trade handled at its improved harbour to satisfy Brighton demand; but the impressive growth of Hastings, Worthing, Littlehampton and even Bognor (on imperfect figures) strongly reinforced the Sussex claim to pre-eminence. The two largest watering-places alone now accounted for nearly two-thirds of the county's urban population, as defined in the 1851 census. Kent, meanwhile, could claim four of the top ten resorts, with two more in the next five, although Deal's status as a holiday resort was still marginal. Growth in Kent had been much less impressive

Table 2. Seaside resorts in England and Wales ranked by percentage population growth-rate, 1801–51

1	Hove	3963.4 b	23	Cleethorpes	195.4 b	46	Cromer	102.1	
2	Weston-super-Mare		24	Aberystwyth	195.2	47	Ilfracombe a	100.1 d	
		2808.7 b	25	Lytham	193.3	48	Rottingdean	99.6	
3	Worthing a	(1184.7) b	26	Lowestoft	190.8 d	49	Lyme Regis	96.6	
4	Brighton a	793.4	27	Dover a	188.5 df	50	Scarborough a	93.1 cf	
5	Torquay a	740.0	28	Portishead	180.1	51	Broadstairs	89.7	
6	Clevedon	470.4 b	29	Sidmouth	174.8	52	Bridlington	88.8 d	
7	Hastings	455.0 c	30	Cowes a	170.2	53	Great Yarmouth	81.1 df	
8	Blackpool	442.1 b	31	Morecambe	169.4	54	Hornsea	77.3	
9	Rhyl	440.8 b	32	Burnham	160.5	55	Lymington	75.9 d	
10	Ryde a	(376.5)	33	Teignmouth	155.9	56	Paignton	74.3	
11	Littlehampton	317.1 b	34	Herne Bay	151.1	57	Skegness	70.8 b	
12	Southport	314.8 c	35	Dawlish	149.0	58	Brixham	61.7 b	
13	Ventnor	279.5	36	Budleigh Salterton	141.3 d	59	Harwich	61.2 d	
14	Gravesend	266.4 d	37	Redcar	139.4	60	Swanage	54.8 d	
15	Bognor	265.5 d	38	St Bees	132.6 d	61	Bridport	49.3 d	
16	Llandudno	255.7 be	39	Weymouth a	127.5	62	Clacton	41.7 d	
17	Ramsgate a	255.5	40	Exmouth	126.2	63	Minehead	32.1 d	
18	Tenby	253.3	41	Lynton	120.2	64	Dartmouth	31.2 d	
19	Shanklin	238.1 b	42	Margate a	111.9	65	Deal	30.4 d	
20	Walton-on-the-Naze	229.9 b	43	Southend	105.8 d	66	Allonby	24.8	
21	Shoreham	224.2 e	44	Eastbourne	103.8 c	67	Seaford	17.7	
22	Filey	199.2 b	45	Folkestone	109.2 d	68	Whitby	7.4 df	

a Listed in 1851 Census Report.
b Growth-rate inflated by low 1801 base figure.
c Base figure inflated by relatively large non-resort population.
d Growth-rate reduced by relatively large non-resort population throughout.
e Holiday industry not main direct influence on growth.
f Growth-rate reduced by high 1801 base figure.
Brackets indicate that calculations are based on an estimate.

than in Sussex, with Margate, in particular, well down the list; but the county's five leading resorts now accounted for nearly one-third of its urban population.[33] As in Sussex, this was a considerable advance since 1801. Taken together, the 18 Kent and Sussex resorts accounted for nearly 44 per cent of the total seaside resort population in 1851.

The predominance of the south coast was further emphasized by the emergence of the Isle of Wight as a major resort area during this period. Ryde and Cowes grew conspicuously enough to be included in the Census

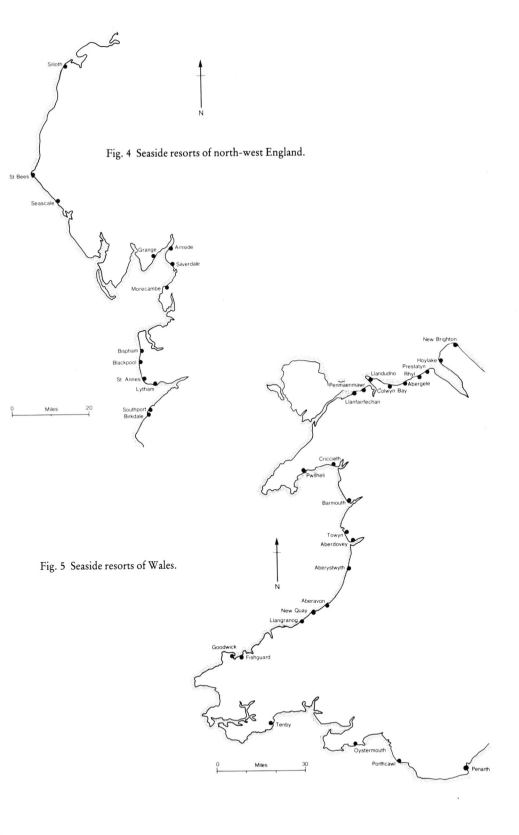

Fig. 4 Seaside resorts of north-west England.

Fig. 5 Seaside resorts of Wales.

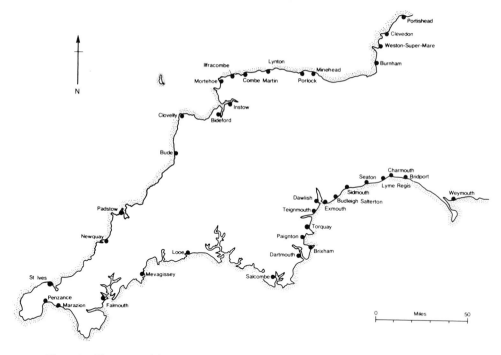

Fig. 6 Seaside resorts of the West Country.

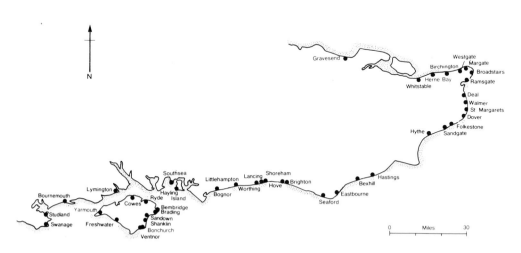

Fig. 7 Seaside resorts of south-east England.

Fig. 8 Seaside resorts of north-east England.

Report calculations, and Ventnor was prospering on its winter season. All this reflected the continuing importance of London-based demand to the growth of the national holiday market.

Despite the railway invasion of the West Country in the 1840s, however, resort development west of the Isle of Wight did not live up to its eighteenth-century promise in this period. As Bath changed its character in the early nineteenth century,[34] it ceased to be a forcing-house for seaside holiday demand, while Bristolians began to colonize resorts closer to home on the Somerset coast, stimulating rapid growth from new beginnings at Weston-super-Mare, Clevedon and Portishead. As new resorts also began to compete for London demand, the established centres in the West Country showed relatively sluggish expansion, and most of them are clustered half way down table 2, growing more slowly than the national urban average. Only Torquay, with its distinctive climate, overcame these competitive disadvantages, almost keeping pace with Brighton in percentage terms as it rose from small beginnings to seventh place among the nation's seaside resorts.

Elsewhere, the main challenges to the established pattern were only just emerging at mid-century. Aberystwyth and Tenby remained the only Welsh resorts of any size, although Rhyl and (at the very end of this period) Llandudno were beginning to respond to new sources of demand, mainly in Lancashire. Much of Llandudno's growth, however, was due to copper mining. Scarborough remained pre-eminent among the northern watering-places, although its development in this period was unspectacular. Southport was becoming an important rival for the affections of the Lancashire middle classes, and Blackpool and Lytham were also competing successfully for a similar market. Nearer home, Filey was beginning to provide a quiet alternative at the select end of the market. Further north still, a string of fishing hamlets on the north-east coast were beginning to attract sea-bathers, but in very small numbers. Only Tynemouth had pretensions to a visiting season on any scale, and despite industrial growth in the parish generally, the resort itself was still 'little better than a village' in 1851. Cumbria was more backward still.[35]

In Lincolnshire and East Anglia, too, resort development remained sluggish and limited in scope. The fastest apparent growth, at Cleethorpes and Walton-on-the-Naze, came in villages which still had fewer than a thousand regular inhabitants in 1851; and at Lowestoft, where the figures look more convincing, fishing and harbour improvements were at least as important as the holiday industry. Great Yarmouth was second only to Brighton in total population, but here the bathing season was still a subordinate, if growing, sector of the economy. As elsewhere in the provinces, the general indications are unimpressive.

Tables 1 and 2 cover a long and turbulent period, and before we can sum up their implications we need to pay attention to shorter-term trends which may so far have been obscured. A decade-by-decade analysis of population change suggests that the best years in many places came early in the nineteenth century, and that growth-rates were slowing down quite sharply in certain areas by the 1830s and 1840s, in absolute terms as well as in percentages. The widespread middle-class prosperity associated with the French wars, coupled with the temporary inaccessibility of the Continent and its watering-places, ensured that most of the fashionable south coast resorts, from Kent to Devon, achieved their highest rates of growth in the first two decades of the nineteenth century. At Hastings, admittedly, the 1820s were the peak decade, and most of the Thanet resorts, fed by the new Thames steamers, also grew fastest in the aftermath of the wars: Margate in the 1820s, and Broadstairs, Herne Bay and the more plebeian Gravesend in the 1830s. By this time, however, much slower growth was general on the south coast. Margate was already stagnating, Brighton, Hastings and Weymouth all grew much more slowly than before; and further west the population of Dawlish and Teignmouth actually fell. Apart from Brighton, Torquay and to a lesser extent Hastings and Folkestone, all of which reaped swift and rich rewards from early railway access, the 1840s were little better. Most of the Devon resorts stagnated; so did the smaller Sussex centres, such

as Littlehampton and even Worthing; and the Thanet steamer boom had run
its course, even in Gravesend, while Margate actually showed a net
population loss between 1841 and 1851.[36] Along the Bristol Channel, as on
the south coast, demand flowed along the pioneer rail routes, and Weston-
super-Mare grew rapidly in the 1840s at the expense of Clevedon and
Portishead. In Lancashire Southport's rise was similarly halted after spectacular growth at the end of the turnpike and canal age, while Blackpool
doubled its population between 1841 and 1851 after the early arrival of a
direct line from the textile towns to the Fylde coast. In Yorkshire the 1840s
also saw accelerated growth, although here increased demand was spread
more evenly as the railways came to all the main resorts almost simul-
taneously.

A closer look at the chronology of population change reminds us that
resort growth in this period was far from being a straightforward linear
progression, and it suggests that temporary advantages in transport could
make a significant short-term impact on the direction of demand flows, even
at the upper end of the market. More generally, however, the persistence of
an established pattern remains clear, even though there were significant
changes in the detail. The influences of London and the fashionable world
remained paramount, and the established south coast watering-places continued to dominate the national hierarchy of resorts, despite temporary
setbacks in the disturbed 1830s. Only on the south coast were resorts able to
tap national demand flows as well as being well placed to attract London
patronage. A few fashionable provincial resorts, especially Scarborough and
Aberystwyth, could attract wealthy visitors over long distances, but most
resorts away from the south coast continued to rely on limited regional and
local hinterlands. Where these hinterlands were experiencing rapid economic development of a kind which distributed wealth and pretensions more
widely among a locally-rooted middle class, as in Lancashire and the West
Riding, provincial resorts could begin to grow quite quickly; but even where
the early railways were opening out new markets, this growth had not
progressed very far by the mid-nineteenth century. In most of Wales and
much of northern and eastern England it was negligible. London and the
'leisure class' were still the main sources of demand for seaside holidays, and
their continuing importance ensured that Kent and Sussex, in particular, still
contained most of the nation's leading resorts at mid-century.

The next 30 years brought significant changes, as the holiday market
reached lower down the social scale to include white-collar workers and
petty tradesmen, and the expansion of demand in the provinces stimulated
sustained resort growth on a substantial scale in new areas away from the
south coast. The increasing availability of railways, as the mesh of lines
thickened in the industrial areas, was important here, and by 1881 few
resorts remained isolated from the national railway network. Rising demand
lower down the social scale also meant the growth of working-class
excursion traffic, which provided additional opportunities in some resorts
but also posed problems where conflicting approaches to enjoyment were
brought into contact.[37] As a result, new resorts appeared to cater for
refugees from the plebeian throng of aspiring clerks and shopkeepers, and

the often rowdy *bonhomie* of working-class trippers. Hitherto, most resorts had shared a visiting public drawn from the solid middle classes, with a leavening of gentry and aristocracy. Now, the widening spectrum of demand meant that resorts increasingly sought to specialize in a particular kind of visitor; and such socially specialized resorts, especially the upmarket ones, grew impressively in this period, in size when close to major population centres, and in numbers on the remoter coastlines. With the aid of tables 3, 4 and 5 we can now examine these developments more closely.

The railways were obviously important to the pattern of resort growth in

Table 3. Seaside resorts in England and Wales, 1881, ranked by population size

1	Brighton	107546	36	Rhyl	6029	72	Penmaenmawr	2212	
2	Hastings	42258	37	Ventnor	5739	73	Southwold	2107 a	
3	Great Yarmouth	37151 a	38	Dartmouth	5725a	74	Aldeburgh	2106 a	
4	Southsea	34226 a	39	Penarth	4963	75	Llanfairfechan	2041	
5	Southport	33763	40	New Brighton	4910	76	Clacton	1963	
6	Scarborough	30504	41	Clevedon	4869	77	Abergele	1916 a	
7	Dover	30270 a	42	Llandudno	4807	78	Seaford	1887	
8	Torquay	24767	43	Tenby	4750	79	Hornsea	1836	
9	Gravesend	23302	44	Paignton	4613	80	Whitley Bay	1800	
10	Ramsgate	23068	45	Broadstairs	4597	81	Shanklin	1780	
11	Eastbourne	21595	46	Dawlish	4519	82	Minehead	1774 a	
12	Hove	20804	47	Herne Bay	4410	83	Skegness	1675	
13	Folkestone	19297	48	Lymington	4366	84	Rottingdean	1673 a	
14	Margate	18226	49	Walmer	4309	85	Sandgate	1669	
15	Bournemouth	16859	50	Hythe	4173	86	Saltburn	1646	
16	Lowestoft	16781 a	51	Lytham	4122	87	Newquay	1600	
17	Whitby	14086 a	52	Morecambe	3931	88	Cromer	1597 a	
18	Weymouth	13715	53	Littlehampton	3926	89	Hunstanton	1516	
19	Ryde	13012	54	Bognor	3920	90	Barmouth	1512	
20	Blackpool	12989	55	Hoylake	3681 a	91	Porthcawl	1397 a	
21	Weston-super-Mare	12872	56	Burnham	3645	92	Birchington	1393 a	
			57	Shoreham	3505 a	93	Walton-on-the-Naze	1371	
22	Penzance	12499 a	58	Oystermouth	3487 a				
23	Worthing	11821	59	Sidmouth	3475	94	Lancing	1341 a	
24	Deal	8500 a	60	Pwllheli	3242 a	95	Hayling Island	1334	
25	Exmouth	8224	61	Budleigh Salterton	2856 a	96	Marazion	1294 a	
26	Bridlington	8117	62	Cleethorpes	2840	97	Seaton	1221	
27	Southend	7979	63	Redcar	2818	98	Lynton	1213	
28	Harwich	7842 a	64	Freshwater	2809 a	99	St Annes	1179	
29	Teignmouth	7120	65	Portishead	2730	100	Grange	1150	
30	Aberystwyth	7088	66	Bexhill	2452	101	St Bees	1142 a	
31	Brixham	7033 a	67	Colwyn Bay	2418	102	Silloth	1056	
32	Cowes	6772	68	Swanage	2357 a	103	Withernsea	872	
33	Bideford	6512 a	69	Filey	2337	104	Clovelly	787 a	
34	Ilfracombe	6255	70	Lyme Regis	2290	105	Mablethorpe	640	
35	Whitstable	6139 a	71	Looe	2221 a	106	Silverdale	489 a	

a Population includes a substantial non-resort element.

this period. Without a cheap and capacious form of rapid transport, resort growth would have been limited in extent and confined to a narrow range of locations. Actual railway influence was, however, less pervasive than this might suggest. A few resorts were called into being by railways, but almost invariably these were incidental by-products of schemes for commercial ports, and railway companies hardly ever played an active part in the creation of holiday towns themselves.[38] Generally the railways accentuated existing trends rather than creating new ones, or provided incidental opportunities which were often grasped by landowners and speculators long after the initial opening of the line. Only in north Wales and (on a much smaller scale) in Cumbria did coastal rail routes enable new resorts to multiply on virgin sites; and even here the time-lag was often considerable.[39]

Railways came later to some resorts than others, and we have seen that some favoured places were already growing faster than their competitors in the 1840s. By 1881, however, most of the temporary differentials had been

Table 4. Seaside resorts in England and Wales ranked by incremental growth, 1851–81

1	Brighton	41977	31	Morecambe	2630	62	Shoreham	915
2	Southport	25069	32	Ilfracombe	2578	63	Pwllheli	911
3	Hastings	24637	33	Dartmouth	2578	64	Hornsea	891
4	Eastbourne	18162	34	Exmouth	2263	65	Seaford	890
5	Scarborough	17589	35	Whitstable	2153	66	Filey	826
6	Hove	16700	36	Walmer	2144	67	Bideford	737
7	Bournemouth	16164	37	Bridlington	2131	68	Clacton	682
8	Folkestone	11748	38	Bognor	2007	69	Walton-on-the-	642
9	Torquay	11000	39	Cleethorpes	2001		Naze	
10	Blackpool	10425	40	Cowes	1986	70	Withernsea	600
11	Great Yarmouth	10271	41	Teignmouth	1971	71	Rottingdean	589
12	Lowestoft	10000	42	Burnham	1944	72	Lancing	513
13	Weston-super-	8858	43	Aberystwyth	1899	73	Birchington	508
	Mare		44	Paignton	1867	74	Looe	505
14	Ramsgate	8215	45	Redcar	1786	75	Aldeburgh	479
15	Dover	8026	46	Tenby	1768	76	Seaton	455
16	Margate	7227	47	Portishead	1646	77	Budleigh Salterton	409
17	Gravesend	6669	48	Broadstairs	1622	78	Mablethorpe	310
18	Worthing	6451	49	Hythe	1498	79	Bexhill	304
19	Whitby	6026	50	Littlehampton	1490	80	Silverdale	249
20	Ryde	5865	51	Deal	1433	81	Minehead	232
21	Southend	5517	52	Shanklin	1425	82	Cromer	231
22	Weymouth	5485	53	Lytham	1424	83	Swanage	218
23	Penarth	4848	54	Freshwater	1416	84	Lymington	184
24	Rhyl	4466	55	Whitley Bay	1369	85	St Bees	171
25	Llandudno	3676	56	Herne Bay	1316	86	Lynton	154
26	New Brighton	3627	57	Llanfairfechan	1232	87	Sidmouth	34
27	Harwich	3391	58	Brixham	1097	88	Southwold	−2
28	Penzance	3285	59	Hunstanton	1026	89	Marazion	−85
29	Clevedon	2964	60	Skegness	1010	90	Clovelly	−150
30	Ventnor	2684	61	Dawlish	973	91	Lyme Regis	−562

evened out, although a few established resorts, especially Lyme Regis, still languished for want of a branch line, and variations in the quality of railway services might have a marginal effect on the relative prosperity of competing resorts such as Blackpool and Southport.[40] The railways did make possible, and indeed encouraged, a continuing increase in the number of resorts, especially in Wales, East Anglia and the far south-west. Most of the additional entries which bring up the number of listings in table 3 to 106 (compared with 71 in 1851) were situated in these fringe areas, which were now made much more accessible. The railways thus made it easier for remote fishing villages to add a resort element to their economies, and thus widened the range of choice in the middle-class holiday market, although the season in such places was inevitably dominated by seekers after seclusion and natural beauty. The new transport system also offered even the most impecunious holidaymakers from the major population centres a choice of

Table 5. Seaside resorts in England and Wales ranked by percentage population growth, 1851–81

1	Penarth	4626.7	31	Freshwater	101.7	61	Herne Bay	42.5
2	Bournemouth	2425.8	32	Walmer	99.0	62	Cowes	41.5
3	Eastbourne	529.0	33	Hornsea	94.3	63	Gravesend	40.1
4	Hove	406.9	34	Mablethorpe	93.9	64	Pwllheli	39.1
5	Blackpool	406.6	35	Seaford	89.3	65	Teignmouth	38.3
6	Shanklin	401.4	36	Walton-on-the-		66	Great Yarmouth	38.2
7	Llandudno	325.0		Naze	87.9	67	Exmouth	38.0
8	Whitley Bay	317.6	37	Ventnor	87.9	68	Aberystwyth	36.6
9	Southport	288.3	38	Ryde	82.1	69	Dover	36.1
10	Rhyl	285.7	39	Dartmouth	81.9	70	Penzance	35.7
11	New Brighton	282.7	40	Torquay	79.9	71	Bridlington	35.6
12	Cleethorpes	238.5	41	Harwich	76.6	72	Shoreham	35.3
13	Southend	224.1	42	Whitby	75.2	73	Aldeburgh	29.4
14	Weston-super-		43	Margate	71.6	74	Looe	29.4
	Mare	220.7	44	Ilfracombe	70.1	75	Dawlish	27.4
15	Withernsea	220.6	45	Paignton	68.0	76	Deal	20.3
16	Hunstanton	209.4	46	Weymouth	66.6	77	Brixham	18.5
17	Morecambe	202.2	47	Brighton	64.0	78	St Bees	17.6
18	Redcar	173.1	48	Lancing	62.0	79	Cromer	16.9
19	Folkestone	155.6	49	Littlehampton	61.2	80	Budleigh Salterton	16.7
20	Clevedon	155.6	50	Seaton	59.4	81	Minehead	15.0
21	Llanfairfechan	152.3	51	Tenby	59.3	82	Lynton	14.5
22	Skegness	151.9	52	Birchington	57.4	83	Bexhill	14.2
23	Portishead	151.9	53	Hythe	56.0	84	Bideford	12.8
24	Lowestoft	147.5	54	Ramsgate	55.3	85	Swanage	10.2
25	Hastings	139.8	55	Filey	54.7	86	Lymington	4.4
26	Scarborough	136.2	56	Broadstairs	54.5	87	Sidmouth	1.0
27	Worthing	120.1	57	Rottingdean	54.3	88	Southwold	nil
28	Burnham	114.3	58	Whitstable	54.0	89	Marazion	−6.2
29	Bognor	104.9	59	Clacton	53.2	90	Clovelly	−16.0
30	Silverdale	103.7	60	Lytham	52.8	91	Lyme Regis	−19.7

several alternative resorts within easy travelling distance. As a result, although the railways were largely responsible for releasing a greatly increased volume of demand from a wider range of social strata than before, they did little to affect its precise direction. The relationship between Morecambe and the West Riding woollen towns, created by an accident of railway alignment and strengthened by the efforts of the Midland Railway to create traffic by offering low fares, is the exception which proves the rule.[41] In general, the fortunes of resorts within easy reach of population centres were determined not by accidents of geography and transport, but by the manner of their response to the widening range of opportunities open to them. Landowners, builders, local authorities, wealthy residents and en-trepreneurs could shape the nature of individual resorts, and strongly influence their rate of growth, by deciding (sometimes after bitter conflict) which of a variety of potential visiting publics would pay best, or which development strategy would be most congenial. Once the railway had become almost universal, these local factors were the really significant influences on particular places. Hence, in this period, the success of Eastbourne and Folkestone, where landowners and leading citizens chose to create and maintain a protected environment for the upper reaches of the fashionable market; or of Southport, where an affluent residential sector was already emerging alongside an increasingly genteel holiday season; or of Torquay and Bournemouth, whose success reflected the growing numbers of mid-Victorians, mainly elderly and female, with private incomes and delicate health. At the other end of the social scale, the adaptability of Blackpool and Southend to working-class needs was already beginning to pay off, and here, too, growth-rates were particularly high, especially in the 1870s. Apart from Brighton and Scarborough, which were big enough to cope with a wide range of lifestyles without undue conflict, as specialized areas developed within their boundaries, and which continued to outpace most of their rivals in absolute terms if not in percentages, established resorts catering generally for the substantial middle classes showed less spectacular growth. By mid-Victorian times, specialization was fast becom-ing the key to success.

The other main theme to emerge from the tables is the growing import-ance of provincial resorts drawing on regional sources of demand, especially in Lancashire and North Wales, and along the Bristol Channel. Admittedly, only a handful of the 20 or so most populous resorts fitted this bill in 1881: Southport, Blackpool and Weston-super-Mare most prominently, Scarbor-ough increasingly as the West Riding of Yorkshire and neighbouring industrial areas became more important to its prosperity, Whitby more debatably because so little of its economy was holiday-centred, and Great Yarmouth more debatably still, because of the importance of visitors from London as well as those from Norwich, the Midlands and Sheffield. Among the second-rank watering-places, however, we find Bridlington well-placed, and Rhyl, New Brighton, Clevedon, Llandudno, Morecambe and Burnham all rising from being mere villages at mid-century to boast populations of well over 3,000 in 1881. These dynamic little towns all featured strongly behind the specialized, up-market south coast centres of Bournemouth,

Eastbourne and Hove among the fastest-growing mid-Victorian resorts in percentage terms, as table 5 makes clear. Moreover, the leading position here was taken by Penarth, which had grown up from nothing as a marine suburb of Cardiff, and smaller places showing rapid growth from tiny beginnings included Whitley Bay, which served the Newcastle area, Cleethorpes, which was fed by Yorkshire and the East Midlands, Withernsea, which depended heavily on Hull, Redcar with its mainly north-eastern clientèle, and Skegness, again serving the East Midlands. In north Wales, too, Colwyn Bay, Llanfairfechan and Penmaenmawr appeared as holiday towns in their own right during the 1860s and 1870s, also catering for essentially regional demands. The rising prosperity of the provinces was at last beginning to be expressed in a wide enough diffusion of disposable income to enable the industrial districts to generate substantial resort development in their own right.

These were significant changes, and they occurred in a period of rapid resort expansion. Between 1851 and 1881 the out-of-season population of the 91 watering-places covered by table 4 increased by about 400,000. In 31 seaside resorts the population more than doubled during the 30 years; in 17 of them it more than trebled. The 31 include Hastings, Scarborough, Southport, Folkestone and Lowestoft, which were already sizeable towns in 1851. But this evidence of growth should be set in perspective. Nearly half the total increase was channelled into the ten towns which saw the highest growth increments; and Brighton, still growing much faster than its rivals in absolute terms, and two-and-a-half times the size of its nearest competitor, was the only seaside resort among the 40 provincial towns in England and Wales with populations of over 50,000 in 1881.[42] Only 12 seaside resorts could claim more than 20,000 residents at an early spring census. Seaside resorts remained prominent in the urban hierarchies of the southern coastal counties, especially Sussex; but in other areas they paled into insignificance beside the leading commercial and industrial centres. Moreover, in spite of the stirrings in the provinces, most of the largest resorts remained concentrated in the south-east, where Margate and Ramsgate faltered but Eastbourne, Folkestone and Bournemouth came forward to match them in importance. More than half the population growth in mid-Victorian seaside resorts was concentrated into Sussex, Kent and Hampshire, which also accounted for about half of the total seaside resort population in 1881. This should remind us that London-based demand was still of central importance, and still increasing, as transport improvements (steamer services as well as trains) enabled the metropolis to stimulate swift and substantial expansion in Essex and East Anglia, especially at Southend and Lowestoft. London's influence persisted as a strong continuity alongside the important new developments of this period; but the form it took was changing, as its enormous lower middle-class population ensured that the extended social range of the holiday market would be felt particularly strongly in parts of the south-east.

The mid-Victorian period saw a marked increase in the scale of seaside resort development, and a distinct acceleration in its pace; but the golden years of the English seaside resort came in the late Victorian and Edwardian

Table 6. Seaside resorts in England and Wales, 1911, ranked by population size

Rank	Resort	Pop.	Rank	Resort	Pop.	Rank	Resort	Pop.
1	Brighton	131237	49	Aberystwyth	8411	98	Aldeburgh	2405 a
2	Bournemouth	78674	50	Littlehampton	8351	99	Hayling Island	2309
3	Southend	62713	51	Bognor	8142	100	Sandgate	2294
4	Hastings	61145	52	Whitstable	7982 a	101	Withernsea	2278
5	Blackpool	58371	53	Brixham	7954 a	102	Birchington	2275
6	Great Yarmouth and Gorleston	55905 a	54	New Brighton	7871	103	Bispham	2244
7	Eastbourne	52542	55	Herne Bay	7180	104	Grange	2232
8	Southport	51642	56	St Ives	7170 a	105	Walton-on-the-Naze	2172
9	Dover	43645 a	57	Dartmouth	7006 a	106	Budleigh Salterton	2170
10	Southsea	43201 a	58	Hythe	6387	107	Abergele	2121
11	Hove	42173	59	Clevedon	6111	108	Barmouth	2106
12	Torquay	38771	60	Oystermouth	6098 a	109	Towyn	2063
13	Scarborough	37201	62	Bridport	5919	110	Bude (estimate)	(2037)
14	Lowestoft	33777	62	Ventnor	5787	111	Prestatyn	2036
15	Folkestone	33502	63	Shoreham	5731 a	112	Salcombe	2032
16	Worthing	30305	64	Sidmouth	5612	113	Lancing	2022
17	Ramsgate	29603	65	Sandown	5551	114	Spittal	1925
18	Margate	27085	66	Walmer	5347	115	Mevagissey	1849 a
19	Weston-super-Mare	23235	67	Burnham	4948	116	Lynton	1770
20	Weymouth	22324	68	Seaford	4787	117	Combe Martin	1733a
21	Cleethorpes	21447	69	Dawlish	4762	118	Seaton	1694
22	Birkdale	18000	70	Shanklin	4751	119	Brading	1563
23	Penarth	15488	71	Swanage	4689	120	Frinton	1510
24	Bexhill	15330	72	Felixstowe	4440	121	St Bees	1436 a
25	Whitley Bay	14407	73	Newquay	4415	122	Bembridge	1428
26	Bridlington	14334	74	Tenby	4368	123	Criccieth	1376
27	Hoylake	14029 a	75	Lymington	4366	124	Aberayron	1342a
28	Harwich	13622 a	76	Skegness	4286	125	Silloth	1340
29	Penzance	13478 a	77	Cromer	4073	126	Aberdovey	1253
30	Falmouth	13132 a	78	Penmaenmawr	4042	127	Marazion	1237 a
31	Colwyn Bay	12630	79	Pwllheli	3731	128	Mablethorpe	1232
32	Morecambe	12131	80	Westgate	3538	129	New Quay	1191 a
33	Exmouth	11962	81	Minehead	3458	130	Arnside	1090
34	Deal	11295	82	Porthcawl	3444	131	St Margaret's	1072
35	Paignton	11241	83	Sheringham	3376	132	Mortehoe	908
36	Whitby	11139 a	84	Portishead	3329	133	Yarmouth (I.o.W.)	847
37	Ryde	10508	85	Saltburn	3322	134	Sutton-on-Sea	835
38	Redcar	10508	86	Filey	3228	135	Mundesley	770
39	Llandudno	10469	87	Freshwater	3192	136	Porlock	744 a
40	St Annes	9837	88	Hornsea	3024	137	Silverdale	713 a
41	Clacton	9777	89	Llanfairfechan	2973	138	Llangranog	708
42	Cowes	9635	90	Fishguard	2892 a	139	Seascale	699
43	Lytham	9463	91	Lyme Regis	2772	140	Instow	648 a
44	Teignmouth	9215	92	Looe	2718 a	141	Clovelly	623 a
45	Bideford	9078 a	93	Southwold	2655	142	Charmouth	575
46	Rhyl	9005	94	Goodwick	2612 a	143	Studland	543
47	Ilfracombe	8935	95	Wells-next-the-Sea	2565 a	144	Alnmouth	542
48	Broadstairs	8929	96	Hunstanton	2511	145	Bonchurch	530
			97	Padstow	2408 a			

a Population known to include a substantial non-resort element.

years, as the price fall of the late nineteenth century released a new flood of working-class holiday demand, especially in the northern textile districts, while the middle-class visiting public also continued to expand. Resort populations were being swollen more and more by commuting business-

Table 7. Seaside resorts in England and Wales ranked by incremental growth, 1881–1911

1	Bournemouth	60067	43	Seaford	2900	86	St Ives	725
2	Southend	54734	44	Cowes	2863	87	Lancing	681
3	Blackpool	45382	45	Newquay	2815	88	Sandgate	625
4	Eastbourne	30947	46	Deal	2795	89	Portishead	599
5	Brighton	23691	47	Ilfracombe	2680	90	Barmouth	594
6	Hove	21639	48	Skegness	2611	91	Mablethorpe	592
7	Hastings	18887	49	Oystermouth	2611	92	Lynton	557
8	Cleethorpes	18607	50	Bideford	2566	93	Southwold	548
9	Worthing	18484	51	Cromer	2476	94	Looe	497
10	Southport	17879	52	Sandown	2431	95	Pwllheli	489
11	Lowestoft	16996	53	Swanage	2332	96	Lyme Regis	482
12	Folkestone	14205	54	Shoreham	2226	97	Mortehoe	478
13	Torquay	14004	55	Sheringham	2217	98	Seaton	473
14	Dover	13375	56	Hythe	2214	99	St Margaret's	460
15	Bexhill	12788	57	Sidmouth	2137	100	Combe Martin	415
16	Whitley Bay	12607	58	Teignmouth	2095	101	Mundesley	393
17	Penarth	10525	59	Porthcawl	2047	102	Freshwater	383
18	Weston-super-		60	Shanklin	2011	103	Aldeburgh	299
	Mare	10363	61	Minehead	1999	104	St Bees	294
19	Hoylake	10348	62	Penmaenmawr	1920	105	Silloth	284
20	Colwyn Bay	10212	63	Whitstable	1843	106	Budleigh Salterton	262
21	Great Yarmouth and		64	Saltburn	1676	107	Dawlish	243
	Gorleston	9665	65	Goodwick	1609	108	Silverdale	224
22	Southsea	8975	66	Frinton	1460	109	Abergele	205
23	Margate	8859	67	Withernsea	1406	110	Criccieth	163
24	St Annes	8658	68	Aberystwyth	1323	111	Porlock	84
25	Weymouth	8609	69	Burnham	1303	112	Yarmouth (I.o.W.)	60
26	Morecambe	8200	70	Dartmouth	1281	113	Ventnor	48
27	Clacton	7814	71	Clevedon	1242	114	Alnmouth	7
28	Redcar	7690	72	Hornsea	1188	115	Instow	−9
29	Scarborough	6697	73	Bude (estimate)	(1101)	116	Lymington	−37
30	Paignton	6628	74	Grange	1082	117	Charmouth	−51
31	Ramsgate	6535	75	Walmer	1038	118	Marazion	−57
32	Bridlington	6217	76	Falmouth	1001	119	Studland	−64
33	Harwich	5780	77	Hunstanton	995	120	Llangranog	−78
34	Llandudno	5662	78	Penzance	979	121	Wells-next-the-Sea	−80
35	Lytham	5341	79	Hayling Island	975	122	New Quay	−134
36	Littlehampton	4425	80	Llanfairfechan	932	123	Bonchurch	−140
37	Broadstairs	4332	81	Brixham	921	124	Clovelly	−154
38	Bognor	4222	82	Filey	891	125	Mevagissey	−337
39	Exmouth	3738	83	Fishguard	883	126	Tenby	−382
40	Herne Bay	3370	84	Birchington	882	127	Bridport	−876
41	Rhyl	2976	85	Walton-on-the-		128	Ryde	−953
42	New Brighton	2961		Naze	801	129	Whitby	−2947

men, commercial travellers and clerks, while seaside retirement was beginning to distort the age-structure of a growing number of watering-places,
especially but not exclusively in the south and south-west.[43] But the summer
season was still the lifeblood of almost all resorts. Even Torquay and
Bournemouth, which had risen to fame as winter retreats for invalids and the
elderly, succeeded in building up a pleasure-seeking summer clientèle as
well.[44] Seaside resorts were able to grow more rapidly than ever in this
period without becoming dominated by the elderly and infirm, as was
already the case in the spas, or by businessmen whose economic loyalties lay
elsewhere. Between 1881 and 1911 the aggregate population of the resorts
covered in table 7 grew by well over 600,000 to just over 1.6 million: nearly
$4\frac{1}{2}$ per cent of the total population of England and Wales. In absolute terms,
this was a considerable acceleration compared with the previous 30 years.
We shall now see how it was achieved.

Over 40 per cent of the seaside resort population in 1911 still lived in
Sussex, Kent and Hampshire, most of them in Sussex; and Eastbourne,
Brighton, Hove, Hastings and Worthing all featured among the ten
fastest-growing resorts in absolute terms (see table 7) while Bexhill and
Seaford grew impressively from small beginnings. All the five major resorts
continued to attract middle-class visitors from all over the country while
depending heavily on London; and the same was true of Bournemouth,
where the West Midlands and the West Country were becoming particularly
important by the turn of the century, and the larger Kentish resorts. But
most of the newly-liberated demand from the provincial lower middle and
working classes flowed into resorts which were closer to home, and this
period saw the swift and emphatic rise of the specialized working-class
resort. London played its part here, as Southend grew explosively in the
Edwardian years, but commuters were the most important ingredient in its
rise to third place in the national resort hierarchy. The seaside resorts of
Lancashire (especially), North Wales and Yorkshire, building on firm
mid-Victorian foundations, were the most obvious beneficiaries, with the
Lincolnshire coast (Cleethorpes apart) responding more slowly to the less
urgent promptings of the East Midland industrial towns.

Above all, these were spectacular years for Lancashire. Blackpool became
the fifth largest resort in the country, and attracted far more visitors than
any of its rivals, though most had very limited resources in free time and
spare cash; Southport, catering increasingly for business commuters and
retired residents, would have more than doubled its population and over-
taken Southend and Hastings if adjoining Birkdale had been included in
the figures; while Morecambe, essentially a working-class resort, joined
up-market St Annes and Lytham to complete a quintet of watering-places
which showed a combined population increase of over 100,000 to nearly
treble the 1881 figure. The rising prosperity of suburban Manchester and
Liverpool played its part in all this, but Blackpool's success owed much to
its increasing ability to attract working-class visitors from far beyond the
bounds of its original Lancashire catchment area, as its publicity machine
spread posters and propaganda into Yorkshire, the Potteries, the Birmingham area, the East Midlands and beyond.[45] Blackpool's success was

achieved partly at the expense of rivals for the same working-class market, especially Rhyl and Bridlington, but industrial Yorkshire generated sufficient demand, when coupled with the suburban expansion of Grimsby, to

Table 8. Seaside resorts in England and Wales ranked by percentage population growth, 1881–1911

1	Frinton	2920.0	45	Herne Bay	76.4	89	St Bees	25.7
2	St Annes	734.4	46	Oystermouth	74.9	90	Clevedon	25.5
3	Whitley Bay	700.4	47	Folkestone	74.1	91	Walmer	24.1
4	Southend	686.0	48	Harwich	73.7	92	Dartmouth	22.4
5	Cleethorpes	655.2	49	Shanklin	73.4	93	Looe	22.4
6	Bexhill	521.5	50	Hayling Island	73.1	94	Scarborough	22.0
7	Colwyn Bay	422.3	51	Hunstanton	65.6	95	Brighton	22.0
8	Clacton	398.1	52	Hornsea	64.7	96	Portishead	21.9
9	Blackpool	349.4	53	Shoreham	63.5	97	Lyme Regis	21.0
10	Bournemouth	322.8	54	Birchington	63.3	98	Great Yarmouth and	
11	Hoylake	281.1	55	Weymouth	62.8		Gorleston	20.9
12	Redcar	272.9	56	Sidmouth	61.5	99	Aberystwyth	18.7
13	Penarth	212.1	57	New Brighton	60.3	100	Pwllheli	15.1
14	Morecambe	208.6	58	Walton-on-the-		101	Aldeburgh	14.2
15	Sheringham	191.3		Naze	58.4	102	Budleigh Salterton	13.7
16	Newquay	175.9	59	Torquay	56.5	103	Freshwater	13.6
17	Withernsea	161.2	60	Hythe	53.1	104	Criccieth	13.4
18	Goodwick	160.4	61	Southport	53.0	105	Brixham	13.1
19	Worthing	156.4	62	Lancing	50.8	106	Porlock	12.7
20	Skegness	155.9	63	Rhyl	49.4	107	St Ives	11.2
21	Cromer	155.0	64	Margate	48.6	108	Abergele	10.7
22	Seaford	153.7	65	Lynton	45.9	109	Falmouth	8.3
23	Porthcawl	146.5	66	Silverdale	45.8	110	Penzance	7.8
24	Paignton	143.7	67	Llanfairfechan	45.7	111	Yarmouth (I.o.W.)	7.6
25	Eastbourne	143.3	68	Exmouth	45.5	112	Dawlish	5.4
26	Minehead	137.0	69	Hastings	44.7	113	Alnmouth	1.3
27	Lytham	129.6	70	Dover	44.2	114	Ventnor	0.8
28	Llandudno	117.8	71	Fishguard	44.0	115	Lymington	−0.8
29	Bude (estimated)	(117.6)	72	St Margaret's	42.9	116	Instow	−1.4
30	Littlehampton	112.7	73	Ilfracombe	42.8	117	Wells-next-the-	
31	Mortehoe	111.2	74	Cowes	42.3		Sea	−3.0
32	Bognor	107.7	75	Bideford	39.4	118	Marazion	−4.4
33	Mundesley	104.2	76	Barmouth	39.3	119	Tenby	−8.0
34	Hove	102.7	77	Seaton	38.7	120	Charmouth	−8.1
35	Saltburn	101.8	78	Filey	38.1	121	Ryde	−8.3
36	Lowestoft	101.3	79	Sandgate	37.4	122	Llangranog	−9.9
37	Swanage	98.9	80	Burnham	35.7	123	New Quay	−10.1
38	Broadstairs	94.2	81	Deal	32.9	124	Studland	−10.5
39	Grange	94.1	82	Combe Martin	31.5	125	Bridport	−12.9
40	Mablethorpe	92.5	83	Whitstable	30.0	126	Mevagissey	−15.4
41	Penmaenmawr	90.5	84	Teignmouth	29.4	127	Clovelly	−19.6
42	Weston-super-		85	Ramsgate	28.3	128	Whitby	−20.9
	Mare	80.5	86	Silloth	26.9	129	Bonchurch	−20.9
43	Sandown	77.9	87	Southsea	26.2			
44	Bridlington	76.6	88	Southwold	26.0			

push Cleethorpes very rapidly up the resort hierarchy, despite competition from the west coast. In the north-east, largely out of Blackpool's reach, Redcar and Whitley Bay were growing nearly as quickly. Meanwhile, the success of Colwyn Bay and Llandudno, which developed along similar lines to residential Southport and genteel Lytham St Annes, offers a further reminder that middle-class demand remained buoyant, in the north and midlands just as further south.

A glance at table 7, and especially table 8, will show that the fastest-growing resorts were much more widely spread through the country in this period than hitherto; but the really substantial growth was still reserved for places within easy reach of major population centres. The resorts of mid- and west Wales, Cornwall, Cumbria and the remoter parts of East Anglia continued to proliferate numerically, but they still attracted a narrow range of visitors, and growth was accordingly limited. Newquay and Bude in Cornwall, Mortehoe in north Devon, Cromer, Sheringham and Mundesley in Norfolk, all doubled their resident populations, but from very small beginnings. So did Goodwick in west Wales, but its rise owed much to the development of the port of Fishguard. Indeed, poor railway communications and distance from population centres ensured that established resorts had difficulty in maintaining their position in this area, as Aberystwyth stagnated and Tenby suffered an actual fall in population. These apart, only Newquay and Cromer among the select resorts on remote coastlines had topped 4,000 residents by 1911, and each was felt by its original *habitués* to have lost its pristine attractiveness. A popular guide to *Seaside Watering-places* listed 20 Cornish resorts in 1895 as against five in 1876; ten in Northumberland instead of one; ten in Norfolk instead of three; and ten in north Devon instead of three; but many of these were tiny farming and fishing communities whose gentle decline was moderated by the additional income from summer visitors like those who frequented Happisburgh in Norfolk because of its 'comparative remoteness', wanting to be 'out of the regular tourist beat.'[46] Palling, not far away, is a typical example of these new resorts of the 1880s and 1890s:

> There are no [bathing-]machines, but the fishermen readily rig up a rough tent if requested to do so . . . There are no regular lodging-houses . . . but as a pleasant substitute . . . the residents, both in the farm-houses and the better-class cottages, receive visitors during the summer months . . .[47]

Practically all the major English seaside resorts had, in fact, been established by the 1870s; and the new foundations of the late nineteenth and early twentieth century were more modest adaptations of existing village economies, with little new building beyond the occasional new hotel, villa or terrace of lodging-houses. The 30 years after 1881 saw a rapid multiplication of small resorts in new areas, but they were patronized mainly by refugees from the perceived formality and artificiality (and the concomitant expense) of the successful resorts close to the population centres. By definition, they appealed to a small minority, and most of their visitors

Fig. 9 A slow and late developer among resorts: fishing boats and deckchairs mingle at Southwold, Suffolk (reproduced from *Pictures of East Coast Health Resorts*, ed. A. Peaton, no date).

sought to keep them as they were. The middle-class invasion of distant coastlines was muted in tone, and had little visible impact in terms of population change and building development.

The mid-Victorian trend towards specialization in increasingly well-defined visiting publics thus came to fruition at the turn of the century, and the fastest-growing resorts were those which chose, and succeeded in attracting, the fastest-growing categories of visitor. Almost all of the larger resorts had to hedge their bets to some extent, of course: Blackpool with its quietly affluent North Shore; Southend with its similar Cliff Town and later Westcliffe and nearby Leigh; Bournemouth with its increasingly plebeian summer season; Brighton, Scarborough and Great Yarmouth with their complicated informal systems of internal social zoning. Some found the upper reaches of the market, with their possibilities for the development of suburban and retirement functions, sufficient, and Hastings, Eastbourne, Southport, Hove and Folkestone were among the 20 leading resorts in 1911. By this time, too, the largest resorts had extended their geographical catchment areas so as to draw on more than a single city or industrial hinterland. Southend's dependence on London, and the East End at that, is the only significant exception, for even Margate was attracting Midlanders in some numbers before the First World War.[48] The failure of Devon to match the sustained resort growth shown in the south-east, Lancashire and North Wales, and on parts of the east coast, may well be largely due to the lack of accessible population centres to boost demand in the changing circumstances of the later nineteenth century.

It was during this period that the seaside resort really came of age as a nationwide phenomenon, as mature towns grew up specifically to cater for visitors on all but the most distant coastlines. Eight resorts counted over 50,000 residents in 1911, and 39 were substantial towns of over 10,000 people. Only Cumbria, Cornwall (leaving aside Penzance and Falmouth, which were far from being specialized resorts), north Devon, Wales beyond Penarth and Llandudno, and the east coast between Cleethorpes and Great Yarmouth and north of Whitley Bay, could show extensive tracts of coastline without a resort of this size. Between 1881 and 1911 the distribution map of English seaside holiday towns became firmly and fully defined. The subsequent expansion of the holiday industry has taken the form of caravan, chalet and camping provision rather than a full-scale urban infrastructure, with all its implications for the growth of a resident population; and the growth of existing resorts has become increasingly dependent on provision for the retired and the business commuter. The seaside holiday town, as such, was and remains an essentially Victorian and Edwardian phenomenon, and its development reached an appropriate climax with the triumphantly successful visiting season of 1913.

Crude population figures, of course, do not tell the whole story. Ideally, some indication of the changing importance of the holiday season to different resort economies should also be provided. We shall look at the occupational structure of resorts in the next chapter; but the most direct method of comparison, over time and between places, ought to lie in the size of the visiting public. Unfortunately, figures for the number of visitors present at any given time, or during a given season, are scarce, occasional, imprecise in definition, and untrustworthy in magnitude. Most are mere guesses, and none discriminate adequately between long-stay visitors, short-stay visitors and excursionists. The most plausible-looking estimates come from the minutes of parliamentary select committees on disputed proposals for railways, piers and municipal improvements, where the temptation to distort was restrained by the other side's ability to challenge a tendentious statement. Such evidence, filled out with press comments and the estimates put forward by an analyst of seaside water supplies in 1878, permits a few tentative conclusions about the size of visiting publics in the popular resorts in the late nineteenth and early twentieth century.[49] The more select side of the holiday industry was even more resistant to quantification.

Most obviously, Blackpool's position as the most successful of the popular resorts is brought into sharp relief. Already in 1865 it could claim over 20,000 staying visitors at a time, about four times its winter population, and as many (though not as affluent) as Brighton in 1840. By 1884 the figure had risen to 70,000, supplemented by up to 40,000 day-trippers, as Blackpool began in earnest to exploit a hinterland containing 4.5 million people within 50 miles, 5.5 million within 60 miles, and 6.5 million within 70 miles: statistics which help to explain the rise of the Lancashire resorts more generally. This brought Blackpool well ahead of any of its competitors, and growth continued to accelerate until the turn of the century, when estimates of 150,000 or more visitors at a time were commonplace.

Estimated visitor totals for the season rose from 850,000 in 1873 to nearly two million in 1893 and nearly four million in 1913.[50]

No other resort could match Blackpool for sheer numbers, although most attracted visitors who stayed longer and spent more as individuals. Southend claimed between 40,000 and 50,000 staying visitors at the height of a short season in 1895, and a few years later 30,000 at a time were said to stay for a week or a fortnight. August Bank Holiday brought spectacular peaks: between 1901 and 1910 arrivals by train and steamer between Saturday and Monday varied between 88,772 and 124,545, and in 1913 the figure was over 160,000.[51] Ramsgate and Margate each attracted up to 30,000 staying visitors at a time in the 1870s, and Margate's Medical Officer of Health reckoned in 1904 that a winter population of 24,000 was increased to 100,000 by visitors and additional residents in August.[52] Scarborough's estimated 15,000 to 20,000 visitors at a time in 1865 put it on a par with Blackpool (which had a much lower base population), and in the 1890s it was claiming a staying visitor population of 20,000 at the season's height, along with Weston-super-Mare and Llandudno.[53] Rhyl had joined the big league by 1913, with up to 50,000 visitors to augment a base population of under 10,000.[54] It will be obvious that the relationship between size of resort and maximum visitor numbers was far from clear-cut, and this remained true lower down the resort hierarchy. Barmouth in 1890 claimed 5,000 visitors in August, compared with the 4,588 recorded four years earlier by a local census at Ilfracombe, where the base population was nearly four times as large. Newquay in 1906 fell neatly in between, with 3,821 visitors to 3,776 residents.[55]

Estimates of the number of visitors per season also bring out the extent of Blackpool's ascendancy. Great Yarmouth claimed up to 800,000 visitors in 1897, 430,000 of them staying for several days at least; various estimates for the late 1870s put Margate's annual visitor total at between 460,000 and 700,000; and Scarborough lagged still further with 450,000 in 1890, 250,000 of them staying overnight.[56] Comparisons using different years for different resorts are clearly unsatisfactory, for visitor numbers in many resorts grew rapidly in a short time during the late nineteenth century, and the evidence does not allow a proper comparison of like with like. Railway arrivals at Cleethorpes, for instance, increased from 320,000 in 1873 (including 72,000 excursionists) to 451,000 eight years later (120,000 excursionists).[57] All we can do is try to establish a notional pecking order among the largest of the popular resorts at around the turn of the century, with Southend in eager pursuit of Blackpool, and Great Yarmouth, Rhyl, Scarborough, Cleethorpes and Margate prominent among the rest. Our very limited and unsatisfactory evidence will take us no further; but the magnitude of the figures quoted should remind us that seaside resorts, though accounting for only $4\frac{1}{2}$ per cent of the population in 1911, exerted an attraction and an influence over many times that number of transient visitors in the course of a single season.

The overall pattern of resort development emerges clearly enough from the population figures, and the evidence on visitor numbers is too sparse and inconclusive to modify it significantly. The increasing importance of easy access from the major population centres is brought out by the proximity of the fastest-growing resorts to extensive urban and industrial hinterlands, although the most successful resorts of all generally had to attract visitors from further afield as well. The rise of the lower middle-class and working-class seaside holiday made quick, cheap transport all the more important, but as resorts became increasingly specialized, the upper reaches of society also congregated in select, protected resorts of their own, with equally comfortable access to the great cities. At all levels of the market, seaside resorts grew fastest, and largest, when close to their main sources of demand. This was true of the provinces as well as the resorts in London's orbit. Hence, it might be argued, the failure of the Devon resorts, Torquay excepted, to build on their early advantages; hence the provincial predominance of Lancashire and North Wales over Lincolnshire and Yorkshire. Such conclusions may seem obvious, but they did not hold good for the leisured, genteel visiting public of the late eighteenth and early nineteenth century. Rather, they were produced by the changing social structure of the holiday market as it became increasingly plebeian and provincial in the age of the railway. Even then, this is far from being the whole story. We have seen that the pace and extent of resort growth varied in different parts of provincial England, and this was strongly affected by differences in the level of demand for seaside holidays, differences which were largely determined by occupational structure, wage-rates, and attitudes to the spending of money and the use of free time. Not only must these regional variations be explained, however; we must also consider the differing fortunes of resorts within each region, which might seem equally well placed to tap a given reservoir of potential demand. How, for example, do we account for the contrasting experiences of Blackpool and Southport, and why did they grow so much faster than Lytham or New Brighton? Why did Brighton, Bournemouth and Eastbourne become giant resorts while Littlehampton, Bognor and Seaford stayed firmly in the third or fourth rank? Why did Abergele and Pensarn stagnate while Colwyn Bay grew spectacularly? Why did Weymouth fail to emulate Brighton? Bath, after all, had outshone Tunbridge Wells in an era of slow, uncomfortable, expensive transport. Many specific questions of this kind cannot yet receive a satisfactory answer; but they draw our attention to the limited value of any attempt to explain the pattern of resort development purely in terms of geography and transport. We must also consider the internal social and political structure of the resorts themselves, and how this affected their responses to the increasingly complex and often conflicting impulses to growth which were transmitted from the outside world. As a witness remarked in 1855 of the South Eastern Railway's influence on Folkestone: 'They have brought the people there – the town has made itself.'[58] Our starting point, before examining the crucial parts played by landownership, local government and entrepreneurial activity, must be a closer study of the social structure of the resorts themselves, and how it changed over time.

4 Resort society: structure and problems

This chapter will develop a theme already introduced in chapter 3: the wide variety of economies and social structures which can be lumped together under the heading 'seaside resort', and the ways in which they changed over time, usually as a concomitant of increasing specialization. Many resorts, as we have seen, had mixed economies, living by fishing, shipping and even manufacturing, and providing services as market centres and dormitory towns, as well as catering for visitors, wealthy residents and the retired. Such mixtures of opportunity made for complexity at the level of the household economy, as well as that of the town as a whole. Moreover, the holiday industry itself was often divided into sectors with sharply divergent attributes, attitudes and needs. Landladies and entertainers catering for working-class visitors had very different characteristics and interests from the providers of opulent hotel and residential accommodation for high-class visitors and long-term residents. As we shall see these divisions often engendered conflict, and they also make generalization difficult. In spite of problems of classification and source interpretation, however, it will be possible to venture some general statements about the distinctive social characteristics of resorts; but they will have to pay a wary respect to the complexity of the subject.

Seaside resorts are particularly intractable as objects of social analysis. The high level of seasonal fluctuation, especially in the large popular resorts, poses problems by encouraging, indeed imposing, multiple occupations and even seasonal migration. This reduces the value of census evidence on social structure, as the printed returns (which are only available for the largest individual resorts) are based on a single occupational label for each person, and short-term occupations related to the holiday season tend to be excluded. The mid-Victorian census enumerators' returns give more detail, but still understate the importance of the holiday industry in domestic economies. Even in 1871, entertainers are hardly visible in the enumerators' books, and local directories consistently list far more landladies than can be found in the census. The directories, indeed, give much fuller coverage to the holiday industry, but variations in quality between firms, and even within individual directories,[1] make them difficult to use for comparative purposes. Moreover, the coverage of directories becomes steadily fuller through the nineteenth century, making changes over time difficult to document, as apparent increases in the numbers engaged in particular occupations will reflect improvements in the sources as well as higher levels of activity. For the accommodation industry itself, visitors' lists in local newspapers provide the fullest coverage, but this source poses problems of its own, as newspaper policy and presentation varied considerably over time and between places, and the temptation to fraud was strong. None of these sources gives any indication of the size of individual enterprises, and the same applies to shopkeeping and other trades which were much more fully recorded in the census as well as by the local directories. The sources for seaside social structure are particularly patchy and unreliable before the early Victorian period, and even when they grow rapidly in volume and coverage after mid-century they provide no simple answers, and often contradict each other.[2]

Even so, we can identify some important common social characteristics which were shared by most, if not all, of the larger resorts, although the degree of specialization varied widely over time and between places. Seaside resorts were centres of wealth and conspicuous consumption, and had more than their fair share of comfortably-off residents. The requirements of the holiday and residential sectors combined to ensure that personal services were well-represented, in the form of domestic servants and laundry workers as well as the inevitable provision of board and lodging. Entertainers were also well to the fore, although until the late nineteenth century few of them took root at the seaside outside the holiday season; and in more exalted vein the peculiarities of the seaside gave ample scope to the legal and medical professions, to teachers and private tutors, and to those engaged in what the census labelled 'art, music and drama'. Retailing, transport and building were disproportionately important for obvious reasons, and some seaside resorts had important fishing fleets or military garrisons. Manufacturing industry was rarely a significant influence on mature resort economies, although unobtrusive workshop crafts or domestic industries were capable of surviving strongly into the resort era, especially when the products were attractive to visitors, as with jet ornaments at Whitby or Honiton lace at Exmouth.[3] Shipbuilding and fish processing were the most common seaside manufactures, but they declined steadily in the resorts through the second half of the nineteenth century. Mines, heavy industry and large factories, of course, created conditions inimical to resort growth, although bathing seasons survived into the 1870s at Maryport and Flimby in West Cumberland, and in the North-East Tynemouth, South Shields and Sunderland all

had flourishing late Victorian resort districts, while Spittal, near Berwick,
boasted three manure factories as well as a specialization in fish-curing. A
national guide-book of 1895 even recommended Seaham Harbour, where
'There are bottle works, chemical works, *etc.* in the neighbourhood, which
. . . depends for its prosperity mainly on the coal trade.' Little seems to have
come of this recommendation, and few resorts prospered as such with
large-scale industry in their immediate vicinity, except when they catered
mainly for day-trippers.[4]

The occupational peculiarities of resorts also made for a distinctive
demographic structure. Women were strongly in the majority, as their
numbers were boosted in all but the youngest age-groups by servants,
landladies, and widows and spinsters with private means. Children became
increasingly scarce in the 'better-class' and specialized accommodation areas
of resorts, except where private boarding schools produced concentrations
of them, while the older age-groups grew in numbers, especially around the
turn of the century. Jobs for young men, especially, were in short supply,
and resorts saw a high incidence of out-migration among local men in their
teens and twenties.[5] But the main tide of migration flowed strongly in the
opposite direction, as the rapid growth of the leading resorts was fuelled by
in-migration, often over long distances, rather than natural increase. Seaside
resort populations, indeed, were older and more transient than those of
most provincial towns, even if we ignore the large number of seasonal
migrants; but by the last quarter of the nineteenth century many of them
were also becoming remarkable for low birth-rates. More surprisingly at
first glance, death-rates also fell as the distinctive age/sex structure of the
resorts evolved; but the prevailing level of infant and child mortality, and the
high risks associated with childbirth, meant that an older (and relatively
affluent) population was more likely to produce the low mortality levels on
which the resorts thrived.

Most of these features of seaside social structure and demography are
predictable enough in outline; but it will be instructive to look more closely
at the pace of change over time and the extent of variation between places,
before examining some of the problems arising from the peculiarities of the
seaside, and drawing out some wider implications.

In the first place, some of the larger seaside resorts were clearly becoming
centres of wealth and conspicuous consumption for residents as well as
visitors by the second quarter of the nineteenth century. Brighton, indeed,
had long been attracting wealthy London commuters. In 1821 Dr John
Evans praised the stage-coaches which performed the journey in six hours,
and expected balloons to reduce the time by two-thirds in the foreseeable
future; and in 1823 Cobbett described 'stock-jobbers . . . [who] skip
backward and forward on the coaches, and actually *carry on stock-jobbing*,
in 'Change Alley, though they reside in Brighton'.[6] Health-seekers with
private incomes had long been building houses at the seaside, especially in
and around the south Devon resorts, and by the late 1840s the results of
these migrations of the wealthy were becoming apparent in tax returns. *Per
capita* payments of taxes on luxury items in 1847–8 stood at £0.51 for six of
the leading watering-places (including four seaside resorts) as against £0.42
for London itself, and an average of £0.23 for the 110 towns analysed.[7]

The 1831 census suggests that wealthy residents were already congregating conspicuously in some of the south coast resorts, from Devon to Kent, and in a few other favoured places; and the surviving architectural evidence of opulent middle-class villas in places like Sidmouth and Lyme Regis bears this out.[8] Table 9 shows a marked over-representation of the élite category of 'capitalists, bankers, professional and other educated men' in several resorts. The figures may have been distorted in some places by early visitors, as this was a May census; but on the other hand some of the smaller resorts include considerable surrounding rural populations which would tend to depress the percentages. The criteria for inclusion among this élite may have varied somewhat from place to place, but this evidence is well worth using.

Table 9. Elite groupings as a percentage of the male population in resorts, 1831, with location factors[9]

	%	Location factor		%	Location factor
Weymouth	9.00	3.47	Lyme Regis	5.86	2.26
Tenby	8.50	3.27	East Budleigh	5.82	2.24
Margate	8.05	3.10	Aberystwyth	5.55	2.14
Hornsea	7.30	2.81	Deal	5.40	2.08
Hastings	6.92	2.67	Broadwater (Worthing)	4.95	1.91
Teignmouth (East and West)	6.86	2.64	South Bersted (Bognor)	4.95	1.91
Sidmouth	6.25	2.41	Brighthelmstone	4.90	1.89

The location factor in this case is found by dividing the percentage of the local population in a given category, by the percentage of the national population in the same category. This forms a crude but useful index of the concentration of particular occupations in particular places or areas.

These are very impressive figures, although there are some surprising omissions from this leading group, and Hornsea, which must already have been attracting commercial residents from Hull, is a remarkable inclusion. Exmouth, Dawlish and even Tor-moham, the emergent Torquay, all fell well below the figures displayed by their Devon rivals, and Ramsgate, North Meols (*alias* Southport) and Scarborough fell around or even below the national norm. But the importance of wealthy residents to many resort economies, especially within easy reach of London, or where climatic advantages were well-known, is clearly apparent even at this early stage.

Subsequent censuses unfortunately abandon the convenient, if rather vague, élite category employed in 1831, and attempts to identify the affluent become increasingly perilous. The higher commercial occupations are no longer presented separately, and contemporaries were clear about the dangers of trusting the superficially attractive label of 'independent means' as an indicator of wealth and status. It included:

not merely the wealthy, or even those in easy circumstances, but all who support themselves upon their own means without any occupation. It will, therefore, afford no test of the relative amount of wealthy people in different localities . . . as while it includes in the more rural districts many poor widows or aged men living upon their savings, it omits many large capitalists who are returned under their proper heads in the list of 'occupations'.[10]

In the absence of more convincing evidence, however, the proportion of the population claiming 'independent means' has some validity as an indicator of resort social structure. As the passage quoted above suggests, the poor people living on their savings who swelled the national total were probably mainly rural, while the effort of moving to a resort and sustaining the high cost of living in a fashionable setting suggests that those claiming 'independent means' at the seaside were likely to be comfortably off. The figures in table 10 will therefore tend to understate the relative importance of the affluent and unoccupied in resort populations, especially as a high proportion were probably heads of households.

Table 10. People of 'independent means' as percentage of population over 20 years old in seaside resorts, 1841, with location factors[11]

| | Males | | Females | |
	% of male population	Location factor	% of female population	Location factor
Brighton	7.32	2.51	12.50	1.82
Weymouth	6.80	2.33	10.69	1.55
Margate and Ramsgate	9.23	3.16	13.32	1.94
Great Yarmouth	3.90	1.34	10.28	1.50
Hastings	5.35	1.83	11.63	1.69
Scarborough	6.71	2.30	12.11	1.76
Tenby	8.33	2.86	15.43	2.24

This evidence reinforces the findings in table 9, and also brings out the importance of female annuitants and property-owners in resort populations. Scarborough and Brighton show up significantly better on the 1841 criteria than they did in 1831, but the low figures for Great Yarmouth offer a reminder that the town's economy was still dominated by maritime and related interests as the demand for high-class housing continued to grow slowly in face of the rival residential attractions of Norwich.[12] One caveat should be entered. As in 1831, the holiday season had already started in Margate and elsewhere, and some of the people of 'independent means' recorded in the census were certainly visitors rather than residents.[13] Even so, prosperous residents were already becoming important to many resorts in the second quarter of the nineteenth century, especially as their needs and resources as employers and consumers made a disproportionate impact on the local economy and social structure.

After 1841 information about individual resorts in the printed census returns almost dries up, although evidence from Brighton, Dover and Great Yarmouth suggests that existing trends and divergences of experience were maintained. The census enumerators' books shed a clearer light on the importance of the residential interest in some of the smaller resorts around mid-century: at Lytham in 1861, for instance, 15.5 per cent of all household heads claimed 'independent means', while at Ilfracombe in 1851 the figure was 13 per cent, with a further 18.3 per cent returning no occupation. In this latter case these proportions had fallen by 1871, to rise again over the next 40 years as an influx of comfortably-off spinsters, widows and retired civil servants and military men took place.[14] At Brighton and Hastings, and no doubt in many other resorts, the mid-Victorian years saw a steady expansion of the affluent residential sector; but the Ilfracombe pattern of accelerating growth in the late nineteenth and early twentieth century was probably general, although changing census categories make it very difficult to document. Table 11, however, shows that in 1911 all of the leading resorts had a high proportion of retired or unoccupied men in the population. Bournemouth, indeed, had the highest proportion of unoccupied males over ten years old of any English county borough in 1901. The figures for women

Table 11. Proportion of population per 10,000 over ten years old labelled 'retired' or 'unoccupied' in the 1911 census[15]

	Men	Women
All urban districts, England and Wales	1579	6569
Blackpool	1897	6147
Bournemouth	2171	5939
Brighton	1970	6269
Eastbourne	2260	5617
Hastings	2280	6144
Southend	1964	6866
Southport	2014	6170

were complicated by the unusually large number of job opportunities in accommodation, catering and domestic service. The increasing importance of the retired at the turn of the century will also become apparent when we look at the changing age-structure of seaside resort populations, although the impact of retirement was patchy and limited compared with developments between the wars.[16]

Retirement, even to the seaside, did not inevitably connote opulence. Increasingly, all it needed was a modest competence; and the same applied to seaside commuting in resorts close to the main population centres. Retired tradesmen in new streets behind the sea-front at Blackpool's North Shore, and commercial travellers and office workers at Southend and Blackpool's South Shore, jumped at the chance of poky, often jerry-built semi-detached or even terraced houses at relatively low rentals in the 1890s and early twentieth century.[17] Much more effective as a measure of affluence is the level of servant-keeping, which will also serve to illuminate another aspect of the distinctive nature of seaside social structure.

Servants are another problematic census category, as definitions and sub-divisions changed over time; but we can provide comparative figures for several resorts in 1841 and 1911, although the printed returns between 1851 and 1891 only offer evidence on Brighton, Dover and Great Yarmouth. The 1841 figures are not, of course, directly comparable with those for

1911; but in each year the highest location factors are very impressive indeed if we bear in mind the high base figure for domestic servants as a proportion of the national female population. Again, comparisons between the resorts are instructive. As we might expect, Brighton almost topped the list in 1841; but it was outshone by Tenby, the only small resort with an elevated social tone to creep into the census listings, and this offers a reminder that Brighton had already outgrown exclusivity, and that its sprawling back streets contained a very numerous lower middle-class and working-class population. Even so, domestic servants bulked larger in Brighton's economy

Table 12. Female domestic servants as a percentage of the female population (over 20 years old in 1841, over ten years old in 1911) in seaside resorts, with location factors[18]

| | 1841 | | 1911 | |
	%	Location factor	%	Location factor
Weymouth	18.55	1.75	—	—
Margate/Ramsgate	17.16	1.62	—	—
Great Yarmouth	8.51	0.80	7.74	0.90
Brighton	20.15	1.90	10.93	1.28
Hastings	18.70	1.76	14.02	1.64
Scarborough	14.19	1.34	—	—
Tenby	21.42	2.02	—	—
Southend	—	—	12.60	1.47
Blackpool	—	—	6.82	0.80
Southport	—	—	13.47	1.57
Bournemouth	—	—	16.76	1.96
Eastbourne	—	—	16.58	1.94

than in the successful but less prestigious resorts of Margate, Ramsgate, Weymouth and even Hastings, and the social primacy of Brighton and Tenby in the census report's rather eccentric list is reinforced by location factors of 2.27 and 2.20 for manservants, an even clearer indication of high status, although the vagueness of this category in 1841 is sufficient to inhibit its elevation into a full table. Mid-Victorian Brighton also showed high location factors for specialized categories of female servant. Scarborough and Great Yarmouth, on the other hand, provincial resorts with strong port and harbour interests, were far adrift of the more specialized southern resorts, confirming the suggestion in table 9 that wealthy residents were most in evidence in the resorts of Kent, Sussex and south Devon.

The 1911 listing, drawn from the eight resorts with populations of over 50,000, brings out the spectacular success of Bournemouth and Eastbourne (both in their infancy in 1841) as high-class residential resorts, eclipsing Hastings and even Southport, which performed similar functions for prosperous Lancashire businessmen and retired people. Brighton was now well down the list, even below Southend, where the needs of London commuters must have made a considerable impact; while the other resorts with a mainly working-class visiting public, Blackpool and Great Yarmouth, actually fell below the national average for female domestic servants.[19]

Table 13, which covers a wider range of resorts, brings out the variation at the turn of the century even more clearly, though with a different basis for the calculation.

The concentration of the servant-keeping classes into particular places and tracts of coastline was the product of many years of evolution and adaptation. Sussex and Devon were still particularly highly favoured, while the high figures for some of the smaller Lancashire resorts reflect a strong regional demand for seaside residence and retirement in more socially salubrious surroundings than could be provided even by the 'better-class' areas of Blackpool or Morecambe. East Kent, Essex and the Yorkshire coast

Table 13. Number of domestic servants as a percentage of the total number of separate households in resorts in selected counties, 1901[20]

Sussex		Kent		Essex		Lancashire	
Hove	65.3	Folkestone	41.4	Southend	28.9	St Annes	53.4
Eastbourne	43.8	Broadstairs	38.2	Clacton	26.8	Birkdale	48.8
Worthing	41.0	Margate	31.9			Lytham	40.6
Bexhill	37.4	Herne Bay	31.9	Devon		Southport	34.2
Hastings	35.6	Ramsgate	25.9	Exmouth	43.2	Blackpool	21.0
Brighton	25.8	Dover	24.5	Torquay	42.8	Morecambe	13.5
Littlehampton	24.1			Paignton	39.1		
				Teignmouth	37.5	Yorkshire	
				Ilfracombe	32.2	Redcar	29.3
						Scarborough	28.4
						Bridlington	25.7
						Whitby	22.1

suffered from climatic disadvantages and a reputation for plebeian holiday-makers. At the top end of the scale, the level of servant-keeping in Hove challenged comparison with the fashionable West End of London, or with high-class Kentish residential suburbs such as Chislehurst; while even Littlehampton and Bridlington were better-endowed with servants than a county town and market centre such as Chelmsford. Only Morecambe of the resorts in table 13 fell below this frame of reference, and even here the level of servant-keeping was much higher than in the specialized manufacturing towns. Hove and St Annes, Exmouth and Eastbourne were exceptionally opulent even among the seaside resorts; but a generally high incidence of servant-keeping expressed the relative affluence of even the more unfashionable provincial watering-places.

In many seaside resorts, however, the provision of accommodation for holidaymakers became the single most important economic activity in the course of the nineteenth century; but its suppliers are difficult to fit into social categories, and even to count. This is due partly to stratification within the trade, in terms of size of business and standard of accommodation, partly to the varying place of income from visitors in household economies, and partly to the vagaries of the sources, which cannot be collated to produce a convincing overall picture until the very end of our period. Throughout the nineteenth century, local directories usually listed more landladies than the census, while visitors' lists and local enumerations by surveyors and medical officers find more lodging-houses than either. The position is further complicated by the fact that, although almost all the landladies, as such, were self-employed tradespeople (a very few managed houses on behalf of others), many depended on additional income from husbands whose occupations ranged from the professional to the unskilled manual. This undermines the conventional approach to analysing social structure through the occupation of a male head of household.

The seaside accommodation industry took four forms in this period, if we discount the mainly Edwardian vogue for camping and the similarly late appearance of the first precursors of the holiday chalet.[21] From the beginning, the more opulent visitors took whole houses, often for long lets, and catered for themselves, often bringing their own servants.[22] By the late eighteenth century, however, the apartments system was becoming common, and it rapidly became the norm during the nineteenth century as visitors of limited means grew rapidly in numbers and put pressure on existing accommodation. It involved taking a suite of rooms (increasingly often a single room, or even a shared room at the working-class end of the market), buying food at shops and markets, and entrusting the cooking and cleaning to a resident landlady and her servants, most of whom were taken on solely for the season.[23] Full board, with meals provided by the landlady, was a more expensive option, offering the landlady an opportunity to make a profit on catering as well as accommodation. It was already appearing in some resorts during the late eighteenth and early nineteenth century,[24] but its spread thereafter was patchy and generally slow, with wide variations between resorts. At the top end of the scale came the opulent purpose-built hotels, which really began to proliferate in mid-Victorian times, providing spacious amenities which distinguished them from the older inns, whose cramped quarters had generally been used as temporary bases from which to look for cheaper and more congenial long-term accommodation.[25]

Seaside accommodation was already big business in the larger resorts at the beginning of the nineteenth century. Accommodation accounted for nearly 40 per cent of all entries in Cobby's Brighton directory for 1800, when nearly 300 landladies accounted for about 20 per cent of the town's households.[26] Soon afterwards, indeed, Brighton lodging-house keepers had to step in against 'the system of forestalling or jobbing lodgings', as profiteering middlemen tried to interpose themselves in what was perceived to be a highly lucrative trade. As a remedy, a registry of apartments was set up, and the lodging-house keepers resolved 'not to let them excepting to the party immediately occupying them.' By this time London agents had long been offering to procure Margate lodgings for intending visitors on a commission basis.[27]

Unusually full and revealing directories enable us to say a little more about the supply of accommodation in two rather smaller and less specialized resorts which were probably closer to the mainstream of seaside experience.[28] The 108 lodging-houses listed for Weymouth in a guide-book published in 1800 accounted for roughly one house in every seven. Scarborough's list in 1808 was slightly longer, but worked out at one house in every 11 or 12 in a larger population. These lists certainly excluded many occasional holiday caterers, but probably included most of those who depended on letting apartments or whole houses to visitors for a significant proportion of their income. Even so (and as in Brighton) many had additional occupations.[29] At Scarborough, half of the proprietors listed were also shopkeepers or tradespeople of various kinds, and one was a surgeon. At Weymouth all except the keepers of inns and boarding-houses had additional resources, at least among the men, and only one lodging-house keeper appeared as such in the 1812 poll-book.[30] More than 70 per cent of those listed in both resorts were men, a pattern which was to change sharply later in the century. This evidence suggests that at this stage seaside accommodation was more a property transaction than a service industry, although the catering rôle of wives was probably growing in importance.

Even in major resorts such as these, however, the holiday industry had yet to stimulate a high level of specialization in accommodation. Most families found it safer to keep another iron in the fire, in spite of the high seasonal rents which could be charged. The standard rate for apartments at Scarborough was 10s. 6d. or 12s. per week per room, with half price for servants. This included bed- and table-linen, but washing and use of kitchen and utensils were added to the bill. At Weymouth the rates per room were broadly comparable to this for houses ranging from four rooms to 13, 16 and even 18. With regular long lets, houses of this kind could generate a handsome income, even when it was spread over the whole year. It was possible for William Stone of Margate to retire in 1777 and invest his savings in a lodging-house which brought in a low rent (by Weymouth standards) of between 2 and 3½ guineas per week, but still provided a steady gross income of £1 per week or more throughout the succeeding 19 years.[31] Not surprisingly, many lodging-houses in Scarborough were said to 'afford a most desirable quietness' because no other business was carried on, and it was claimed that, 'Many of the best houses are the property of persons truly respectable.' But Scarborough, like Southampton and Great Yarmouth, also had a useful reservoir of relatively cheap accommodation, which G. S. Carey explained in terms of their size and the mixed nature of their economies.[32] In the smaller resorts, most of the accommodation was cheap and unpretentious, offering little more than a supplement to existing sources of income. Exmouth in 1782 was still a village 'composed of cot-houses, neat and clean, consisting of four or five rooms, which are generally let at a guinea a week.'[33] Even in the most sophisticated centres, however, the supply of specialized accommodation was inevitably slow to respond to peaks of seasonal demand, as Carey remarked of Brighton:

Here Lords and Ladies oft carouse
Together in a tiny house;
Like Joan and Darby in their cot,
With stool and table, spit and pot.[34]

In this case, however, high levels of demand among free-spending visitors brought correspondingly high prices and windfall profits for those whose

Fig. 10 The upper levels of the accommodation hierarchy in 1913–14: the Gogarth Abbey Hotel, Craig-y-Don Boarding House, Ormescliffe Boarding Establishment, and Kingston House 'Superior Private Apartments' (reproduced from *Lovely Llandudno*, 1913–14).

main sources of income lay elsewhere. Full commitment to the accommodation industry in the early nineteenth century, even in Brighton, was still largely confined to a minority of caterers for the higher levels of the market; and this was much more apparent elsewhere.

National trends in the seaside accommodation industry are almost impossible to trace through the nineteenth century. All the general indicators point to rapid and accelerating growth and specialization, but we cannot provide quantitative documentation of even reasonable accuracy. The census is a broken reed, for the printed returns offer hardly any material on individual resorts, and the 'lodging- and boarding-house keeper' category includes purveyors of all manner of accommodation, from common lodging-houses upwards, throughout the country. Between 1891 and 1901, a period of unprecedented expansion in the seaside holiday industry, the census report recorded a 2.2 per cent drop in numbers in this category.[35] Rightly, the report itself urged caution in interpreting this strange phenomenon, and even in the early twentieth century the census seems to provide information only about lodging-house keepers whose level of commitment to the trade was great enough to enable them to set aside alternative occupational labels, including for those with small private incomes the seductive designation 'independent means'.[36]

The occupational returns for resorts in the 1841 census reflect chronic under-recording of lodging-house keepers at a national level, and especially in some individual resorts.[37] Weymouth, with 108 lodging-house keepers listed in a turn-of-the-century directory, returned only five in this census, and Scarborough only 29. At Great Yarmouth, 132 landladies had been listed in a directory of 1845, but the census found only 55.[38] Only in the combined parishes of Margate and Ramsgate did lodging-house keepers account for more than 2 per cent of the female population (there were hardly any men), and in most resorts, including Brighton, the recorded figure was less than one per cent. We can make little of evidence like this; but for the rest of the century the census offers even less, with unconvincing returns for Brighton, Dover, Great Yarmouth and later Hastings which are not worth pursuing.

Local directories vary so much in quality and coverage that they are equally unhelpful in piecing together a general pattern, although as they offer increasing space to the accommodation industry over the second half of the nineteenth century, some at least begin to provide plausible minimum figures for the number of households whose domestic economy was significantly influenced by income from letting rooms to visitors. The Post Office Directory for 1865, for instance, lists well over one-third of all Blackpool families as lodging-house keepers, although at Morecambe and Lytham the proportion falls below one in six and at residential Southport to 9.3 per cent. An attempt at nationwide coverage for the late 1880s and early 1890s, using directories in the British Library, produced an even wider range of results, but aroused the suspicion that the exercise was really comparing the quality and policy of different directories rather than the reality of accommodation provision in different resorts. Table 14 presents the findings for a selection of resorts in five regions, with the warning that these are to be seen as minimum figures, and that some of the directory compilers were clearly not very interested in lodging-house keepers.

Table 14. Lodging- and boarding-houses listed in various directories, 1886–95, as percentage of all houses, occupied and unoccupied, at 1891 census

South-east and South		*East Anglia*		*North Wales*	
Eastbourne	5.0	Clacton	11.9	Bangor	3.0
Hastings	8.8	Cromer	15.9	Criccieth	9.2
Brighton	3.3	Hunstanton	39.8	Llandudno	36.5
Worthing	3.4	Sheringham	6.7	Llanfairfechan	19.6
Bournemouth	13.8			Penmaenmawr	19.5
Ryde	2.4	*South Devon*		Colwyn Bay	21.0
Sandown	16.3	Torquay	6.7	Rhyl	15.4
Shanklin	25.9	Paignton	3.4		
Ventnor	15.1	Teignmouth	3.6	*Lancashire*	
		Dawlish	7.3	Southport	11.7
				Morecambe	20.3
				Blackpool	34.6

The overall pattern is not surprising, even though the actual figures need to be taken with a handful of salt, especially the lower ones.[39] Even in Blackpool, the Medical Officer of Health's attempt at a comprehensive survey in 1884 suggested that 54 per cent of the households took in visitors, far more than even the most comprehensive directory could identify.[40] The low percentages for Sussex and South Devon reflect the importance of the prosperous residential side of the seaside economy, and the continuing prevalence of the practice of letting whole houses to wealthy upper- and middle-class families. At Sheringham (where most lodging-house keepers doubled as fishermen), Ryde and Bangor, the holiday industry took second place to other economic activities. The highest levels of penetration occurred in recently-developed and largely purpose-built resorts catering for the mainstream middle-class and emergent working-class markets. If we bear in mind that the percentages for Hunstanton, Llandudno, Shanklin, Colwyn Bay and Morecambe, all over 20 per cent, are likely to be understated just as are the Blackpool figures, we obtain a clear picture of the potential importance of the accommodation industry to the economy of a specialized late Victorian resort.

The 1911 census provides useful comparative material on those who depended most heavily on the accommodation industry in the eight largest seaside resorts, and table 15 shows the importance of this hard core of specialists to the local economies.

Table 15. Lodging- and boarding-house keepers as a percentage of the male and female population over ten years old, with location factors and as a percentage of all households in eight resorts, 1911[41]

| | Men | | Women | | All lodging-house keepers as % of all households |
	%	Location factor	%	Location factor	
Blackpool	3.47	18.90	12.27	19.95	30.94
Southport	0.70	3.82	3.81	6.19	9.65
Bournemouth	1.05	5.68	3.06	4.98	9.11
Eastbourne	0.75	4.10	3.12	5.08	8.90
Hastings	0.73	3.95	2.80	4.55	7.10
Southend	0.54	2.96	2.84	4.61	6.69
Brighton	0.70	3.82	2.42	3.94	5.91
Great Yarmouth	0.39	2.11	2.58	4.20	5.35

Blackpool stands out at once as a special case among these leading resorts. It was unique in growing beyond the 50,000 population mark without seeing its specialization in holiday catering significantly diluted by residential or industrial elements; and although its accommodation industry was unique in sheer scale (4,174 lodging-house keepers recorded in the 1911 census) and economic importance, many smaller resorts could have shown similar levels of involvement, especially when they catered for the lower reaches of the market. Blackpool was far from being the wildly untypical case that table 14 appears to indicate;[42] and many householders in the other leading resorts undoubtedly took in visitors during the season without this additional source of income percolating through to the printed census tables.

What sort of people became lodging-house keepers at the seaside? In the early stages of resort development, accommodation was an additional source of income for the families of local tradesmen, although the bounty was distributed more widely at peak periods. This was true in the early nineteenth century even at such well-established resorts as Scarborough and Weymouth. As the holiday season became more firmly established, however, the accommodation business began to attract migrants into the resorts, especially middle-aged widows and spinsters of limited means, and families with members in failing health who had been prescribed sea air by a medical adviser. Lodging-house keeping was particularly attractive as one of the few respectable occupations open to the legion of unattached women from the less affluent levels of the middle classes, whose incomes were insufficient to maintain them in the style to which they aspired. Under these new influences, seaside lodging-house keeping became more visibly a woman's business as the middle-class holiday market expanded in mid-Victorian times. By 1865 the original core of local tradesmen was already being outnumbered in the leading Lancashire resorts by a combination of un-attached women and families headed by men with no alternative occupation.

Table 16. Sex and marital status of lodging-house keepers listed in the Post Office Directory (1865) for four Lancashire resorts

	'Mr'		'Mrs'		'Miss'		'Misses' and other female partnerships	
	No.	%	No.	%	No.	%	No.	%
Blackpool	277	63.0	98	22.3	48	10.9	17	3.9
Southport	68	21.6	162	51.4	67	21.3	18	5.7
Morecambe	50	58.1	23	26.7	11	12.8	2	2.3
Lytham	51	53.7	21	22.1	21	22.1	2	2.1

Where the lodging-house keeper listed in the directory was a man, he was almost invariably in partnership with his wife; and even in Blackpool, where the proportion of male lodging-house keepers was highest, only a small minority (61 out of 277) recorded alternative occupations. Most of the women listed with the prefix 'Mrs' would be widows, supplemented by wives separated from their husbands. Women left to fend for themselves dominated the Southport entries, as befitted the most select and successful of the mid-Victorian Lancashire resorts; but everywhere, already, a strong impression is conveyed of heavy dependence on the holiday season among the listed lodging-house keepers. Other kinds of evidence would present a less clear-cut picture, for many other sources of income must have gone unrecorded in the directories; but the booming seaside holiday market was already drawing large numbers of migrants to the seaside in pursuit of an income from lodging-house keeping, and this in turn gave a considerable impetus to the building trades.[43]

By the late 1880s and early 1890s these trends had advanced much further in the Lancashire resorts; but as table 17 shows, there were remarkable variations in the directory evidence from other parts of the country.

By this time women dominated the listings in Lancashire and the leading south coast resorts, where spinsters were particularly strongly in evidence. Bournemouth, with its long season, large capital-hungry villas and demand-ing clientèle, is an instructive exception, for here the requirements and opportunities associated with a booming holiday industry brought in additional capital and active participation from husbands. At the top end of the scale in 1891, hotel proprietors included two doctors of medicine (one was also a *F.R.G.S.*), and others had been 'for many years manager of the Guards' Club, London', and for ten years chef to the earl of Tankerville. Another hotelier boasted of his collection of Japanese objects. Such affluence was exceptional, but Bournemouth was unique in that almost all

Table 17. Sex and marital status of lodging-house keepers listed in directories, 1886–95, as percentage of total number of entries for each resort

	'Mr'	'Mrs'	'Miss'	'Misses' and other female partnerships
High-class south coast resorts: hotels and boarding-houses:				
Bournemouth	61.6	22.2	12.1	4.0
Brighton	23.0	52.5	21.3	3.3
Hastings	24.0	44.2	15.4	16.3
Eastbourne	13.6	45.5	31.8	9.1
High-class south coast resorts: lodging-houses:				
Bournemouth	47.6	28.3	12.9	11.3
Brighton	38.5	38.7	19.4	3.4
Hastings	37.5	36.0	20.4	6.0
Eastbourne	38.1	37.2	18.2	6.5
Isle of Wight: lodging-houses:				
Sandown	51.7	43.2	5.1	—
Shanklin	62.0	27.5	8.8	1.8
Ventnor	44.6	40.1	12.1	3.2
North Wales: lodging-houses:				
Llandudno	40.9	39.8	15.3	4.0
Llanfairfechan	63.3	20.2	15.6	0.9
Penmaenmawr	69.0	22.1	8.0	0.9
Colwyn Bay	49.7	23.5	21.3	5.5
Rhyl	48.4	33.2	14.8	3.6
Lancashire: lodging-houses:				
Blackpool	36.7	47.6	10.2	5.5
Morecambe	26.5	55.7	13.4	4.5
Southport	29.5	51.2	14.3	5.0
East Anglia: lodging-houses:				
Clacton	55.8	27.4	13.7	3.2
Cromer	54.3	28.4	16.0	1.2
Hunstanton	49.0	37.8	10.2	3.1
Sheringham	84.6	11.5	3.8	—

the houses had names rather than numbers, and even the humble letters of apartments in the smaller villas were, no doubt, a cut above their colleagues in the less-impressive terraces of rival resorts.[44]

The increasing predominance of women in the Lancashire listings conceals an important change of pattern at the lower levels of the holiday industry, as the rise of the brief but crowded working-class season drew in working-class married couples, especially from the cotton towns, who depended on a second source of income from the husband's outside work in order to make ends meet, and put directory entries and other public announcements in the wife's name.[45] The very high proportion of entries in the 'Mrs' column reflects this new trend, although widows who might depend more completely on the holiday industry remained important, especially in the 'better-class' areas.

Elsewhere, and especially in the more recent middle-class resorts, male lodging-house keepers remained in the majority, or very nearly so. Llandudno, select and already well-established, conformed to the high-class south coast pattern, but it seems to have been unusual. Second and even third occupations were strongly in evidence in some of the directories. For example, they accounted for more than half of the men listed at Cromer, Sheringham and Hunstanton, and over one-third at Clacton and Paignton. Most second incomes (which probably dominated the household economies in question) still came from retail trades and crafts, though variants included a postman, a railway guard, a reporter, an architect, a butler, a commercial traveller, gardeners, fishermen and a bricklayer, while in North Wales the lists included at least ten nonconformist ministers. The generally *petite bourgeoise* background which our patchy evidence suggests for most seaside lodging-house keepers contrasts with the evidence from Blackpool, where unequivocally working-class migrants were already moving into purpose-built 'company-houses' in large numbers; but the Lancashire experience was clearly exceptional.

By 1911 the core of heavily-committed lodging-house keepers who featured in the census returns for the eight largest resorts were predominantly female, though many of the married women listed no doubt had resident husbands who contributed to the family budget. Most were middle-aged or elderly, as no doubt had long been the case, for the capital, freedom and incentive to set up in business by the seaside tended to appear late in life, especially for women. By 1911, too, a high proportion were spinsters. This represents the culmination of a striking transition in the demography of the seaside accommodation industry over the previous century, as it became a specialized occupation and a female preserve.[46] Table 18 brings out the extent of the changes, though we must remember that they were probably far less advanced in many of the smaller and less specialized resorts.

One or two variations call for comment. We can point to a substantial over-representation of spinsters among the women, but the standard south coast pattern of spinster predominance, though replicated at Southport, is broken in the more down-market resorts of Blackpool and Great Yarmouth. The high proportion of married women at Blackpool reflects the importance of married couples at the working-class end of the accommodation industry. The census probably identified a higher proportion of all lodging-house keepers at Blackpool than elsewhere, too, because the unusual length of the working-class season there gave greater scope for specialization in accommodation at this level. At Southend and Great Yarmouth, especially, large numbers of married women who took in summer visitors were probably recorded under other headings. The figures do confirm the general predominance of the middle-aged and elderly, especially at Great Yarmouth, where sailors' widows may help to account for the unusual distributions, and Hastings. This evidence also gives support, very broadly, to the late Victorian and Edwardian stereotypes of the prim south coast spinster and the formidable northern working-class landlady with her downtrodden husband.

The mainstream holiday accommodation industry thus saw significant changes in its relationship with the family economy over the century before

Table 18. Lodging-, boarding-, eating- and coffee-house keepers in the eight largest resorts, by age and sex, 1911[47]

	No. of men	%	No. of women	%	% of men under 35	35–54	over 55
Blackpool	717	17.2	3457	82.8	10.5	51.2	38.4
Bournemouth	264	16.9	1300	83.1	10.2	46.2	43.6
Brighton	338	18.5	1487	81.5	15.7	49.4	34.9
Eastbourne	132	13.7	833	86.3	11.4	51.5	37.1
Great Yarmouth	77	10.9	632	89.1	23.4	41.6	35.1
Hastings	148	14.4	879	85.6	10.1	43.9	45.9
Southend	116	12.3	829	87.7	21.6	49.1	29.3
Southport	121	10.6	1106	89.4	14.0	43.0	43.0

	% of women Unmarried	Married	Widowed	under 35	35–54	over 55
Blackpool	38.9	39.4	21.7	21.3	50.1	28.6
Bournemouth	48.6	26.8	25.2	15.2	54.0	30.8
Brighton	39.6	28.6	31.8	18.0	50.0	32.1
Eastbourne	50.2	23.8	26.1	17.3	49.9	32.8
Great Yarmouth	35.9	19.5	44.6	10.9	40.3	49.4
Hastings	47.4	25.4	27.2	12.9	44.6	42.5
Southend	46.2	23.2	30.6	16.0	52.2	31.7
Southport	48.0	26.2	25.8	18.3	47.0	34.6

the First World War; but there were significant continuities in the nature of the services provided. The apartments system prevailed throughout the period in almost all resorts. Only at Douglas (Isle of Man), which was noted for informality and easy mixing, did the more sociable boarding-house system become the norm by late Victorian times, as the impressive purpose-built houses along the Loch Promenade took in between 50 and 150 visitors at a time, with common dining- and drawing-room accommodation, and a prevailing habit of sitting for a smoke and a gossip in the porches and along the flights of entrance steps. This gregarious approach to holidaymaking was in sharp contrast to the usual middle-class concern for privacy and exclusiveness, and contemporaries remarked upon it as a curiosity.[48] Elsewhere, boarding-houses catered more expensively for a higher and less informal class of visitor, but they were becoming numerous in south coast resorts like Bournemouth, Brighton, Hastings and even Margate by the 1890s, although Blackpool still had only 13 in 1901.[49]

At the top end of the scale the amenities offered by the larger boarding-

houses, especially at Bournemouth, overlapped in character with those of
the hotels which increasingly catered for the more affluent visitors during
the second half of the nineteenth century. Some were purpose-built, others
were conversions of existing mansions; some were the speculations of
individuals or partnerships, and some were railway company ventures, but
many were promoted by independent limited companies, some of which had
share capitals running into tens of thousands of pounds and challenging the
leading entertainment companies for sheer scale of investment. Activity of
this kind reached a peak in the 1860s, at the height of the mid-Victorian
middle-class holiday boom, as enormous Gothic or Renaissance or
architecturally hybrid hotels appeared in all of the major resorts and some of
the minor ones, accompanying a parallel boom in pleasure pier investment.[50]
Brighton's Grand Hotel, completed in 1864 at a cost of £160,000, dwarfed
the town's earlier and less ostentatious hotels and dominated its section of
the sea-front; while the impact of Scarborough's Grand, with its elevated
site, was even more spectacular, and its cost also ran into six figures. Some
lesser resorts saw similar ventures on only a marginally smaller scale, such as
the Imperial at Blackpool and the Ilfracombe Hotel.[51] These enormous
purpose-built hotels marked a transition from the provision of 'private suites
of serviced rooms' to 'a wider range of services and facilities, such as public
restaurants and smoking rooms' featuring 'the latest in interior design and
domestic technology.'[52] During the 1880s and 1890s similar new ventures
spread to up-and-coming resorts like Bexhill, and to remote seaside villages
in Devon, Cornwall and north Norfolk; while the takeover of the Duke of
Athol's Manx residence, Castle Mona, by a hotel company in 1888 was only
the most spectacular of many similar developments.[53] At resorts like
Bournemouth and Eastbourne, meanwhile, palatial new hotels continued to
multiply. At Bournemouth the 119 hotels and boarding-houses listed in a
directory of 1891 included the Bourne Hall, with its 125 bedrooms for
visitors, its library, ballroom, theatre, billiard room and ten bathrooms; the
Mont Dore with its medical baths, ballroom, winter gardens and covered
tennis courts; and the Grand Fir Family Hotel, 'furnished throughout by
Messrs. Shoolbred of London'.[54] The largest hotels triumphantly advertised
the patronage of gentry, nobility and even royalty, but the *nouveaux riches*
were more in evidence in Brighton, while David Cannadine cites a description of Eastbourne hotel life which has a much wider applicability, including
as it did 'the usual clergyman and his family, the usual landowner with his
invalid wife', Anglo-Indians, an assortment of widows and spinsters, 'a
stockbroker, some Jews and the usual horrible fill ups.'[55] Industry and
commerce would have bulked larger in northern England, and the professions, with a leavening of artists and Americans, in rural Devon or north
Norfolk, but everywhere the hotel-visiting public was upper middle class at
best, and often less exalted.

At the lower end of the social scale the swelling working-class demand of
the last quarter of the nineteenth century was stimulating the development
of street upon street of three- and four-storey 'company-houses' in the
popular resorts, especially in northern England and north Wales, but also,
for example, at Weston-super-Mare. Even in these larger establishments,

Fig. 11 Seaside entertainers: Llandudno's Pier Pavilion Orchestra, 1913 (reproduced from *Lovely Llandudno*, 1913–14).

however, and even in Blackpool with its long working-class season and remarkable range of late Victorian attractions, the working-class landlady faced a difficult struggle to make ends meet.[56] A higher-class clientèle staying for longer periods imposed heavy overheads and offered no guarantee of solvency, and many households continued to combine lodging-house keeping with other sources of income in a complex family economy. Widows and spinsters without resident relatives who were capable of earning, and with little or no independent income, were likely to come off worst, and it is no surprise to find the desperate income-increasing expedients of the hard-pressed landlady passing into English middle-class folklore through the pages of *Punch*. Jokes about overcrowding, overcharging and the frequent practice of charging extra for such items as 'boots, lights, cruets, fire, table-linen, sheets, blankets and kitchen fire' reflected the fears of visitors anxious for value for money, but the commonest theme was the quiet embezzlement of the food and drink which had to be left in the landlady's custody.[57] Crowded accommodation and 'extras' were indeed commonplace, and not just at the lower end of the market; but visitors could be dishonest too, and the apartments system involved endless complications of cooking and storage, and very long working days, for an income which could be as little as a shilling per person per day, or even less.[58]

The accommodation industry generated a great deal of additional work for servants; but most was seasonal, and as much as possible was kept within the family to keep overheads down to a minimum, especially in the back streets of the less prestigious resorts. Even in the April census of 1911, however, servants in hotels, lodging-houses and eating-houses accounted for about 4 per cent of the female population over ten years old in Eastbourne and Bournemouth, and nearly 3 per cent in Blackpool. The figures elsewhere were less impressive, but numbers were enormously swollen everywhere by summer migrants and local people looking for temporary work. Laundry workers were also well represented in the high-class resorts, accounting for 3 per cent of the female over-tens in Brighton, and not much less in Eastbourne and Hastings, although Blackpool and Great Yarmouth recorded figures below the national average.[59]

Seaside entertainment was even more dependent on itinerants, summer migrants and opportunistic locals temporarily turning their attention to a lucrative and attractive field of activity. The seaside resorts soon became part of the regular itinerary of the street musicians, hawkers and petty showmen who were so numerous in Victorian England[60] and a *Punch* contribution from 'Shingleton, near Dulborough' gave a long list of 'our daily programme of music' in the streets, concluding, 'I shall return to Town to-morrow, for surely all the street tormentors must be out of it, judging by the numbers that now plague the sad seaside.'[61] Actors and music-hall entertainers were equally peripatetic, and it was not until the turn of the century that it became worthwhile for professional entertainers to live at the seaside all the year round. The June census of 1841 found only a single actor and an exhibition or show keeper in Brighton, and these categories were completely absent from the other resorts whose occupations can be analysed, including Weymouth, Margate, Ramsgate, Scarborough and Hastings.[62] By 1871, Brighton itself was becoming a minor stronghold of the theatrical world, with 53 men and 21 women returned as working in theatres, exhibitions or shows. The 79 photographers must also have depended heavily on the custom of visitors, and a considerable number of entertainers must have been included among the 211 musicians and music teachers.[63] But these were a minute proportion of the town's population, and Brighton was exceptional. Great Yarmouth, for example, counted only five theatrical and other show people at this early spring census, and six photographers; and at Blackpool and Ilfracombe the enumerators' books recorded only a handful of pier attendants, toll collectors, musicians and the like.[64] The really rapid growth in this sector came after 1871, and especially between 1891 and 1911.[65] By the latter year, at another early spring census, Brighton counted 1438 entries under the heading of 'Art, music and drama', which included architects, engravers, photographers, artists and 'professors of music' as well as actors, singers, musicians and their ancillaries. This was well over 2 per cent of the over-ten population, however, against a national norm of less than 0.8 per cent; and, Great Yarmouth apart, the other leading resorts recorded similar proportions, with Blackpool recording 178 'performers and showmen'.[66] By this time quite a large number of beach entertainers and stallholders were permanent Blackpool residents, although they lived in the less salubrious parts of the town. In any case, at Blackpool and no doubt elsewhere, the summer influx multiplied these figures many times over, and occupationally mobile locals were also drawn into the entertainment industry.

"BY THE SAD SEA WAVES"

Landlady (who has just presented her weekly bill). "I 'ope,
ma'am, as you find the bracing hair agree with you, ma'am, and
your good gentleman, ma'am!"
Lady. "Oh, yes, our appetites are wonderfully improved!
For instance, at home we only eat two loaves a day, and I find,
from your account, that we can manage eight!"
*[Landlady feels **uncomfortable**.*

Fig. 12 Reproduced from *Mr. Punch at the Seaside.*

At the top of the scale Blackpool's theatrical and music-hall artistes were
themselves nomadic, for the resort was only one among many ports of call in
a year spent touring the commercial and manufacturing centres as well as the
seaside. Musicians for the various orchestras came in for the season just as
did the buskers in the streets, and the orchestras were supplemented at need
from Manchester in Edwardian times. As early as 1878 100 musicians were
employed at three of the entertainment centres, and by 1908 an estimate of
500 for the major shows went uncontested. Most beach traders and hawkers
were also summer visitors, and by 1895 316 people had 'standings on the
foreshore' for stalls and entertainments, while the mid-1880s saw estimates
of up to 200 street musicians and 400 hawkers thronging the central streets at
a time. Moreover, the entertainment companies required large numbers of
scene-shifters and supernumaries for their shows, and these provided
opportunities for locals as well as migrants. The Raikes Hall pleasure
gardens employed schoolboys by the dozen in the 1870s, but there was
plenty of scope for adults of both sexes, especially men laid off from the

local building trades, where summer was (unusually) the slack season.[67] Blackpool was unusual in the extent of its hunger for seasonal labour in entertainment, but the same forces operated to some extent in all but the smallest late Victorian and Edwardian resorts.

Accommodation and entertainment were central and distinctive elements in resort economies, but less idiosyncratic occupations were also very important to a high proportion of family incomes. Building and transport were over-represented almost everywhere, though both were particularly prone to seasonal fluctuation at the seaside.[68] Building found work for between 12 and 20 per cent of males over ten years old in most resorts at the turn of the century; but it was vulnerable to frost, and curtailed by limited daylight, in the winter months, and operations were restricted during the holiday season, while the early spring saw feverish activity.[69] The transport needs of the summer season in a large popular resort demanded armies of cabmen, additional porters at the railway station, luggage cart operators, charabanc drivers and, late in the century, tram crews. At the turn of the century Blackpool licensed up to 400 cabs annually, most of which probably plied only in the season, and by 1911 the Corporation tramways took on an additional 150 temporary drivers and conductors for the summer. Locals were given preference, especially in cab licensing, and some occupational mobility took place in the season from the building trades into transport.[70]

Shopkeeping was the other major seaside employer; and again it was subject to the inevitable seasonal variations, as shops changed their trade for the season or even went into hibernation for most of the year. Shopkeepers and their workforces are impossible to identify as such from census evidence, but they obviously bulked disproportionately large in resort economies. Blackpool had more than 2,000 shops in the 1911 summer season, of which nearly half sold food, including 238 sweetshops and 96 fish-and-chip shops. Otherwise, clothing and souvenirs predominated, and the jewellery trade, significantly, was divided into high-class and excursionist sectors.[71] In the more up-market resorts, such trades as booksellers, hairdressers and picture-frame makers flourished, and Brighton in 1888 found room for such exotica as five artificial florists, two 'seaweed florists' and an equestrian photographer.[72]

Manufacturing industry was not absent from the seaside, but it was rarely obtrusive. Ship-building, fish-curing and allied activities declined steadily in the older-established towns, and everywhere the preparation and manufacture of food, clothing, furniture, trinkets and ornaments developed to service the holiday industry. A return of 1911 found 178 'factories' and 514 'workshops' in Blackpool, nearly two-thirds of them involved in food (including ice-cream and rock) and clothing (especially cheap shoes).[73] Margate, by this time a much smaller resort, had 374 premises on its register of workshops in 1905, though 73 were laundries.[74] These small establishments were themselves subjected to the rhythm of the holiday season, but as Blackpool commentators realized, more orthodox industrial activity, even if capital were forthcoming, would buy more stable winter employment only at the cost of pollution and impaired amenities.[75] Few resorts were as fortunate as Brighton, with its railway works; or Worthing, where the growth of market gardening under glass in the late nineteenth century provided extensive employment as well as additional attractions for visitors; or even those East Anglian resorts where the autumn herring season followed conveniently in the wake of the departing holidaymakers.[76]

Along with the wealthy élite of independent residents and those who ministered to their needs, there were a few other characteristic sectors of resort populations for whom seasonal fluctuations held no terrors. Above all there were the private schools which proliferated at the seaside, and especially in the more salubrious south coast resorts, during the second half of the nineteenth century. Already in 1851 Brighton had more than twice its fair share of schoolmistresses, with the masters not far behind; and in 1871 the census notes listed private school populations for several south coast resorts. At Lancing nearly 20 per cent of the small population were returned in private schools; and among larger resorts Hove and Margate each had over a thousand children in private schools, amounting to 8 and 10 per cent of the towns' respective populations, while Brighton's 1,607 came to less than 2 per cent.[77] Preparatory schools predominated, and their numbers grew rapidly over the next 30 or 40 years. At Bexhill, for example, independent schools multiplied in step with the town's overall development from small beginnings after 1885, and by 1900 there were more than 30, specializing in the children of Imperial civil servants.[78] At Folkestone, too, 'a host of small exclusive private schools sprang up at the turn of the century', when crocodiles of children taking exercise became a characteristic sight on the Leas.[79] The climate and social tone of these aristocratically controlled south coast resorts, coupled with their proximity to London, gave them special advantages, but most Kent and Sussex resorts developed strong secondary specializations in private education. Directories of the late 1880s and early 1890s listed 125 private schools at Brighton, 70 at Hastings, 67 at Eastbourne and 50 at Bournemouth. Unkinder climates, lower prestige or greater distance from population centres meant less impressive listings: Torquay 26, Rhyl 13, Southend 12, Llandudno six. These are very impressionistic figures, giving no indication of the size, status and financial condition of the schools in question; indeed, many of the proprietors can have been little more secure in their vocations than most landladies. By the early twentieth century the leading south coast resorts counted up to two-and-a-half times their fair share of teachers of all kinds, in spite of overall populations which were strongly weighted towards the middle-aged and elderly. At the other extreme, Blackpool and Great Yarmouth fell on or below the national average.[80] Even so, the education 'industry' clearly helped to smooth out the fluctuations of the season in most resort economies, though its influence was least in those popular resorts where seasonal fluctuations were sharpest.

Not surprisingly, doctors and lawyers were also much in evidence at the seaside. Indeed, as table 19 makes clear, the national distribution of these élite professions was being increasingly strongly skewed towards the resorts.

As might be expected, the medical profession bulked larger in 1841, except at Tenby; but by 1911 the balance had tilted the other way except in resorts with a particularly large invalid population, such as Bournemouth and Hastings. High levels of population mobility and large numbers of land and housing transactions made plenty of work for the legal profession at the seaside. Moreover, death-rates might be low, but a high proportion of the deaths followed long periods of ill-health and meant the disposal of considerable amounts of property, especially in the 'better-class' resorts. These visible opportunities help to account for the over-representation of doctors and lawyers, although the inflated numbers may well have generated

Table 19. Location factors for doctors and lawyers in seaside resorts, 1841 and 1911[81]

	1841		1911	
	Attorney, solicitor, writer, law student, barrister, conveyancer	Physician, surgeon, apothecary, medical student	Barrister, solicitor	Physician, surgeon
Weymouth	1.92	1.94	—	—
Margate and Ramsgate	1.98	2.34	—	—
Great Yarmouth	1.25	1.31	0.91	1.05
Brighton	1.38	1.81	1.96	1.73
Hastings	0.91	2.15	1.57	2.92
Scarborough	1.27	1.95	—	—
Tenby	2.54	1.45	—	—
Southend	—	—	2.55	1.56
Blackpool	—	—	1.21	1.56
Southport	—	—	3.09	2.83
Bournemouth	—	—	2.80	3.74
Eastbourne	—	—	2.86	2.38

intense competition and insecurity in spite of the generally favourable economic and demographic circumstances. Even in the early twentieth century, the elevated status of medicine and the law was no guarantee of universal prosperity for seaside practitioners.

Apart from the wealthy residents, and the retainers and tradespeople who depended on them (and groups like Torquay's 'villa residents' might themselves spend their money elsewhere for long periods of the year[82]) the seaside population was generally vulnerable to seasonal fluctuations, competitive pressure or a combination of the two. Most families needed two or three sources of income, and many of the small businesses which were so important to resort economies had limited capital and few reserves. To make matters worse, the distinctive seaside occupational pattern created imbalances in the age/sex structure of the resorts, and the resulting predominance of female and ageing elements in resort populations posed problems of its own.

The characteristic resort age/sex structure, with a shortage of children and a strong over-representation of women, especially at the peak ages for domestic service between the late teens and early thirties, was already emerging in the larger resorts by 1851; indeed, an isolated return from

Brighton shows that it was becoming apparent there in 1821.[83] By 1871, mid-Victorian developments had brought about a wider divergence from the national averages in most resorts, especially in the 15–19 age-range; but a specialization in elderly residents, which later became another distinguishing

Table 20. Age/sex structure in seaside resorts, 1851–1911: percentages of whole population[84]

	Under 15		15–39		40–59		Over 60	
[1851]	Male	Female	Male	Female	Male	Female	Male	Female
England and Wales	17.8	17.6	19.6	20.9	8.2	8.6	3.4	4.0
Brighton	16.4	16.0	17.4	26.2	7.5	10.0	2.7	3.8
Great Yarmouth	16.3	16.7	16.5	24.0	7.8	10.0	3.5	5.2
Scarborough	17.3	16.4	16.4	22.9	7.8	10.1	3.8	5.2
Southport	18.4	19.1	16.9	22.2	7.3	9.1	2.8	4.2
Torquay	15.7	16.3	17.5	26.5	7.5	9.9	2.7	4.0
[1871]								
England and Wales	18.1	18.0	18.8	20.3	8.4	9.0	3.5	4.0
Brighton	16.1	16.2	16.6	24.8	7.7	10.8	3.1	4.7
Eastbourne	18.3	18.4	16.9	22.5	7.8	9.2	3.2	3.8
Great Yarmouth	16.7	16.7	17.9	21.5	8.2	10.3	3.6	5.0
Ilfracombe	16.8	16.8	15.1	21.6	7.4	10.3	5.0	7.0
Lowestoft	17.3	18.1	20.8	19.1	8.4	8.7	3.4	4.1
Margate	19.5	17.1	15.9	22.9	6.8	9.4	3.4	5.1
Scarborough	17.0	16.9	16.2	23.4	8.2	10.1	3.3	4.9
Southport	17.0	16.9	15.5	25.9	6.9	10.3	3.1	4.4
Torquay	15.4	15.9	15.2	26.1	7.7	11.3	3.5	4.8
Worthing	17.8	16.7	15.5	22.3	7.6	10.5	3.9	5.6
[1911]								
England and Wales	15.3	15.3	20.1	21.7	9.3	10.2	3.6	4.5
Urban districts	15.2	15.3	20.2	22.4	9.2	10.2	3.2	4.2
Blackpool	12.3	12.7	17.2	24.1	10.5	14.1	3.6	5.6
Bournemouth	10.6	10.8	15.9	28.6	8.2	14.6	4.2	7.2
Bridlington	12.9	13.1	15.3	24.9	8.9	13.2	4.6	7.0
Brighton	13.1	13.1	17.7	23.3	9.6	12.8	4.1	6.3
Budleigh Salterton	10.5	9.6	12.1	28.2	8.3	15.4	5.6	10.4
Cleethorpes	17.1	17.6	19.0	23.6	8.1	9.3	2.3	3.2
Eastbourne	13.0	12.3	16.6	27.8	8.5	13.0	3.4	5.4
Grange	9.5	8.9	14.9	30.7	9.1	15.3	4.6	6.9
Great Yarmouth	15.1	15.1	17.3	22.1	8.9	10.8	4.5	6.2
Hastings	11.7	12.2	15.2	24.0	9.0	14.4	4.9	8.5
Hove	10.6	10.9	13.7	28.9	8.4	15.4	4.2	7.9
Hunstanton	14.1	11.1	14.5	30.1	7.0	13.0	4.1	6.1
Ilfracombe	11.4	12.1	14.8	24.4	9.2	14.6	5.1	8.4
Lowestoft	17.0	16.8	17.3	23.1	7.7	9.9	3.4	4.7
Margate	15.2	13.9	18.7	24.6	7.6	11.2	3.2	5.6
Scarborough	12.8	12.7	15.3	24.6	9.1	13.5	4.8	7.3
Southend	13.9	14.4	17.5	24.9	9.2	12.0	3.2	4.9
Southport	11.3	11.5	16.5	26.8	9.0	13.9	4.0	6.9
Torquay	9.8	10.1	20.4	24.3	8.9	14.1	4.8	7.6
Weston-super-Mare	11.6	11.9	15.1	27.6	8.4	14.0	4.0	7.5
Worthing	12.3	12.1	15.2	24.7	8.2	14.5	4.5	8.4

feature, was only just beginning to appear in a few climatically favoured places. At Ilfracombe 12 per cent of the population already consisted of over-60s; but the highest figures elsewhere were 8.6 per cent at Great Yarmouth (for inscrutable reasons probably unconnected with the town's resort function) and 8.5 per cent at Worthing, against the national total of 7.5 per cent. The cases of Margate, where the large schoolboy population affected the age/sex structure to a marked degree, and of Lowestoft, where a high-class holiday industry failed to counterbalance the influence of fishing and other seafaring occupations, are interesting variants from an already-established resort pattern.

It was between 1871 and 1911, however, that most seaside resorts became really distinctive demographically, though the range of variation between different resort types also increased as specialization in particular markets advanced. Some (but not all) high-class residential resorts displayed the conventional demographic distortions to the point of caricature by 1911, as at Grange, where only 18.4 per cent of the population were under 15, or at Budleigh Salterton, where the over-60s accounted for 16 per cent of the population as against a national urban figure of 7.4 per cent, and 70 per cent of the 15–39 age-group were female. The elderly were heavily over-represented in several much larger resorts by this time, including Ilfracombe, Torquay, Hastings, Worthing and Hove in Devon and Sussex, all with over 12 per cent; but Scarborough also fell into this category, and Bridlington, Bournemouth and Weston-super-Mare were not far behind. Residential Southport, interestingly, was further down the list, and Eastbourne and Folkestone stood close to the national average. But these figures bring out the wide distribution by 1911 of a specialization in seaside retirement which had been little in evidence before the turn of the century.[85] The middle-aged were also well-represented in most resorts, though never spectacularly so. Landladies and wealthy residents boosted the 40–59 age-group to nearly 25 per cent of the population at Blackpool and Grange, with several other places not far behind. A strong predominance of women, especially in the 15–39 age-group, was also almost universal, although they generally accounted for about 60 per cent of this age-range rather than the freakish Budleigh Salterton figure cited above.[86] A strikingly low proportion of children was also general, despite the presence of large numbers of private schools, and only the fishing and industrial communities of Cleethorpes and Lowestoft bulked large enough to reverse the trend in individual resorts. By the eve of the First World War the seaside resorts had acquired a distinctive population profile, coupled with a remarkable combination of low birth-rates and low death-rates.[87]

A corollary of the rapid fall in seaside birth-rates in the later nineteenth century was that population growth in the resorts was based almost entirely on migration rather than natural increase. Seven of the eight most populous seaside resorts in 1911 featured among the 35 towns of over 50,000 people in which immigrants outnumbered the locally born; and table 21 shows how heavily the natives were outnumbered in some of the fastest-growing resorts.

Most of the other 'towns' in this category were suburbs of London,

Birmingham and Liverpool. In Brighton, at least, out-migration was also heavy, and there is no doubt that resort populations generally were footloose and unstable. Moreover, they included unusually high proportions of long-distance migrants, many of whom came from vulnerable groups. There was a strong predominance of young single women and a large proportion of elderly people of both sexes; and an unusually high proportion had travelled long distances, including foreign-born British subjects (who were especially numerous in Cornwall, as Falmouth and its neighbours cast their spell over returning overseas civil servants and their families) and foreigners, who were especially attracted to hotel service.[88] Together with their peculiar demographic structure, the resorts' high levels of population turnover and mobility must have created or exacerbated serious problems of personal isolation and insecurity.

Table 21. Locally-born per 1,000 of each sex in seaside resorts, 1911[89]

	Male	Female		Male	Female
Blackpool	294	227	Eastbourne	382	280
Bournemouth	286	185	Southend	206	164
Brighton	533	447	Southport	437	312
Hastings	515	375			

Even without these added difficulties the peculiarities of seaside occupational structure, and the vagaries of the holiday season, would have combined to generate serious enough social problems in many resorts. Winter poverty was endemic, and in bad years soup kitchens and special relief funds were brought into operation not only in places which depended on a short summer season, such as Blackpool and to a lesser extent Scarborough and Ilfracombe, but also in high-class residential resorts such as Hastings, Brighton and even Eastbourne. Recipients included lodging-house keepers as well as labourers, and 'genteel poverty' was widespread.[90] Difficulties of this kind were exacerbated by high rents and a shortage of cheap cottages, which necessitated seasonal overcrowding (as families packed in large numbers of visitors to make ends meet) or the permanent sub-division of modest houses whose rentals were beyond the reach of labourers. At Southend in the summers of the 1890s children were regularly sent out to sleep in wooden sheds at the backs of houses, and everywhere whole families spent the summer crowded together in attics or basements to maximize visitor numbers. Long hours of work also prevailed, especially among lodging-house keepers and hotel workers. Medical Officers of Health in the popular resorts complained regularly about these conditions at the turn of the century, and blamed the high infant mortality rates in such resorts as Blackpool, Margate and Southend on the pressures of the summer season.[91] In similar vein schoolteachers bemoaned the frequent incidence of seasonal truancy, especially among girls who were pressed into service by their parents, and by the Edwardian years the authorities were becoming aware of a problem of teenage unemployment after early years in dead-end jobs associated with the holiday trades.[92]

There was thus some general validity in Robert Tressell's grim Edwardian portrait of the south coast resort of Mugsborough, where 'the majority of the inhabitants existed in a state of perpetual poverty which in many cases bordered on destitution', and even the tradesmen and boarding-house keepers were hit hard by exorbitant rents and rate demands.[93] On the credit side, the holiday industry rescued many ailing seaside economies from steady decline and ultimate collapse, as transport innovations threatened the viability of ancient seaports. The tradition of multiple occupations in a town like Ilfracombe could readily be carried over into the visitor trades.[94] But the advantages of seaside living were at best precarious for those below the ranks of big business and the affluent retired. A successful entrepreneurial career in seaside catering or entertainment could, indeed, bring affluence in its wake, as the Blackpool evidence makes clear. Probate valuations show six of the town's leading businessmen, all of whom had risen from modest beginnings *via* the entertainment and building industries in late Victorian times, leaving estates of over £100,000, with W. G. Bean of the Pleasure Beach amusement park topping £350,000 to qualify as one of the hundred richest British corpses of 1929. Lower down the scale, six lodging-house keepers who had been active in local politics left comfortable estates of between £1,595 and £4,693; but these were among the very small proportion of successful survivors in this demanding trade.[95] For many, the only advantage of lodging-house keeping was the additional living space provided for most of the year by occupying a larger house than could otherwise have been afforded. At Southend, and no doubt elsewhere, the extra income from accommodation made seaside living possible (often precariously) for many London clerks and supervisory workers who could not otherwise have afforded to commute.[96]

These were themselves precarious benefits, however, and for most families the opportunities of the summer season had to be set against the irregularity of work for most of the year, with the over-supply of labour generating bitter competition for jobs. Many men, indeed, sought winter work inland. Meanwhile, the numerous middle-aged and elderly widows and spinsters continued the lonely struggle to eke out their annuities without compromising their gentility. The impressive top-dressing of elegant houses and wealthy families, and the bustling prosperity of the holiday season, should not be allowed to disguise the fact that even in the most successful resorts, financial stringency coexisted with an insecurity and rootlessness which contrasted sharply with the steady routines and neighbourhood life of many maturing industrial communities. For many, the health and amenities of seaside residence were undermined by poor living conditions, high overheads, uncertain incomes and lack of resources; and for most, they were dearly bought.

5 Planning and building: landownership and development

We have seen that the pace and timing of seaside resort growth varied sharply in different parts of England, region by region and at the level of the individual town. Within a common frame of reference, there were also significant variations in the social structure and economic organization of resorts. We shall now attempt to account for these differences; and in explaining why some resorts grew faster than others, and why some specialized in the 'better classes' while others came to cater for a largely working-class market, we shall shed further light on the general causes and consequences of the rise of the English seaside holiday town.

We must begin by looking at the shaping of the resorts themselves, for quality of layout, architecture and building were vitally important in moulding the perceptions of visitors or residents, potential or actual, and thereby regulating the flow of demand. The higher the class of visitor sought, the more important was the creation and perpetuation of a planned, controlled environment, if we except that cultured or adventurous middle-class minority who actively sought the primitive and the picturesque. Three main influences dictated the pattern and quality of urban growth at the seaside, as elsewhere: these were topography, the structure of demand, and the policies of landowners and developers. We shall see that the operation of these forces was affected by additional variables, especially changes in transport technology and policy, and an increasing degree of local government intervention; but these tend to modify the picture in detail without affecting the broad sweep of events.

David Cannadine has recently argued that 'the physical appearance of a town – the quality and location of its housing, and the overall pattern of its spatial evolution – was largely determined by forces other than land-ownership and the nature of the land law.'[1] The dominant influences on nineteenth-century urban development were 'market forces – topography and location, numbers and social structure – which, mediated by speculative builders, seem to have been most important in creating suburban appendages to London and the great provincial towns.' He suggests that the seaside was different, because 'the creation of an extension to an established town was a less uncertain or demanding enterprise than the making of a resort, out of nothing, in the middle of nowhere . . . Of necessity, during the first 10 or 20 years in the life of a resort town, investment had to be greater, the return was smaller, and the threat of failure was more omnipresent than in the case of suburban development.' As a result, aristocrats became 'the most frequent initiators of seaside town development' in Victorian times. They had access to capital on a large scale, and they could afford to ride out the inevitable early difficulties. 'In the seaside towns, it was the aristocratic landowners themselves who actually had to initiate the process, attract the people, and create the market.'[2]

These sweeping statements about the seaside are founded on the experience of eight resorts: Eastbourne, Folkestone, Torquay, Bournemouth, Bexhill, Southport, Llandudno and Skegness. In several of these towns the presiding landowners were substantial gentry rather than aristocrats, and if we extended the list to include other resorts where established individual landowners played a formative part in development, such as Exmouth, Teignmouth, Weston-super-Mare, Clevedon, Littlehampton, Lytham, Birkdale, Minehead, Penarth, Cromer and Hunstanton, the 'mere' gentry would bulk rather larger.[3]

Even this fuller list of resorts developed on the estates of aristocratic or genteel families, and under the supervision of their agents, leaves them in a very small minority. Moreover, very few resorts were created 'out of nothing, in the middle of nowhere'. Most of the successes of the pre-railway era were enjoyed by established towns which spread piecemeal, field by field, small estate by small estate, into areas of fragmented landownership. Torquay, Southport and Weston-super-Mare are prominent exceptions, but the active rôle of the landowners here was very limited until the 1830s and 1840s. Even in the railway age, when resort development came to be seen as a worthwhile speculation by the established owners of extensive coastal estates, relatively few resorts were created as separate entities on virgin sites. Most of these were in North Wales and Cumbria, where land companies and railways were more in evidence than aristocratic or genteel landowners.[4] Elsewhere, Bournemouth and Penarth were the most important new creations by landowners in the railway age, although the former had attained a considerable size before the railway actually arrived. Where a pre-resort settlement existed, admittedly, it was sometimes on a very small scale, and aristocratic endeavours were important to the creation of impressive new resorts from tiny beginnings at Eastbourne and Skegness. But it remains the case that most resorts grew up within, around or alongside established villages or small towns, as at Bexhill and Folkestone, and as we have seen, a few doubled as residential suburbs on the fringes of large maritime towns such as Portsmouth and Sunderland.[5]

The early and mid-Victorian years did see the eager and successful promotion of several resorts by large aristocratic and genteel landowners, and it was then that their claims to pre-eminence were strongest. By 1881 Southport was fifth, Torquay eighth, Eastbourne eleventh, Folkestone thirteenth and Bournemouth fifteenth in the resort hierarchy, by the crude measure of census population size. Five of the ten fastest-growing resorts, measured incrementally, between 1851 and 1881 were dominated by aristocratic or gentry families, and in percentage terms the three most favoured resorts all fell into this favoured category, with two more in the top ten. This was an impressive showing, but it was not sustained in late Victorian and Edwardian times. By 1911 Bournemouth ranked second only to Brighton in census population, and it had far outpaced its rivals in incremental growth over the past 30 years. Eastbourne and Southport were seventh and eighth respectively by this time, and Torquay, Folkestone, Weston-super-Mare, Penarth and Bexhill were among the top two dozen resorts; but most of the fastest-growing centres by this time were either dominated by land companies or had sub-divided landownership, limited building controls and an increasingly working-class clientèle.[6] Most of the 'aristocratic' resorts were well-planned and carefully controlled, and almost all appealed to the 'better class' of seaside visitors and residents; but they were neither as numerous nor as relatively significant as the emphasis of Cannadine's argument suggests.

It is true that landownership patterns mattered more to urban development in the seaside resorts than elsewhere; but the advantages afforded to a small minority of resorts by aristocratic control provide only a small part of the explanation. Within each resort, just as in the inland towns, the pull of topography in conjunction with perceptions of prevailing levels of demand could often exert a strong and even predominant influence on zoning patterns; but there was a crucial difference between resorts and other kinds of town, which inflated the importance of landownership at the seaside. Resorts were in competition, particularly at the top end of the market, for a visiting and especially a residential public which had a wide choice of locations for holidays, second homes, retirement or suburban residence. At the seaside, the additional amenity and security provided by controlled development on a large scale could make a difference to the character and fortune of whole towns, as well as affecting zoning within resorts. Under these circumstances, tenure might also became important, as restrictive covenants supervised by an estate office could enhance the appeal of a leasehold estate by safeguarding amenity and social status. These advantages were not essential to the creation and perpetuation of a high-class resort, especially in the early years, for a consensus among developers on small or unsupervised estates that the high-class market was also the best-paying could also ensure the emergence of a desirable resort environment, even without the wide roads and long perspectives of a master plan. In any case, aristocratic oversight was not essential to the development of planned, controlled estates or the emergence of an effective system of social zoning, for the same effects could be achieved by land companies, land syndicates (some of whose efforts predated almost all of the aristocratic ventures), individual land speculators and institutional landowners of various kinds.[7] The policies of landowners were vital to the nature of resort growth, but only in mid-Victorian times did the aristocracy really stand out in this rôle. Even then, their influence was significant only in a small minority of highly visible cases.

Landownership must not be seen in isolation as an influence on resort development. Estate offices might set minimum values, impose well-defined building styles and practices, and proscribe undesirable activities; but all this often left considerable leeway for builders and developers, who could build to the minimum prescribed standards or, if they chose, aim much higher. On the other hand, the attempted imposition of unrealistically high standards on an estate invited the nemesis of empty plots and bankrupt builders, as élite demand proved insufficient, or purchasers went elsewhere in the resort or sought a more congenial setting beyond its boundaries, impelling the landowner to consider lowering his sights. Market forces could be as hard a taskmaster at the seaside as inland, and not only on the sub-divided freehold estate with minimum building controls. The large estate was not exempt.[8] We have seen that the level and structure of demand for seaside holidays and seaside residence varied significantly from region to region, and this obviously affected the creation of the built environment in the resorts. Especially in the provinces, there might be narrow limits to the extent to which landowners and resort promoters could 'attract the people, and create the market'. Within each town, too, topography provided constraints and opportunities of its own, and we ought to look a little more closely at this most basic influence, before examining the policies of landowners and developers in greater depth.

Local topography set out the likely pattern and style of development in a resort, and often set limits to the potential range or balance of visiting publics; but these predisposing influences were always vulnerable to countervailing pressures from landowners, developers and local government, as they tried to interpret the signals from the demand side of the resort economy. These influences determined the timing of development on a given site, and the changing fashions in residential building over a century and a half meant that the treatment of an estate might vary enormously depending on when it came on to the market. Changes in the social structure of visitors and potential residents had even more fundamental implications.

The likeliest topographical recipe for success on a large scale remained constant throughout the period, though its treatment by developers altered considerably. For the early devotees of therapeutic sea-bathing, for the middle-class Victorian families, and for the excursionists of the later nineteenth century, the most important consideration was comfortable access to a clean sandy beach. A straight shoreline with gently-sloping cliffs was particularly desirable, because this enabled visitors of different classes and attitudes to spread laterally along the beach and share the same resort with a minimum of mutual antagonism and conflict. Brighton itself, Blackpool and Great Yarmouth were prominent among the successful popular resorts which shared this characteristic, and a double bay, as at Scarborough, could be even more effective.[9] A lack of steep gradients (which Scarborough did not share) was particularly valuable to resorts which sought the patronage of young families and the retired. Rhyl was recommended in

1899 to 'Paterfamilias, with . . . a rising family of disproportionate length to his purse', because 'the bairns will thoroughly enjoy themselves on mile upon mile of good, firm sand, on which there is no fear of their being surrounded by the tide or tumbling off anywhere – because there is nowhere to tumble off'.[10] The flat resort with a long frontage – the 'elongate' resort, as Barrett calls it – could thus have the best of almost all worlds. What it often lacked was the picturesque appeal of rocks, coves and cliffs; and local guide-books often made every effort to overcome this admitted defect. At Blackpool much was made of the distant views of Snowdonia, the Furness peninsula and (according to a fanciful Abel Heywood guide of the early 1860s) 'the fair Cheshire county'. The Corporation's first guide-book in 1880 laid special emphasis on the sea itself ('the distinctive glory of Blackpool') and the sunsets.[11] Blackpool had artificial attractions of its own by this time to set against the absence of the picturesque; but where this was not the case, otherwise well-endowed elongate resorts might languish in competition with prettier or more arresting rivals. Withernsea, for instance, remained only potentially 'elongate', suffering as it did from a shortage of scenery and objects of interest. Black's *Guide to Yorkshire* pronounced in 1862 that, 'There is nothing to attract the visitor to Withernsea except the sea', and nearly half a century later Baddeley's *Thorough Guide* perpetuated the condemnation: 'Withernsea has a pier, a lighthouse and fair bathing, but no elements of the picturesque.'[12] This bad press helped to condemn Withernsea to slow and limited growth throughout the period.

Natural deficiencies of this kind mattered relatively little to the middle-class families and working-class excursionists who made up the most numerous of the late Victorian visiting publics, however; and most of the large popular resorts of the nineteenth century varied only marginally from the classic elongate type. For resorts in general, however, the commonest patterns saw the spread of new development along the cliff tops on either side of an established harbour or fishing village, as at Ramsgate or Whitby, or the appearance of a seaside offshoot to an existing inland village or small town, as at Bexhill and Bridlington.[13] In this latter category fell the picturesque resorts whose social range of appeal was most severely restricted by their topography: the villages which straggled along a steep and rocky valley to a narrow bay with very limited bathing facilities. There was little scope here for the invalid or elderly of limited agility, for the young family, or indeed for the working-class excursionist; and too eager a pursuit of building development was likely to deter those seekers after the picturesque who dominated the visiting public. This perception inhibited Ilfracombe's growth in the later nineteenth century, for example, as did the lack of safe bathing and sandy beaches.[14] At Clovelly even narrower topographical constraints were reinforced by persistent isolation from the railway system, though steamers were calling regularly by the 1880s, and in the early twentieth century 'the one street is sometimes so crowded with visitors as to resemble a queue awaiting entrance at a theatre'; but the crucial influence against development, even here, was the unwillingness of successive occupants of Clovelly Court to sacrifice 'the irregular quaintness of the place' by allowing alterations and expansion 'to meet the supposed needs of the omnipresent tourist'.[15] We cannot discount the influence of topography on the pace and overall character of resort growth, especially where the educated and discriminating middle classes bulked large among the potential visiting public; but in the vast majority of cases the lie of the land was subordinated to other considerations.

Topography was more important as it affected differences within resorts than as an explanation for differences between them, except at a purely visual level; and even here, the preferred architectural idioms of purpose-built resort housing owed little to the precise nature of their surroundings, apart from a tendency for romantic wooded hillsides to attract fanciful detached villas in the more opulent resorts. Variations in height along the shoreline were particularly significant in affecting quality of development in the larger resorts.[16] Here, as in Hampstead, 'gradient analysis is the key to urban social morphology',[17] although behind the sea-front the relationship is complicated by the tendency for social tone to fall with distance from the sea, especially in the many cases where a railway line intervenes running parallel to the shore.[18] Cannadine shows how Eastbourne's 'opulent houses, costing between two and ten thousand pounds, which belonged to the wealthiest inhabitants', became concentrated in the south-west of the town, 'ascending the wooded, undulating slopes towards Beachy Head, and basking in the reflected glory of proximity to Compton Place', the duke of Devonshire's mansion; while on the other side of the pier and central entertainment district, artisan terraces were concentrated into the east end, 'low, marshy and liable to flooding'. Although the Devonshire estate was in a position to dictate this zoning pattern, 'it seems probable that Eastbourne might have evolved according to a similar spatial pattern regardless of ownership'.[19] In Blackpool, with its patchwork of small estates, it was on the northern cliffs that a land company chose to engross several small plots of land to develop a high-class, protected estate, containing the resort's most impressive hotel and setting a standard which was never challenged by the less elevated middle-class area at South Shore, the opposite end of the town.[20] Examples could be multiplied, for the sea views and bracing air of a cliff-top position were perceived by developers to be attractive to a wealthy class of visitor and resident, while in many resorts the low-lying land was already occupied by the often picturesque but always insanitary dwellings of the old village. Where this was not the case, the low-lying areas were often marshy and vulnerable to inundation, and their beaches tended to attract trippers who preferred to take a downhill route to the sea. The obvious and immediate need of expensive sea defences was also a deterrent to speculators at the top end of the market, and sometimes such land was not even deemed fit for working-class terraces. At Paignton in 1898 the sea-front near the station was still disfigured by a patch of land three feet below sea level, which lay fallow as 'a foul blot upon the sanitation' of the town, frightening away newly arrived visitors and attracting 'shows, gipsies, circuses and so on'.[21] In less extreme cases, as at Blackpool's South Beach, such land became filled with tightly-packed working-class terraces, especially at the east ends of rapidly-developing south coast resorts, downwind of the most populous part of the town.

The usual positive relationship between relatively high land and high social status was complicated in the resorts which catered particularly for invalids, especially in winter, by the fact that here shelter from the wind was often at a premium, though medical advice often recommended that the tubercular patients who were so important in some resorts should be kept back from the sea front itself.[22] Ideas about the influence of climate on disease could thus affect the zoning patterns of a specialized health resort, as sufferers sought micro-climates appropriate to their condition, aided by a torrent of medical literature.[23]

Much more important was the way in which ideas about climate affected the fortunes of entire resorts, and even of whole tracts of coastline. The great prize was the development of a winter season of wealthy sojourners, and, indeed, the attraction of free-spending permanent residents of independent means; and throughout the nineteenth century resorts competed with increasing attention to detail in providing carefully-selected statistics of minimum temperature, temperature range, humidity and shelter from unhealthy winds. Southeast Devon was particularly fortunate at an early stage, as the discovery of the 'mild and genial softness of the air' made its resorts attractive to a wide range of invalids from the late eighteenth century.[24] Subsequently several south coast resorts, especially in west Kent and east Sussex, began to compete successfully in the expanding market of the early nineteenth century, and the Isle of Wight's Undercliff around Ventnor achieved widespread medical recommendation for the management and treatment of consumption, which so preoccupied contemporaries. Further west, Bournemouth began its spectacular rise in the 1840s, assisted by a remarkable eulogy from Dr Granville in 1841.[25] Subsequent aspirants to winter resort status appeared on the south coast, where Folkestone, Worthing and Eastbourne (for convalescents) vied with the established reputations of Hastings and Dover, and later in south Cornwall, where winter mildness attracted many residents, temporary and permanent, to Falmouth and Penzance in the later nineteenth century.[26] Elsewhere, very few resorts were perceived to have special climatic advantages in winter, although Minehead and Tenby failed to build on early reputations, and a volume put out in 1912 by the Royal Society of Medicine had kind words for Hunstanton, sheltered from the east winds which generally made the east coast 'bracing' and unsuitable for most invalids in winter, and the little Cumbrian resort of Grange-over-Sands.[27] A winter season offered such obvious advantages that the popular summer resorts collected medical testimony avidly to advance their claims. Blackpool, with its open aspect and 'bracing' reputation, achieved little until the early twentieth century, after the publication of Dr Carr's *Blackpool as a Health Resort* in 1901; but the rising popularity of golf was more important to the growing numbers of winter week-end visitors at the big hotels, and the brief but developing Christmas season was similarly based on the pursuit of amusement.[28] Margate's efforts to attract winter health-seekers were less successful still, and even Ilfracombe, which eventually obtained a sympathetic medical press, failed to overcome the prejudices aroused by its northern outlook.[29] By the late nineteenth century Switzerland and the Riviera were becoming formidable competitors, and only those English resorts which offered obvious winter comfort, supported by explicit medical recommendation, could hope to sustain a satisfactory winter season. Elsewhere most winter visitors appeared briefly in search of pleasure and recreation rather than health. Here was an aspect of the seaside holiday market in which natural endowment counted for a great deal in channelling high-class development into particular parts of the country, and the residential nature of this demand ensured that a premium was set on spaciously-arranged villas at an early stage, rather than the terraces of boarding-houses which predominated longer in resorts which depended on a short summer season.

Summer climates varied too, of course, but the pattern of resort development does not suggest that intending visitors paid much attention to differences in hours of sunshine or inches of rainfall. Perceptions of resort climates were probably based on individual experience or the reports of acquaintances rather than on published figures; and although the resorts of Kent, Sussex and the Isle of Wight had a clear statistical advantage over other areas, we should not read too much into the figures.[30] A sunny summer climate may have given the south-eastern resorts an additional, if marginal, long-term advantage in attracting and retaining the loyalty of Londoners, and in competing for prosperous middle-class custom from further afield; but the significance of this was limited and secondary. We cannot ignore the influences of topography and climate, but it is clear that the main determinants of the pace and character of resort growth were social and economic.

This brings us back to the central theme of this chapter: how English seaside resorts were developed, and how the process varied between places and changed over time. At the outset, we must draw attention to the 1840s as an important watershed. Until then, the largest and fastest-growing resorts arose from the transformation and expansion of existing towns. In the vast majority of cases landownership was heavily sub-divided, and building was left in the hands of individuals or small syndicates with little or no external control. Indeed, the main legal instrument of controlled development, the 99-year building lease with restrictive covenants, was still being perfected over most of this period, and many landowners found difficulty and expense in breaking out of legal constraints which had not envisaged the opportunities provided by urban development.[31] The piecemeal exploitation of small estates remained important after the 1840s, of course, even in some of the more fashionable resorts; but by the early Victorian years large landowners were increasingly prepared to invest substantial sums in turning their coastal estates into planned, high-class resorts, while land syndicates and even individual speculators were moving into the seaside land market with similar ends in view. The incidence of large-scale planned development increased in late Victorian and Edwardian times, but on a smaller scale, as building operations passed into the hands of estate companies, though many of these aimed no higher than grid-pattern terraces and small semi-detached houses for the lower middle class. By this time aristocratic influence was beginning to wane even in the resorts where it had shone most brightly, and the changing structure of the holiday market was increasing the pressure to build unpretentious houses at relatively high densities in the rapidly-expanding popular resorts. The most significant and clear-cut changes, however, came in the early railway age, as it became clear to landowners and speculators of various kinds that tempting opportunities could be exploited in a well-established and rapidly-expanding holiday industry.

The originators of seaside resort development in the mid-eighteenth century had been much more tentative. Even in Brighton, the transition from fishing port to resort came about in the first instance through the conversion, rebuilding or replacement of old houses in the existing built-up area. Local copyholders responded cautiously to new opportunities, and although by the early 1760s 'wealthy people' were building 'substantial houses on the Steine', we are told that 'much of the process of development from the 1760s took place by selling or by sub-division for inheritance rather than by consolidation to build on large areas. Brighton was built by the small owner, builder and investor'. Professionals and gentlemen, as well as craftsmen and retailers, were becoming involved in building and improvements, and mortgage capital came increasingly from Lewes and rural East Sussex; but even when the town began to expand in earnest into the surrounding open fields in the last quarter of the eighteenth century, the spread of resort housing was piecemeal and effectively unsupervised.[32] At Margate, too, the early years of sea-bathing encouraged conversion, demolition and rebuilding in the old town rather than ambitious expansion on the outskirts, and in 1770 a guide-book remarked that many of the lodging-houses were 'now applied to a Use for which they were not originally intended.' Already, however, a new square had appeared, 'lately erected by Persons of Fortune', and in the 1860s Kentish gentry families were already becoming involved in building speculations on the small freehold plots, alongside local lawyers and traders.[33]

The other pioneer seaside resorts probably saw similar cautious, small-scale beginnings. Indeed, away from the strongest currents of metropolitan demand, extreme caution prevailed well into the nineteenth century. In about 1840 fewer than 20 Southport householders accepted Sir Henry Bold-Hoghton's offer to convert their life-leases into freeholds for £40 apiece, and it was alleged in 1837 that Blackpool's hotel-keepers had refused to release their farmland for development in the early nineteenth century for fear that their own trade might suffer.[34] In such southern resorts as Brighton and Weymouth, however, the ambitions of developers and the tempo of development began to increase sharply as confidence grew towards the end of the eighteenth century.

The early years of the sea-bathing fashion had offered little inducement to large-scale speculation in house-building, despite the occasional complaints of visitors at the standard and expense of their accommodation. Until the 1790s an existing urban fabric was adapted to meet the basic requirements of a visiting season, but no major new departures were undertaken. The opportunities afforded by the French wars, by the expanding demand for seaside holidays and residence among the prosperous middle classes, and more specifically by the drawing power of royal patronage at Brighton and Weymouth, encouraged speculation on a much more ambitious scale, and resorts began to compete in architectural magnificence and formality of layout. Even when new squares and crescents began to spread across the fields and along the cliffs, however, the pattern of landownership remained relatively unimportant. The most successful late Georgian resorts, indeed, did not need the oversight of a large estate. Their architectural splendours were created by speculators who developed relatively small estates which were increasingly carefully controlled internally, but which were not part of any master plan for the town as a whole. The appearance of homogeneity was fostered by a community of taste and expectation among the developers, stiffened by a common awareness of the needs and desires of the fashionable clientèle which offered the greatest rewards, and given expression, in Brighton and elsewhere, by the extensive employment of a limited number of successful local architects, who increasingly speculated in their own right.[35] This approach to high-class development was pioneered in Bath, beginning in the later 1720s and reaching a climax in the building boom of the late 1780s and early 1790s. Here, as at the seaside, the 'key figures in land promotion were the developers', as opposed to the original landowners. Many were architects and builders, with local attorneys and 'well-to-do tradesmen' also prominent, and a heavy dependence on metropolitan capital. These speculators were responsible for imposing uniformity of elevation and building materials on their promotions. They 'handled several acres at a time, and prepared schemes which were complete in themselves, but often unrelated to neighbouring schemes.' As Chalklin points out, 'Georgian Bath is a unity, but it is a unity created by its building material, stone, and by the classical uniformity of its architecture, not by its general planning.[36] In this respect as in their provision of amenities and entertainment, the early seaside resorts followed precedents laid down in eighteenth-century Bath.

Brighton, in its flimsier brick-and-stucco idiom, was the closest seaside emulator of Bath, and royal patronage here helped the national building boom of the late 1780s and early 1790s to be sustained into the new century, as London capital encouraged the rapid extension of the built-up area. Even here, however, individual projects long remained small-scale, und it was not until well into the nineteenth century that developers' ambitions began to match Bath speculations of the 1750s and 1760s, as expansion on to the cliffs to east and west offered new opportunities for display and opulence of layout. This trend was foreshadowed by the West Indian planter J. B. Otto's Royal Crescent of 1798–1807, with its fourteen 'elegant lodging-houses'; and over the next two decades Bedford Square, with 42 houses, and Regency Square, where 70 building leases were issued, demonstrated the growing capacity and confidence of Brighton speculators. But it was not until the 1820s, when Brighton achieved a higher percentage population growth-rate than any other British town, that squares and terraces were conceived on a scale to match the largest Bath promotions. Kemp Town, begun in 1823, and Brunswick Town a year later, were built on substantial cliff-top estates (Brunswick Town was 35 acres, Kemp Town considerably larger) at either extremity of the built-up area. The estates were owned by Thomas Scutt, a clergyman of retiring disposition, and T. R. Kemp, who came from a Sussex landed family and was M.P. for Lewes and Arundel; but in both cases the planning was done by Brighton architects, C. A. Busby and the Wilds, father and son, who were strongly influenced by Nash's recent work in London's West End. Kemp Town was a particularly spacious and opulent development, with 105 very large houses behind the impressive facades of Sussex Square and Lewes Crescent, whose span was 200 ft wider than the Royal Crescent at Bath. These estates were planned as self-contained units, with their own churches, sea defences, gardens and (as originally envisaged) housing for the lower orders, and their own self-governing institutions for the wealthy residents. Each was, indeed, a resort within a resort, and Kemp Town's ambitious major terraces took over 20 years to complete. Development of this kind required access to very large reservoirs of capital, especially at Kemp Town, and this scale of activity was only possible in a resort with very strong connections with London and the fashionable world. Even in Brighton, it was exceptional, although the creation of Kemp Town stimulated the infill building of less ambitious but still opulent new crescents to its west. But most development remained small-scale and piecemeal, especially in the back streets where the new slum areas were 'in all respects as bad as those of the industrial towns of the north'.[37]

Most of the other pre-railway resorts had fragmented landownership and experienced piecemeal development, without seeming to suffer by it. Margate and Gravesend may have adapted more easily to an increasingly plebeian clientèle because of the lack of a restraining landowning or wealthy residential interest. The other major resorts prospered and met the expectations of their visitors on the Brighton model, with some substantial controlled developments, but without any need for overall planning. Even in the very few cases where a large resort developed from scratch in this period on a site dominated by a single aristocratic or genteel landowner, the pattern of development was much the same as at Brighton or Ramsgate. At Torquay, the Palk family exercised no effective control until William Kitson took over as estate steward in 1833. Until the mid-1830s, conflict between the various agencies of manorial and parochial government allowed near-anarchy to prevail: 'Tenants built their houses without any attempt at preserving a uniform street front, actuated only by the desire to make the most of the ground allotted to them, while sanitary precautions were not thought of.' The town's attractions arose from a consensus of developers, guided by two architects who took on 'the lion's share' of the building work in the formative half-century after 1810.[38] At Southport and Lytham the landowners remained aloof until the 1840s, and the Rolles at Exmouth did not interfere significantly until the 1860s.[39] At Weston-super-Mare the Pigott family handed over responsibility for early development to the largest tenant farmer and two allies.[40]

In a few resorts the municipal corporation was a major landowner; but only at Weymouth did it involve itself in the organization and planning of new building, alongside the Duke of Gloucester and Sir William Pulteney. Here, as elsewhere, most of the risk-taking fell to the holders of the building leases, and such architectural unity as Georgian Weymouth came to possess owed more to the widespread employment of a single architect, James Hamilton, than to controls exercised by the landowners.[41] At Great Yarmouth and Aberystwyth extensive Corporation estates were developed piecemeal, with no concern for status, layout or even drainage.[42] Until early Victorian times, at least, municipal holdings at the seaside were as indifferently managed as aristocratic estates.

By the 1820s and 1830s a few established landowners were beginning to plan new seaside resorts on their estates. At Clevedon the Elton family began to lease out building land in the 1820s, although it is not clear whether their mid-Victorian policy of strict building controls originated at this time.[43] Nearby Portishead is a more clear-cut case of controlled development by a single landowner, as Bristol Corporation, Lords of the Manor since 1577, laid out a full-scale resort of 'marine villas' in 1827, with entrance lodge, hotel and landing stage.[44]

These speculations by established landowners were far outnumbered by the efforts of syndicates or individual speculators to plan seaside resorts from small beginnings in this period. Bognor, probably the earliest, was sub-divided among several proprietors after the death of its promoter, the London hatter Sir Richard Hotham, and failed to live up to its early promise;[45] the Colchester Quakers who set up Walton-on-the-Naze as a resort in the 1820s and 1830s made no impression outside a limited area of north-east Essex;[46] the syndicate which developed Royal Terrace, the first specialized resort housing at Southend, in the early 1790s, was bankrupt by 1795;[47] and at Filey the 35-acre 'estate of elegant lodging houses and hotels,including a grand crescent', which was projected by a Birmingham solicitor, took over 30 years to complete.[48] Herne Bay and New Brighton likewise fell short of the expectations of speculative promoters of the 1830s.[49] Only Burton's St Leonards, which really stood in the same relationship to Hastings as Kemp Town to Brighton, was really successful; and this reminds us that the fastest-growing resorts of the pre-railway era were established towns with resort functions grafted on, with divided landownership, unsupervised development and no overall plan. Their success in meeting the wishes of a prosperous and discriminating clientèle arose from a consensus of builders and developers as to the identity of the best-paying market, and the best way of gratifying its tastes.

This manner of development produced results which satisfied the architectural and spatial requirements of most resort users, whether the prevailing idiom was the monumental terrace, the villa or the *cottage ornée*. There were exceptions. In 1799 G. S. Carey found Margate's streets narrow and filthy, remarking that its Parade had 'little to boast of in respect to elegance or even cleanliness'; and 30 years later Blackpool, too, was found to be lacking in architectural dignity: 'It is a pity but what [sic] there had been some kind of uniformity observed, as all sea-bathing places ought to have their houses built upon a plan entirely unique.'[50] These were unusual cases, and the widely prevailing taste for the picturesque and romantic ensured that the second comment expressed a far from universal perception. Sidmouth, for example, was described as 'generally neat, occasionally highly picturesque, and in some parts positively handsome', despite being 'irregularly built'.[51] By the 1830s, the ideal resort needed a judicious mixture of formal, imposing sea-front terraces and fanciful villas scattered in their own shrubberies, to cater for the differing needs and tastes of an increasingly complex market. St Leonards achieved this in a planned way, with a visible unity of architectural conception, despite Burton's eclectic approach to villa-building, as the Italian, Gothic and Lombard rubbed shoulders in the fashion of the 1830s and 1840s; but the case of Torquay shows that a similar, and to most eyes indistinguishable, effect was possible without an overall plan, especially when nature was kind.[52] The only sufferers from irregular development at this stage were those resorts whose developers lacked the space and confidence, and perhaps the capital, to build terraces and crescents on a sufficiently impressive scale, or to indulge in the provision of the exotic villas in their own grounds which the work of Loudun and his imitators was making fashionable.[53] This helps to explain the failure of such resorts as Blackpool and Margate to compete effectively for high-class patronage in the early Victorian years, when the growth rates of rival centres were accelerating rapidly. In other resorts, however, the prevailing vice of over-building at the top end of the market caused problems at this time. Ramsgate suffered in this way, and so did Brighton, where the terrace remained the dominant architectural idiom, perhaps to the resort's disadvantage. It also gained an unfortunate reputation for jerry-building, which Granville helped to further in 1841: 'Brighton is over-built, and houses are constantly on sale. It is a curious sight . . . to behold some of these, with their showy exterior, but stripped of their internal fineries . . . and to see how flimsily they are built.'[54] At most resorts, as inland, small builders with slender resources predominated, and a lament from Ventnor in 1841 probably had widespread validity: 'The land has been let in small portions to needy people, who have run up cheap small houses for immediate gain.' Below the level of the great crescents and opulent villas, this was a common problem.[55] The new pressures and opportunities of the railway age were to increase its intensity in some resorts, while bringing about a much stricter supervision of development in others.

By opening up the seaside to a far wider range of income groups than before, the railways posed problems for developers as well as offering new opportunities. As the lower reaches of the holiday market displayed growing spending power, the provision of cheap lodgings and amusements became attractive options for entrepreneurs. In the early and mid-Victorian years, however, the best-paying and most reliable visiting public overall, almost everywhere, was still drawn from the wealthy upper and solid middle classes, and too obvious a willingness to cater for the lower orders was likely to drive away the main support of the existing resort economy. What might be profitable for the individual entrepreneur in the short run, could well prove disastrous in the long term for the resort as a whole. It was at this point that the pattern of landownership, and the policies of landowners, became crucial influences on resort development. When the visiting public in most resorts was reasonably homogeneous in tastes and expectations, the market could be left to find its own level; but when the railways imported, or threatened to import, the unacceptable manners and styles of enjoyment of clerks, shopkeepers and working-class excursionists in large numbers, they posed a palpable threat to the existing status and future prosperity of the resorts. Moreover, even where the pressure of new kinds of demand was limited and occasional, greatly improved travelling facilities increased the effective range of the existing visiting public, providing a wider choice of resorts and increasing the competitive importance of architecture, layout and amenity provision. In mid-Victorian times, especially, the most success-ful resorts were those which were capable of preserving or creating the standards and amenities which the established visiting public required. Local government played an important part in this, but the basic competitive requirement in a rising resort (less so in an established one) was the ability of a large estate to impose high minimum standards on new building, to determine the location of working-class housing, to assist the provision of necessary services and amenities with an eye to the resort's general attrac-tiveness, and to enforce restrictive covenants against undesirable practices and activities which might tend to lower the social tone. At this stage, unless the imperatives of the market were still unequivocal in demanding high-class development, only the large landowner had sufficient power to impose these requirements; and the presence or absence of a substantial estate could effectively determine the manner of the future development of a mid-Victorian resort, or, indeed, whether a given site would be used for resort purposes at all. At a time of agricultural uncertainty, urban investment of this kind was particularly attractive to landowners who hoped to be able to finance improvements on the land out of rapidly-swelling urban ground-rents.[56]

It is no coincidence, then, that the new market conditions towards mid-century brought about a revolution in estate management in those resorts where large landowners predominated. The pioneer in many ways was Sir George Tapps-Gervis at Bournemouth, who commissioned Ben-jamin Ferrey to lay out a high-class watering-place in 1838. Neighbouring landowners soon joined in, and strict controls on uses and minimum values were imposed from the beginning.[57] A change of régime also precipitated more active landed involvement at Torquay, where William Kitson took over as Palk estate steward in 1833 and two years later began a 25-year reign as chairman of the new Improvement Commissioners. He was active in encouraging and controlling new roads and villa development, and his policies were soon emulated by the rival local gentry family, the Carys.[58] The mid-1830s also saw the beginning of Sir Peter Hesketh Fleetwood's ultimately unsuccessful attempt to create a select watering-place at Fleet-wood in Lancashire, fed significantly by a new railway from Preston.[59] These were straws in the wind, anticipating the stronger economic impera-tives of the 1840s, when large landowners began to take a serious and sustained interest in encouraging high-quality resort development at Folke-stone, Eastbourne, Llandudno, Lytham, Weston-super-Mare and South-port. In the first five cases, new policies of controlled leasing were directly associated with the arrival or approach of railways. At Folkestone, Lord Radnor had been providing 'neat houses in judicious situations' for bathers since the 1820s, but the resort's full potential only became apparent with the arrival of the South Eastern Railway in 1843, and in the mid-1840s Sydney Smirke was commissioned to draw up a series of development plans, the third of which, in 1849, proved highly successful.[60] At Eastbourne there had been a false start in the late 1830s, but it took the building of the Hastings railway to within a few miles of his estate to persuade the Duke of Devonshire to take the plunge ten years later, when his first priority was to obtain a branch line.[61] At Llandudno the Mostyn estate's decision to create a tightly-controlled resort in which building was classified 'by locality, assigning one neighbourhood for large houses and another for a smaller description, thereby giving protection and security to the former without depreciating the value of the latter', was taken as the arrival of the Chester and Holyhead Railway became imminent.[62] At Lytham and Weston-super-Mare the initial aims of the landowners were less ambitious, but here, too, the approach of railways coincided with the introduction of policies of controlled leasing on the Clifton and Pigott estates.[63]

Southport is a more complicated case. Again the change of policy came in the 1840s, but it occurred some years before the advent of the town's first railway, and it arose from the passing of both the main estates into new hands in 1842. Sir Peter Hesketh Fleetwood, financially embarrassed by his attempts at resort promotion further north, sold his Southport holdings to his younger brother Charles Hesketh, the local rector; and Sir Henry Bold-Hoghton's 2,700 acres were bought up by Charles Scarisbrick, an aggressively entrepreneurial landowner who was eager to provide a secure inheritance for his three illegitimate children. Hesketh was personally attached to the estate, but his brother's experiences left him unwilling to take any speculative risks; while Scarisbrick's sole concern was the maximization of profit with the minimum of outlay, and he really falls into the category of outside speculator rather than established aristocratic landowner. The two estates imposed high minimum values and plot sizes, and a formidable array of restrictive covenants; but they left the burden of road-making and drainage to fall on the lessees. As John Liddle says, 'It was considered a small price to pay for the haven of exclusive middle-class respectability which the estate's social policies were intended to guarantee'; and demand of this kind was buoyant enough in mid-Victorian Lancashire to assure the success of this novel policy of social exclusiveness.[64]

Southport's landowners were unusually unaccommodating in their attitude to potential developers and residents; but even here the Heskeths, at least, were prepared to 'donate land for churches or public parks as and when it suited their own religious, moral, political or financial ends'.[65] Elsewhere a much more positive line was taken, especially where resorts were being developed from small beginnings and the dominant landowning family had more extensive resources than the Heskeths. Eastbourne is certainly the most striking case, with the Devonshire estate making itself responsible for almost all of the promenades and sea defences, bailing out the Local Board when the sewerage scheme encountered serious difficulties, and rescuing all manner of local companies from financial embarrassment, from the waterworks to the pier, the college and what became the Parks and Baths Company. All this was in addition to the more usual donations of sites for parks, churches and a library.[66] Only the Earl of Scarbrough's efforts at Skegness from the late 1870s onwards, and the De La Warr estate at Bexhill, came near this level of self-interested munificence, however, and most landowning dynasties at the seaside confined themselves to setting out exacting ground rules for development and waiting for demand to do its work.[67] Sometimes they had to give ground a little as the pattern of demand changed in the later nineteenth century. At Weston-super-Mare the Pigott estate and its neighbours were felt by some to be unduly flexible in the 1880s: 'In Weston as soon as anything like a building site could be procured every inch of it was covered with small tenements, and there appeared to be great rivalry among speculative builders as to who could run up the greatest number of houses of a maximum rent of £25 *per annum*.'[68] At Southport

Fig. 13 A classic example of Victorian resort planning under the auspices of a landed family: the Mostyn's Llandudno (reproduced from *Two Hundred and Fifty Views of North Wales*).

flexibility took another form, as by the 1880s the Scarisbrick estate, in particular, was allowing restrictive covenants to be broken 'in exchange for a fixed ground rent or payment of a substantial fine.'[69] Landowners operating on a leasehold system were usually unwilling to take this kind of policy too far in case it damaged the reversionary value which made high-class development attractive on those estates where it was a realistic proposition; but the imperatives of demand, and sometimes the financial needs of landowners, could become insistent enough by the later nineteenth century to enforce changes even in resorts which had aimed at the higher reaches of the market.

Even so, the persisting concern with high minimum standards ensured that working-class housing was provided particularly grudgingly and belatedly in 'aristocratic' resorts, and in inadequate numbers. At Torquay the 'beautiful vale of Ellacombe' was eventually turned over to artisan dwellings

in 1859, when the town's population was already over 15,000, after the
failure of a model lodging-house for single men which had been intended to
ease the labour supply problem.[70] By 1871 Eastbourne's needs were being
met partly by cottage-building in the neighbouring hamlet of Willingdon,
just as those of a closed agricultural village might have been; and in 1883
most of Bournemouth's working men allegedly had to travel long distances
to work from outlying villages.[71] High rents and a shortage of small houses
posed problems in most resorts into the twentieth century, but the
difficulties were probably at their most acute wherever large estates supervised leasehold development with an eye to reversionary value.

After the efflorescence of planned resort development by aristocratic and
genteel families in the 1840s, several other landed estates followed suit in
mid-Victorian times, including the Lestranges at Hunstanton, the Windsors
at Penarth, the earl of Scarbrough at Skegness and, last but particularly
successful, the De La Warrs at Bexhill. Not all landed families were eager to
embrace the new opportunities, however. The preservation of Clovelly is a
case in point, but the best-documented example is at Abergele and Pensarn,
in north Wales. In the late 1850s the pressure on accommodation in the old
market town and minor resort of Abergele became so great that local
tradesmen petitioned Thomas Hughes of Kinmel to release coastal land at
Pensarn for building, and over the next few years a Chester syndicate
erected over 100 houses there. In 1864 sanitary problems led the inhabitants
to petition successfully for a Local Board of Health to embrace both
Abergele and Pensarn; but soon afterwards an agitation against the new
arrangement began, orchestrated by the leading local landowner Mrs
Jones-Bateman. According to a Local Government Act Office inspector,
she 'appears to resent with great indignation any attempt to invade or
diminish the seclusion of her dwelling house at Pentre Mawr, which is about
a quarter of a mile from Pensarn'. Abergele opinion was roused against the
threat of heavy rates for sea defences and drainage which would benefit only
the Pensarn people, and the established Local Board was eventually
overturned (the first such occurrence) on a legal technicality. Mrs Jones-
Bateman, meanwhile, acquired two fields across which any Pensarn water
supply would have to run, and used all her local influence to prevent
Pensarn from becoming a Local Board district by itself. In 1867, however,
majority opinion in Pensarn prevailed, and the fields were included within
the new Local Board boundary; but the continuing resistance of Mrs
Jones-Bateman and her neighbour R. B. Hesketh of Gwrych Castle
effectively prevented Pensarn from growing beyond its existing boundaries,
and it stagnated while nearby Rhyl and Colwyn Bay grew rapidly in the later
nineteenth century.[72] This example is a reminder that where large landowners preferred the preservation of their own residential amenity and
political power to the risks and discomforts of resort promotion, they had
the power to suppress development as well as the opportunity to initiate and
control it; but the evidence for such activities tends to be buried in the
archives, while the success stories are visible to all.[73]

Even in the first half of the nineteenth century, not all planned or
supervised resorts were presided over by established gentry families, and in

the railway age other unifying influences on resort development came strongly to the fore. Railway companies, land speculators, syndicates and estate companies all grew in importance as promoters of new resorts, and companies increasingly took over the planning and control of extensions to late Victorian and Edwardian resorts, even where a high-class clientèle was not envisaged.

The railways themselves were the least important of these agencies. Only three English resorts were founded and controlled in their formative years by railway companies, and none achieved more than modest success. Silloth, in north Cumberland, was founded by Carlisle businessmen who built a railway to the Solway Firth in search of an independent outlet to the sea, and it was planned as a resort when delays in dock building and commercial traffic generation brought financial embarrassment to its promoters.[74] At Seascale, further south on the same coast, the Furness Railway optimistically conceived an opulent settlement of villa residences in the early 1870s, at the height of Barrow's industrial prosperity, but most of the land was never built on.[75] On the east coast Withernsea owed its being to the Hull and Holderness Railway, which was completed in 1854 as a vehicle for the resort promotion schemes of the Hull merchant Anthony Bannister; but his dreams of wide streets and prosperous villas proved illusory, and most of the limited building took place in a modest, haphazard way on a small yeoman estate to the north of Bannister's holdings.[76] In a few other resorts, especially Cleethorpes, railway management of strategically-placed estates was important to overall development; but direct railway involvement in the planning and building of resorts at national level was negligible.[77]

As well as marking the high point of landed estate involvement in resort promotion and planning, the early and mid-Victorian period also saw a marked increase in similar activities by outside entrepreneurs; but only Charles Scarisbrick at Southport really profited spectacularly from exerting a formative influence on an important resort, and he allowed most of the infrastructure to be provided by lessees and local government. On a smaller scale, at Westgate in Thanet successive purchasers of the 350-acre building estate profited handsomely by a policy of high-class development, and here the owners supplied gas and water as well as laying out the roads, no doubt responding to the more competitive environment of the south-east. Elsewhere, we find an almost universal story of frustration and financial embarrassment, of half-finished projects and ambitious schemes scarcely begun. This was true of the effects of London capitalists at Seaford and Swanage, of businessmen from Manchester and the West Midlands at Colwyn Bay, Towyn and Pwllheli, and even of Col. George Tomline, backed as he was by broad Suffolk acres, at Felixstowe.[78] Most of these entrepreneurs bought their way into only part of the potential resort area, and found themselves with insufficient resources to finance the expensive infrastructure of a resort. At Seaford Dr Tyler Smith and his associates tried to promote development without securing their sea defences, with unhappy results, although their discomfiture was less than that of the Lancastrian land speculator Mr Hubbard, whose building estate at Lowestoft was actually washed away because of an inadequate sea wall.[79] Significantly, many estate promoters on the fringes of the larger resorts were having to be bailed out by local government in the late nineteenth century, as the construction and maintenance of sea defences proved too much for them, in neat reversal of the situation at resorts like Eastbourne and Bexhill.[80] Some outside speculators failed even to make a start. At Pwllheli, William Potts of Birmingham bought three miles of sea-front adjacent to the old town in about 1870, but was unable to raise the capital to develop it, effectively sterilizing the land until the estate was resold to a Mr Churton from Rhyl, whose trustees eventually initiated a successful scheme in 1890.[81] It took the capital resources and borrowing power of the great railway contractors and civil engineers to make a success of large-scale resort development. Peto at Lowestoft is the best example, though Hudson himself set the tone for future development at Whitby, and on a smaller scale Peter Bruff of Ipswich gave a considerable impetus to the growth of Walton-on-the Naze, though he soon abandoned his attempts to do the same for Clacton.[82] The ambitious individual developer tended to run into trouble when he went beyond the safety of the established infrastructure provided by an existing resort.

The limited success of speculative outsiders in resort promotion arose from their failure to emulate the unity of ownership, continuity of management and financial stability of the best-placed landed estates, or to generate sufficient income from early leases and agreements to bring about self-sustaining expansion without incurring a crippling burden of debt. In the middle decades of the nineteenth century substantial established landowners were clearly in the best position to stimulate and sustain high-class resort growth from small beginnings. From the 1860s onwards, however, the ready availability of limited liability encouraged a further change in the pattern of resort foundation and growth, as speculators banded together in estate companies, taking the provision of sea defences, streets and drainage into account when deciding or expanding the authorized capital of the undertaking. At Colwyn Bay, Clacton and St Annes, sizeable resorts eventually grew out of schemes of this kind, where the land company's powers and financial resources enabled it to adopt the same policies as an aristocratic landowner, with minimum values, zoning, prescribed building styles and densities, restrictive covenants against undesirable users, and the power to prohibit or restrain boisterous activities and unwanted amusements on the company's promenades and open spaces.[83] Several smaller resorts prospered more modestly on the same basis, including Saltburn, Westward Ho!, Frinton and Bridport's West Bay.[84]

High-class resort planning was thus far from being the sole prerogative of aristocratic landowners. Land company promoters included Manchester businessmen at Colwyn Bay, Rossendale industrialists at St Annes, the London Steam Boat Company at Clacton and the Pease family of ironmasters at Saltburn. Even so, the most sustained and successful endeavours came from established landed families; and even at the turn of the century the three largest company towns lagged far behind Eastbourne, Torquay and even Bexhill in social tone as well as sheer size. But the influence of estate companies was not confined to the creation of new resorts; it was also becoming significant in the established centres in the later nineteenth century, as the activity and direct influence of the landed estates declined, and as the many large resorts with divided landownership became separated out into distinct social areas.

The entrepreneurial vigour of the major landed estates declined steadily as their towns became firmly established and the pattern of development defined. At Torquay the Palk estate influence collapsed altogether, as the second Lord Haldon, succeeding in 1883, found that 'the expenses incurred in developing Torquay, and principally by the construction of the Harbour and the Teign Valley Railway,' had left intolerable mortgage debts, and in 1885 extensive land sales began, reaching a peak in 1894 and culminating in the sale of the last of the Torquay property in 1914.[85] Elsewhere, withdrawal was a slower and more nuanced process, its timing depending partly on the stage of development reached and the capacity and attitude of local government. At Bournemouth and Weston-super-Mare, and perhaps elsewhere, the initiative in promoting new extensions, and the interest in supervising them, seems to have been passing to land companies and syndicates by the late nineteenth century, when the demand for large houses was declining. The wealthiest residents began to move abroad, and pressure for commercial development on central sites was accompanied by changes in the housing market which favoured small semi-detached and terraced dwellings for a less demanding class of resident. Landowners under increasing financial pressure began to look for short-term profits, while their superintendence of new development became less necessary; and these

Fig. 14 St Annes as envisaged by its Land Company.

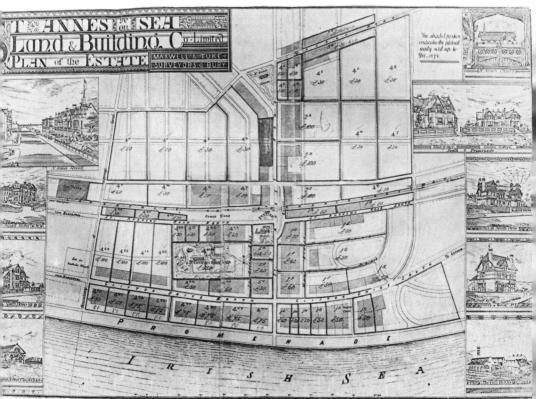

changes were expressed in resort politics as agitations for leasehold enfranchisement began, coupled with running conflicts between landed estates and local government.[86]

The land company or syndicate also became an increasingly important vehicle for development in the many popular resorts which had grown up piecemeal and unsupervised; but here their rôle was often to raise the social tone by creating protected enclaves of 'better-class' housing. Blackpool's Claremont Park and Southend's Cliff Town helped to set this trend in the 1860s, and although they were far less impressive than the best of Brighton or Bournemouth, their residents presented a common front against all attempts to introduce unseemly amusements.[87]

Over wide areas of those resorts which attracted extensive working-class patronage early, however, fragmented landownership gave rise to a lowest-common-denominator approach to building. Speculators were unable to go up-market in the absence of controls on the surrounding land, in resorts where the structure of demand ensured that small terraced houses or unpretentious purpose-built boarding-houses would find ready takers, for a lower outlay and at less risk than high-class development. This theme runs through Blackpool's building history, and Southend followed suit in the late nineteenth century, as speculative builders from the East End of London moved in on land whose agricultural value had collapsed in the Great Depression. Whole estates were often laid out without a single sewer, as arrangements were left to individual speculators, and houses were sometimes occupied within ten weeks of building commencing.[88] Here, the active intervention of the local authority was necessary to preserve minimum building standards, and at Blackpool the pressure of demand, and the strength of the builders' and speculators' lobby on the local council, was such that by-laws as to yard space and wall thickness were set aside as a matter of course even in the main accommodation district, as efforts were made to cram the maximum number of bedrooms on to each site.[89]

Not only might a swelling influx of working-class visitors, and of residents of limited means, ensure the covering of broad acres of the unsupervised popular resorts with 'endless perspectives of bay windows' fronting undistinguished and often jerry-built terraces built to the most unimaginative of grid-plans by small speculators on individual plots; it might also threaten the status of existing 'better-class' areas, as excursionist demand for entertainment and accommodation spread outwards from the town centre, helped on its way by sea-front tramways. Such pressures were at their most acute in late Victorian and Edwardian Blackpool, where the Land, Building and Hotel Company resisted the temptation to go down-market, preferring to allow plots to lie fallow, and successfully enlisting the support of the Corporation to protect its northern flank against fairground amusements. At South Shore, on the other hand, the respectability of quiet streets of unassuming semi-detached houses was threatened at the turn of the century by the fairground which became the Pleasure Beach. Here, a modest residential selectness had been achieved by developers' consensus, but this was undermined as trippers poured along the electric tramway after its opening in 1885, providing opportunities for noisy open-air amusement caterers at the terminus; and the absence of restrictive covenants, or of the will to enforce them on freehold estates, enabled a rapid conversion of premises into cheap lodging-houses at the south end of the promenade. Blackpool's own local élite found sanctuary inland, as Enoch Read's 48-acre estate at Bonny's Farm and the adjoining Raikes Hall estate imposed high minimum values, controlled materials, facades and lawn areas, and prohibited any uses other than the purely residential, after the manner of sea-front estates at Brighton and Hove. The avoidance of the central and southern promenades by Blackpool's leading citizens from the 1870s onwards is itself an indication of their visible vulnerability to commercialization and tripper penetration.[90]

Blackpool was an extreme case even among the popular resorts, but here as elsewhere Corporation controls were beginning to make a significant impact by the late nineteenth century, especially in the defence of North Shore amenities, but also in the regulation of the Pleasure Beach fairground in the early twentieth century, when noise was reduced, undesirables evicted and Sunday operation prohibited. In some places Corporation intervention was already much more wide-ranging in defence of residential amenity, especially at Great Yarmouth, where extensive sea-front estates were in Corporation hands and there was a strong vested interest in regulating the streets and foreshore to protect rents and property values, with most outdoor entertainment being confined to the town centre, away from the villas on the Denes and their sensitive inhabitants.[91] In all resorts, local government in the second half of the nineteenth century was becoming an increasingly important and controversial influence on building patterns and the evolution of social areas, as streets were replanned and realigned, and sites had to be found for sewer outfalls, public conveniences, tramways, gasworks, cab stands and a variety of other essential services which affected sea views, local amenities and the expectations of builders and residents, while local authorities became responsible for sea defences, the regulation of amusements, and the provision of public parks and libraries, as well as the basic public health, public order and public utility functions. Where the policies of landowners, or the lack of them, had often exerted a crucial influence on resort development patterns in mid-Victorian times, by the turn of the century this rôle was swiftly passing to local government. We shall explore this point further in the next chapter.

Landownership thus became an important formative influence on resort development in the early Victorian period, but the scope and motivation for the active intervention of major landowners of all kinds declined towards the turn of the century, as the importance of local government increased. The years when landownership really counted, however, were years in which the destiny of many resorts was shaped; and Cannadine is right to argue for a positive relationship between unified landownership (especially in aristocratic hands) and successful high-class development. He himself enumerates significant exceptions: resorts like Brighton, Hastings and Worthing where high standards were achieved by consensus rather than prescription, although here the die was already cast before the railway revolution complicated the expectations of developers. Elsewhere, as he points out, resorts failed to match their promoters' expectations, as at Fleetwood, where competition and confusion of aims were crucial. There is also the maverick example of Skegness, where unified and spacious planning by an aristocratic landowner was accommodated from the beginning to the realities of Midland working-class demand, and excursionists were encouraged in large numbers.[92] In a few other cases, perceptions of demand and imperfectly arranged estates inhibited or sabotaged pretensions to high-class development. Southend's Lord of the Manor, Daniel Scratton, led the party of expansion there in the early 1860s but took the substantial profits on his 'large quantity of land' and retired to his Devon estate without trying to impose a controlled development policy,[93] and at Cleethorpes the Sidney Sussex College estate owned over half the township but did not control the whole of the sea-front, and though building controls imposed high maintenance standards and prohibited offensive trades, the nature of Grimsby suburban housing demand ensured that artisan terraces would predominate.[94]

This may seem a long roll-call of exceptions; but it is short in relation to the total number of resorts under investigation, and the positive relationship between unified landownership and high-class development, and the association between land sub-division and the ready assimilation of working-class visitors, can be admitted. Tenurial arrangements seem to have worked in a similar way: a freehold resort like Blackpool or Ramsgate succumbed more readily to pressure for change than a leasehold town, although the example of Westgate is a reminder that the freehold system was not incompatible with a very high social tone indeed. In these respects, seaside resorts contrasted strikingly with other kinds of town.[95] Indeed, it seems clear that certain resorts grew rapidly in late Victorian and Edwardian times precisely because of the lack of regulation by landowners, and because they had failed to develop an established, protective residential interest during the mid-Victorian heyday of the controlled middle-class resort. By this time, however, the rôle of local government was becoming increasingly important, and it becomes more and more misleading to examine the significance of landownership in isolation.

Before we proceed to an analysis of local government at the seaside, a final point should be made about key influences on resort character. The relationship between landowners, speculators and perceived demand, operating under the constraints imposed by local topography, determined the quality of a resort's built environment, with increasingly effective intervention from local government; but the visible results of this interaction were expressed in architectural idioms which owed more to extraneous fashions than to the circumstances of a given site. At the top end of the market, in particular, the slow and uncoordinated transition from the monumental terrace to the detached villa, and the successive waves of architectural innovation from the Classical through the Italianate and the Gothic to the vernacular and Norman Shaw styles which appeared at the seaside at the turn of the century, made a particularly strong impact in those resorts which competed for the fashion-conscious and educated public. The niceties of style might matter little in a Blackpool dominated by unpretentious terraces;

indeed, a lack of architectural distinction might even foster an illusion of homeliness attractive to working-class visitors. But even a provincial resort like Clevedon might suffer from the vagaries of architectural fashion; in 1900 its recent stagnation was ascribed to the preponderance of 'stuccoed semi-Italian villas on the Ladbroke Grove model that became discredited a generation ago.'[96] In Brighton the impact of this revolution in taste was also noticeable. The West Brighton estate in Hove, for example, suffered from its initial attachment to the monumental terrace, which was beginning to look anachronistic by the 1870s, and the developers soon changed over to villas, so that by the 1890s 'what began as a bastard Georgian estate without Georgian architecture was ending as a garden suburb without gardens', as tile-hanging and Norman Shaw took over. In nearby Brunswick Town houses which had let at 40 guineas a week in 1877 could be had for five guineas 20 years later.[97]

Despite these occasional problems, building styles were a marginal influence on the social development of most resorts, and they tended to be a function of landowners' and developers' interpretations of the market rather than an autonomous variable in themselves. The pattern and character of resort development depended most obviously on demand, landownership and local government, and the third of these influences, which came into its own during the second half of the nineteenth century, will receive extended treatment in the next chapter.

6 Local government at the seaside

During the nineteenth century urban local government institutions became increasingly sophisticated. Their powers, financial resources and accepted spheres of influence expanded spectacularly, especially after mid-century, as reformed municipal corporations and Local Boards of Health took on new functions while retaining a remarkable degree of executive autonomy, although new legislative initiatives were subjected to close and critical scrutiny by central government, which also vetted most projects which involved substantial capital expenditure. From early Victorian times public health as well as public order became an accepted responsibility of increasingly representative local government bodies, while the legitimacy of municipal trading became more generally acknowledged, allowing local authorities to provide a wide range of services which might not have been attractive speculations to private investors, but which could be seen to benefit the town as a whole.[1]

These developments were particularly important at the seaside, for the health and comfort of visitors was an essential part of a resort's stock in trade. The existence of a direct relationship between sanitation and disease was becoming widely appreciated in the 1830s and 1840s, and this was reflected in resort propaganda. 'Whereas eighteenth century guides extolled the advantages of their particular resort for bathing, the guides of the mid-nineteenth century are largely concerned with drainage systems.'[2] Water supply also became a matter for assertive competition. Rivalry apart, an absolute standard had to be pursued; as Tenby's civic leaders were warned by a Board of Health inspector in 1850, a high-class resort 'should not only be clean, but remarkable for cleanliness.'[3] The standard of other utilities and services, especially paving, lighting and internal transport, also provided fuel for propaganda and controversy. Resorts might therefore be expected to bulk large among the pioneers in municipal enterprise, initiating utilities or buying them up from private companies to control the standard of service, as well as to cut prices or plough back profits in relief of the rates.[4] In fact, this was not the case, at least where orthodox 'gas and water socialism' was concerned. Table 22 shows that by 1902 the 22 seaside resorts with borough status owned fewer gas and water undertakings than the national average, though they were more likely to control the more recent tramway and electricity services. Resorts had an early and obvious need for lighting and water supplies, and in many cases private enterprise arrived on the scene before the local authority was sufficiently large or self-confident to intervene.

Table 22. Proportion of seaside resorts incorporated before 1902 operating specified municipal enterprises at that time, compared with all English boroughs[5]

	Total	Waterworks No.	%	Gas No.	%	Electricity No.	%	Tramways* No.	%
Seaside resorts	22	12	54.5	4	18.2	9	40.9	4	18.2
All English boroughs	286	171	61.2	90	31.5	81	28.3	24	8.4

*Worked by local authority.

Despite competitive pressures, many early and mid-Victorian resorts were slow to respond to the need for improved sanitation and basic services. We shall see that *laissez-faire* attitudes and resistance to local rates could be as great a barrier to improvement as in the commercial and industrial centres, and it was not until the last quarter of the nineteenth century that some of the seaside resorts really began to blossom as centres of municipal innovation and enterprise. This belated efflorescence, which continued strongly into the twentieth century, was based as much on the provision of special attractions and amenities, on direct participation in the holiday industry, as on the efficient provision of basic services.

It soon became apparent that seaside resorts had special needs which could not readily be met by private enterprise, unless public-spirited local investors were prepared to forego the likelihood of a return on their capital by underwriting a seemingly unprofitable project in the hope of indirect benefits to their businesses or lifestyles.[6] Sea defences and promenades were the most obvious and important examples of this kind of essential amenity, for construction costs were so great that private investors were unlikely to find them attractive as speculations unless they formed part of the necessary infrastructure of a high-class building estate. At Bexhill, Eastbourne and other 'aristocratic' resorts the dominant landowners were willing and able to make the necessary provision on an opulent scale, and this was a major advantage to such resorts in their formative years, before urban growth had generated a sufficient rateable value to make large-scale municipal borrowing a legal and political possibility.[7] Elsewhere land syndicates, companies or even individual developers with long sea frontages were sometimes able to take care of themselves. Otherwise, public subscription was the only alternative; and this had the dual disadvantage of seeming to tax the visitors (whose contributions were eagerly solicited) in order to provide a patched-up and inferior product.[8] Very occasionally, the prospect of toll revenue was in itself sufficiently attractive to encourage speculative investment in a marine promenade. At Llandudno in 1873 the extensive carriage trade led local investors to support a Marine Drive Company, which spent £14,000 on a 4½-mile toll road. Even in this favourable setting, however, dividends did not rise above 1½ to 2½ per cent, and when the Urban District Council sought to buy the company out in 1897 the price quoted was only £9,000.[9] This was a most unusual case, and even in those resorts where sea defences had been provided in generous measure by landowners and estate companies in earlier years, the responsibility for upkeep and extensions was passing to the local authorities in the late nineteenth century, especially where tolls and other restrictions on company property inhibited free access by respectable members of the general visiting public.

By this time local government was becoming more generally involved in the provision of attractions and entertainments, stepping in where private enterprise feared to tread, or taking on responsibilities which had hitherto been met by the unreliable and divisive means of voluntary subscription. In some places large landowners had provided essential financial backing for approved forms of entertainment, and given land for parks, libraries and churches, especially in the early days of the 'aristocratic' resorts. At Eastbourne, and to a lesser extent elsewhere, such assistance was still being provided in the early twentieth century, when a mature local government system was well established.[10] As in other spheres, however, local authorities generally began to take over the initiative around the turn of the century, especially where there was no dominant landowner and a limited level of private investment. Municipal bands became almost universal, and resorts began to take over ailing entertainments, such as piers, winter gardens and concert halls. Some even promoted large-scale undertakings of this kind from scratch. Such use of ratepayers' money long remained controversial, especially where municipal entertainments competed with established interests; and several schemes had a rough passage in parliamentary committees. Even more contentious were the parallel attempts to obtain power to advertise resorts on the rates, in the wake of an accidentally-successful Blackpool proposal of 1879; and we shall see that other local authorities adopted a variety of subterfuges in their eagerness to evade legal restrictions on the use of public money to advertise their towns as a whole, rather than depending on the limited perspectives given by the advertisements put out by particular interests, or the fluctuating generosity of voluntary subscribers.

Local government at the seaside thus became increasingly important to the health, comfort and enjoyment of visitors and residents. By the turn of the century, indeed, resorts were becoming prominent as innovators in health care and disease control, as well as extending municipal activity into more unusual territory. Just as important as a healthy environment, however, was a reputation for order and security; and here, too, the influence of municipal government was becoming increasingly pervasive during the second half of the nineteenth century. Here again, resorts had special problems of their own. 'Better-class' visitors and residents had increasingly high expectations. They sought a well-regulated environment in which they could mix comfortably with their equals and betters. Until the middle decades of the nineteenth century most resorts could provide this without too much difficulty, and often with mainly voluntary policing arrangements, although the regulation of bathing was often controversial. But the new lower-class visitors of the railway age disrupted this socially secure environment. They brought noise and bustle to central streets and beaches, and in their wake came hawkers, stallholders and showmen, causing congestion and discomfort, and bringing middle-class families into contact with undesirable sights and sounds. To keep the patronage of established visitors, resorts needed powers of prohibition and restraint, to curb excesses and to confine offensive activities to the least sensitive parts of town. Problems of jurisdiction made this inevitably largely a matter for local government, although outside magistrates and the county police were often important, especially in the smaller resorts. Landowners might regulate promenades, streets and open spaces which remained their own property, and Lord Radnor's policeman still patrolled the Leas at Folkestone with his short cane at the turn of the century.[11] Restrictive covenants might control the use of private houses and gardens, preventing the development of forecourt trading; but the public streets and beach, and usually most or all of the promenade, were the responsibility of the local authority, although we shall see that control of the beach was often a legal minefield in itself. Everywhere, the common law soon proved too imprecise and unwieldy an instrument for the control of excursionists and those who ministered to them, and local authorities (landowners too, where appropriate) had to seek special by-law powers to prohibit activities which annoyed or impeded 'better-class' visitors, tradesmen and residents, and to license beach or street traders who might prove dangerous, obstructive or a nuisance. This was not always straightforward. Even the largest resorts had to obtain the consent of a critical Local Government Board or its predecessors when seeking new by-laws, or even to obtain a local Act from Parliament. After 1894 the Urban District Councils which replaced the old Local Boards had to send their draft by-laws to the County Council, and Llandudno complained bitterly in 1897 of the three-month gaps between meetings of the relevant committee.[12] Legal difficulties were common even when by-laws had been duly ratified, and they were often compounded by policing problems. Even in the early twentieth century most resorts did not have borough status, and some of the remainder preferred not to incur the expense of running their own police force. This left them dependent on the county police, who were not always responsive to demands for extra staffing at peak periods, especially in their early years in the 1840s and 1850s. At Blackpool, the town's leading citizen, John Cocker, guaranteed the cost of an extra constable for the season in 1850, and three years later the new Improvement Commissioners felt obliged to do the same.[13] In the early 1870s there were frequent complaints that the county police would not enforce Blackpool's by-laws, and the only effective authority was vested in 'a nuisance inspector and a couple of carriage inspectors'. Even when offenders were summoned, the magistrates dismissed a large proportion of the cases on legal technicalities. It took the setting up of a separate borough police force in 1887, and the appointment of additional magistrates from the ranks of the town council, to make Blackpool master of its public order machinery; and most resorts never reached this level of independence.[14]

The public order policies of seaside resorts were particularly important because, in spite of all the practical difficulties and limitations, they helped to determine social tone. Repressive by-laws effectively enforced could drive away working-class visitors, who might be encouraged elsewhere by a tolerant legal framework or by the existence of problems of jurisdiction and enforcement. We shall explore this theme further in chapter 8, when we shall look more closely at the problem of integrating working-class visitors, in particular, into an established recreational culture at the seaside. In the meantime, the increasing strategic importance of local government to the fortunes of Victorian and Edwardian resorts should be clear enough. It remains for us to chart its growth, describe its components, and assess the significance of the conflicts which were engendered along the way.

Until the 1830s and 1840s, at best, local government at the seaside remained patchy in organization and limited in scope. Improvement Commissioners were already making some inroads into problems of paving, lighting, sewering and watching in the late eighteenth century in some of the larger centres, and at Brighton (especially), Margate, Weymouth, Worthing and Southampton their powers and financial resources were significantly increased in the early nineteenth century. Even so, street improvements and sea defences still depended heavily on public subscriptions even in the best-governed resorts, and public order was generally left in the hands of a few superannuated watchmen, although resorts with municipal corporations at least had some of the relevant judicial machinery. Gas and water usually came from private enterprise, and drainage was universally neglected. Where no municipal corporation or Improvement Commission existed, the powers of the manor and the vestry were even less relevant to the provision of urban sanitation and amenities, although there was little contemporary complaint until the 1840s, when public health reform became an increasingly fashionable topic.[15]

As yet the quality of local government mattered greatly only in the largest resorts, where a systematic approach to cleansing and sanitation was becoming all too visibly necessary. But size brought benefits as well as problems, and it is no coincidence that the largest and most successful resorts were capable of sustaining the most sophisticated and expensive local government systems. The quality of services was far from uniform, but even the worst-governed of the leading resorts were paved, lit and watched by the 1830s, and in some cases the influence of local government already extended much further. Such advantages in turn fuelled further growth, and no doubt they helped Weymouth, for example, to outpace Lyme Regis and Lymington, or gave Scarborough an additional edge over Filey and Bridlington. But the quality of resort local government, like that of planning and layout, did not become a major competitive issue until the 1840s. A certain level of provision became necessary in the leading centres, but the expectations of visitors remained relatively limited until the great expansion of the early railway age.

The heightened perception of problems of public health and public order in early Victorian England made a significant impact in the resorts, as in other rapidly-growing towns; and the reformed municipal corporations after 1835 were in a better position to take action on these issues. Improvement Commissioners also continued to proliferate, and the 1848 Public Health Act offered a further option, the Local Board of Health, with powers specifically geared up to the attack on sanitary problems. During this period, too, attitudes to municipal trading began to mellow, and the operation of utilities which were naturally monopolistic, especially the supply of gas and water using mains running through the public streets, was coming to be seen as a legitimate local government activity.[16] The seaside resorts might have been expected to grasp eagerly at the new powers, but in practice their response was unimpressive. Despite the efforts of reformers, basic public health defects were still painfully apparent in some resorts in the 1870s, and a similar lack of initiative was often visible in the provision of adequate promenades, sea defences and even street lighting, although the pursuit of enhanced powers for crowd regulation and public order mainte-nance was undertaken significantly earlier. We must now explore these points a little further.

The unhealthy sanitary state of most resorts was brought into sharp relief by the cholera epidemic of 1849, which occurred at the height of the season in several places, and by a spate of damning reports issued by inspectors from the General Board of Health in the years immediately following; but a groundswell of unease had been growing for several years, as visitors found themselves bathing in contaminated water and inhaling noxious effluvia as they strolled along the promenade. The late summer of 1849 saw 26 cholera deaths recorded at Southport, 65 at Hastings, 124 at Margate and a very large but unknown number at Great Yarmouth, which had also been badly hit in the first epidemic in 1832.[17] In the small resort of Ilfracombe the outbreak was alleged to have cost £8,000 to £10,000 in lost income from visitors.[18] From 1850 onwards the Board of Health reports, some of which had been commissioned in direct response to the damage done by cholera, painted a grim picture of inadequate drainage, contaminated foreshores and bathing grounds, leaking cesspools and polluted wells. For all the energy of its commissioners, Brighton fared as badly as anywhere. It had over five miles of sewers, but these were for surface water only, and householders were forbidden to discharge from privies or watercloses into them, so that the town still depended on cesspools. The inspector provided a long catalogue of defects and abuses in 'the worst-conditioned houses', and made extensive proposals for improved drainage and water supply.[19] At Margate, where the Paving Commissioners had quite a good record on street improvements and spent £455 in 1849 on their police force, the sewers were similarly reserved for surface water drainage; but here the concern to protect bathing beaches from pollution went even further, as householders were forbidden to remove nightsoil from their cesspools between February and

November. This was unenforceable, but it added to the problems of Margate residents; and by 1851 defective drainage was coming to be seen as a genuine threat to the resort's economy.[20]

In many resorts the drains carried a high proportion of the sewage straight into the sea; and here the problem was more visible, as rivulets of sewage meandered across the beach and pipes discharged their noxious contents among the bathers. At Worthing eight wooden troughs deposited all of the town's sewage directly on to the beach below the esplanade, and in 1850 a considerable increase in sickness was alleged since the 1830s, especially among the poor. Hastings had a similar system, with seven large sewers emptying themselves below the promenade.[21] Thus even where the houses themselves were effectively drained, the problem was merely transferred: instead of cesspools polluting the subsoil and water supply, drains concentrated the sewage to pollute the bathing beaches.

Conditions in the smaller resorts, many of which still lacked formal urban local government institutions, could be equally unpleasant. At Blackpool, B. H. Babbage found 45 sewers and open drains emptying on to the beach.[22] At Littlehampton the visitors' area of the town was the worst off for drainage, and an attempt to drain Beach Terrace had stopped short of the river after the subscription money had run out.[23] Even Clevedon, where the dominant Elton family contributed to the building of the principal sewer, had serious problems, for many houses drained directly over the cliffs, creating an 'intolerable nuisance' in the summer as privy refuse accumulated on the beach. In dry summers the river became 'one long cesspool', and the two main drains discharged near the centre of the Parade. The overall death-rate was as high as 31.7 per 1,000.[24]

Examples of this sort could be multiplied almost endlessly. Even the largest resorts lacked a coherent sewerage system with an outfall at a safe distance from the bathing beaches. But this was far from being the only problem. Water, too, was dubious in quality and limited in supply almost everywhere. At Blackpool pumps were padlocked and chained, and householders paid 1. 6d. per barrel for water, or up to 5s. 6d. *per annum* for use of a pump. The well water was very hard and almost certainly contaminated.[25] At Tenby the Corporation's supply was praised for its purity, but it was only available for eight hours daily during the season, when the shortfall was worsened by the demand for the washing of carriages brought into the town by wealthy visitors.[26] Public water supplies were still unusual, whether they were operated by municipalities or, as at Hastings and St Leonards, by recently-established water companies.[27] The Blackpool example was nearest to the norm, and even as large and important a port and resort as Great Yarmouth still depended on wells and rainwater in 1850.[28]

The old fishing and agricultural settlements, around which most early resorts developed, posed the worst sanitary problems. At Hastings Cresy remarked on the overcrowded conditions under which 'a very large proportion of the inhabitants', mostly fishermen, lived in poverty and squalor, while Babbage found 181 pigsties at Blackpool, 'about 1 to every $2\frac{1}{3}$ houses'.[29] Brighton, of course, had added newly built slums to its fishermen's cottages by this time, and insanitary hovels and their malodorous adjuncts added to the problems of public health almost everywhere. The seaside was by no means immune from the general problems of large-scale urbanization which were making themselves felt throughout Britain at this time.

Paving and lighting were rather better served. Improvement Commissioners had long been active in the larger centres, and by the 1830s gas companies were beginning to appear in the lower reaches of the resort hierarchy, at Lymington and Ilfracombe as well as obviously flourishing places like Torquay.[30] Even Littlehampton had a gas company by 1847, though public street lighting took several years longer.[31] By this time the Improvement Commissioners at Southport and Lytham were starting their own gasworks, although as late as 1856 Lytham's street lamps were still being taken down for the summer and stored in the market house, leaving the visitors to rely on moonlight and lanterns.[32] Tenby's Corporation also ran its own gasworks, but private enterprise was still the norm at mid-century for gas as for water, and many smaller resorts, such as Clevedon, remained unpaved and unlit in the absence of private or public initiative.[33]

It is not surprising that up to the mid-century resorts were paved and lit more effectively than they were sewered and watered. The former services were less capital-hungry, and less controversial in legal and technological terms, than the major schemes which were required for adequate drainage and constant pure water; and their amenity value was obvious to the casual observer. They interfered less abrasively with private interests and property rights, too, although disputes about the responsibility for road making and maintenance remained endemic everywhere. Respect for individual property rights also ensured that while the scavenging of the public streets was one of the first public health functions to be organized by local authorities (especially where, as in Brighton, contractors were willing to pay heavily for the privilege),[34] the control of conditions inside houses was effectively impossible, even where their occupants catered for visitors. This was to become a contentious issue in the late nineteenth century.

At mid-century seaside local government was not remarkable for enterprise, quality or range of services in public health, utilities or amenities. Problems were usually much less pressing than in the commercial and industrial centres, but this was largely due to the limited scale of growth and the nature of housing demand and economic activity. Lively responses such as the great Liverpool and Manchester water schemes were not yet finding echoes in resorts with limited financial resources and a complacent self-image which was only just coming under challenge.[35] Even sea defences were still left largely to estate promoters, and even at Brighton subscriptions from developers still accounted for a high proportion of expenditure.[36] More significant innovations were occurring in the field of public order. But those resorts which had acquired the power to license street and beach traders, and to make and enforce by-laws regulating public behaviour, were distinctive at mid-century more for their range of specific prohibitions and powers than for the general tenor of their overall policy. Some of the larger resorts had been obtaining the power to license cabs, bathing-machines, donkeys and even sedan-chairs from the early nineteenth century, and hawkers and street singers also began to find life more difficult. Bathing was increasingly being formally confined to machines on fixed sites, and after 1832 the Hastings Commissioners even prohibited the drying of clothes on the beach.[37] The new Improvement Commissioners of the 1830s and 1840s were, indeed, keen to assume such powers at the outset.[38] Apart from its specific seaside aspects, however, most of this tightening up of the regulation of streets and other public places ran parallel to the essentially similar activities of Watch Committees, magistrates and Improvement Commissioners in the inland towns, where efforts were being made to clear the streets of undesirable loiterers and to stamp out activities like nude foot-racing which were now being seen as indecent as well as disorderly.[39]

The need for more effective regulation of behaviour in public places, especially after the coming of the railways, helps to explain the promotion of several Improvement Acts during the 1840s at resorts which had depended on parochial and manorial institutions, such as Blackpool (where the attempt was unsuccessful), Lytham and Weston-super-Mare. By this time the public health motive was becoming at least as important in the new climate of sanitary opinion, and local leaders began to pay heed to arguments like those advanced by Babbage in this concluding remarks on Blackpool: 'The above deficiencies (sc. in drainage and water supply) are not only very inconvenient to the inhabitants, but . . . in many cases they inflict pecuniary injury upon them by driving visitors away from the town.'[40] As a visiting land agent remarked of the evil smells on Blackpool's sea-front in 1846, 'It is impossible for Blackpool to maintain its position if these nuisances are not removed.'[41]

Despite these pressures, Improvement Acts were sometimes hotly opposed, in resorts as elsewhere. The commonest problem was a widespread unwillingness to incur liability for increased or additional rates, and this proved particularly thorny where those directly involved in resort activities were expected to benefit at their neighbours' expense. At Ilfracombe the anti-improvement party in the 1840s was also opposed to further resort development, and this group was strong enough to defeat a campaign for an Improvement Act.[42] Similar attitudes were still in evidence at Bridlington in 1863, when a campaign for a Local Board had to contend with resistance from the farmers, who had been strong enough a few years before to prevent the introduction of gas lighting, and 'the elder portion of our inhabitants', who had 'set their faces against all alteration and improvement.' The Local Board party took care to explain that sea defences would remain the responsibility of individual proprietors, and their arguments eventually won the day. Die-hard opponents insisted on a poll, however, though the most outspoken of them, the farmer James Vickerman, carried tightfistedness to its logical conclusion by refusing to guarantee the cost. The influence of such objectors tended to decline as resorts grew and became more specialized, although they were still capable of blocking improvements in new resorts like St Annes in the 1880s.[43]

The Public Health Act of 1848, which became the usual vehicle of improvement, was controversial for further reasons, although it merely provided a package of enabling clauses 'for complete coverage of health problems, as then defined', and provided 'wide rating and loan powers' to overcome the financial shortfalls which had bedevilled many Improvement Commissions with limited borrowing allowances. The power of enforcement and oversight from the General Board of Health in London was limited and mainly advisory, and the package was very much cheaper than an ordinary Improvement Act.[44] Even so, fears of Chadwickian centralization on the Poor Law pattern were current before the passing of the Act, and some local Improvement Acts were propelled on to the statute book in the mid-1840s as local leaders sought to avoid central control by putting their own house in order independently. Reformers were sometimes not averse to helping the process along by conjuring up the spectre of 'a Government Commissioner, who would do as he liked and tax them as he pleased.'[45] Long after the actual measure appeared in all its permissive mildness, popular mythology held the General Board's powers to be much stronger than they actually were. In 1849 William Squire of Great Yarmouth told the Board that, 'Our application to you have [sic] moved the Town Council to a perfect terror of your advent', and subsequently he himself had to be reassured that the Board was not empowered to impose a drainage scheme of its own devising against the wishes of the local authorities.[46] Local autonomy was a potent focus of resistance, and confusion over the extent of the General Board's powers may help to explain the continuing preference of some small resorts, such as Rhyl in 1852, for expensive Improvement Acts.[47] Existing Improvement Commissions were often defended by those who had vested interests in their limited rating and spending powers and oligarchical organization;[48] and the advocates of purely local legislation were given additional support for several years by the failure of the 1848 Act to provide by-law powers for the regulation of streets and beaches. Blackpool, for example, had to seek a supplementary Improvement Act for these purposes only two years after the establishment of its Local Board. This problem was resolved by the Public Health Act of 1858.[49]

Even at the seaside, resistance to the introduction of a Local Board was usually unsuccessful. Many resorts had death-rates above the 23 per 1,000 at which a Local Board became compulsory (until 1858), if 10 per cent of the ratepayers petitioned for it.[50] But the establishment of a Local Board was no guarantee of active or even efficient local government, and in some places sanitary problems remained unchecked for many years. At Tenby a Local Board was set up in 1851 but voted at its first meeting that 'it is inexpedient at present to carry out the Health of Towns Act for the borough of Tenby.' In 1853 the surveyor was dismissed, complaining that there was 'not one sufficient sewer in the town and not one house in ten that has anything like a proper drainage.' He described his successor as 'an ignorant printer'. Two years later a local doctor complained that the Local Board's own inspector had told him that 'the Board of Health could put a broom in our hands, but could not make us use it.' No drainage loan was applied for until 1861, and at the beginning of 1867, as central coercion was beginning to be applied to delinquent authorities by the Board of Health's successor, the Local Government Act Office, the drainage system was still incomplete.[51]

Tenby was an unusually recalcitrant case, at least among resorts; but the reasons for its unwillingness to pursue public health improvements were not peculiar to itself, and an examination of them will help to explain why many other resorts dragged their feet on public health issues through the 1850s and 1860s, and, in some places and respects, even longer. Most obviously, 'the habit of regarding the minimum of rates as the maximum of happiness', as the Tenby doctor called it, died hard even at the seaside, as the citizens were slow to detect the positive correlation between sanitary expenditure and visitor numbers which G. W. Wigner suggested in an attack on the local authorities in some resorts at the end of the 1870s:

> I incline to . . . the opinion that the neglect of the sanitary authorities is in most instances the cause rather than the effect of the paucity of visitors . . . (in some cases) the local authorities would be much better called unsanitary authorities, because, held back by their parsimony or by the pressure of the municipal electors . . . they practise economy where economy is folly, and by that means prevent their town attracting the visitors, who would ultimately furnish they money needed to repay that which has been spent in making the necessary sanitary improvements.[52]

To quote the Tenby doctor again, 'In small towns and borough towns especially power is generally lodged in the hands of obstruction.' At Tenby, and even at Scarborough, this meant substantial property-owners with little interest in resort development. At Blackpool or Morecambe, at least until the mid-1860s, it meant farmers, small landowners, petty tradesmen and, in the latter case, fishermen, making for a chronic lack of enterprise, expertise and even mere competence.[53] The social composition and economic attitudes of local government bodies clearly had a strong negative influence on resort development in many places in mid-Victorian times.

Complacency was also a widespread problem, as it was often difficult to shake the confidence of leading citizens in the natural healthiness of their resort. In 1849 Tenby sheltered behind the Pembroke Union's medical officer, who blandly asserted that the town had been 'remarkably free from infectious diseases since I have known it'.[54] The statistical movement had made no impact here, and the same was true of Margate, where local doctors testified to the town's 'almost entire exemption from Epidemic Diseases' two years after a major cholera outbreak.[55]

Where the will to improve was present, expertise was often lacking, in councillors and their officials alike. Tenby's unfortunate surveyor complained of 'unwarrantable interference' from Local Board members, with 'each one deeming himself *master* and giving orders and directions as his whim or his stupidity might guide him.' Elsewhere, if not in this case, surveyors themselves were often ill-qualified and visibly incompetent. Blackpool had a chequered history in this respect. Its first Local Board surveyor caused consternation at the Board of Health offices by sending the required town plan, at 10 ft to the mile, on an undivided sheet of paper more than 30 ft long. His eventual dismissal was for 'misconduct' and 'defalcation', but his successor was a popular local man who combined the office with keeping a pub in nearby Poulton-le-Fylde, and prepared plans which the General Board found 'so unsatisfactory . . . as to render them of little use.' He was dismissed, controversially, after a dispute with a Local Board member over turf-cutting rights, and described his prospective replacements as a provision dealer and a Methodist preacher. Blackpool was no more fortunate in its drainage contractors, and a long stretch of sewering had to be relaid in 1856 after negligent installation had led to leakages and obstructions.[56] It took a long time for local authorities to come to terms with the technology of drainage, and the same applied to water supply. Difficulties were exacerbated in many cases by disputes between rival advisors over the proper course of action. The daunting capital cost of essential public works, especially sea defences, made these problems loom all the larger, and there was plenty of fuel for the petty personal spite and jealousies which all too often made up the substance of small-town politics, at the seaside as elsewhere. Conflicts were at their worst in towns with divided landownership and a preponderance of small property-owners, and they could prove especially pernicious when co-operation was needed on a major project like a sea wall or promenade, which involved a large number of properties.[57] Even where this was not the case, the cost of essential improvements could actually remain beyond the reach of small mid-Victorian resorts with low rateable values, and Eastbourne's drainage scheme had to be rescued by the Duke of Devonshire in the early 1860s for want of £2,500 on top of an existing debt of £7,000.[58] It was during the early and mid-Victorian period, indeed, that the investment, patronage and unifying influence of an interested large landowner was most visibly important to an aspiring resort.

Worst off of all were the little resorts which lacked a separate administrative identity of their own even after the establishment of a Local Board. Silloth, for instance, formed only a part of one of four mainly rural wards when the Holme Cultram Local Board was formed in 1863, and the farmers who predominated were most unwilling to spend heavily on the resort's streets and sewers when the North British Railway abandoned its responsibilities there in the late 1870s. The result was a hiatus which adversely affected the visiting season.[59] In Wales the rival neighbouring resorts of Aberdovey and Towyn came under the same Local Board, which also covered an extensive rural area. The result was exemplified by two contributions to a discussion in 1874. Mr Hunt: 'But you don't expect the people of Towyn to provide seats for Aberdovey.' Mr J. Williams: it was unfair for the Local Board to spend ratepayers' money on resort amenities 'for the sake of a few who kept lodging-houses.'[60] Under such circumstances it was especially difficult to escape from the narrow economic outlook of the petty tradesman and small property-owner, often with no interest in or sympathy with the needs of the holiday industry.

Most of these obstacles to sanitary reform and general urban improvement are familiar to students of manufacturing and commercial centres. What is remarkable is their strength in towns whose stock in trade was a healthy and attractive environment, and the high cost of drainage and sea defences in the resorts was only partly responsible for this. The strength and pervasiveness of the early and mid-Victorian attachment to the rights of locality and private property, and the problems arising from the rule of the petty bourgeoisie, are brought into sharp relief by the experience of the seaside resorts. Persistent delinquency was still widespread in the late 1870s, as Wigner's report on seaside water supplies makes clear. Of 107 places he examined, 53 had 'first-class' water, but five were 'third-class' and 15 more depended on wells, most of which were dangerous. The bad supplies were concentrated into the smaller resorts: Filey's water company offered a product which gave off 'when warmed, an offensive smell, which gave a strong suspicion of urine'; Littlehampton's well water was 'of an absolutely dangerous character'; and at Clacton the hotel well was 'full of particles of suspended matter . . . decomposing muscular fibre and hairs.' Some larger centres came in for criticism. Margate and Weston-super-Mare had salt and vegetable contamination; and Aberystwyth's supply was 'unsatisfactory . . . probably due to neglect on the part of the authorities.'[61] Some resorts had genuinely serious natural disadvantages, and the typhoid epidemic which ruined the season at Worthing in 1893 was not a fair reflection of the work of a local authority which had faced up to a particularly intractable sea defence problem as well as a shortage of natural water resources;[62] but elsewhere neglect was indicated by reliance on wells or by the failure to intervene against an unsatisfactory private company. The same could also apply to sewering: several important resorts retained an unhealthy dependence on cesspools into the 1870s and 1880s, but Southport, at least, could attempt to justify its apparent complacency by pointing to its flat site and extensive sands, which posed potentially expensive problems of gradient and outfall.[63]

This stress on the obstacles to mid-Victorian improvement should not be allowed to obscure the fact that most of the larger resorts did spend heavily, by the standards of the time, on drainage, water supply and sea defences. Beyond this, a few responded promptly and fully to criticism and undertook remarkable burdens of municipal debt, while others rescued themselves from parsimony and ineptitude at some point during the 1850s and 1860s, as the attitudes, expectations and personnel of local government were transformed. Worthing's new Local Board spent £19,000 on drainage and waterworks during its first eight years, and it followed on in 1859 by obtaining extended powers for sea defence work which enabled it to reconstruct on an impressive scale after storm damage in the mid-1860s.[64] This level of expenditure compares interestingly with inland Lancashire, where Ormskirk, a slightly larger town with a population of just over 6,000 in 1861, was highly praised by Eric Midwinter for its unusual enterprise in completing a £4,500 reservoir by the mid-1850s: a further reminder of the high comparative costs of seaside improvements.[65] Pride of place, however, must go to Blackpool, which broke out in the mid-1860s from the deadening cycle of limited investment, inefficiency, ratepayers' reaction and retrenchment which so often held sway, and from the fear of debt and lack of confidence in the future which so often prevented large projects from being undertaken.[66] Here, a confident group of prospering shopkeepers and professional men on the Local Board set aside the protests of a Ratepayers' Association to carry out a promenade extension and widening scheme whose cost went up from an estimated £32,000 in 1867 to nearly £60,000 (a sum

which required special borrowing powers) on completion in 1870.[67] Its
success in attracting additional visitors and residents was immediately
apparent, creating a climate of opinion in which further large projects and
innovations could be pursued.

By this time a few local authorities were also making ambitious moves for
the provision of amenities to delight their visitors. Fittingly, Brighton led
the way in spectacular style, as in 1850 the town commissioners bought the
Pavilion from the Commissioners of Woods and Forests, saving it from
probable demolition and rescuing its grounds from the speculative builder.
The £53,000 cost was covered by a local Act, and a further £4,500 was soon
spent on furnishing and making good, in readiness for a series of balls and
other entertainments which confirmed the Pavilion as a major municipal
asset.[68]

Brighton's commissioners had financial resources on a scale unique among
resorts, and the Pavilion purchase was backed by sentiment as well as
business sense. Other resorts moved much more cautiously, but in 1856 the
infant Improvement Commissioners at the still tiny resort of Bournemouth
set an example by taking immediate steps to obtain and lay out extensive
pleasure gardens. By 1861 they had also taken advantage of a clause in their
Act which empowered them to spend £5,000 on a pier, although their
wooden structure proved disastrously vulnerable to storm and teredo
worm.[69]

These examples were not widely heeded until late in the century, although
many local authorities laid out small parks and offered guarantees to
approved bands, and sea defence works almost invariably involved the
creation of promenades embellished by gardens, bandstands and shelters.
The one area of universal concern was still the preservation of order and
decorum through the licensing and regulation of open-air activities, for this
was inexpensive and clearly essential to the prosperity of a season based on
the 'better-class' visitor.[70]

The initiatives at Worthing, Blackpool, Brighton and Bournemouth were
straws in the wind, but it was only after 1870, and often not until the 1880s
and 1890s, that the full necessity and scope for local authority intervention
at the seaside was realized, as Wigner's remarks on the need for a high level
of investment in public health and amenities came into closer harmony with
the spirit of the age. Some of the increased activity took the form of
large-scale improvements to existing services: the provision of a fully-
planned sewerage system with an outfall at a safe distance from the bathing
beach, the extension and enlargement of sea defences and promenades, the
purchase and improvement of private gas and water undertakings, and the
extension of this principle to tramways and electricity works. But local
authorities were also moving into a wide range of novel activities, some of
which were looked upon askance by central government in the form of the
Local Government Board. They began to provide, and even to inaugurate,
amenities and even entertainments on an altogether novel scale, sometimes
competing briskly with private enterprise in the process. Municipal piers,
concert halls, golf courses and even Winter Gardens began to appear, and
resorts found ways of diverting money from the rates into advertising their

A DELICIOUS DIP

Bathing Attendant. " Here, Bill! The gent wants to be
took out deep—take 'im *into the drain ! !* "

Fig. 15 *Punch* long remained preoccupied with the drainage problems of seaside resorts
(reproduced from *Mr Punch at the Seaside*).

EVIDENCE OLFACTORY

Angelina (scientific). " Do you smell the iodine from the
sea, Edwin? Isn't it refreshing ? "
Old Salt (overhearing). " What you smell ain't the sea,
miss. It's the town drains as flows out just 'ere ! "

attractions inland. All these innovations were spurred on by the increasingly
fierce competition between resorts, as falling prices, lengthening holidays
and improved transport enabled holidaymakers to travel further and resorts
to try to extend their established catchment areas. Under these conditions all
aspects of a resort's environment and entertainment came under scrutiny,
and wherever private enterprise failed to provide or maintain the necessary

improvements and facilities, an increasingly vocal and influential holiday industry urged that local government should step in.

The point of transition from parsimonious caution to active intervention varied from resort to resort. Southend's was a common experience among the more popular and successful centres; its Local Board, founded in 1866, practised 'strict economy' for several years, but was brought on to the high road of improvement in the mid-1870s by a 'society of earnest townsmen' with experience of the wider world, who by 1890 had succeeded in their aim of 'making the town into a favourite resort of Londoners of modest means'.[71] At Weston-super-Mare the Local Board similarly decided to spend its way out of trouble at the end of the depressed 1870s.[72] Ilfracombe's historian identifies a similar watershed with the transition from Local Board to Urban District Council in 1894, and the quickening tempo of competition and opportunity had similar galvanizing effects in many other resorts at this time, after widespread depression in the 1880s.[73] Often, of course, the process was gradual and cumulative, but the victory of the party of expansion and improvement was apparent in the council chambers of almost all of the larger resorts by the turn of the century.

Drainage was the top priority, and the turning point here came in the 1870s in most resorts, even those whose local authorities remained unregenerate in other respects. Margate spent over £40,000 on its sewers in the 1870s, as a successful campaign against cesspools began to make headway;[74] Scarborough was catapulted into activity by bad publicity when the Prince of Wales caught typhoid fever while staying at Londesborough Lodge in 1871, although it remained in a 'primitive' state with over 6,000 old-fashioned privies surviving in 1890;[75] Brighton abolished its eight foreshore outfalls and despatched its sewage four miles up the coast to Rottingdean in a great burst of investment between 1871 and 1874; Bridlington at last invested in a full-scale sewerage system in 1878–85, after many years of complaints;[76] Torquay's new drainage works were completed in 1878, ending gross pollution of the beaches which had inhibited the development of a summer season;[77] and three years later Blackpool began to relay and enlarge its old Local Board sewers, which were already inadequate to cope with the needs of an enormously inflated summer population.[78] Everywhere, indeed, the stresses of the season exacerbated drainage and pollution problems at the worst possible time, and imposed a much higher-capacity sewerage system than would have been necessary with a stable population. Significantly, all the major schemes of this period involved the removal or extension of unhappily-sited outfall pipes. Such improvements were delayed well into the twentieth century in some second-rank resorts, and at Ilfracombe, for example, the foreshore remained badly polluted until 1904.[79] Cesspools could also be persistent, and they were still very much in evidence at Paignton at the turn of the century.[80] Even where drainage improvements were pursued diligently and vigorously, moreover, there were limits to the conscientiousness of most resort authorities. Sewage farms and treatment systems were rare indeed, and the two most virtuous resorts in this respect, Southend and Southport, had virtue forced upon them. Southend was forced to treat its sewage in Edwardian times after a prosecution from the Kent and Essex Sea Fisheries Committee, while Southport was obliged to take similar measures in 1910 as a condition of a long-desired amalgamation with adjacent Birkdale.[81] In most places the capaciousness of the sea remained too tempting, and sewage remained untreated, with sad results for those who consumed the local shellfish, as Blackpool, Southend and Margate all saw typhoid cases from this source at the turn of the century.[82]

Despite these limitations, the logic of their circumstances had imposed a high level of investment in efficient sewering at most large resorts by the early twentieth century; and in other spheres of public health activity some resorts became increasingly innovatory. Admittedly, the late nineteenth century saw some surprising survivals. The urban pigstye was still common-place in Aberystwyth in 1884, when one district was affectionately known as 'Piggy-square'; and in 1898 Paignton was still trying unavailingly to rid itself of pigs. As its Medical Officer of Health urged, 'It is not the right thing whether a pigstye is kept clean or dirty that you should have a herd of pigs in the middle of a health resort.'[83]

In some of the larger and more specialized resorts, however, local government intervention was already becoming effective on a broad front. Blackpool had banished its urban pigs by the end of 1873, and from the late 1870s its Corporation began to intervene energetically in several fields where public health and the holiday industry overlapped directly. Refuse collection and nuisance inspection were stepped up in summer during the 1880s, and by 1901 some parts of the town saw daily visits from the dustmen, whose job was made easier by the rapid replacement of ashpits by water-closets. In 1879, mindful of the danger of an epidemic raging through crowded lodging-houses in mid-season, Blackpool became the first borough to adopt a clause in the 1875 Public Health Act empowering the compulsory notification of several infectious diseases. At the same time certificates of healthiness were offered to lodging-houses under a voluntary inspection scheme, although only a handful of landladies took up the offer. From 1890 onwards Blackpool pioneered the systematic testing of drains for sewer gas leakages, and at one point six drain-testers were regularly employed. In the early twentieth century the problem of high infant mortality, common to many resorts, was tackled successfully by a programme of paving yards and back entries and controlling milk supplies, and through the appointment in 1907 of a female Health Visitor.[84]

Blackpool was, no doubt, unusually energetic. The prevalence of jerry-building and summer overcrowding meant that it needed to be. Margate, with very similar problems, was matching Blackpool in its campaign against infant mortality by the early twentieth century, when the calibre of the local Medical Officer of Health was of central importance.[85] Not that a high social tone and generally strict building conditions bred complacency, for Bournemouth, like Blackpool, went in for house-to-house drain-testing in the early 1890s, and in 1892 the Corporation sought the power to make this compulsory. Concern for the protection of visitors and invalid residents could go much further than this, and in 1892 Bournemouth also obtained the power to regulate the burning of garden refuse, on the grounds that the smoke was trapped by the town's famous pine trees and caused annoyance to sufferers from lung disease.[86] This was an extreme example of local government intervention, and it was only allowed after some debate; but it illustrates a growing tendency for the needs of resorts to spawn a widening range of public health legislation which cumulatively extended the scope of local authority jurisdiction over private property in significant ways.[87]

The record of resorts in operating municipal utilities was less distinctive, though often controversial. Some were among the pioneers of municipal gas and water, but we have seen that private enterprise predominated in these spheres during the mid-Victorian period, and subsequent change was gradual, although local authorities were quick to move into tramways and electricity supply in the late nineteenth century. Even in 1900, however, only Blackpool among the 22 seaside boroughs operated all four of these mainstream utilities, while Brighton, Southport and Torquay ran three each. A municipal takeover was a major item of expenditure, and it may be significant that the purchase of waterworks, and their subsequent improvement, inaugurated an era of ambitious municipal activity at such resorts as Rhyl and Weston-super-Mare.[88] Where municipal enterprise could be seen to be efficient and profitable, ratepayers were prepared to look more benignly on expenditure elsewhere. Again, Blackpool is the most remarkable example. Here, the gasworks, opened by the Local Board as early as 1853, was expanded in the late 1870s at well over £10,000, and thereafter its capacity kept pace with the number of consumers, which was doubling every six years at this time. The profits were already handsome, and in 1879 the Corporation obtained power to apply them as it saw fit for the benefit of the inhabitants. They were used thereafter to fund a series of fêtes and celebrations, to buy land for the new library and pictures for the Art Gallery, and in 1914 they provided £500 towards the illuminations. From 1898 to 1915 the profits were always in five figures, in spite of very low gas prices and the free supply of meters and grills.[89]

The conspicuous success of the gasworks by the late 1870s encouraged the Corporation to move into further trading ventures. As early as 1877 municipal tramways were being considered, and in 1885 the Corporation was responsible for Britain's first full-scale electric tramway, although for the first few years a Halifax-dominated company was grudgingly allowed to work the services. In 1893 Blackpool became the third borough in the country to own and operate its tramways, and a vigorous programme of service extension and improvement followed, with unusually low fares, as the trams' value as an attraction to visitors was fully appreciated. Like the gasworks, the trams proved remarkably profitable, comparing very well with the national average for municipal undertakings in 1900. So did the electricity works, which had been one of the first handful in the country to supply municipal current to domestic users in 1893, at a cost of £26,000. Again, however, the key decision had been taken in the late 1870s, and in 1879 £5,000 had been spent on the first permanent electric street lighting in the country, which drew thousands of sightseers to the promenade and salvaged a disastrous season. In all these fields the Corporation's enterprise was encouraged by the need to provide attractions for visitors, to keep up-to-date and obtain favourable publicity, and to keep potentially lucrative and useful monopolies in local hands and free from private competition. The quartet of municipal utilities was completed in 1899 when Blackpool, in partnership with neighbouring towns, bought out the Fylde Waterworks Company.[90]

Blackpool Corporation was unique in combining the will, ability, resources and popular support necessary for municipal innovation and expansion on this scale. The record of even the largest rival resorts in the management of staple utilities was pedestrian by comparison, and the spectacular aspects of this case-study must not be allowed to distort the picture. Many resorts admittedly, suffered from financial inhibitions due to the heavy borrowing requirements imposed by necessary sea defences. This did not inhibit Blackpool itself, however, where the sheer scale of municipal expenditure on promenades and sea defences was probably unmatched even in the largest and most opulent of rival resorts. After the success of the original scheme which was completed in 1870, more than £60,000 was spent at North Shore in the mid-1890s after the Land, Building and Hotel Company had disclaimed responsibility, and in 1901–5 a long-debated widening of the main promenade by 100 ft throughout its length was carried out at a cost of £350,000. By 1912, when a further linking section was opened by Princess Louise, the *Blackpool Gazette* could congratulate its readers because 'the fact that we have spent over £600,000 upon our marine promenades has been announced all over the country', and in 1913 a £66,000 scheme for a southward extension was agreed, only to be delayed by the First World War.[91]

Spending figures from other major resort authorities put this achievement in perspective. Llandudno's total municipal spending between 1895 and 1913 was put at £424,000.[92] Torquay was said admiringly in 1915 to have spent 'close on £200,000' on its sea-front, including harbour, pier, gardens and terraces.[93] Scarborough spent £40,000 on what became the Royal Albert Drive at North Cliff in the late 1880s and early 1890s, and ten years later contemporaries were impressed by the £140,000 eventually laid out on a new Marine Drive round the castle rock. This gave Scarborough a 2½-mile sea-front promenade, still much shorter than Blackpool's.[94] Margate borrowed £140,000 for sea wall and street improvements in 1877, but there was no subsequent activity on the Blackpool scale.[95] This was, of course, major expenditure by leading resorts; and lower down the hierarchy Bridlington was pushed into a similar scale of activity by ferocious erosion.[96] Where this was not a problem, expenditure could be much lower. Southend's local authorities undertook considerable promenade improvement and extension work between 1878 and 1903, but the three new esplanades of 1899–1903 cost only £55,000, and the earlier schemes were unremarkable. There was no promenade widening scheme on the Blackpool model, partly because some of the land was still in private hands.[97] Weston-super-Mare spent over £40,000 on promenade widening and extension in the early 1880s, but this, again, was not followed up to any significant extent, even though the next decade saw a rapid increase in population while the rates remained stable.[98]

These were substantial capital sums even for resorts with rapidly-rising rateable values, and promenade expenditure was often highly controversial. A high level of investment was essential, however, for the protection of property as well as the comfort of visitors. Much more contentious, especially in its early stages, was the movement of resort local government into the provision of entertainment and amenities such as parks and open spaces. Here, Blackpool took a back seat, for the rapid development of the working-class holiday habit encouraged a remarkable surge of private investment into heavily-capitalized entertainment companies during the last quarter of the nineteenth century, and the promenade and foreshore were felt to be park enough, without luring visitors away from the main entertainment complexes.[99] Elsewhere, local authority involvement took three forms: the buying up of bankrupt or ailing concerns, to be leased out or exploited directly, sometimes after refurbishing; the funding of existing activities, especially bands, which had previously relied on public subscription; and, most controversial of all, the establishment of new entertainment facilities from scratch.

If we set aside the Brighton Pavilion as a special case, the first major example of a local authority taking over an existing attraction was at Southend, where the Pier, begun in 1829, was bought by the Local Board for £12,000 in 1875, after a chequered career involving several changes of ownership and gradual dilapidation. After several years' wavering, during which attempts were made to lease the pier out, and sale was seriously considered, a complete reconstruction was begun in 1888 and completed in August 1890. The new pier included a Pavilion for entertainments, and also shops and a bandstand.[100] A spectacular increase in receipts followed: from £2,906 in 1890 they rose to £5,251 in 1891 and £9,340 in 1892, levelling off thereafter. By 1909 the local authority had spent over £128,000 on the pier, but £40,000 in profits had been ploughed back in relief of the rates.[101]

Southend's Pier, like many others, was important to the town's economy as a landing place for passengers, as well as being an attraction in its own right; but after reconstruction its promenading and entertainment functions predominated, as was the case with several other municipal ventures into pier operation which followed Southend's success. Bournemouth's Local Board had already spent £21,600 in replacing their existing pier in 1880, and between 1890 and 1914 further piers were taken over by local authorities at Clevedon, Great Yarmouth, Ilfracombe, Bognor, Boscombe and Rhyl, while Torquay and Great Yarmouth also saw municipal pleasure piers built on to existing harbour works.[102] This is not a complete list, and commercial success was far from universal, especially in the smaller places. The Local Government Board took a cautious line with the extensive Great Yarmouth proposals of 1897, urging that, 'Experience has proved that pier under-takings in the hands of local authorities frequently involve a serious drain on the resources of the district', in order to provide a service which was not a usual responsibility of local government. As a result, loan sanction depended on a good record of basic public health provisions.[103]

Piers apart, until the 1890s most local authority activity was confined to the less controversial provision of parks and gardens, although often on a much grander scale than inland, and with the holiday and residential interests very much in mind. At the top end of the scale Scarborough was spending about £4,000 per year on the maintenance of five parks and gardens, while Bournemouth in the early twentieth century had over 400 acres of public open space in Corporation hands.[104] The pressures were strongest where a reputation for scenic beauty had to be protected from the speculative builder, and Ilfracombe's Local Board began buying up key plots of land from 1872 onwards, spending £12,000 on three estates by the turn of the century. By 1914 'with one or two exceptions . . . the Council controlled all of Ilfracombe's open spaces and beauty spots.'[105] The smaller resorts did what they could, and Barmouth in 1891 was 'using land . . . originally acquired for sewerage purposes as a pleasure ground.'[106] Donations from landowners often helped, and not only in 'aristocratic' resorts like Eastbourne and Southport (where the most impressive gift was designed to stimulate high-class development on the Hesketh estate); at Southend, for example, a similarly self-interested but useful grant of 20 acres came from a speculative building syndicate in 1895.[107]

By the 1890s the bands which played in parks and on promenades were increasingly being funded by local authorities, although official parliamentary sanction was not always forthcoming when sought. As early as 1871 a Southport Improvement Act allowed £100 per year on a municipal band. In 1879 Blackpool obtained the power to devote a twopenny rate to band and advertising purposes; but almost all of the proceeds from this freakish piece of generosity went on advertising.[108] Over the next decade only a handful of similar requests were allowed, with maximum rates ranging from $\frac{1}{4}$d. at Hastings and Eastbourne to 1d. at Ventnor, Weymouth and Weston-super-Mare. Powers were allowed more readily in the 1890s, as committees came to realize that 'a band of music is of very vital importance in a watering-place';[109] but in any case some local authorities managed to evade the legal restrictions on this use of ratepayers' money. Bridlington and Bournemouth eventually obtained the necessary powers, but most of their band income came from admission charges to their pleasure gardens and (in Bournemouth's case) the municipal pier; while at Great Yarmouth a mayoral salary of £300 was voted in 1894 for band purposes.[110] This was a common strategy elsewhere, and by the turn of the century municipal music in a municipal park or on a municipal promenade had become a commonplace of seaside entertainment, although it had plenty of rivals in most resorts.

During the 1890s several local authorities went into the entertainment business on a much more ambitious scale, and here again the climate of legal, parliamentary and ratepayer opinion moved rapidly in their favour. Bridlington's Local Board bought up the Victoria Rooms there as early as 1879, with attractions including baths and a roller-skating rink; but the most impressive innovations began about a decade later, when Southend Local Board opened its Pier Pavilion, Southport began a fashion for marine lakes which was later copied by Rhyl, Aberystwyth and Portishead, and Ilfracombe built its Victoria Pavilion, which was intended as a Winter Garden but soon began to provide a necessary supplement to a limited private enterprise concert programme.[111] In 1892 an important watershed was crossed when a deeply divided parliamentary committee allowed Bournemouth Corporation the right to develop Winter Gardens from scratch, after stress had been laid on the special needs of the resort and the failure of private enterprise to meet them.[112] In the event, the Corporation chose instead to lease the existing Winter Gardens, which had been moribund for several years, as a concert hall, and in 1893 they inaugurated the nation's first municipal orchestra, which put on the first of many symphony concerts two years later.[113]

After this expensive but successful venture, the flood-gates opened at the beginning of the new century. Torquay, Brighton, Hastings and even Margate felt the need to fund municipal orchestras of their own, and Torquay and Margate housed their new acquisitions in controversial pur- pose-built pavilions, Torquay's costing £20,000 in 1909.[114] Brighton also spent £32,000 in buying up the ailing Aquarium, which had been in voluntary liquidation for several years, and by 1913 the Corporation had lost £45,000 on the first eleven years' operations.[115] Rhyl's local authority purchased its pier in 1913, to add to a municipal marine lake, funfair and bands, none of which made a profit.[116] Pavilion and concert-hall ventures at such resorts as Bridlington, Great Yarmouth and Weston-super-Mare may well have been more successful financially; but the point was less to make a profit than to provide and maintain a service to visitors or residents which private enterprise was unwilling or unable to fund, whether by risking initial capital or by persisting in the face of trading losses. A *Brighton Gazette* editorial made this point in 1900, in support of the Aquarium purchase: 'We draw a distinction between conducting an establishment for the sheer sake of making a profit out of it, and administering an institution that constitutes a legitimate and powerful attraction to the town, from which all classes may derive direct or indirect benefits.'[117] In this way pavilions and winter gardens were brought within the pale of acceptable local government activity, alongside more orthodox public utilities such as gas and water- works. Private enterprise could never have contemplated the narrow margins envisaged by the Great Yarmouth pier and pavilion proposals of 1897, when a profit of £650 *per annum* was envisaged on an investment of £42,000.[118] Where municipal proposals requiring parliamentary sanction conflicted directly with established private interests, a strong presumption in the latter's favour persisted, and Weston-super-Mare was not allowed to promote a pier in competition with two existing companies in 1896.[119] Where decisions could be made locally, the complaints of private enterprise were less effective. Torquay Corporation voted to go ahead with its Pier Pavilion scheme in 1897 in spite of the forebodings of an alderman and theatre company director, who explained his abstention by remarking that he 'could not be expected to take an active part in his own extermination'.[120] Margate's restaurateurs were a much stronger lobby, but in 1913 they only just prevented the Corporation from going into the catering trade on a large scale in its new Pavilion. The argument that every shilling taken there would come out of the pockets of the town's tradesmen prevailed by only one vote against Councillor Reeve's demand that the Pavilion be used to bring maximum benefit to the ratepayers at large.[121] By this time Margate Corporation ran the Pavilion, with its concerts and municipal orchestra, further concerts at the Oval, the Westonville Pavilion and the Queen's Bandstand, the bathing at Westonville and Palm Bay, and the deckchairs, bowling greens and tennis courts.[122] This level of involvement could be matched or challenged at several other important resorts, including Great Yarmouth, Brighton, Bournemouth, Torquay, Bridlington and Ilfracombe, where local authorities at the turn of the century (and earlier in a few cases) had shown themselves willing to invest heavily in the entertainment industry, filling the gaps left even in otherwise prosperous resorts by shortages of private capital and entrepreneurial drive.

In an increasingly competitive world, the power to levy an advertising rate was also eagerly sought by local authorities towards the turn of the century. Here again, Blackpool set the pace. In 1879, by some oversight, the Corporation was allowed to devote a twopenny rate to 'the cost of maintaining at railway stations and in other public places advertisements stating the attractions and amusements of the town'.[123] This provided £500 *per annum*, which grew in step with the town's rateable value to yield over £2,500 in 1900 and well over £4,000 in 1914. From its earliest years, shareholders and directors of the entertainment companies had a strong voice on the Advertising Committee which allocated this income, and for a critical period in the 1890s it was dominated by an inner circle of Tower Company representatives and their allies. The result was a concentration of resources into the extension of the catchment area through the classless and (in the early 1880s) novel medium of the coloured picture poster. Blackpool was able to capture the best positions on the hoardings, and eagerly invaded the territory of its rivals. In 1889 there were complaints that, 'They lately have been placarding their attractions all about Scarborough, and Scarborough wants to retaliate by advertising in Blackpool.'[124] Only when Blackpool's working-class catchment area had been firmly extended over a wide area of the Midlands and industrial Yorkshire did the Advertising Committee turn its attention thoroughly to season extension at the turn of the century, after a building boom had greatly inflated its income and the entertainment company presence had been diluted by an admixture of high-class shopkeepers and estate agents from the Tradesmen's Association. After experiments with motor racing and an aviation meeting, a 'better-class' autumn season was successfully established by the development of a musical festival and the inauguration, in 1912, of the autumn illuminations.

Policies were often criticized in detail, but the money spent on advertising by Blackpool Corporation was begrudged only by a small minority. Municipal economists generally found juicier targets elsewhere. Blackpool held a privileged position, however, and for many years its rivals strove unavailingly to wrest similar rating powers from unsympathetic legislators and civil servants. The Local Government Board was unwilling to accept rate-supported advertising as a legitimate function of local authorities, and there were also the prejudices of parliamentary committee members to overcome. Thus Mr Kenrick in 1889: 'It struck me as rather undignified for the Local Board to be advertising their attractions.'[125] Concessions before the First World War were relatively few and limited, with a long list of rejections in the 1880s and 1890s.[126] As late as 1912 Brighton was refused a

halfpenny rate for posters and placards, being confined to leaflet and
newspaper advertising financed from deck-chair and bandstand profits.[127]
Some local authorities were able to use funds from other sources: Scarborough voted a mayoral salary for advertising, and Great Yarmouth was able
to allocate £1,100 to advertisements in 1913, mainly from the Corporation's
Race Committee.[128] Most resorts also benefited from railway publicity, as
the companies began to take an active competitive interest in promoting
their coastlines from the 1890s; but such publicity was aimed at the
passenger first and the holidaymaker second, and it usually focused on a
group of resorts rather than a single town, as in North Wales or on the Great
Western's Cornish Riviera. Entertainment companies in the popular resorts
were also advertising busily inland by this time, but they only presented a
partial picture of a town's attractions. For advertising geared up to the
interests of the resort as a whole, most places still depended in 1913 on
public subscriptions administered by *ad hoc* committees or organizations
like the Chamber of Commerce, often in alliance with local government,
and sometimes in confederation with other resorts. The limitations of this
approach for planning and continuity of purpose were epitomized by the
case of Brighton's Publicity Association, whose income declined from £628
in 1905 to £217 in 1908, and stayed at the lower figure. No alternative
system could sustain an income for advertising which generated more than a
fraction of Blackpool's twopenny rate. In this sphere especially, a general
drive towards increasing municipal activity was still being frustrated by the
legal, administrative and ideological barriers which were already crumbling
at the turn of the century where municipal attractions and amusements were
concerned.

As well as venturing into new fields of municipal enterprise, seaside local
government was confronting new problems of public order and social
regulation in the late nineteenth century, as armies of trippers brought
ever-growing numbers of stalls, showmen, hawkers and other undesirables
in their wake. Resort authorities often responded by seeking Draconian
powers of suppression and restraint; but here again, legal ambiguities
abounded, and ambitious plans were often thwarted by the Local Government Board and the legislature, always anxious to safeguard individual
liberties against the possibility of local tyranny, and often setting aside the
resorts' interpretations of the greatest happiness of the greatest number. The
struggle to come to terms with large numbers of working-class visitors in an
essentially middle-class environment was one of the most important aspects
of local government activity; but it is a major theme in itself, and will be
explored in chapter 8. Here, it must be taken as read, reinforcing the theme
of increasing local government enterprise, commitment and range of activity
in late Victorian and Edwardian times.

This period, indeed, saw a revolution in municipal government in the
larger seaside resorts: a revolution with far-reaching implications for the
economies of towns whose prosperity depended on the face they presented
to the world, a face whose charms depended increasingly on municipal
skills, investment and cosmetic treatment. This realization dawned on local
authorities in almost every resort at some point during the last third of the

nineteenth century; and municipal spending and intervention grew in
volume and importance accordingly. Even in the 'aristocratic' resorts, the
balance of spending, and therefore the balance of power, tilted away from
landowners who became increasingly concerned with profit-taking at the
expense of political influence, and towards local authorities who assumed
the cast-off responsibilities of landed families, while often continuing their
policies. Again, the timing of the process varied, but the results were
becoming apparent at the turn of the century in resorts like Bexhill, Lytham
and even Eastbourne itself.[129] We have described the development of
municipal enterprise and involvement, from unpromising beginnings, at some
length; we must now try to explain the late Victorian transformation of
seaside local government.

In the first place, the new tolerance of sustained high municipal expenditure was made easier in most of the leading resorts, and in many smaller
ones, by rapidly rising rateable values as building extensions went on apace,
greatly increasing the product of local taxation without hitting the pocket of
the individual ratepayer. In the fastest-growing resorts a feedback process
developed whereby growth fed municipal investment, which in turn fed
further growth. Blackpool's high levels of expenditure were made politically
tolerable not only by the conspicuous success of key municipal activities,
but also by a rateable value which had already grown from £9,000 to £43,000
between 1853 and the completion of the first promenade scheme in 1870,
and then increased tenfold between 1870 and the start of promenade
widening in 1901. By 1912 it had reached £544,000.[130] At Southend the
rateable value rose from £11,000 to over £80,000 between 1866 and 1892,
and then increased fivefold over the next 17 years, reflecting the enormous
building boom at the turn of the century.[131] Even where growth was much
less spectacular than this, significant economies of scale could still cushion
the impact of municipal spending; the rateable value of Weston-super-Mare,
for instance, doubled between 1876 and 1896, while that of Seaford trebled
between 1895 and 1915.[132]

Resorts also benefited, like other towns, from the growing expertise and
professionalism of local officials, and from the rapid improvements in
appropriate technological and financial skills. Sometimes a pugnacious and
well-informed campaign originating outside the council chamber was necessary to bring these skills into effective use, as at Southend in the late 1880s,
when drainage improvements were precipitated by the Rev. Dr T. H.
Gregg, a bishop of the Reformed Church of England who also held a
Scottish medical degree.[133] Gregg enlisted the local Ratepayers' Association
on the side of improvement on this issue, but this was most unusual, and
pressure from groups of this kind was usually exerted in favour of
economy.[134] The most important impetus to municipal activity, in an
increasingly favourable environment, came from within the council chamber, and the key to the improved record of seaside local government must be
sought in the social composition and attitudes of the councillors, although
sustained improvement of course depended on their ability to retain the
confidence of the electorate.

Growing resources did not guarantee the will to municipal enterprise, and even the most successful resorts saw persistent movements for economy, retrenchment and caution, usually expressing the perceived interests of retired residents and small tradesmen on the fringes of the holiday industry. Seaside local government flourished most spectacularly where the holiday and building trades dominated the council chamber, forming a coalition of interest-groups with a common expansionist aim. Blackpool is the most clear-cut example of this pattern. Here, occupations in the holiday industry accounted for more than 20 per cent of entrants to the council between 1876 and 1914, and if hotel and entertainment company directorships are taken into account, 36 per cent had a strong and identifiable direct interest in the holiday trades. Many more had shareholdings in entertainment companies, and it would be difficult to find a councillor who did not benefit at least indirectly from the holiday season. Building was also well-represented. Again, more than 20 per cent of entrants were active as builders or in allied trades, and at least half of all council members during this period were engaged in property development or land speculation. The drink interest was also strong, accounting for nearly a quarter of all entrants if hotel directorships are included. Several leading local politicians had fingers in all these pies, of course, and this was particularly apparent during the peak years of municipal innovation and economic growth between 1876 and 1898, when the Corporation came to be dominated by directors of the major entertainment companies in alliance with publicans and property specula-tors. The ethics of some of their activities were sharply called into question on occasion, but their successful rule engendered an atmosphere of confi-dence and optimism which was rarely threatened after the mid-1880s. Only when Council membership was doubled in 1898, after a series of land speculation scandals had provoked sustained opposition to the ruling group, was the political strength of the entertainment companies diluted; and the retailing and trading interests who then began to make their presence felt were happy to continue an expansionist and interventionist municipal policy, although the emphasis shifted from the attraction of trippers to the improvement of amenities for the 'better-class' visitor, retired resident and commuter.[135]

The extent to which Blackpool was run by and for the holiday industry is almost certainly unique. Bournemouth's vigorous municipal activity in late Victorian times was promoted by its 'Progressive' faction, 'an informal group of councillors, composed of tradesmen and builders', but opposition from the powerful residential lobby was strong enough to delay the adoption of much-needed Pavilion and Undercliff Drive schemes for many years, although problems with landowners also played their part.[136] The building lobby was also well-represented at Eastbourne and Torquay, but here their interests were bound up more closely with the wealthy residents who put public order, social regulation and low rates ahead of improved amenities.[137] Here, as elsewhere, the holiday industry as such was long of little account. This was true of Ilfracombe, too, where local government was dominated by professionals, men of independent means, and retailers, although the trading and holiday interest gained ground at the turn of the century, when the new Urban District Council began to pursue livelier policies.[138] Even Morecambe, superficially so similar to Blackpool, saw its local authorities dominated by professional men, commuters and the retired.[139]

More impressionistic evidence from Exmouth, Brighton, Seaford and New Brighton confirms the impression that at the seaside the best recipe for active and innovatory local government was the eager participation of a holiday industry with whose interests shopkeepers and the powerful builders' lobbies could identify, while when left to themselves retailers and residents put economy first.[140] A strong residential interest, indeed, was likely to limit the extent and scope of local government action in support of the holiday industry. Investment in amenities at Torquay was held back at the turn of the century by 'the acute and permanent division of opinion . . . between the mass of the residents on the one hand and the traders and boarding-house keepers on the other.'[141] Similar divisions were endemic in Brighton throughout the second half of the nineteenth century, and appeared in late Victorian times in resorts as diverse as Ramsgate, New Brighton, Paignton, Lynton, Weston-super-Mare and even Southend.[142] Torquay's experience showed that residential opposition could be overcome even when well entrenched, in the changing economic circumstances of the turn of the century; but in some resorts opposition on grounds of economy and residential amenity was fuelled by depression or the fear of depression. Bridlington's dilemma in 1879 was representative: necessary improvements meant higher rates, which would antagonize existing residents and deter intending ones. Broadstairs and Towyn were similarly unwilling to spend their way out of trouble in the early 1880s; and to a large extent municipal success was a matter of confidence as well as competence.[143]

Residential lobbies might be the most potent expressions of seaside opposition to municipal improvement, but they were certainly not the only ones. Farmers, fishermen and other opponents of amenity expenditure were still powerful in some places in the late nineteenth and early twentieth centuries. At St Annes the Local Board was dominated by farmers from its inception in 1878 until the early 1890s, so that roads were unmade and sewers non-existent, and the infant resort was nearly abandoned to be engulfed by the encroaching sandhills.[144] Geographical divisions within resorts could also generate bitter conflict, as at Hastings, where 'east' argued with 'west' over promenade improvements, or at Southend, where 'Old Town' was pitted against 'Upper Town', or indeed at Blackpool, where 'North' *versus* 'South' bedevilled park and library schemes as well as promenade work.[145] The cautious, legalistic attitudes of parliament and the Local Government Board, custodians of the doctrine of *ultra vires*, provided a receptive environment for opposition or complaint from such sources, and these bodies laid additional snares of their own for municipal adventurers.

Blackpool was able consistently to unite a convincing majority of its citizens under the banners of 'Progress' (the town's motto) and 'Improvement', basing a clear and sustained policy of municipal expansion on an appeal to enlightened self-interest. Here was no 'civic gospel' of 'effective moral action' through local government, as in Birmingham or Bristol; and here were no party plans of improvement, as in late Victorian Leeds, for in

Blackpool parties were irrelevant in the council chamber. The idea of the town as 'a solemn organism through which should flow, and in which should be shaped all the highest, loftiest and truest ends of man's moral nature', would have provoked unseemly ribaldry at the Clifton Arms before a council meeting. Blackpudlians preferred the less metaphysical analogy of the public company, with the council as directors and the ratepayers as shareholders having a common interest in efficient management on sound commercial lines. Extreme specialization in the holiday industry made this goal all the easier to achieve.[146]

Elsewhere, divisions and doubts made local authorities less single-minded. At Southend it was still possible to assert in 1880, à propos a Local Board proposal to take over and protect the Cliffs, 'Such improvements as these can only be carried out by the generosity of a private individual.'[147] Such attitudes were especially long-lived in the smaller resorts, and in those where a large landowner had made the early running. Despite all obstacles, however, what is remarkable is the extent of the expansion of local government activity at the seaside after 1870, and especially after 1890. The transformation is all the more remarkable, coming as it does after the general lethargy of mid-Victorian times. Seaside local government still had its limitations in the early twentieth century. It was especially slow to improve services to the poorer residents, who were often viewed with embarrassment and even aversion, particularly in the high-class resorts.[148] Correspondingly, Labour politicians were slow to appear, and even slower to enter the council chamber, at the seaside. Industrial relations, one suspects, were often conducted after the manner of *The Ragged-Trousered Philanthropists*. But the perceived needs of visitors and residents drew seaside local government into a remarkable range of activities, even though many of them provided direct benefits only for the wealthier of its constituents, and resorts were more dilatory than most towns in providing services for their less opulent inhabitants, as befitted towns whose economies were dominated by small tradesmen.[149] When local authorities woke up to the fact that seaside resorts had special needs which could only be met by the public sector, they began to meet them in style, but only in so far as they related to the holiday season and the attraction of wealthy residents. Here, however, important precedents were set for local government bodies elsewhere, as local government became the most important influence on the character and fortunes of late Victorian resorts.

There remained ample scope for private enterprise to cash in on the booming holiday market of these years, in building, retailing and entertainment. We have seen that municipal intervention was essential in the entertainment industry in some resorts to make up for the shortcomings of private enterprise, or perhaps of demand; and we have also seen that Blackpool, at the other extreme, was effectively taken over by its entertainment companies for a crucial transitional period in the late nineteenth century. But we need to know more about the provision of entertainment by private enterprise, which could be very important to a resort's fortunes; and we shall pursue this theme in the next chapter.

7 *Seaside entertainment*

From the beginning the seaside, like the spas, catered for seekers after pleasure, recreation, novelty and status as well as votaries of health and rest; and many of the latter themselves found resorts more attractive if they offered amusement and society to family and friends, if not to the invalid himself. A minority of visitors expressly preferred quiet and seclusion, or put natural attributes above all other considerations in choosing a resort; but most wanted artificial amusements and opportunities for carefully-regulated social mixing. Their expectations had been formed by their experience of polite society in London and spa towns, and in the many provincial towns which were also acting as centres of fashion, display, conspicuous consumption and the marriage market by the third quarter of the eighteenth century.[1] As seaside resorts took on similar functions, growth beyond a very small scale became conditional on the provision of institutions and entertainments which were already well established in the urban culture of the provinces as well as that of London and the spas. The assembly room and the circulating library, with their adjoining coffee and newspaper rooms, became the dominant social institutions of the seaside, and the social life of the pump room was faithfully reproduced in the similar suites which became attached to the bathing rooms of the larger resorts.

By their specialized nature, the resorts provided greater concentrations of these services than the county towns and provincial capitals; but their early attractions were derivative, and even activities directly related to sea-bathing were assimilated to an established model of organization and behaviour. It was only towards the middle of the nineteenth century, when the seaside holiday was becoming increasingly open, middle-class and family-centred, that a distinctive pattern of organized entertainment began to emerge, centred on the beach and pier rather than the assembly room and circulating library. The coming of the working-class excursionist gave a further, and stronger, impetus to change, encouraging eager investment in heavily-capitalized entertainment companies in some of the larger resorts, aiming at the popular market. This trend became clearly marked in places during the 1870s, and culminated in the enormous pleasure palaces of the 1890s, which offered everything from menageries to music-hall in giant buildings with exotic furnishings and embellishment. Here again, however, the form and content of the shows and spectacles had been developed elsewhere, in London and the great industrial towns, although the seaside Towers, Kursaals and Winter Gardens were remarkable for the scale of their conception, the scope of their operations and the extravagance of their architecture.[2] The foreshore fairgrounds and sideshows which came to characterize many late Victorian and Edwardian resorts were similarly inland forms of entertainment, swollen and concentrated at the seaside in response to seasonal demand. The spectacular new technology which they began to adopt at the turn of the century was mainly transatlantic in origin.[3]

The seaside did evolve its own distinctive modes of entertainment during the nineteenth century, but these were developed mainly during the mid-Victorian heyday of the middle-class family. The pier itself was *sui generis*, although the promenading rituals and the music, dancing and entertainment it provided conformed to established models. Only the widely popular swimming displays and aquatic shows gave a maritime flavour to the bill of fare. On the shore, the 1870s saw a vogue for Aquaria, in which the wonders of the deep were displayed with musical accompaniment for the rational recreation of a respectable public; but this proved transitory, and the proprietors had to diversify their attractions and move down-market in order to survive. Most of the early Winter Gardens had the same aims and underwent a similar evolution. But the characteristic seaside entertainments, to contemporaries, were outdoor, beach-centred and smaller in scale and capital outlay than this: the nigger minstrel show and later the pierrots, and lower down the scale the donkey ride and Punch-and-Judy show. Seaside motifs might pervade the general recreational culture, providing themes for songs, jokes and cheap fiction,[4] but only in the mid-Victorian period did the seaside nurture distinctive modes of commercial entertainment. Otherwise, it was more important as a carrier and concentrator of existing trends and fashions than as an initiator of new ones. Throughout the period, however, the quality of a resort's range of commercial entertainment was an important competitive weapon. The ability to attract and reward investment in entertainment became a highly significant influence on the economic fortunes and social standing of resorts. These issues demand sustained attention.

The spas provided a successful model for entertainment for the upper and prosperous middle ranks. The early seaside resorts adopted the assemblies for dancing and cards, the circulating library and the coffee house readily and naturally, and in most places these formal and exclusive institutions, often regulated by a Master of Ceremonies, dominated visitor society until the early railway age. Many resorts also had pump rooms of their own, for Scarborough was only the earliest of many resorts to combine spa water with sea-bathing.[5]

Entry into the charmed circle of 'the company', as defined by participation in the round of balls, card parties, raffles and public assemblies which made up the season, was regulated less by social status in the abstract than by ability to pay the expensive subscriptions and participation fees, although the social perceptions of the Master of Ceremonies, and the elaborate rules of dress, conduct and precedence which governed assemblies, were intended to filter out those *nouveaux riches* whose manners did not match their financial resources. In practice, however, it was very difficult to shut out the social climber, as the spas had already found. The anonymity of the large resort with wide catchment area combined persuasively with the lure of profit and the need to maximize returns on high levels of investment to ensure that the only effective control on admission was the ability to pay. At Margate as early as 1777 a satirist could remark on the Master of Ceremonies' 'strange predilection for haberdashers, mantua-makers and milliners', and in the early nineteenth century a fashion for masquerades encouraged more intimate social mixing, as disguised tradesmen danced with 'dignified misses'.[6] This was in spite of seasonal subscriptions of up to 10s. 6d. (in 1799) for the main Assembly Rooms, and 5s. for the circulating libraries, with heavy charges even to subscribers for tea, cards, dancing and lotteries. For those who could afford the journey and accommodation, however, a moderate measure of participation in amusements could be taken as a matter of course, and Margate, following Bath and other spas, was only the first of many seaside resorts in which the growth of the holiday market brought an inevitable broadening of the social base of entertainment facilities which had originally been intended for an exclusive clientèle.[7]

Early investment in entertainment was cautious and tentative. The first formal assemblies were usually run by hoteliers or innkeepers on their own premises, and theatres were improvised in barns or stable blocks. It took a generation for purpose-built establishments to appear, even in the fastest-growing resorts. Scarborough pioneered in many ways, but its early accumulation of the paraphernalia of a genteel season owed much more to its spa rôle than to sea-bathing. The first public assembly rooms appeared here in the 1720s, supplemented by a coffee house and bowling green; and by 1733 a theatrical season had begun. Amenities at the spa itself were still primitive, with a communal ladies' lavatory providing a supply of leaves to cope with the purgative qualities of the waters. More important than any improvement in this department, perhaps, was the appointment of a Master of Ceremonies in 1740, and by 1767 a purpose-built theatre was completed.[8]

The first specialized seaside resorts were already catching up rapidly by the 1760s. Brighton's first regular assemblies began at the Castle Inn in 1754, and later in the decade balls were held twice weekly during the season. By 1760 two circulating libraries were operating, and a second assembly room opened in the following year. In 1764 a barn was converted for theatrical use by a Chichester company of actors, and in 1767 the town acquired a Master of Ceremonies.[9] Margate was close on Brighton's heels. The New Inn assembly rooms had 429 subscribers by 1762, and a purpose-built Assembly Room opened in 1769, letting for up to £600 *per annum*. By this time two circulating libraries were also in being, and a Master of Ceremonies was appointed in the same year. A regular theatrical season was already well established, again in a converted barn, and there were five bathing rooms which also provided coffee, newspapers and evening amateur concerts. Southampton, which had begun its fashionable career as a spa in the 1740s, was almost keeping pace with this flowering of amenities in the 1760s and 1770s.[10]

These were the pace-setters, and early development elsewhere was patchier and more uncertain. A 'sea-water Bathing House' opened in Portsmouth as early as 1754 at a cost of over £1,000, while Yarmouth saw a similar level of investment in a 'Bath-house' five years later.[11] These towns were important enough to attract county society and prosperous company in their own right, and in a similar way the early Assembly Rooms at Weymouth in the 1760s may have been intended as much for fashionable society from the vicinity as for more distant visitors attracted by the towns' growing but subordinate reputations as health resorts.[12]

Margate and Brighton consolidated their advantage in the late eighteenth and early nineteenth century, as visitor numbers continued to grow and high levels of investment could be rewarded in entertainment as well as building and accommodation. By 1816 Margate offered eight bathing rooms, with increasingly lavish appointments, from which over 40 bathing-machines operated, each of which had probably cost £60 when new. The town's main Assembly Room was described in 1803 as 'a truly splendid apartment', measuring 87 ft by 43 ft, and elegantly furnished. Its public breakfasts, music, dancing and gambling were rivalled by the circulating libraries, which offered 'reading, shopping, socializing, promenading and entertainment', with concerts and evening assemblies of their own. As early as 1787 Samuel Silver's catalogue listed over 5,000 books, and auction records suggest very high levels of investment in stocks of jewellery, hardware, morocco and ivory goods and maps. Theatre investment increased rapidly in the 1770s and 1780s, and after fierce competition between rival entrepreneurs in 1785 Francis Cobb, a leading local brewer, secured a royal charter for his chosen protagonist, incurring heavy legal costs in the process. As a result, in 1787 the new Theatre Royal was opened at a cost of £4,000, with a capacity of 700 which brought in £60 per performance at the standard charges. This was big business, and it is no surprise to find London interests taking a dominant rôle as Covent Garden and Drury Lane entrepreneurs bought out the original proprietors in 1790. Leading London performers made regular appearances, and in 1797 Mrs Jordan was paid £300 for six nights. By the 1780s Margate also boasted a rural pleasure garden, Dandelion, which was capable of attracting several hundred people at a time to its public breakfasts.[13] The new century saw investment on a still grander scale, as £100,000 was spent on the replacement of Margate's landing pier, which was used for promenading and extended by the addition of Jarvis' Landing Stage in 1824. At the same time work began on the Clifton Baths, which involved extensive sea defences and the excavation of 40,000 tons of chalk.[14]

Brighton followed a similar path, culminating in the building of the Chain Pier (aimed at passenger and goods traffic, with promenading at first a lower priority) in 1822–3 at a cost of £30,000, and in the disastrous Antheum project at Hove in 1832–3, when the botanist Henry Phillips planned an enormous winter garden under a dome of cast-iron and glass, which collapsed as soon as it was completed.[15] £2,500 had been spent on a new theatre in 1788–90, but the building which superseded it in 1806 cost £12,000, seating 1,400 people and challenging the largest provincial towns for sheer opulence.[16]

Brighton and Margate were unmatched in the range and scale of their commercial entertainments at this stage; but rival resorts, especially on the south coast, were pursuing them eagerly by the turn of the century. Southampton was already falling out of favour, but Weymouth did very well out of its royal visitors, with a fashionable new Assembly Room opening in 1785, a theatre in 1773 (rebuilt on a grander scale a few years later), and three circulating libraries by 1800. Sea-water baths were also provided at a cost of £500. G. S. Carey was cynical about some of this activity, remarking that much of it had failed to attract the anticipated royal patronage, and describing the rebuilt theatre as 'on a *contracted* scale, built in the shape of a wig-box, and not much bigger'.[17] Scarborough had a similar range of amenities at this stage, and Yarmouth in 1778 had seen £1,500 invested in a theatre which met with Carey's approval, although he decried the Assembly Room of 1788 as 'not of the first order' in elegance or company.[18] Worthing was making giant strides at the turn of the century, with two circulating libraries and a bath-house by 1798, and in 1806 its first permanent theatre cost £6,992, a level of expenditure which put it on a par with Newcastle-upon-Tyne and King's Lynn.[19] Ramsgate, Hastings, Bognor, Eastbourne and Exmouth were also expanding their artificial attractions appreciably at this time, while Gravesend was beginning its rise to popularity as pleasure gardens and circulating libraries multiplied, although their heyday was reserved for the steamer boom of the 1820s and 1830s.[20]

Scarborough and Yarmouth apart, resorts away from the south coast and the pull of London showed much slower progress. Swansea was enjoying a brief spell of genteel prosperity in 1803, when it offered a bathing-house with ballroom and accommodation, two more rival sea-water baths, and two circulating libraries with billiard rooms attached.[21] Bridlington had an Assembly Room, bathing-rooms and a theatre by 1813.[22] But in most provincial resorts substantial development did not take place until the 1820s and 1830s. Weston-super-Mare's Knightstone Baths, with billiards and reading room, opened in 1822, and Assembly Rooms followed four years later.[23] Southport had 'several fancy shops' by the early 1820s, when a theatre also made a brief appearance, fighting a losing battle against hostile local leaders; but there was no full-scale Assembly Room until 1831.[24] Blackpool's assemblies remained hotel-based until 1837, and the Victoria Terrace and Promenade of that year proved unsuitable for concerts.[25]

By the eve of the railway age, however, all but the most unpretentious and disadvantaged of resorts had acquired the basic institutions which were still deemed necessary to sustain a genteel holiday season on the model which had been passed down from Nash's Bath. In some of the smallest resorts, admittedly, they might be so unpretentious as to be barely recognizable. Allonby was very proud of its baths and reading-room on their opening in 1836, but a few years later the 'handsome and massy' building, 'in a style of elegance surpassed by few watering-places in the kingdom', was the victim of an affectionate but devastating caricature by Charles Dickens himself:

> Let Mr Idle carry his eye to that bit of waste ground above high-water mark, where the rank grass and loose stones were most in a litter; and he would see a sort of long ruinous brick loft, next door to a ruinous brick outhouse, which loft has a ladder outside, to get up by. That was the reading-room, and if Mr Idle didn't like the idea of a weaver's shuttle throbbing under a reading-room, that was his look out . . .[26]

Even when we have adjusted for the satire, this was a far cry from Brighton or Margate; but Allonby was quite remarkably isolated, with a visiting public drawn almost entirely from northern Cumberland, and most resorts made much more effective concessions to genteel tastes and expectations. This involved a measure of speculative investment; and we must now consider where the capital came from for the Assembly Rooms, baths, theatres and libraries which sprang up at so many points along the English coastline between the 1760s and the 1830s.

Hard evidence on investment is difficult to come by, but a few tentative conclusions can be drawn for these formative years. As in house building, much early enterprise was local, especially the provision of bathing facilities.[27] The first visiting theatres were offshoots of existing provincial circuits: Great Yarmouth's was serviced from Norwich, Brighton's from Chichester, and Margate's from Sittingbourne, Canterbury and finally Dover, with an interlude when the key figures were local men, a former ostler, a currier and a tailor.[28] Capital from the surrounding district became important to other enterprises at an early stage: thus Brighton's first Assembly Room, at the Castle Inn, was set up by a Lewes innkeeper.[29] As projects became more ambitious and capital-hungry in the larger resorts, and syndicates or incorporated associations began to supplement individual enterprise, capital from resort hinterlands became important. London money, especially, began to flow into entertainment as well as building on the south coast, as metropolitan resources helped to fund the new theatre at Margate and the Chain Pier at Brighton.[30] In the provinces, Bristol capital was behind the origins of the Knightstone Baths at Weston-super-Mare in 1820–2, and the £25 shareholders in Southport's 1831 Assembly and News Rooms were 'gentlemen resident in Manchester, Liverpool, Bolton, Wigan, etc.' Even little Allonby required the aid of 'a few gentlemen who were occasional visitors and saw the necessity of improvement' for its baths and reading-room.[31] There is a hint of patronage rather than profit-seeking in this last example, and even at this early stage a few resorts benefited from the munificence of large landowners or other interested parties. In the early nineteenth century Tenby's M.P., Sir William Paxton, ploughed money from his Indian fortune into baths and an unsuccessful theatre; while Teignmouth's first theatre was built on land given by the Courtenay family.[32] Despite the growth of external influences, however, much of the momentum for the growing seaside entertainment industry still came from tradesmen in and around the resorts.

Hugh Cunningham has recently described the Assembly Room and circulating library as institutions of 'rational recreation' in a 'deliberately exclusive' middle-class culture.[33] We have seen that the seaside and its formal entertainment did exclude those who were unable to afford the high cost of travel, subscriptions and necessary 'extras'; but the intrinsic 'rationality' of this kind of seaside diversion must be questioned. Seaside circulating libraries were notorious repositories not only of cheap and disreputable novels, but also of trinkets and frivolities. At Jane Austen's Sanditon, 'The Library, of course, afforded every thing; all the useless things in the world that could not be done without'.[34] Assembly Rooms provided not only good music and serious conversation, but also gossip, gambling and dancing.[35] It was possible to use these institutions in 'rational' and 'improving' ways, but this was to work against the grain of the prevailing seaside culture.

At this stage, indeed, the most 'rational' of seaside pleasures were informal and alfresco. All resort guide-books, from their earliest days in the 1760s, provided long lists of excursions to places of historic interest or natural curiosity; and the wonders of modern technology were not neglected. One of the highlights of the diarist Mr Denham's Ramsgate holiday in 1829 was a visit to the gasworks; while visitors to Swansea were urged in 1803 to take a walk along the canal, where there were 'many capital objects . . . large smelting copperworks, an iron forge, tin and brass works, a fine copper rolling mill . . . and a most stupendous steam-engine.' Other resorts catered specially for geologists, and Lymington was presented as a botanist's paradise, with the sundew and other rarities occurring close by.[36] These were minority tastes, but trips to picturesque ruins and noblemen's houses, and the collection of seaweed, shells and pebbles, were generally enjoyed; and tea gardens grew up around the most popular attractions. It was this sort of activity, combining exercise with the garnering of information, the enhancement of knowledge and the appreciation of beauty, which made the seaside acceptable to the prophets of 'rational recreation', especially when sea air and sea-bathing brought health into the equation.

The early railway age, indeed, found paternalistic employers, Sunday schools and temperance organizations eager to give their dependants and members a taste of the improving pleasures of the seashore; and the middle decades of the nineteenth century were the heyday of the middle-class family holiday, with the main focus of attention shifting away from the Assembly Room and theatre to the beach. We must not exaggerate this change of emphasis, however. Investment in the established institutions of polite resort society continued throughout this period; indeed, it revived in subtly different forms in the late 1860s and early 1870s. At Bridlington a joint stock company invested £8,000 in the Victoria Rooms, on the Assembly Room pattern (though with a 'museum' attached) just as the railway arrived in 1846.[37] At Worthing the two circulating libraries of 1798 had grown to four or five by 1859, and similar increased provision was apparent elsewhere.[38] In the same year Blackpool at last secured a permanent theatre building, and in 1867 investment from industrial Lancashire (especially Manchester) flowed readily into new Assembly and Concert Rooms, accounting for most of the £10,000 capital.[39] At Great Yarmouth and Margate, Assembly Rooms still flourished into the 1870s and beyond, advertising services which would have raised no eyebrows a century earlier. In some places, indeed, the title 'Assembly Rooms' was used for new promotions in the 1880s and 1890s, though by this time it denoted a concert hall with no particularly select attendance.[40] On a more raffish plane, pleasure gardens on the lines of London's Cremorne and Ranelagh, which had appeared at Margate and elsewhere by the 1770s, still flourished beyond the mid-century in places, and in the popular resorts new ventures in the 1870s harked back to the older pattern. Margate's Tivoli Gardens (dating from 1829) and Broadstairs' own Ranelagh (founded in the early 1770s) attracted up to 2,000 visitors at a time to their dances, outdoor concerts and firework displays in 1850, and the former was still flourishing in 1868, though it was soon to disappear in a cloud of scandal.[41] Great Yarmouth's Royal Victoria Gardens still offered fireworks and balancing acts in 1860, and Shoreham's Swiss Gardens, opened by a local shipbuilder in 1838, flourished for half a century with a wider range of attractions which included an aviary and reading room as well as dancing and boating.[42]

At Margate, as we shall see, and no doubt elsewhere, entertainment of this kind was offered to a mixed but increasingly proletarian audience throughout the nineteenth century, as 'Lord' George Sanger's Hall-by-the-Sea took over where Tivoli had left off. Horse-racing survived throughout the period in some resorts, too, although an attempted revival at Scarborough in 1861 encountered opposition on grounds of public order and morality. On the whole, indeed, the early and mid-Victorian trend was for seaside recreations to become more decorous, 'improving' and family-centred, as gambling, dancing and even the theatre became increasingly suspect to a widening cross-section of the visiting public. The cock-fighting, bear-baiting and prize-fighting enjoyed by Brighton visitors in the 1780s had long disappeared from the public life of the seaside. The most important capital-intensive developments of this period, the promenade piers and later the Aquaria and early Winter Gardens, reflected these trends.[43]

Piers built for commerce had been used as fashionable promenades from the early days of the seaside holiday, although until the later nineteenth century most piers probably derived the majority of their revenue from the landing and embarkation of passengers and goods. Margate's new pier began to charge a penny toll for promenading in 1812, an innovation which was greeted initially by riots; and Brighton's Chain Pier charged twopence, rapidly becoming 'popular as a place of fashionable resort.'[44] A steady trickle of pier promotions followed over the next three decades, tapping the ever-growing steamer traffic and becoming important transport arteries in their own right as well as attracting promenaders and loungers; but the real boom in pier construction began in the 1860s, when at least 21 were completed, while work on several others was well advanced by the end of the decade. Four of the 21 were in large and well-established resorts: second piers at Brighton and Great Yarmouth (emulating Margate, whose second pier dated from 1856), and pioneering ventures at Scarborough and Hastings; five more made the south coast total up to seven: Worthing, Southsea,

Bournemouth, Folkestone and Bognor; two (Weston-super-Mare and Clevedon) were in the Bristol catchment area, and another (Aberystwyth) in mid-Wales. But the most impressive concentration came in the fast-growing resorts of Lancashire and North Wales: two at Blackpool, and others at New Brighton, Rhyl, Southport, Lytham and Morecambe, while Douglas (Isle of Man), with its Lancashire clientèle, effectively makes an eighth. These piers were responses to demand; the twenty-first, at Saltburn, was part of an attempt to create it, by a land company which was attempting to found a new watering-place. Like the similar venture at Herne Bay in the 1830s, and the subsequent one at Westward Ho!, the result was not very successful; but the pier boom was more usually an expression of robust health in seaside economies rather than a sign of mere aspiration.[45]

Several factors lay behind this sudden rush of pier-building. Technology was important, and the necessary ironwork swiftly became cheaper and more reliable as experience accumulated and the engineering industry consolidated its position. The railways helped in both respects. The design for Southport's pier in 1859 was based on the recently-completed railway viaduct over Ulverston sands, and the same engineers were employed in the planning and erection.[46] By 1869 it was possible for Clevedon's pier to be 'built . . . from factory-made components assembled on the site', and Morecambe's was also prefabricated, having been originally intended for Valparaiso.[47] Such innovations helped to reduce capital cost; and investment does seem to have been more readily forthcoming in the 1860s than before, for Southport and Weston-super-Mare were not alone in seeing a series of proposals coming to nothing in the 1840s and 1850s.[48] Risks were reduced by improved technology, and by the availability of limited liability after 1856. But piers remained expensive and perilous enterprises, vulnerable to storms and shipping accidents as well as to the trade cycle. The cost of Weston-super-Mare's Birnbeck Pier soared to nearly £70,000 after tidal problems were encountered, but this was a remarkably high figure. Indeed, it amounted to crippling over-capitalization, and the shareholders received no dividend for 17 years.[49] Most pier promotions aimed to raise between £8,000 and £20,000 from shareholders, though some soon found it necessary or desirable to increase their demands. Brighton's West Pier raised its share capital from £20,000 to £25,000 almost immediately, while Southport Pier expanded its resources from £10,000 in 1860 to £40,000 in 1868. In the seven cases where shareholding returns have been analysed, a remarkably high proportion of the capital was subscribed locally, suggesting that the fear of competition from rival resorts was a significant motive alongside the expectation of profit. Rhyl's first pier company was completely dominated by local money, and at Aberystwyth, Scarborough, Southport and Brighton more than half the investment came from residents. The two Blackpool piers showed lower figures of about one-third, but demand for shares was buoyant in the town's industrial hinterland, and Lancashire's enthusiasm for piers extended further afield, for its investors accounted for more than one-sixth of the Brighton West Pier share capital in 1864. London investment was unimportant except at Aberystwyth, where it provided the initial impetus.[50]

Who were the pioneering investors who enabled these piers to be built? Everywhere, local shopkeepers and tradesmen were well to the fore, and at Rhyl, Aberystwyth, Morecambe and Blackpool they were the single most important element in the early shareholders' registers. The holiday industry as such was not very strongly represented, though lodging-house keepers formed a noticeable minority among the small investors at Scarborough, Southport and Blackpool. A strong local professional interest was evident at Scarborough, while at Brighton more than 40 per cent of the shareholders seem to have had independent means, and the professions were again well represented. Blackpool's piers attracted considerable investment from Preston tradesmen and Manchester manufacturers, but the most remarkable register came from Southport. Here businessmen from inland Lancashire were conspicuous, as were professionals and men of independent means; but among the investors were many small tradesmen, and the list also included farmers and fishermen, and a barmaid, a waiter and a domestic servant. Working-class investors in seaside entertainment companies were to become commonplace in the next generation, but these were very early and unusually lowly.

The seaside piers of the 1860s were thus attracting investment from people who knew the resorts well. Most of the shareholders lived locally (as did most of the promoters), and many had very limited financial resources. Their willingness to risk their savings on an enterprise of this kind clearly reflects an informed perception of what the visitors wanted; and they themselves could hope to benefit from any improvement in the holiday season.

What, then, did the piers have to offer? As yet they promised little or no artificial entertainment. The articles of association drawn up by the promoters of Blackpool's North Pier expressed a widely shared but limited set of aims: to provide an 'extensive and agreeable promenade' at high water, and to give 'access to and landing from pleasure boats and other machines.'[51] The attractions of a healthy walk above the waves in comfort and safety, and of the view of the shore from the pierhead, were sufficient in themselves in most mid-Victorian resorts, and they were enhanced by the scope for display, discussion and flirtation which the pier, like other promenades, provided. An air of frivolity was encouraged by the early adoption of exotic architectural styles, with Oriental motifs much in evidence;[52] but apart from the inevitable band, there was at first little or no artificial amusement. Brighton's Chain Pier had soon found room for shops and silhouettists in the 1820s,[53] but the piers of the 1860s were purely for promenading, fulfilling similar functions to the Assembly Rooms and circulating libraries, but doing so cheaply, in the open air, and without dubious distractions or imposed formality.

The promenade pier was a healthy and sometimes a visually stimulating environment, but in itself it did little to satisfy the growing numbers of educated middle-class visitors who sought to occupy their time with pursuits savouring of self-improvement. The seaside provided excellent opportunities for dabbling in popular science through the collection of specimens, satisfying a need to accumulate possessions as well as a desire to understand and appreciate the riches of the natural world. As we have seen, the earliest sea-bathers had collected shells and seaweed, and hunted (usually casually) for fossils and butterflies, but the mania for specimens reached a peak in the third quarter of the nineteenth century. A guide to the resorts in 1876 recommended Weymouth, Freshwater, Southwold and Sheerness for geology, Falmouth for shells and seaweed, and West Lulworth for lepidoptera; but every resort had its speciality in the realm of natural curiosities.[54] A fashion for marine biology was stimulated by Philip Gosse's *A Naturalist's Rambles on the Devon Coast* (1853) and a stream of successor volumes. The resulting pillage of the rock-pools was vividly described by Gosse's son, who recorded his father's 'great chagrin' at the unforeseen outcome: 'An army of "collectors" has passed over them, and ravaged every corner of them. The fairy paradise has been violated . . . crushed under the rough paw of well-meaning, idle-minded curiosity.'[55]

The vogue for fern-collecting which followed the publication of Charlotte Chanter's *Ferny Combes* in 1856 was shorter-lived and less damaging; but, like Gosse's work, it helped to bring a high tide of mid-Victorian prosperity to the Devon resorts.[56] So did the popular success of Kingsley's *Westward Ho!*, which even inspired the promotion of the resort of the same name, although Kingsley himself was dismayed by 'the Northam Burrows scheme for spoiling that beautiful place with hotels and villas', which would 'frighten away all the sea-pies and defile the Pebble Ridge with chicken bones and sandwich scraps.'[57]

Westward Ho! itself languished, despite a famous golf course, but the established north Devon resorts saw visitor numbers greatly augmented by Kingsley devotees. Blackmore's *Lorna Doone* later had a similar effect. Further west, an element of popular anthropology crept into Cornwall's appeal, as Penzance's market day was recommended to the curious tourist: 'The dress of the many fishwomen is peculiar, and the visitors from St Just and the other remote mining towns are very odd looking.'[58]

For a few, these 'improving' seaside pursuits were seriously undertaken as ends in themselves. For most, no doubt, they were a specific against idleness and a salve to the work ethic. Tenby's newspaper struck an appropriate chord in 1873 when it urged visitors to seek true recreation, refreshment and invigoration through walking, botany, fern-gathering, rowing and fishing, through the study of ancient monuments and the 'physical and still more the moral' features of the neighbourhood.[59] Competitive sport had yet to come into its own at the seaside, but plenty of strenuous physical outlets were available. The result of this wide range of socially acceptable and morally laudable outdoor activities, superficial though the veneer of culture and scientific knowledge might often be, was that in some of the remoter and better-endowed resorts, natural attractions and places of interest made artificial entertainment effectively redundant. This was still the case in south Devon, among other places, at the turn of the century; the Ward Lock guide to Torbay remarked on the emptiness of the towns during the day, adding: 'Most of the more plebeian caterers for the amusement of holiday-makers have deserted the south Devon seaside resorts, because visitors have other and more healthy ways of filling up their hours than listening to nigger songs or watching the antics of the puppets of a Punch and Judy show.'[60]

Fig. 16 Rational recreations for all ages: pillaging the rock pools at Felixstowe (reproduced from *Pictures of East Coast Health Resorts*, ed. A. Peaton).

This was unusual. Most middle-class holidaymakers in most mid-Victorian resorts spent their time on beach, promenade and pier, surrounded by their children. Bathing-machines were in great demand: Brighton had over 300 in 1866, and some of its rivals were not far behind.[61] But most of the time was devoted to the idleness which was deplored by the serious-minded, to strolling and lounging, or at best reading and sewing, even on the beach. As Walvin remarks, 'Many people merely transferred to the resorts . . . the style of life they led at home.'[62] The seaside shows us a mainstream middle-class culture which was much less earnest and more hedonistic than some of the stereotypes, although inhibited and circumscribed in expression by convention and propriety. Nigger minstrels and itinerant bands provided informal entertainment for this passive majority, and vendors of food and trinkets ministered to their needs. Donkeys were available to amuse the children, buckets and spades sold well, and boat- and stage-coach trips catered for the enterprising. This mainstream holiday market attracted safe, stylized, predictable, lowest-common-denominator entertainment, often of poor quality and execution, as complaints testified.[63] A competent troupe of minstrels in a popular resort, capable of amusing children without offending parents, could make a good living. The Royal Margate Minstrels could divide £50 per week between 11 members, and the leader augmented his income by selling his own songs.[64] But this group survived and prospered for over 30 years, and most seaside performers could not approach this level of continuity, stability and, no doubt, talent. The pickings even in a small resort could be lucrative enough to generate fierce competition among itinerant entertainers, and the unskilled efforts of the weaker brethren provoked complaints of nuisances. At Llandudno in 1863 three rival bands each played different kinds of music, often within earshot of one another, while Southend in 1874 saw a direct confrontation between the established band of Mr Curtis and some intruding Italian musicians for possession of one of the best 'pitches', with each side playing at full volume to try to drown the other's performance. Soon afterwards a town committee was formed to collect subscriptions in the hope of offering a guaranteed income to a good band, shutting out the existing 'discordant Tin Pot Bands'.[65] This had long been a common practice elsewhere, but in practice the caco-phonous results of free trade in music were to remain a universal feature of resort life for some time to come.

The bland staple fare of seaside entertainment was enlivened in places by the surviving pleasure gardens or by music-hall, but the latter's clientèle was probably dominated by local lesser tradesmen and working-class people at least until the 1870s, although one of Ramsgate's music-halls was on the sea-front in 1867.[66] There were also occasional special attractions. Annual regattas, organized by voluntary committees and funded by subscriptions, remained popular in many resorts, and at Folkestone in 1860 the crowds attracted showmen with swings, roundabouts, Aunt Sallies and other amusements which were coming to be permanent beach attractions in the most popular resorts.[67] Occasional shows and exhibitions ranged from circuses to lectures on phrenology or geography, 'Dioramas' and 'Panor-amas' of famous scenes and current events, of a kind familiar enough inland.[68] Putting the regular and the occasional together, the amusements of the week at a major resort could make impressive reading. Apart from the bathing machines and baths, the carriages and riding horses, the pleasure boats, circulating libraries, assembly rooms and subscription pleasure grounds, all familiar from the late eighteenth century, Hastings in 1856 could offer, at the height of the fashionable season in September, a grand archery meeting, Haswell's panorama of the Crimean War, fireworks at the Tivoli Gardens, Macarte's equestrians, a lecture on American slavery, three subscription bands, and a motley array of itinerant singers and musicians.[69] Hastings' strait-laced rulers had made the town inhospitable to the theatre, and as yet there was no pier, but otherwise this programme of undemanding but generally respectable entertainment, tinged with edification, was typical of most of the larger mid-Victorian resorts.

Sunday, of course, was special. By this time commercial entertainment was effectively proscribed, and the lack of alternatives made the style and content of religious services all the more important. The divisions within the Church of England meant that the presence of a High Church or Low Church clergyman, with no alternative available, might deter a significant proportion of the potential visiting public. At Lowestoft in 1876 the kind of visitor who might be attracted by the town's freedom from 'that low species of amusement to be found in most watering-places', would certainly find it important that 'both the evangelical and ritualistic schools of Churchmen are represented', and until 1867 Evangelicals were deterred from visiting Bournemouth by the High Church monopoly there.[70] The importance of a 'popular clergyman' was readily recognized by resort promoters, who encouraged the building of churches on their land, often giving sites and financial assistance. Wealthy residents and visitors also contributed. Most resorts acquired a wide range of churches and chapels during the generally expansive mid-Victorian period, and growth and diversification continued into Edwardian times.[71] Services were well-attended, especially during the season, but the need to charge pew-rents to sustain the expenses of a new parish meant that accommodation for short-stay visitors was often limited, as free sittings were hard to find. Anyway, it was impossible to provide sufficient room for thousands of additional worshippers for a few weeks at the height of the season, and many visitors took the opportunity to escape from a churchgoing routine which derived more from social constraint than from genuine conviction. At Blackpool in 1873 the extensive use of cabs for Sunday joy-riding was explained in this way, as visitors were freed from the censorious supervision of their neighbours; while at Scarborough the pull of fashion was stronger than that of worship, as the Sunday morning parade of fancy hats and leather-bound prayer-books along the Esplanade began before the services had finished.[72] Churchgoing remained an important feature of resort routine for a significant minority, but, as we shall see, many visitors used the relative anonymity and flexibility of seaside life to seek some relaxation from the restraints of middle-class convention which governed behaviour in their home towns.

Even so, Sundays remained particularly quiet; but the general régime of the mid-Victorian seaside resort was often criticized for dullness. This was especially true of the smaller places. Silloth's daily routine was neatly encapsulated by its local newspaper in 1860: 'We eat, we drink, we bathe, we walk, we sleep; and then we eat and drink and bathe and walk and sleep again. Only for variety's sake sometimes we bathe before we walk, and sometimes we walk before we bathe.'[73]

Some larger resorts were felt to be equally uninspiring, especially where invalids predominated, as at Bournemouth and Torquay, or where local leaders put religion, morality and public order before entertainment, as at Southport, where the regatta was suppressed by the Lords of the Manor in 1853, the Improvement Commissioners refused to let the Town Hall to a theatre company, and the local authorities showed steady hostility to nigger minstrels and other open-air performers. Even here, however, plenty of outdoor entertainers remained, and in 1872 the Promenade itself featured clowns, nigger minstrels and performing dogs, while theatrical companies regularly found premises and there were frequent indoor concerts after 1860.[74] In any case, one man's dullness was another's decorum. The mid-Victorian period saw the final demise of the old resort régime, based on the Master of Ceremonies, the formal subscription-based Assembly Room and the organization of entertainment for a relatively wealthy élite who could be expected to share each other's company and exchange visits without undue embarrassment.[75] It also saw the decline of the raffish amusements of the late eighteenth and early nineteenth century, with their masked dancing at the pleasure gardens and gambling at the circulating libraries. The proprieties were upheld with increasing attention by the evangelical consensus which dominated public discourse and which, though never unchallenged and often quietly ignored, exercised a powerful influence on local government.[76] Instead, a distinctive family-centred, open-air seaside culture emerged, less formal and less derivative of metropolitan and spa models; and with all its limitations, it offered satisfactions of its own, as is suggested by the rapidly rising popularity of the seaside in these years.

Seaside entertainment during the third quarter of the nineteenth century required energy, organizing ability and entrepreneurial flair; but apart from the piers and some of the new assembly and concert rooms, it was conceived on a very limited scale. Nigger minstrels and promenade bands were labour-intensive rather than capital-hungry enterprises, and visitors had to create a lot of their own amusement. It was not until the 1870s that the ever-growing demand for seaside holidays began to encourage the development of large-scale leisure complexes requiring purpose-built premises. When these appeared, they began by building on the existing interest in the wonders of nature, making exotic plants and the marvels of the deep accessible to a wider public in buildings which also offered the promenading and musical facilities of Assembly Rooms. The Aquaria and Winter Gardens which in many ways pioneered commercial mass entertainment at the seaside thus began with an overtly didactic purpose, and fitted quite convincingly into the category of 'rational recreations'. But they were profit-seeking concerns, and the exigencies of the market soon forced sharp changes of emphasis and content away from the world of the Mechanics' Institute towards that of music-hall: a transition less startling than it first appears, for Bolton's leading music-hall of the 1850s had also contained a museum of natural curiosities, and the word 'exhibition' had often been used to cover a multitude of sins with a largely spurious veneer of educational merit.[77]

Winter Gardens were being mooted at Torquay, without success, as early as 1864, and Southport had a short-lived Zoological Gardens in the 1860s, but the first major scheme of this kind to come to fruition was the Marine Aquarium at Brighton, which was promoted in 1868, and opened in 1872 by the Duke of Edinburgh at the visit of the British Association for the Advancement of Science. These auspices were fitting, for the original Memorandum of Association simply envisaged the setting up of an Aquarium near the West Pier, with classes, lectures and research on the contents.[78] Over the next few years speculators in several other resorts followed suit, promoting Aquaria, Winter Gardens (often in the hope of creating a winter season), or a combination of the two.[79] The abortive Margate proposal of 1874, and Dr Cocker's Aquarium at Blackpool in the following year, followed the Brighton model closely on a smaller scale, and Bournemouth's first Winter Garden at Southbourne was merely 'a glass pavilion filled with flowers and ornamental plants'. Its second, more ambitious scheme, opened in 1877, offered ornamental gardens and 'general

Fig. 17 Church parade at Scarborough (reproduced from *One Hundred and Sixty-One Views of Scarborough and District*).

opportunities to the public for reading and mental and physical self-cultivation.'[80] Southport's Winter Gardens, in similar vein, promised to support the study of zoology, ornithology, geology and mineralogy.[81] Even where company promoters spread their nets wider to include concert and music halls, ballrooms and skating rinks, some of the schemes kept a strong didactic element. Thus the Tynemouth Aquarium and Winter Gardens Company in 1875: 'To promote the advancement and exhibition of Floriculture, Music, the Fine Arts, Practical Science, and other objects for promoting Education, Recreation and Amusement.'[82]

In almost all cases, the commitment to 'improvement' soon faded. The emergent mass market demanded lively and spectacular entertainment with a strong flavour of the music-hall; and from an early stage, alongside the Aquaria and Winter Gardens, rival entertainment companies sprang up to provide it in some of the popular resorts. In 1871 a syndicate of Blackpool and Halifax businessmen set up the Raikes Hall Park, Gardens and Aquarium Company, with 51 acres on which to lay out gardens with conservatories and rooms for concerts, dancing, theatrical productions and other entertainments. From the beginning, it followed the old London pleasure garden pattern, concentrating on dancing and spectacular shows involving acrobats, tightrope-walkers, fireworks, giant pictures and pageants. In 1874 a liquor licence was obtained to cover the entire park, and prostitutes and pickpockets became uncomfortably evident. Some lip service was paid to 'improvement' in the early years, but the conservatories were unsuccessful, and subsequent investment went into novelties such as mechanical racehorses, a roller-skating rink, bicycle track and miniature railway. Handsome dividends of up to 12 per cent resulted.[83] At Margate 'Lord' George Sanger, the circus proprietor, created a similar pleasure centre by his transformation of Hall-by-the-Sea, a concert- and dance-hall which had been converted from a disused railway terminus by the London restaurateurs Spiers and Pond in 1866.[84] When Sanger took over ten years later he laid out extensive Italian and Zoological Gardens at the back of the building, introduced fishponds, steam roundabouts, a 'cosmorama', shooting galleries, waxworks and a wizard, and put on regular 'balls' and concerts. A sixpenny admission fee covered the whole premises from 10 a.m. to 6 p.m. A flood of complaints followed about Sunday opening, salacious and blasphemous comic songs and the nude 'classical' statues, which were said to give rise to 'immoral' conversations between the sexes; but Sanger's enterprising mixture of Cremorne and Canterbury Hall survived and prospered beyond the turn of the century.[85]

Competition of this kind merely accelerated inevitable changes. Blackpool's Winter Gardens, as originally proposed in 1875, was cast firmly in the prevailing mould of gentility and 'rational recreation', promising gardens, a library, reading-rooms and a picture gallery as well as an indoor promenade and concert hall.[86] At the formal opening in 1878, these ideals still bulked large; but it soon became clear that the summer season would generate almost all the revenue, and that some concessions would have to be made to excursionists drawn in by the sixpenny flat rate which was necessary to maintain an adequate turnover on a capital investment of over £50,000. In 1879 popular variety was already invading the concert hall, with a 'female human cannonball' at Whitsuntide and August Bank Holiday. The following year saw the near-collapse of the company, but it survived to earn increasingly healthy dividends from 1883 onwards. The transition to popular variety shows was completed in 1887 by the appointment as manager of William Holland, who had more than 20 years' experience in London music-hall. He was responsible for the introduction of 'ballets' and variety programmes with such themes as 'Our Empire', and for the Empress Ballroom, a monument to the Lancashire working-class love of dancing, which he did not live to see completed. The Opera House of 1889 provided Gilbert and Sullivan, and sometimes more rarefied fare; but the Holland régime between 1887 and his untimely death in 1895 successfully completed the transition to concentration on spectacular entertainment for the masses.[87]

Blackpool's Winter Gardens had Raikes Hall to contend with, but its transformation was echoed in several other popular resorts, at Scarborough, Rhyl and for a time at Brighton itself, and to a lesser extent at Tynemouth and Southport. At Margate several Aquarium schemes produced only a roller-skating rink, which folded up in 1881 and reappeared five years later as the Marine Palace concert- and music-hall. At Great Yarmouth the Aquarium had 'a chequered career in its original capacity – fish being

Fig. 18 Interior of Blackpool's North Pier Pavilion, 1913 (reproduced from *The North Pier Blackpool 1863–1913*).

sufficiently to the fore at Yarmouth without a supply of captives in tanks'; but it prospered when converted into a variety theatre.[88]

The general process of adjustment was hindered in several cases by legal difficulties which became intolerable when companies sought the power to entertain as well as to exhibit. Bournemouth's second Winter Gardens found itself hamstrung by restrictive covenants imposed by the ground landlords, the Tregonwell estate, which forbade dancing or any form of entertainment other than fireworks and amateur theatricals, and imposed closing hours of 8 p.m. in winter and 10 p.m. in summer. Not surprisingly, the company soon collapsed, but the original acceptance of these restrictions sheds further light on initial priorities. It was not until the municipal takeover in 1893 that the Winter Gardens became a going concern.[89] Scarborough's Aquarium and Southport's Winter Gardens encountered similar though less drastic problems with their leases, especially with regard to the sale of alcohol.[90]

Alongside the spread of Winter Gardens and Aquaria, the pier-building boom continued into the 1870s; and here again, an established recreational institution with pretensions to gentility and even 'rationality' began to change its character during the decade. The transition came earliest at Blackpool, Margate and Weston-super-Mare, where the pressures and opportunities of working-class demand were felt particularly strongly; but by the late 1880s and early 1890s new piers everywhere were making provision for commercial entertainment, and existing piers were being re-founded and rebuilt to new specifications.

Blackpool's South Jetty (later the Central Pier) began the new trend soon after its opening. In 1870 a new manager introduced a successful combination of cheap steamer trips and dancing, catering for the excursionists who already congregated at the southern edge of the town. Monthly takings quadrupled, and the pier began to pay healthy dividends. Four years later the North Pier acquired refreshment rooms, shops and a 'spacious pavilion' where a 35-piece orchestra costing £125 per week dispensed high-class music to high-class visitors, as the town's original pier widened the social distance between itself and its increasingly proletarian neighbour.[91] On Margate's Jetty Extension, as improved in 1876, 'they can now get everything down there except their lodgings', or so a local councillor alleged in 1880; and by 1876 Weston-super-Mare's Birnbeck Pier already had 'swings, gymnastics and other games', although the company lacked the capital to complete its refreshment pavilion. Cleethorpes' pier was offering dancing for the 'great unwashed' by 1876.[92]

To some extent, these initiatives were being matched elsewhere by the end of the decade; but Eugenius Birch, *doyen* of pier engineers, was exaggerating when in 1878 he affected not to know of any sizeable pier without refreshment and concert rooms.[93] Southsea (with two pier pavilions) and Skegness were among the resorts to follow the trend in the late 1870s and early 1880s, and Llandudno's ambitious remodelling in the mid-1880s provided space for a 40-piece orchestra and an audience of 2,000 at its pierhead, and a concert pavilion capable of seating 4,000.[94] But the real rush of investment which brought about a general transformation of the seaside pier took place between 1888 and 1896, as opulent pavilions (though rarely on Llandudno's scale), refreshment rooms and arcades of shops became almost universal in the larger resorts. Existing promenade piers were embellished with pavilions, and in many cases widened, at Eastbourne, Brighton, Worthing, Ryde, Sandown, Aberystwyth, Southport, Morecambe and Scarborough, while new pleasure piers of a similar kind were opened at Clacton, Folkestone, Hastings, Southampton, Boscombe, Torquay, Blackpool and Morecambe again.[95] This is not a complete list, and a steady flow of further additions continued into the new century, while promenade piers continued to be built at quiet resorts such as Minehead.[96] Eastbourne's new amenities included a rifle saloon and American bowling saloon, while the reconstructed Scarborough Promenade Pier Company of 1890 was already looking to a controversial future by planning to own or manage automatic machines, procuring them 'by hire purchase or otherwise'.[97] The new century saw a Grotto Railway on Blackpool's Central Pier, and the Palace Pier at Brighton, with its 'golden oriental domes and delicate filigree ironwork arches', its theatre, pavilion and astonishing array of slot-machines, marked the apotheosis of the pleasure pier.[98]

The 1890s also saw a renewed surge of large-scale entertainment investment on dry land. The previous decade had been a period of consolidation and adjustment. Most of the Winter Gardens and Aquaria had endured hard times in the depressed years after the disastrous 1879 season, when the weather and the trade cycle had conspired unkindly against the new companies, many of which collapsed altogether or had to be reconstructed, sometimes more than once. Even before this, many over-optimistic ventures had been abortive, as promoters competed to tap a seemingly inexhaustible flow of demand. Investors often sustained heavy losses. After the collapse of the New Brighton Aquarium, Baths and Hotel Company in 1879, three years after its formation, the shareholders received 6⅔ per cent of their nominal investment; and investors in a string of other companies, which folded up at about the same time, can have done little better. The Aquarium at Tynemouth, founded in 1875, brought down one company in 1879 and a successor in 1880, lying fallow for several years thereafter.[99] Scarborough's Aquarium failed in 1881 and again in 1886, in spite of being excused rates for a year, while two rival concerns never got off the ground at all.[100] Similar sad stories came from Margate, Brighton, Southend, Rhyl, Morecambe, Bournemouth and Torquay, and where the enterprises were not abandoned altogether, the 1880s were occupied in picking up the pieces. Even Blackpool's Winter Gardens had its troubles, as we have seen, and the Borough Bazaar there was yet another casualty of 1879.[101] Entrepreneurs and shareholders alike burned their fingers severely at this time, and it took a spectacular upturn in seaside holiday demand in the early 1890s to revive interest and confidence.

The largest schemes of the 1890s were far more capital-hungry than those of the 1870s. Brighton's Aquarium had expanded its share capital to £120,000 by 1878, and Southend's Marine Palace unsuccessfully sought £75,000, while Scarborough's Spa had nearly £78,000 spent on it after a fire in 1876. But most limited companies ranged from £10,000 for some of the smaller Aquaria to £60,000 for Rhyl's Winter Gardens. Scarborough's Aquarium and the Winter Gardens at Southport and Blackpool expanded well beyond this level during the 1880s, but even they were put in the shade by the £300,000 sought by New Brighton's Tower in 1896, or the half-million pounds required during the 1890s for Blackpool's Tower, Alhambra and Gigantic Wheel, to say nothing of the Victoria Pier and further expansion at the Winter Gardens.[102] All these nominal capitals could, of course, be increased to a varying extent by loan finance, but this probably does not affect the orders of magnitude.

The largest pleasure palace schemes to come to fruition in the 1890s were in the north-west, where the working-class holiday first became a mass experience. Blackpool apart, Southport and Morecambe saw heavy additional investment in existing Winter Gardens, Morecambe acquired a Tower, and Douglas (Isle of Man) continued to expand the enormous ballrooms and pleasure gardens which had already been proliferating in the locally-prosperous 1880s.[103] Elsewhere there were plenty of schemes in the £50,000 to £70,000 range, but only at Brighton and Southend did new enterprises try to raise six-figure sums from shareholders, and both were unsuccessful.[104]

The range of attractions on offer at the largest entertainment centres can be conveyed by a description of the Tower at Blackpool in 1897:

> In the basement of the Tower, bounded by the four legs, is a large variety circus, the arena of which can be filled with water for aquatic spectacles. Two or three performances are given daily . . . On the ground floor are

[*sic*] fine billiard room and restaurant. An aquarium, the tanks being disposed in a series of rocky caverns and passages; a menagerie, with its ever-popular monkeys, gay-plumed birds, lions and tigers; the tropical roof-gardens on the buildings surrounding the Tower; the seal pond and bear cages; such are but a few of the attractive appendages to the Tower itself. The Elevator Hall is quaintly arranged as an old English village . . . From the Entrance Hall one goes upstairs to the Grand Pavilion, perhaps the finest ballroom in England, where, without any extra charge, you are permitted to enjoy one of the finest variety entertainments imaginable. An equally magnificent saloon and refreshment bar adjoins. Electric lighting everywhere reigns supreme.[105]

This rich and varied menu, combining all the fun of the circus, stage and music-hall with dancing, promenading space and a residual commitment to exhibitions with some claim to educational value (though quaintness, spectacle, novelty and sheer attractive power were the key assets) was reproduced with only minor variations in the other great entertainment complexes of the 1890s, and in the new creations of the early twentieth century. At Rhyl, the Palace in 1904 boasted a huge ballroom with 2,500 springs under the parquet floor, extensive roof gardens, 40 shops and offices, a waxwork show, ping-pong rooms, and underneath the ballroom an imitation Venice which featured 'real Gondolas propelled by real Italians.'[106] When Southend's Kursaal eventually provided a southern version of these delights in 1901, it took Blackpool's Winter Gardens as a model; but during the following decade new influences came to the fore, and attention shifted towards switchbacks and novelty rides in the surrounding 26-acre Marine Park. By 1910, when the Luna Park and Palace of Amusements company had taken over, it could describe itself as, 'The largest and most complete American fun park in the country', although it still provided theatrical attractions and maintained a full orchestra even in the winter months.[107]

Luna Park borrowed its very name from Coney Island (in sharp contrast with the pedigree of the word 'Kursaal'), but its claim to pre-eminence would have been hotly challenged in Blackpool, though not by the Tower or Winter Gardens. In 1897 the fairground of nearly 40 acres which became Blackpool's Pleasure Beach began to grow, beyond the southern edge of the existing promenade. In 1901 it came under the control of an Anglo-American syndicate whose front man and manager, W. G. Bean, had several years' experience of the American fairground industry which was already blossoming at Coney Island and elsewhere. Expansion was rapid, despite local opposition which led to regulation by the Corporation. In 1904 the original primitive bicycle railways and roundabouts were augmented by the Sir Hiram Maxim Captive Flying Machine, and over the next ten years a flood of novelties appeared, most of them electrically operated, including a cake walk, 'submarine switchback', oscillating staircase and 'Monitor and Merrimac' battle show. Like the last-named, most of these were American imports, and during the Edwardian years the Pleasure Beach took over from the recently-defunct Raikes Hall gardens as Blackpool's leading outdoor entertainment centre. By 1914 it had a summer staff of 600, and expected up to 200,000 visitors on a Bank Holiday. It could not match the sheer extravagance of its Coney Island exemplars, but it was undoubtedly the most impressive seaside enterprise of its kind in Britain, although rivals were appearing at most of the popular resorts before 1914.[108]

The Pleasure Beach confirmed Blackpool's position, which it had been consolidating since the 1870s, as the nation's leading pleasure resort in terms of sheer quantity and range of large-scale, all-weather entertainment. Indeed, its only serious rival for world supremacy was probably Atlantic City, with its five piers and numerous entertainment houses clustered around the railroad terminals.[109] By the turn of the century Blackpool's three pleasure piers, its Tower, Winter Gardens and Alhambra, formed a complex of commercial amusements which no other British resort could even approach. The loss of Raikes Hall to the builder at the turn of the century would have been a sad blow elsewhere, but Blackpool bore it with equanimity. Other leading popular resorts, such as Rhyl, New Brighton, Morecambe, Scarborough, Bridlington, Great Yarmouth, Southend, Margate and even Brighton itself could provide one or even two pleasure piers, one or even two entertainment complexes with some pretensions (often inflated ones) to emulating Blackpool's pleasure palaces; but Blackpool's pre-eminence relegated them to the second rank. Weston-super-Mare and the Lincolnshire coast resorts, which also aspired to catering for the mass market, had less to offer: little more than pier, pavilion and gardens, supplemented by music-hall and a measure of beach and fairground entertainment.

Even in the booming Blackpool of the 1890s, the giant entertainment companies did not have a uniformly easy ride. The Tower Company nearly fell by the wayside at the outset, and had to be rescued by local businessmen from the clutches of a London-based syndicate whose sole aim was to make a fat profit on the initial land transactions. Later in the decade the Gigantic Wheel proved to have limited dividend-earning power once the initial novelty had worn off, and the Alhambra was hamstrung by over-capitalization, although the Tower Company was able to turn it into a going concern after much of the capital had been written off.[110]

Blackpool's northern rivals made heavier weather. New Brighton's Tower soon proved to be absurdly over-capitalized, and plunged steadily deeper into debt as interest charges swallowed up occasional and meagre working profits. Even the 6 per cent preference shareholders had to forego their dividends, and in 1906 the *Financial Times* commented, 'What object there can be from the point of view of the shareholders in keeping the undertaking alive any longer we cannot imagine, and the sooner it is put into liquidation the better.' This dismal record was partly due to the hostility of the local authority, whose ferry service made no concessions to the Tower's needs, but there were also dark hints of financial mismanagement or chicanery by the original promoter, who seemed to have made an enormous profit in selling the site to the company. A string of dubious financial transactions followed.[111] But New Brighton's Tower survived much longer than most seaside entertainment companies in the north. Morecambe's Tower, still unfinished, went into liquidation after the disastrous local slump at the turn of the century;[112] and Douglas, Scarborough, Bridlington, Rhyl and Llandudno all saw abortive, short-lived or unremunerative schemes, while the refloating of Southport's Winter Gardens on a grander scale at the turn of the century was also followed by liquidation within a few years. Further south, uncertain demand levels and suspicion of outside promoters ensured that very few large-scale projects ever did business. Intervention from landowners (as at Eastbourne) or municipal involvement in the entertainment industry became generally inescapable around the turn of the century.[113]

The leading entertainment companies of the 1890s thus fared no better as commercial speculations than the pioneers of the previous generation. The few successful dividend-earners (mainly in Blackpool and among the piers) were far outweighed by the failures and abortive schemes. But entrepreneurs still found the seaside attractive, and investment was readily forthcoming from the general public beyond the turn of the century, in northern England at least. Further south, the share-buying public was more sceptical.[114] But we need to know more about the nature of entrepreneurial activity at the seaside, and about the identity of the investing public, to see how these influences affected the fortunes of resorts, and whether they changed significantly over the last quarter of the nineteenth century as the popular holiday industry came of age.

An examination of the origins of 60 leading seaside entertainment companies suggests that their sources of inspiration changed noticeably between the 1870s and the 1890s.[115] In the earlier period, the projects most likely to be carried out were those promoted mainly or entirely by tradesmen within the resorts themselves, shopkeepers, builders, brewers and the like. Solicitors, doctors and people of private means were also represented, but local commercial interests predominated. Several northern companies included Lancashire or West Riding manufacturers or merchants among their promoters, and in a few cases (most noticeably Tynemouth's Aquarium and the rival schemes for Aquaria at New Brighton) the initiative came from the resort's hinterland. The most pervasive outside influence, however, came from London, as civil engineers, architects and other speculators with appropriate expertise sought to ride the seaside holiday boom. The pier engineer Eugenius Birch, for example, was a signatory to several Memoranda of Association at this time. Most of these projects were in the south, and few were ever completed, as local tradesmen remained unimpressed by the extravagant claims of outsiders.[116] In a few cases, such as Margate's Hall-by-the-Sea and New Brighton's Palace, individual entrepreneurs were responsible for very extensive enterprises; but the limited company depending mainly on share capital was, and remained, the norm at this level.

The new boom of the 1890s saw important changes of emphasis. Local promoters remained active, but mainly in second-rank resorts like Llandudno and Bexhill, where their efforts were largely unrewarded. The capital-hungry enterprises of the second wave of entertainment promotions relied for their initial impetus much more on wealthy outside speculators.

Thus merchants, manufacturers and accountants from Manchester were behind Blackpool's South Shore Pier and Alhambra, while industrialists from Leeds were prominent in Bridlington schemes of the same vintage, and Aberystwyth saw ambitious proposals (which came to little) from the West Midland industrialists Bourne and Grant.[117] Alongside this increased provincial activity, London speculators were also busy, as clerks and minor functionaries came forward to act as front men for grandiose-looking projects hatched by syndicates and holding companies. The most remarkable example was the Standard Contract and Debenture Corporation, which was responsible for further abortive Eiffel Tower schemes on the Blackpool model at Brighton, Douglas and Scarborough, buying prime sites with a view to resale at a vast profit to a client company whose shareholders would be attracted by the *bona fide* presence of leading local businessmen on the board.[118] Not all metropolitan speculations were as cynical as this, but very few resulted in tangible or lasting benefits to the resorts concerned. By the early twentieth century, indeed, the share-buying public was becoming increasingly sceptical of all seaside promotions, and the spate of schemes died away to a trickle.

Where did the original share capital come from for these companies, and who were the (usually unfortunate) investors? Even in the 1870s, the local investment which had been so prominent in the promenade piers of the 1860s was already being outweighed by money from the resorts' catchment areas. London investment was important in the south coast resorts, as we might expect, accounting for about half the share capital of the Margate Aquarium of 1874 and Skating Rink of 1876, and of Bournemouth's Winter Gardens. In the main growth areas of Lancashire and North Wales, local investment was of limited importance (as in the south, it ranged from about 10 per cent to about 40 per cent of the stock of individual companies), and London money was conspicuous by its absence. Here, the leading entertainment companies were funded largely from the prosperous industrial districts of Lancashire and the West Riding, with a strong Liverpool presence in the case of New Brighton. Rhyl, Blackpool, Morecambe and Scarborough followed this pattern, and only Southport, which had already acquired a prosperous residential élite including many businessmen from inland Lancashire, was able to generate most of its own investment. Here, over 60 per cent of the Winter Gardens' shares were locally owned at the outset, and figures for the other promotions of the 1870s ranged from 62.5 per cent to over 95 per cent. Further north, however, the pattern of regional rather than local investment was maintained even more strongly at Tynemouth, where 86.5 per cent of the Aquarium's capital came from Northumberland and Durham.

The second promotion boom in the 1890s saw an even more pronounced dependence on outside investment, except in the less ambitious schemes at resorts like Aberystwyth and Llandudno. London capital now became important to several northern projects, especially New Brighton's Tower, where eight Londoners among the 498 shareholders accounted for nearly half the shares. But the bulk of the investment in northern companies still came from the Lancashire and Yorkshire textile towns, which also helped to fund southern concerns like the Southend Tower scheme of 1898, which later passed into the hands of Allsopp's Brewery (as the Kursaal) and then (as Luna Park) to a Rochdale industrialist. On the south coast, however, London capital was now overwhelmingly important, supplemented at Brighton by a truly national share-buying public, although local residents here, as elsewhere in the south, remained apathetic or suspicious.[119]

Most companies, especially the largest ones, depended for their share capital on a multitude of small investors. Some of the pier companies of the 1860s had registered over 100 shareholders, including many lodging-house keepers and petty tradesmen; but such projects of the 1870s as the Tynemouth Aquarium and Margate Skating Rink required over 250 investors, and the giants of the next generation cast their nets even more widely, as Blackpool's Gigantic Wheel had over 900 shareholders, and the Tower's list topped 1500. There were, of course, some massive individual investors even at the outset, and their importance increased as creditors and speculators acquired blocks of shares in ailing firms; but in almost all cases the show was set on the road by the accumulated savings of tradesmen, professionals, widows, spinsters and (increasingly) clerks and skilled workers. Merchants and manufacturers contributed substantial sums in the northern resorts, no doubt influenced by the late Victorian combination of tight textile industry margins and rising working-class spending power. The contribution of the local holiday industry itself, even in Blackpool, was far outweighed by these outside shareholdings. To a large extent, and increasingly, the resorts' large-scale entertainments were made possible by the investments of their potential customers, buoyed up by the optimism engendered by the sight of summer crowds and high-season activity. To an August visitor, New Brighton's Tower must have seemed a certain financial success; and in 1898 the money rolled in from industrial Lancashire, lured by a guaranteed 10 per cent dividend for the first three years, and in spite of damning comments from the specialist investment press.[120] It took the costly failure of several schemes at the turn of the century to dampen this enthusiasm and persuade these small investors to take their savings elsewhere.

A little lower down the scale, music-halls also multiplied at the resorts during the last quarter of the nineteenth century, and especially after 1890, when the seaside theatre also revived, with considerable investment in new purpose-built premises supplementing the provision of the larger entertainment complexes. In 1875 Blackpool already afforded visitors the joys of the Royal Star Amphitheatre of Varieties in Coronation Street, with a ballet troupe, a female impersonator, a 'flying man' and a highland vocalist, while the minstrel show at the Crystal Palace, Bank Hey Street included 'chaste and racy' dialogues.[121] This was the staple fare of urban entertainment inland, and it found increasing favour at the seaside with the new late Victorian visiting public. The same tastes led established seaside theatres such as Blackpool's own Theatre Royal to offer a diet of farce and melodrama during the season. But there was a parallel tradition of more serious theatre appreciation inland, and when the respectability of the stage began to revive in conventional middle-class circles towards the turn of the century, entrepreneurs like Thomas Sergenson in Blackpool and Jules

Rivière in Llandudno seized the opportunity to provide high-class, purpose-built premises which found room for Gilbert and Sullivan, West End hits, and even Shakespeare and Grand Opera.[122] Individual and family enterprises also found outlets in the many small pleasure gardens, usually attached to public houses, which continued to offer dancing, light entertainment, bowls and strawberry teas on the outskirts of most late Victorian resorts.

The largest theatres and music-halls demanded fixed capitals well in excess of £10,000, and could not afford to alienate potential customers, or to fall foul of the licensing magistrates, by incurring charges of 'vulgarity' or 'immorality' from mainstream representatives of middle-class opinion. Extreme nonconformist or teetotal ire could be rebutted, or even turned to account, as 'Lord' George Sanger (an experienced protagonist) found when his Hall-by-the-Sea at Margate came under fire in the mid-1870s; but comic songs and 'racy' dialogues had to recognize an accepted, if hazy, code of proprieties. This, indeed, was a necessary condition of the growing accepta-bility of music-hall. In the popular resorts, however, these relatively safe pleasures were being supplemented in the late nineteenth century by back-street and open-air entertainments which catered for a less inhibited, largely working-class clientèle, and it was here that the most risqué forms of seaside entertainment flourished. Waxwork shows featured all the latest murderers; exhibitions displayed freaks of nature, human or animal; stalls featured 'sickening prints of skin diseases'; 'art galleries' in wooden sheds showed pictures with such themes as 'The Goddess Diana and her hunting party'; phrenologists, quack doctors and corn-cutters colonized foreshores, alongside more orthodox fairground attractions; penny-in-the-slot

Fig. 19 Edwardian foreshore entertainment: the cadets and other attractions on Scarborough sands (reproduced from *One Hundred and Sixty-One Views of Scarborough and District*).

machines appeared, some exhibiting 'a very suggestive looking picture'; and singing-saloons in back-street public houses posed a more immediate perceived threat to the morality of young visitors.[123] We shall see that local authorities tried hard to curb and regulate activities of this kind; but from the 1870s onwards, the popular resorts saw a rapid proliferation of cheap, informal entertainment aimed at a working-class market, which often survived for a long time with few effective constraints on content and mode of expression. The wholesale transplanting of back-street entertainment and fairground amusements from the inland towns to the rich summer pastures of the seaside posed severe problems of regulation, especially when parts of the beach and sea-front were thereby rendered unacceptable to 'better-class' families. But most working-class visitors revelled in it; as a Blackpool commentator remarked in 1897,

> They expect to see the attractions of their own towns (on market days and at Wakes) glorified, and that is what the sands have been . . . they get this, the one poor pleasure, in the sunlight by the sea, and they like it, with a liking which can only be understood by those familiar with their lives.[124]

In most resorts, however, beach amusements continued to follow the path marked out in their mid-Victorian heyday. The style and appearance of the characteristic open-air entertainers might change, as the pierrots displaced the nigger minstrels during the 1890s; but the need to appeal to all ages without offence, and without over-taxing the intellect, kept approach and content within narrow bounds.[125] Donkeys kept their popularity, and the sands remained a children's playground; but the mid-Victorian mania for collecting pebbles, shells and assorted marine life was on the wane. The most remarkable changes, however, involved the place of bathing in the holiday programme. The rituals of medicinal sea-bathing fell into disuse in the late nineteenth century, and bathing-machines themselves began to decline in use and numbers. In 1899 one observer found them 'still pretty general, but at many places [they] seem to be largely superseded by tents, huts or other conveniences.'[126] Pleasure had supplanted health as the dominant motive for bathing, and this transition encouraged a growing pressure for mixed, family bathing, which was becoming widely acceptable as both sexes began to use 'more or less complete costumes' as a matter of course. Prudery and vested interests long combined to restrict visitors' freedom in most resorts, and conflicts arose as the practice of 'mackintosh bathing' – changing in lodgings or hotel room and 'covering up' for the journey to and from the beach – became current. At Southend, for example, bathing-machines and tents were insufficient to cope with the growing demand for bathing in Edwardian times, and mackintosh bathing was eventually allowed.[127] In many established resorts, bathing became a more relaxed, family-centred activity in the early twentieth century, and it also became much cheaper, although change was slow overall and resorts like Broadstairs and Eastbourne clung to segregated bathing and the bathing-machine long after the First World War.

New attitudes to bathing were symptomatic of a general, though often controversial, relaxation of mid-Victorian taboos and social constraints, as the related influences of narrow evangelicalism, the work ethic and the ideal of self-improvement declined at the seaside as in the wider society.[128] We have seen that commercial entertainment steadily lost its educative pretensions during the late nineteenth century, as idleness on holiday became more a matter for enjoyment than guilt, and as the immediate pleasures of laughter, dancing and (especially on the more sophisticated new fairground rides) unexpected physical movement displaced the intellectual or pseudo-intellectual arts of view-gazing and specimen-collecting. The identification of the seaside in summer with pleasure rather than health, and therefore (to most people) with exuberant enjoyment rather than the quiet of the sick-room, was taking place by the turn of the century even at the great centres for consumptives, Bournemouth, Torquay and Ventnor.[129] We must not draw these contrasts too sharply, of course. *Punch* neatly satirized the educative contribution of mid-Victorian nigger minstrels, putting into a nursemaid's mouth the sententious remark (for her mistress' consumption) that, 'There was nothink to improve the mind, M'm, till the niggers come down!!'[130] On the other hand, aquaria, menageries and exhibitions showing life in foreign lands remained regular features of the Edwardian pleasure palaces, and Blackpool's Winter Gardens found room for Caruso and Melba on its programme in 1909 and 1910.[131] In such resorts as Bournemouth, Eastbourne and Torquay, of course, high-class concerts and drama were an Edwardian commonplace. The culture of the seaside was broadening its range in the late nineteenth and early twentieth century, as the larger resorts proved capable of providing intellectual and aesthetic stimulation for those who sought it, as well as (more obviously) allowing more boisterous opportunities for the pursuit of earthier and less inhibited pleasures. The mix varied enormously from Blackpool and Morecambe to Eastbourne and Bournemouth, and the change of emphasis was less marked in the smaller and more sedate resorts. But a remarkable transition from a preoccupation with health, self-improvement and decorum to an eager pursuit of pleasure and amusement can be charted with some confidence.

But the mid-Victorian seaside culture did not disappear; it was merely made less visible by the rise of more popular and less demanding alternatives. A resort guide of 1899 quoted Sir Edward Sieveling on the joys of Falmouth: 'For the healthy there is every possible attraction – geology, botany, mineralogy, marine zoology.' The spirit of Gosse lived on, though the same guide-book remarked sadly of Tenby's rare shells and marine life, 'The best of this harvest is now gathered.'[132] Devotees of nature and scenery bulked large among the late Victorian and Edwardian refugees to remote fishing villages. But excursions to beauty spots and historic buildings remained important preoccupations of many visitors to larger and more popular resorts. The Great Eastern Railway's sumptuous guide to 'East Coast health resorts' at the turn of the century devoted 12 of its 16 pages on Great Yarmouth to picturesque buildings and historical associations, and popular productions like the Ward Lock *Red Guides* displayed the same priorities.[133] Steamer and stage-coach trips retained their attractions in this context; in 1907 Llandudno's stage-coach tours into Snowdonia were so popular that advance booking was essential in mid-season, and similar services flourished at Southend as well as in south Devon.[134] Quaint or archaic transport already had a fascination of its own, and in 1894 the narrow-gauge Festiniog Railway was advertising itself to Cambrian Coast visitors as 'the Fairy Line'.[135] The novel sensations of the journey were probably the crucial attraction for many, and the persisting prevalence of excursions to places of historic, literary or picturesque interest may mask a transition from the serious and self-cultivating to the frivolous and pleasure-seeking in the ways in which they were perceived and experienced by visitors; but the strong survival of this mode of holiday activity is important in itself.

Nor was the pursuit of health itself forgotten, though sea-bathing itself took a back seat. What counted now was climate and air, and these still brought visitors as well as retirers to the seaside. Southport still had 18 bath-chair proprietors in 1914, and the new resort of Southbourne, near Bournemouth, boasted a chalybeate spring in 1895. Saltburn, with its mid-Victorian spa, added brine and other medical baths to its armoury in 1891, and Sidmouth likewise offered medical baths for heart disease, rheumatism and gout.[136] In 1888 Clacton's new switchback offered itself as a cure for biliousness, with a medical opinion recommending up to a dozen rides as the proper dose.[137] These initiatives coincided with the late Victorian revival of the inland spas for medical rather than fashionable reasons; and the seaside's distinctive contribution to the nation's health was to be made in a more novel manner.[138]

The late nineteenth century saw a great boom in competitive participant sport, especially among the middle classes; and the seaside holiday provided excellent opportunities for the polishing of skills and the pursuit of associated social goals. The rapid rise of tennis and golf, especially, took the boredom out of the conventional seaside holiday for many adolescents (and indeed their parents), and any nagging doubts about the frivolity of the enterprise could be dispelled by thoughts of health and invigoration. Moreover, the cost of equipment, time and access to courts and courses necessary to acquire basic skills, ensured the games a social exclusiveness which was increasingly difficult to obtain in most seaside pursuits.[139] Resorts had always offered opportunities for fishing and boating, and yachting, one of the most exclusive activities of all, enjoyed a late Victorian and Edwardian boom which brought additional prosperity to such diverse resorts as Cowes, Torquay, Lowestoft and Brightlingsea. Hunting had long been an option for the wealthy at resorts from Eastbourne to Minehead, and local cricket clubs readily opened their doors to skilled and socially presentable visitors. Less demandingly, and encouraging an attractive mingling between the sexes, the mid-Victorian vogue for archery and croquet also flourished modestly at the seaside.[140] But none of this gave any hint of the explosive growth of golf and tennis, gathering momentum from the mid-1870s and reaching a climax in the 1890s, when they became indispensable adjuncts to the middle-class seaside holiday. In 1891 even the affluent Sussex coast had only two golf courses, but by 1895 they were springing up in the remotest Cornish fishing hamlets, such as Gunwalloe and Boscastle, and in East Anglian villages like Caister-on-Sea, as land-

owners and hoteliers found that the strength of demand amply repaid high
capital and running costs. By the turn of the century almost every seaside
resort was in easy reach of a golf course, and places like Felixstowe,
Hoylake, Lytham St Annes and Westward Ho! owed much of their custom
to the game's popularity. As A. R. H. Moncrieff remarked, 'You can live at
Westward Ho! without being connected with the army or navy; but you
may as well stay away if you are no golfer.'[141] At Bournemouth, the
Corporation was not to be outdone by these upstart competitors for its
chosen market, and laid out golf courses on the old turbary commons in
1894 and 1903–5.[142] Tennis became an urgent priority rather earlier, and by
1895 Eastbourne had between 20 and 30 courts available in Devonshire
Park, while Exmouth and even little Holkham had their tennis tournaments,
and the game had become so essential to a conventional middle-class way of
life that, as with golf, courts were appearing in improbable-sounding
Cornish villages like Downderry and Mevagissey. If all else failed, as in the
remote Welsh hamlet of The Havens, the visitors marked out their own
courts on the sands.[143]

   This was not sport as 'rational recreation', encouraging team spirit and
responsibility, and revitalizing mind and body for further exertions of a
productive kind; for seaside sport in this individualistic mould was clearly an
end in itself, almost an obsession, for many. This was particularly likely in
the smaller resorts, devoid as they were of artificial attractions, and
potentially dull for those who had no bent for rambling, painting, sketching,
antiquarianism or natural history. But the likes of Gunwalloe and Sandsend,
Manorbier and Palling-on-Sea, numerous though they were becoming,
accounted at the turn of the century for only a tiny and rather eccentric
proportion of even the middle-class visiting public. Above them stretched a
complicated hierarchy of resorts, each tier providing a wider range of
entertainment for a widening range of visitor tastes. Almost at the bottom
was Runswick Bay in North Yorkshire, where the Fishermen's Institute was
the sole place of assembly: 'Visitors are welcomed here, generally contribut-
ing a trifle to the box; and, as there is also a piano, they frequently give
concerts for the villagers.'[144] A step higher were resorts like Aldeburgh,
which in 1899 ran to a new Jubilee Hall for subscription dances and
entertainments, or Spittal in Northumberland, where Berwick's town band
played twice weekly during the season.[145] Hotels, where they existed, often
provided a lively social scene of their own, and help to bridge the gap to the
relative sophistication of Barmouth, for example, with its Assembly Room
for concerts and its professional 'concert party', heirs to the nigger minstrel
tradition, on the beach.[146] Beyond this comes the fully-equipped small
pleasure resort, usually with a pier and perhaps a pavilion, formal gardens,
minstrels or pierrots and a band, as in the case of Skegness, Bognor,
Felixstowe or Teignmouth. Then, experiences diverge, with the parks,
high-class concerts, opulent theatres and pier pavilions and carefully policed
promenades of Eastbourne, Folkestone, Bournemouth or Lowestoft on the
one hand, and the roistering working-class resorts with dancing platforms
and assorted pleasure palaces, such as Blackpool, Douglas and New
Brighton, on the other. But most of the larger resorts tried to keep a foot in

both camps. Folkestone itself found room for a switchback railway, to which 'Prime Ministers and even Princesses were addicted', Southport allowed a whole fairground to accumulate on its foreshore, while Margate catered for respectability with a municipal orchestra, and even Blackpool itself kept the North and South Shore Piers as havens of well-dressed sophistication, with innocuous programmes featuring such performers as 'Charles Capper, the well-known London Society entertainer.'[147]

Such compromises were the fruit of long years of conflict and accommodation, as interested parties competed over the vexed questions of what kind of visitor was most desirable, both morally and financially, and where the line should be drawn between acceptable and reprehensible modes of entertainment and behaviour. As the larger resorts developed through the stages which were represented at the turn of the century by Runswick Bay, Aldeburgh, Barmouth and Bognor, their evolution was shaped by the outcome of countless battles between conflicting evaluations of their appropriate 'social tone', as landowners, residents, entrepreneurs and holidaymakers sought to define resorts in their chosen image. These disputes were complicated increasingly in the later nineteenth century by railway extensions, changes in railway policy and more general alterations in patterns of demand and responses to them. They form a central theme in seaside history, and in the relationship between the resorts and the wider world; and we shall examine them more closely in the next chapter.

8 Styles of holidaymaking: conflict and resolution

Landowners, local government and the entertainment industry were all essential formative influences on the pace and character of seaside resort growth, but the fundamental variable was the demand for seaside holidays. Resorts responded to changes in the volume and nature of demand in different ways, but at some point they all had to come to terms with the growing importance of the lower middle and working classes. The pressure to cater for quantity as well as quality was far from uniform, but it was almost universal, as cheap steamer and rail fares, lengthening holidays and rising real wages opened up the prospect of day-trips and longer seaside holidays to an ever-widening circle of lower-class consumers. This extension of the holiday market brought conflict in its wake, as many of the new visitors enjoyed themselves in ways which their 'betters' found offensive, but which offered commercial opportunities for those who were able and willing to cater for the newcomers. Even before the coming of the mass market, tension between the raffish and the respectable, the hedonistic and the valetudinarian, had been apparent in the resorts; but the changes of the railway age added a new dimension of class conflict to the existing cultural divisions. Economic vested interests soon coalesced around the cultural polarities, and in most resorts a struggle took place over whether it was more profitable – and proper – to cling to the safety of selectness and respectability, or to encourage the masses and their frivolous amusements. The result of this battle could determine the future character of a resort and, to a large extent, condition its economic fortunes.[1] Moreover, the nature of the conflict brought the seaside resorts into the forefront of the great struggle over the use, content and control of leisure, which has recently emerged as a major theme in the social history of Victorian England.[2]

The second half of the nineteenth century, and especially its last quarter, saw steady improvements in working-class living standards and in the availability of free time which could be enjoyed rather than endured. There were limits to the scope of this improvement, of course, as the poverty surveys at the turn of the century made clear. Unwanted empty hours still hung heavily on the hands of the underemployed casual worker or the ill-paid labourer in the early twentieth century, and overtime was always in demand. As a delegate to a Preston Trades Council meeting pointed out in 1905, 'What they were pleased to call holidays in the third week in August often partook more of the nature of a "lock-out".'[3] On the other hand, long hours for low wages and very limited holidays remained the norm in sweated occupations such as dressmaking, and for shop assistants. By the turn of the century, however, such sufferers were an unfortunate, if significant, minority, and the growing commercialization of mass leisure activities marked the arrival of a generation in which most people were able to commit considerable resources to the pursuit of pleasure in their expanding free time. At the workplace skill dilution, reorganization and new technology might be eating into job satisfaction and shop-floor autonomy in many areas; but in the evenings, at weekends and in the summer a new world of recreational opportunities was opening out to those who had the resources to take advantage. Many thrifty families found themselves able to spend money on enjoyments without prejudicing their ability to save for a rainy day. Immediate gratifications could be pursued with less danger of long-term retribution, and the mechanisms of thrift themselves proved adaptable, in the form of the Christmas club, picnic club or holiday savings club, to budgeting for a special occasion. Under these conditions, seaside visits became an attainable option for a wide spectrum of the working classes, from the spendthrift to the careful, and the behaviour of working-class visitors often reflected this wide range of home circumstances and attitudes.

These developments were significant enough in the eyes of contemporaries to become the focus of serious conflicts. The mid-Victorian middle classes were divided among themselves in attitudes to leisure. Some remained shackled by a persisting belief in the wastefulness and immorality of enjoyment for its own sake, as opposed to participation in a limited range of activities which could be seen to be morally uplifting, intellectually reward-ing or physically invigorating. Others, especially the large number of young and unattached men in London and other major cities, responded eagerly to any opportunity to escape from the confines of a narrow evangelically-dominated respectability.[4] Divisions of this kind remained important throughout the century, although the balance tilted steadily in favour of the pleasure-seekers as the century wore on. Much sharper conflicts of lifestyle and expectations, however, centred on the relationship between the serious-minded, actively religious, self-consciously respectable wing of the middle class, and the apparently unregenerate wing of the working class, whose adherents unashamedly enjoyed drink and its associated pleasures, and saw no reason to modify their behaviour or moderate their language to placate their 'betters'. Wherever these groups came into contact, mutual incomprehension or antipathy was likely to lead to attempts at the restriction or even prohibition of undesirable activities, and to passive or even violent resistance to such intervention from those whose livelihoods or enjoyments were under threat.[5]

This conflict of lifestyles had obvious class overtones, although the lines of conflict were not clear-cut. There was always some middle-class support for popular festivities and entertainments; and on the other hand the self-improving, thrift-and-temperance side of the skilled working class lent its support to causes like the abolition of fairs and wakes, or the limitation of public-house entertainment. Nonconformists were prominent here, but intervention also came from beyond the bounds of the religious mainstream, as advocates of working-class advancement through rationality, respectability and the pursuit of useful knowledge added their opposition to atavistic amusements.[6] Despite these cross-currents, however, attempts to reform or suppress working-class amusements could usually be identified with propertied middle-class groups, some of whom, as employers and shopkeepers, had visible interests in maintaining continuity of production and undermining competition from stallholders, showmen and publicans.[7]

Usually, however, religion, morality and public order dominated the language of conflict. Religion sometimes provided the main motive for intervention in its own right, especially where a Sabbatarian consensus prevailed among 'respectable' opinion, although the declining influence of earnest evangelicalism was beginning to undermine this standpoint by the later nineteenth century.[8] A more general preoccupation with reducing opportunities for crime and sin, especially those centred on the pub, the beerhouse and the music-hall, was at the root of most of the pressure for legislative interference both at national and local level, and there remained an acute fear of the potential threat to life and property posed by the gathering of large, unruly working-class crowds.

Attempts to reform working-class amusements had a positive as well as a negative side. The provision of educationally stimulating, morally improving or at least harmless counter-attractions was a major preoccupation of reformers, but the results were usually very limited. At best, counter-attractions took their place in a widening range of recreational options, but without ousting existing activities. Where popular amusements came to take less offensive form in the eyes of 'respectable' opinion by the turn of the century, this was due mainly to the emergence of a more tolerant middle-class consensus on the one hand, and on the other to the increasing public acceptability of much working-class recreational behaviour. Developments at the seaside can tell us a great deal about this process.

For many serious-minded mid-Victorians, however, the enjoyments of individuals could not be seen in isolation. The evangelical groups, who were often disproportionately influential in local government, saw themselves as their brothers' keepers, with a duty to assist the unregenerate in resisting temptation. They could not feel happy in their own enjoyment of their chosen lifestyle while their brethren followed the road to perdition by revelling in activities which were tolerated by the laws of man but not, in many people's eyes, by the word of God. This active moral and religious dimension gave a sharper edge to conflict in this sphere, though this was blunted again by the late Victorian drift away from the demanding restrictions on acceptable behaviour laid down by the stricter mid-Victorian religious orthodoxy which had spanned the denominations.[9]

It would be misleading simply to divide the Victorian working classes into 'rough' and 'respectable', just as their social superiors were not straightforwardly polarized between 'frivolous' and 'decorous'. There was an extensive area of morally neutral common ground in recreational activities, and this grew during the late nineteenth century.[10] The more strait-laced among the middle classes, however, automatically excluded themselves, and especially their families, from activities which threatened exposure to boisterous behaviour, drink, gambling and sexual embarrassment. In any case, as the secure environments of late Victorian suburbia proliferated, and as even shopping became a socially segregated activity in the 'better-class' streets which were crystallizing out in the central business districts of the larger towns, direct encounters across the double barriers of respectability and class became increasingly rare. As the suburban paterfamilias became accustomed to a peaceful and secluded home life, he became even more unwilling to expose his family to the more boisterous elements of working-class culture.[11]

The sedate, protected middle-class family was probably the most important constituent of the mid-Victorian holiday market; and the invalids and retired residents who also bulked large in the resorts shared similar priorities of peace and security. The more specialized resorts were, indeed, the outermost satellites of suburbia. The suburb was, however, an environment for privatized domesticity, and its enjoyment required residence and considerable financial outlay. The seaside, on the other hand, depended on public enjoyments which were accessible to anyone who could spare the time and expense of the journey; and the coming of cheap and easy access by steamer and railway made it impossible for many resorts to maintain the social homogeneity of inland suburbia. The opening out of new sources of demand ensured that by mid-century many seaside resorts brought together all the contrasting lifestyle patterns of an increasingly complex society, especially on summer weekends. The established resort users found their predominance challenged not only by raffish elements among the middle and upper classes, but also by excursionists drawn partly from the undeferential, unregenerate working class. The creeping invasion of clerks, petty tradesmen and deferential or aspiring members of the working class was disruptive enough to many status-conscious visitors, but the alien lifestyle of many excursionists posed a direct threat to the secure enjoyment of a family holiday or secluded retirement, and therefore to those who catered for those lucrative markets. Inevitably, the struggle over the content and expression of popular amusement was particularly keenly prosecuted in the Victorian seaside resort.

The spatial organization of most resorts, and the preoccupations of most resort users, exacerbated the tensions and conflicts. At the seaside rich and poor, respectable and ungodly, staid and rowdy, quiet and noisy not only rubbed shoulders in the centres of what were still, in most cases and for most of this period, small towns or mere villages; they also had to compete for access to, and use of, recreational space. In all but the most commercialized of seaside resorts, the first priority of almost all visitors was access to the sea, whether for bathing, paddling, playing on the beach, promenading, looking on or inhaling the ozone. This shared objective transcended other differences; and the result was untrammelled competition for the use of the most convenient areas of foreshore, which in the beginning were usually outside the jurisdiction and control of local authorities and developers with a general interest in the prosperity of the resort. Places like Weymouth and Scarborough, where a long-established Corporation owned the foreshore outright, or Brighton, where the Corporation was able to take out a long lease on the foreshore below high water mark from the Crown in 1861, were exceptionally fortunate.[12] In most places ownership of the tidal foreshore was disputed, usually between the Lord of the Manor and the Crown, and if it was in Crown hands the administrative responsibility might lie with one of several bodies, including the Board of Trade, the Office of Woods and Forests and the duchy of Lancaster. Sometimes responsibility was divided, functionally or geographically, between two or more of these bodies, each of which had different attitudes to the purchase, leasing or regulation of Crown property by other individuals or organizations, local authorities included. Sometimes, indeed, the various Crown agencies fought among themselves over the apportionment of responsibility. The result was a happy hunting-ground for lawyers, and a severe problem for local authorities who were anxious to control their most important assets, but found the behaviour of visitors, stallholders and showmen on the beach very difficult to regulate, especially below high water mark, which was where local authority jurisdiction normally ended.[13]

In most resorts, for most of the nineteenth century, confusion of this kind helped to ensure that the foreshore lay open to all who could afford the journey to the seaside, with few constraints on their behaviour. Wherever the disputed territory lay close to the station and easy of access, the working-class excursionist was able to colonize it, bringing stallholders and showmen in his wake. Central Blackpool was the most extreme case. Here the Town Clerk in 1895 listed 316 'standings on the foreshore', including 62 fruit vendors, 57 stalls selling toys, general goods and jewellery, 52 ice cream stalls, 47 vendors of sweets and refreshments and 21 oyster and prawn dealers. Entertainers included 36 photographers and exhibitors of 'photographs, kinetoscopes, picture views, stereoscopes and telescopes', 24 ventriloquists and phrenologists, six quack doctors, six musicians and five conjurors. These figures almost certainly understate the actual numbers. In 1892 the British Phrenological Association found 35 phrenologists on the beach during Whit-week, noting sadly that only four or five of them were 'fully qualified'; and the Town Clerk's list makes no mention of the Blackpool chiropodists who cut excursionists' corns on the sands before admiring audiences.[14] At Weston-super-Mare the Local Board complained in 1886 that 'of late the noise and annoyances on the Foreshore have become

A STARTLING PROPOSITION

Seedy Individual (suddenly and with startling vigour)—

"Aoh ! Floy with me ercross ther sea,
Ercross ther dork lergoon ! !"

Fig. 20 Reproduced from *Mr. Punch at the Seaside*.

intolerable through the Rabble that frequent there, with their Swing Boats, Shooting Stands and Galleries, Games of "Aunt Sally", "Throwing sticks three a penny for cocoanuts", Costardmongers, Likeness Takers, Shows of every description, Occupants of Tents, etc.'[15] Almost every major resort within easy reach of large centres of population encountered similar problems, from New Brighton to Southsea and from Brighton itself to Rhyl and Llandudno. Even the ubiquitous donkeys and horses could get out of hand, and even Teesside could generate an embarrassing amount of working-class demand, as little Redcar's efforts to control its beach demonstrated as early as 1870.[16]

Developments of this kind could render whole stretches of beach untenable for the sedate and serious-minded, anxious to keep their children away from the moral and even physical dangers of these seashore fairgrounds. Even if we leave the working-class excursionist aside, however, there was ample scope for disagreement within middle-class circles about what constituted proper behaviour and legitimate entertainment, on the beach and elsewhere. Bathing, especially, posed persistent problems into the 1870s and beyond, as the widespread taboo on nudity failed to gain universal acceptance even in the most respectable of professional circles. The Rev. Francis Kilvert's aversion to bathing drawers is well known, but even he might have seconded the outraged complaint from Broadstairs in 1874 about 'the lady who delights in swimming to the head of the pier with her nude and whiskered friend upon her back.'[17] Wherever bathing beaches remained unregulated, middle-class visitors set aside conventional objections to nudity or mixed bathing (though seldom both at once), and regulation was often unwelcome. At Scarborough in 1866 attempts to make bathing drawers compulsory generated furious controversy, as bathing-machine proprietors urged that, 'First-class visitors object to wear drawers when bathing'. The Local Board, on the other hand, could point to numerous complaints of indecent bathing, and argued that, 'The existing practice of bathing without a covering is prejudicial to the interests of the place.'[18] Even in a high-class resort like Bournemouth, however, bathing remained difficult to police with limited resources even when powers were available, and a visiting Scotsman noted in 1885 that a great deal of unofficial mixed and family bathing (with costumes) took place from the bathing-machines themselves. But the high cost of hiring a machine, especially for large families, encouraged the wholesale evasion in many resorts of by-laws which required their use.[19] Such free-and-easy practices were not officially sanctioned until the Edwardian years, and then not everywhere; but long before this a significant proportion of the middle-class visiting public was rebelling in practice against the more strait-laced of its preceptors and would-be

OUT OF TOWN

(UNFASHIONABLE INTELLIGENCE)

Visitor. "What a roaring trade the hotels will be doing, with all these holiday folk!"
Head waiter at The George. "Lor bless yer, sir, no! They all bring their nosebags with 'em!"

Fig. 21 Reproduced from *Mr. Punch at the Seaside.*

spokesmen. The same applied to Sunday observance, as by-laws against Sunday cabs, carriages and donkeys were widely ignored in mid-Victorian times. Sunday bathing was commonplace, and where piers, Aquaria and Winter Gardens opened for promenading and 'sacred concerts' in the later nineteenth century they were eagerly patronized by well-dressed visitors.[20]

Middle-class opinion was also far from unanimous about nigger minstrels and other open-air entertainers. Lowestoft in 1876 presented a forbidding countenance:

> The town and beach are entirely free from that low species of amusement to be found in most watering-places, and which is so repugnant to the feelings of those who are seeking healthful recreation. Niggers, German bands, Aunt Sallies and such like find no abiding place at Lowestoft, thus leaving its visitors entirely free from the annoyance of being asked either to buy or give.[21]

At Westgate, on the Kent coast, 'gates and barriers at all the entrances' ensured protection from such undesirables for City gentlemen and their families; and in 1894 Seaford's Pierrots were forcibly evicted from the beach by the Bay Estate Company, although they reappeared in subsequent years.[22] These inhospitable places were strikingly exceptional, however, and as we saw in chapter 7, there was generally a considerable demand from many middle-class visitors for music and outdoor entertainment of a rough-and-ready kind. When Blackpool tried to banish nigger minstrels and itinerant musicians from the streets in 1877, a lady visitor remarked that her party liked 'something to amuse us going on in the street while we have dinner and tea', and warned that, 'Blackpool is getting too grand. Perhaps you will get a better class of company. Much good may it do you.'[23] Such sentiments would have been widely endorsed in many more securely middle-class resorts of the mid-Victorian years.

The pursuit of self-improvement and 'rational recreations' drew some of the more intolerant visitors away from the main resort centres and the beaches near the railheads; but less mobile elements in the respectable visiting public, invalids, the elderly and families with young children, remained closely tied to central resort amenities. It was for these groups that the problem of the working-class excursionists became most taxing, for the differences in taste and opinion within the middle-class visiting public paled into insignificance beside the perceived impact of the tripper at his worst. The clerks and supervisory workers who formed the lowest form of regular visitor life in many mid-Victorian resorts might be patronized and sneered at, in the local press as well as in *Punch*; but the tripper came to be regarded with aversion and even loathing, for instead of aping the holiday manners of his 'betters' he tended to bring with him his own ways of pursuing enjoyment. As well as patronizing and encouraging stalls and sideshows, he offended against peace and quiet by shouting and blowing tin trumpets and penny whistles; he disregarded the sanctity of Sunday; he paid no heed at all to the bathing by-laws; he offended all too often against the new sensitivity to the sufferings of animals by beating the donkeys which were provided for more innocent amusement, he fuelled his activities by heavy drinking, and just as important, he was visually repulsive to people unaccustomed to grimy chokers, short clay pipes and gaudy holiday attire of doubtful cleanliness.[24]

This stereotype of the tripper was by no means universally shared, and perceptions might change over time as places became accustomed to working-class visitors and made the necessary adaptations. Many early responses were angry and apocalyptic, as at Weston-super-Mare in 1856, when a local newspaper complained that cheap fares at Whitsuntide brought 'the dregs of St Philips, Bedminster and other disreputable neighbourhoods [of Bristol]. They destroyed every quiet retreat . . . If these conditions continue the future of Weston-super-Mare as a fashionable resort is at stake. What invalid would dare to emerge from lodgings on such a day?'[25] The Southend of 1874, on the other hand, showed a remarkably restrained press reaction to a full-scale riot by excursionists from a Plaistow timber-yard, who were eventually put down by the police with the aid of a detachment of artillery from Shoeburyness. The Southend Standard criticized the light sentences imposed on the rioters, but refused to use the incident to reinforce or create an excursionist stereotype, preferring to dwell on the 'hundreds' of working-class visitors 'whose conduct has always been of the utmost propriety and respect.'[26] Where regular working-class visitors had not created a favourable impression of this kind, however, the indignant Weston-super-Mare reaction of 1856 was still being replicated in high-class south coast resorts in the 1890s, as we shall see; and where trippers were not perceived as rowdy or disorderly, they might be criticized for dullness and lack of interest in their surroundings, and blamed for lacking the 'culture' to amuse themselves constructively.[27] At Great Yarmouth, on the other hand, the press as early as 1860 could be quite affectionate in its treatment of the working-class visitor, celebrating the arrival of 'excursionists from the heart of the midland counties, buxom, jolly, holiday-seeking people who pic-nic on the sands, eat very thick sandwiches, and always tell the folks at home that they have been in a bathing machine.'[28] The press is a particularly subjective and unsatisfactory source, but responses to the tripper clearly varied widely according to experience, expectation and economic circumstances.

Not surprisingly, however, the Weston Gazette's worries were shared in many other mid-Victorian resorts. The problem of reconciling incompatible modes of enjoyment was at its most acute on the beach, but we have seen that the streets were also difficult to police, and piers and entertainment companies were increasingly tempted to cater for the more numerous rather than the more select of their patrons. But any transition to concentrating on the noisier and less affluent was fraught with peril even for those few resorts where the pattern of demand made it feasible; and the established visitors had created a formidable body of vested interests in support of a 'better-class' season even in Blackpool by the time the excursionist tide began to flow really strongly. Landladies, especially, preferred to cater for middle-class visitors who stayed for long periods, which gave security, and could afford to pay the 'extras' with which the bill was often augmented.[29] A

working-class season would mean administrative complications, while dis-
rupting the established relationships between landlady and visitor which
were so important to a successful business, and removing the gratifications
obtainable from catering for one's 'betters'. Working-class visitors were
vulnerable to trade depressions and unemployment, and their presence
necessitated sharp reductions in tariffs and expensive alterations to house
interiors as the emphasis shifted from quality to quantity. Established
shopkeepers and tradesmen often shared similar vested interests, and readily
joined forces with the middle-class visitors in resisting any attempt at
encouraging the tripper.

Only the remotest late Victorian resorts lacked an excursionist interest of
some kind, however, and the problem of how to react to an increasingly
obtrusive working-class presence had to be faced. Even Lynton, in north
Devon, which lacked a railway until 1898, was receiving 2,500 seaborne
excursionists per year by the early 1870s, and a running battle over
landing-stage proposals followed between shopkeepers anxious for additional trade, and wealthy residents anxious to protect 'the quiet gentility of
the little watering-place' from the drunken Welshmen who plagued nearby
Ilfracombe.[30] Further up the Bristol Channel, even as obscure a resort as
Watchet was subjected to regular visitations by 'artisans, shop boys and
girls' from Taunton, who '[did] not increase the attractions for quiet loving
or family folk'; while in south Devon August Bank Holiday at fashionable
Teignmouth in 1887 saw 'the ordinary visitors . . . nearly banished by the
crowd which surged upon the promenade, the beach, the machines, the
river'.[31]

In almost all resorts the clash of interests between the established holiday
industry, supported by retired residents and business commuters, and the
supporters of the trippers, added an extra dimension to the universal
Victorian conflict over the use and control of leisure time. At the seaside the
usual considerations of public order and morality were entangled with the
thorny problem of identifying the best-paying visitor market. Morality and
marketing became completely intertwined. This interaction ensured that
struggles over the 'social tone' of resorts would be hard-fought, especially
when a strong pressure of working-class demand made its presence felt in an
already well-established resort, as vested interests lined up in defence of the
religious, moral and aesthetic susceptibilities displayed by the most vocal of
the existing visitors.

There were three phases to the excursionist invasion of the seaside, and we
must distinguish them in examining the resorts' responses to working-class
visitors. The first major problems appeared almost as soon as railways or
cheap steamer excursions reached the resorts, but they were quite readily
contained in the short run. Working-class holidays were insufficiently
developed at mid-century to encourage an effective excursionist lobby, and
the numbers involved were few enough to be susceptible to regulation as
local government obtained additional by-law and policing powers. During
the 1850s and 1860s, anyway, most railway companies lost their early
enthusiasm for very cheap excursions, and Sabbatarian pressure, though
never all-conquering, was at its most effective in restraining the particularly

disruptive Sunday trips.[32] By the early 1860s the situation had stabilized almost everywhere, as established resort interests found ways of coping with a limited and occasional tripper presence. Even Blackpool, where up to 12,000 excursionists might arrive at weekends throughout the summer in the early 1850s, attained a measure of equilibrium during the decade. Here, the rush of rowdy 'barbers' apprentices and shoeblacks', ignorant of 'the decencies of society', who arrived on Sunday excursions and scandalized the 'better classes', led one correspondent in 1849 to argue that the town had almost ceased to be fashionable, and could only survive by catering for 'the throng visits and casual expenditure of the lower orders', with internal regulation kept to a minimum. Events were to prove him wrong, for an Improvement Act in 1853 provided adequate powers (for the time being) for regulating bathing, donkeys, hawkers and other disorderly trades. Three years later the Lancashire and Yorkshire Railway abandoned its Sunday excursions, which had been attractive to thirsty people in search of the status of bona fide traveller, which legitimized Sunday drinking. With the help of an additional policeman hired for the season from the Lancashire Constabulary, Blackpool's trippers were brought under control.[33]

Elsewhere the problems were less serious, and excursionist numbers were much smaller even in resorts with many times Blackpool's base population of fewer than 3,000. Scarborough's crowds might rival Blackpool at times, and the direct railway from Manchester brought Southport a bumper crop of excursionists for several years after its opening in 1855;[34] but the big south coast resorts showed much smaller numbers. In 1854 Brighton's 5,000 excursionist arrivals on an August Monday was said to have broken all records in the town, and in 1860 the August peak was 6,000 on a Sunday. At this stage Hastings' cheap trippers could normally be numbered in hundreds rather than thousands.[35] The Thanet resorts were often livelier, with monster excursions sometimes bringing several thousand Londoners, but here the season was already firmly based on the pleasure-seeking London tradesman, whose Cockney accents and flamboyant ways had already driven away many (though not all) of the more sensitive middle-class visitors.[36]

The second phase of working-class penetration, which began in the 1870s and 1880s, posed deeper structural problems for the economies of resorts within easy reach of the areas of rapidly-increasing working-class demand. During the 1870s full-scale working-class season was emerging on parts of the Lancashire and Yorkshire coast, as visits began to extend beyond the weekend, and London artisans and white-collar workers were beginning to make a similar impact in Thanet, at Southend and Great Yarmouth and even, by the mid-1880s, at Hastings.[37] The excursions of this period, moreover, were increasingly emancipated from the tutelage of employers, Sunday Schools and the temperance movement, although these influences had never been strong in the southern half of England, and attempts to channel and control the activities and behaviour of participants had always been very difficult to bring into practical effect. The Southend riot of 1874 arose from an excursion organized, according to the defendants' solicitor, by 'a very respectable firm, who had given the most worthy men in their employ a holiday.' Reports of drunken temperance excursionists were also

commonplace.[38] Even so, the commercially-organized trips which predominated everywhere by the 1870s and 1880s offered fewer built-in
restraints on behaviour than the paternalistic and counter-attractionist
ventures of the early railway age, though the presence of workmates and
neighbours no doubt continued to set limits to most people's exuberance.

The rising tide of working-class visitors encouraged a significant change of
attitude in some of the larger resorts, which gave a sharper edge to conflicts
over visitor behaviour. Blackpool led the way in this respect, with its
powerful pro-excursionist lobby infiltrating the Watch Committee and later
the magistracy, and enabling the town to present an increasingly welcoming
face to the excursionist in the 1870s and 1880s, in spite of complaints in some
quarters.[39] By this time the new visitors were visibly offering opportunities
as well as posing problems in several other nascent popular resorts,
especially Southend, Cleethorpes and Weston-super-Mare.

No resort could yet hope to live by excursionists alone, however, and
some measure of regulation was essential to protect the enjoyment of the
quieter working-class visitors, as well as those who made up the established
holiday trade. If controls were too effective, however, the growth of the
working-class sector was stunted, and although some south coast resorts did
well out of policies of exclusiveness in the late nineteenth century, most of
the fastest-growing centres succeeded in assimilating the working-class
visitor on a large scale. But the road to development of this kind led through
short-term conflict.

Where it occurred, assimilation was the product of an equilibrium
between countervailing forces rather than the result of a master plan. The
excesses of excursionist behaviour could be discouraged by controls on
building development and land use, and by the efficient policing of public
places using special local by-laws aimed at the peculiar problems of resorts.
Social zoning could also be encouraged, enabling the followers of incompatible holiday styles to avoid each other as far as possible; and this was
aided by the late Victorian proliferation of protected satellite resorts a short
tram ride away from the major centres, by the colonization of remote
coastlines, and by the growing popularity of the Continent among the
wealthy, all of which took sensitive elements among the 'better-class'
visitors out of the firing line, while also depriving the resorts of their
spending power. In themselves, however, these developments do not
completely explain the declining incidence of conflict over holiday styles
which becomes apparent towards the turn of the century. In some places, of
course, the battle had been won and lost by this time; but almost all leading
resorts did keep a socially mixed clientèle. The clinching development was
the general (but not universal) retreat from the strict consensus of expectation about public behaviour which had prevailed among the mid-Victorian
'better classes' and the 'respectable' lower down the scale. This relaxation of
norms made many 'better-class' visitors more tolerant of the activities of
their social inferiors. At the same time the standard of behaviour exhibited
by working-class visitors, who were themselves becoming more accustomed
to life at the seaside, was itself becoming more acceptable. These important
changes reflect the declining significance of leisure as a focus of conflict in
society at large during the same period.[40]

We have seen that strict building controls through restrictive covenants were being widely deployed in the resorts, as in suburbia, by early Victorian times, especially by large landowners who sought to develop substantial building estates for residents who might be attracted by a spacious, well-planned, architecturally imposing and fashionable environment, and deterred by the prospect of objectionable neighbours. Such considerations were particularly important at the seaside, where most intending residents of the propertied class had sufficient resources and mobility to command a wide choice of potential resorts and residential districts. Competition to maximize amenity was therefore intense between resorts, and between different areas within their boundaries, on the residential as well as the visitor front. It was one thing to provide a high standard of housing and planning, however; it was quite another to guarantee the maintenance of a high social tone, especially where parts of a resort were known to be attractive to boisterous excursionists. Covenants prohibiting beerhouses and other offensive trades were reinforced in the late nineteenth century by clauses forbidding the use of front gardens or forecourts for trading purposes. This was the fruit of bitter experience in resorts like Blackpool, where the temptation to erect stalls, sideshows and even steam roundabouts in well-placed front gardens proved irresistible to many who were willing to put income before amenity and take advantage of excursionist demand.[41] Large leasehold estates in which the landlords retained an interest were less vulnerable than the small freehold plots which prevailed in Blackpool; but wherever a strong demand from working-class excursionists was channelled towards a relatively high-class area, especially on the sea-front, the residents needed particularly good defences if they were to preserve the social tone of the district. As in suburbia, tramways were seen as a particularly dangerous threat, on aesthetic as well as social grounds. Residents defended their privacy and amenities against this harbinger of noise, bustle and commercialization in many resorts at the turn of the century, but even in upmarket centres such as Torquay and Bournemouth such campaigns were eventually unsuccessful. Only in a few bastions of the wealthy residential interest, most notably Eastbourne and Folkestone, were trams kept out altogether; and in the former place this involved rejecting a petition of 1,049 signatures from the working-class end of the town.[42]

At Eastbourne the dominant landed estates had the local authority's full support in pursuing and maintaining an elevated social tone; and in general estate policy by itself formed an effective barrier to tripper incursions and excesses only in extreme cases. Small resorts like Westgate, Frinton and St Annes, controlled by individual landowners or companies, might insulate themselves from conflict by excluding every artificial attraction which the tripper craved.[43] In larger resorts such as Southport, however, the rôle of local government became important at an early stage to supplement the powers of large landowners, but here, as in other select resorts, estate policy or more piecemeal responses to early demand had already created a strong mid-Victorian residential interest which could operate through local government to shape the town's social tone in a preferred image, pre-empting or suppressing conflict on this issue by the strict regulation of amusements and behaviour. The creation of an imposing built environment, indeed, may itself have alienated, intimidated and silenced the potentially boisterous tripper.

Every sizeable resort received regular visits from excursion trains, despite efforts to lobby the railway companies for exemption, which occurred in every decade from the 1840s into the early twentieth century. But the resorts where controls were exercised at an early stage by landowners and developers were not, in general, the ones in which working-class demand was strongly felt, though this did not inhibit angry responses to the activities of what excursionists there were. Resorts of this kind were able to pre-empt the worst conflicts of culture and interests by making themselves unattractive to unwanted types of visitor. Prevented from enjoying himself in the well-controlled resorts, the tripper went elsewhere, to places which were more difficult to police, or where he could be accommodated in parts of the town which gradually became accepted as his territory. This colonization was invariably controversial, unless it was confined to the old fishing quarter of a resort; and bitter conflict might arise as excursionist influence extended into new areas. This happened at Blackpool's South Beach in the late nineteenth century, as the tripper presence changed its character from occasional nuisance to complete economic domination, and 'better-class' landladies resisted the transformation of their neighbours' front gardens into fore-courts for stalls and amusements.[44] They sought assistance from the Corporation; and this response reflected a widespread and general awareness of the increasing importance of local government policy in determining the social tone of those late Victorian seaside resorts which were developing a mixed visitor economy.[45]

By the 1870s all but the smallest resorts had urban local government institutions, and it had long been apparent that the proper regulation of conduct in public places was as important to a resort's economy as the proper maintenance of its drains; indeed, in some mid-Victorian resorts it was probably a higher priority.[46] But the changes in the visiting public in the later nineteenth century pushed local authorities into seeking extended regulatory powers to cover new areas and new kinds of activity, and to tighten existing controls. The most frequent kinds of intervention involved the regulation of bathing, stalls and entertainments on the foreshore; the more effective policing of streets, promenades and open spaces, especially with regard to hawkers, musicians and fairground operators; and the protection of religious susceptibilities, especially by limiting commercial activities on Sundays.

Most local authority intervention involved the use of local by-laws, which required the sanction of the Local Government Board and, if they broke new ground, that of parliament itself. But proposals were often controversial in the resorts themselves. The most restrictive of the visitors and residents tended to make their opinions heard with the greatest effect in the early stages of policy-making, and local authorities often went beyond the bounds of popular acceptability in formulating proposals. At Hastings in 1885, for instance, a lively public meeting saw the withdrawal of clauses from an intended Improvement Bill which had envisaged restraints on public speaking on the beach; strict legislation against Sunday games; the compulsory licensing of flower girls; and the punishment of those who touted for custom for cabs and boats. Objectors complained of 'over-regulation', and pointed to the heavy punishments envisaged for minor misdemeanours; and the meeting ended with three hearty groans for the Rev. J. W. Tottenham, the most prominent advocate of restrictions.[47]

Hastings was a relatively select resort which was having to come to terms with a large tripper presence at its east end;[48] but similar conflicts were equally characteristic of more unequivocally popular centres where an organized excursionist lobby was emerging. Only in a few resorts, notably Eastbourne, were economic interests so completely bound up with the 'better classes' that by-laws forbidding all kinds of hawking and unofficial outdoor entertainment were uncontroversial; and in Eastbourne's case they had been inherited from the Devonshire estate, with subsequent embellishments which were fiercely defended against outside ribaldry.[49] In most places, the problem was to reconcile the desire of the excursionist for noise and entertainment with the more sedate needs of the 'better-class' visitor; and even Blackpool had to bear in mind the need to avoid scandalizing those who saw themselves as 'respectable'. Even here, indeed, civic leaders who were prone to regard street traders and open-air entertainers as unfair competition for heavily-rated shops and heavily-capitalized entertainment companies, often erred on the side of undue restraint. So, at least, thought the Local Government Board on several occasions around the turn of the century, when the Corporation went to parliament for tighter regulatory powers and found its tougher clauses rejected as unfair restraint of trade. The Board's willingness to defend the small tradesman posed problems for many anxious civic leaders in the last quarter of the nineteenth century, as resorts sought to come to terms with changing demand patterns in the depressed and uncertain economic climate of the late 1870s and 1880s; and the accelerated growth of working-class demand in the 1890s coincided with an increasingly sceptical central government attitude to draconian proposals for the control and suppression of stallholders and showmen.

Local authority intervention was aimed at reducing or preventing noise, obstruction and annoyance to visitors and residents, whether from excursionists or those who catered for them. The power to regulate activities on private property was very limited, although representations to the magistrates (usually from the temperance movement and religious pressure groups rather than local government as such) could halt the expansion of drinking outlets, and pub and beerhouse provision remained static in most resorts while visitor numbers and resident populations increased rapidly in the late nineteenth century.[50] Pubs could also be prevented from opening outside approved hours, and from diversifying their attractions. This apart, regulation was effectively confined to public streets and open spaces, and it was generally directed against itinerant vendors and entertainers, stallholders and showmen rather than the trippers themselves. In some resorts the generally available provisions against drunkenness, disorder, obstruction and violence were strengthened by the adoption of by-laws against specific abuses, such as the furious riding of horses or cycles, the blowing of horns and the making of noise at unsocial hours; and at Bridlington, Scarborough and

Southend the local authorities deliberately imposed high tolls to impede excursionist access to protected enclaves of peace and decorum.[51]

The need for measures of this kind underlines the difficulty faced by resorts in controlling large numbers of working-class visitors with limited legal and policing resources. But the worst annoyances in terms of noise, obstruction, and even threatening behaviour were caused by importunate and often disreputable hawkers, street musicians and itinerant showmen; and it was against these groups that powers of regulation and even suppression were most eagerly sought, even and perhaps especially by the resorts with the largest working-class presence. The problems were not new, and nor were the attempted solutions: Ramsgate's efforts to put down hawkers under an Improvement Act had provoked a riot as early as 1839.[52] But the numbers involved increased rapidly in the late nineteenth century in resorts from Blackpool to Broadstairs, and tradesmen, residents and 'better-class' visitors were unanimous in their condemnation. By the time, however, the Local Government Board had developed a policy of protecting small traders against attempts at suppression by local government, and the resorts which queued to obtain additional powers in the 1880s and 1890s had to make do with palliatives. Standard by-laws provided restraints on street cries between certain hours, banned the use of noisy instruments by hawkers, and empowered householders to require unwanted organ-grinders, German bands or similar performers to retire out of earshot. Local licensing was sometimes adopted, and some resorts tried to reduce the prevailing cacophony by offering special privileges to a particular band or minstrel troupe; but the seaside remained so attractive to hawkers and itinerant musicians, and the law so difficult to interpret and enforce, that they continued to annoy the tradesmen and 'better classes' into the new century almost everywhere.[53]

Hawkers and musicians were not the only groups to cause annoyance by accosting people in the street, although they were probably the most numerous. Prostitutes are rarely mentioned as a problem at the seaside, partly because public discussion was kept to a minimum for fear of adverse comment inland. Brighton's prostitute population was already several hundred strong (at least) in 1859, with a 'large annual importation' from London in the season; and Blackpool and Great Yarmouth admitted to a prostitution problem in the 1880s, when New Brighton's 'Ham and Egg Parade' was also developing an equivocal reputation; but vice, like gambling and illicit drinking, was never as visible in English resorts as it seems to have been in Atlantic City or Coney Island, and the location and timing of prostitutes' activities did not threaten or embarrass the 'respectable' visiting public as they did in parts of London's West End.[54] Much more frequent were complaints about solicitations from people offering services which were perfectly legitimate and even acceptable in themselves, but which were advertised in the cheapest possible way by touting for custom in the streets and other public places. Accommodation, refreshments, boat and charabanc trips and entertainments were all pertinaciously peddled in this way, and hordes of touters congregated at the railway stations and in the main thoroughfares of popular resorts. This problem was as old as resort life. It

Fig. 22 Royal Prince's Parade, Bridlington, a genteel enclave protected by the local authority from plebeian intrusion by a controversial four-penny toll (reproduced from *A Pictorial and Descriptive Guide to Bridlington and District*, 4th edn).

had been prevalent in eighteenth-century Epsom and Tunbridge Wells, and in early nineteenth-century Scarborough stage-coaches had been besieged by touts with tradesmen's cards. The rise of obscure backstreet lodging- and eating-houses which catered for the less affluent gave an added urgency to an increasing volume of touting in the late Victorian popular resorts, however. A Southend landlady who was fined in 1894 had invested £20 in a house, but took nothing in her first three months, and was subsisting on a few shillings a week sent by her journeyman husband in London; and similar problems were apparent in the back streets of Blackpool, Scarborough and Cleethorpes. Touting was also rife, however, in up-market centres like Llandudno, Hastings, Southport, Barmouth and Aberystwyth.[55] Again, the Local Government Board proved sympathetic to the needs of small businesses, and was unwilling to allow by-laws to prohibit touting altogether when resorts queued for them in the 1880s and 1890s. Blackpool had to tackle the problem early, and its 1879 Improvement Act allowed a £2 penalty for touting for lodging-houses, hotels and various entertainments. Eating-houses were forgotten, and had to be included later; and various legal loopholes were exploited. But subsequent requests from other resorts sometimes had a rough ride in parliament, and Scarborough had to pull out all the stops to obtain similar powers in 1890, stressing the prevalence of misrepresentation, the nuisance caused by litter from handbills, and the employment of professional touts. In any case, enforcement was difficult, owing to the sheer numbers involved and the difficulty of obtaining witnesses, and local magistrates often shared the Local Government Board's concern to protect small businesses which could not afford legitimate

A QUIET DRIVE BY THE SEA
A Brighton bath-chairman's idea of a suitable route for an invalid lady

Fig. 23 Reproduced from *Mr. Punch at the Seaside*.

advertising. Touting remained an important and irrepressible aspect of most resort economies up to and probably beyond the First World War.[56]

Where excursionists were particularly obtrusive, street obstructions came to take on a more permanent form, as stalls appeared in forecourts and in front of shops, to the dismay of advocates of tidiness and uniformity. Even the earl of Scarbrough's Skegness, admittedly 'the noisiest and most crowded of the Lincolnshire seaside places, except Cleethorpes' according to Murray's *Guide* in 1890, acquired a row of stalls outside cottages near the station, selling shellfish, rock, ginger ale and even beer dispensed from metal bath-tubs.[57] The most spectacular developments, however, took place in Blackpool, where stalls spread rapidly through the central entertainment district during the 1890s. By 1901 there were 700, selling everything from fish and garden produce to crockery and bibles, and making the whole area resemble a Lancashire cotton town on market day. The stalls were clearly very profitable, but complaints about them intensified with the failure of an attempt to levy a separate rate on them in 1898, and in its 1901 Improvement Bill the Corporation sought the power to prevent the further spread of stalls (which could not be dealt with under the building by-laws) and even to suppress existing ones. These aims were supported by the Tradesmen's Association and the ratepayers at large, but the well-organized stallholder interest was treated sympathetically by the parliamentary committees. The existing stalls were seen as an established and legitimate form of property, and full compensation was promised for any existing stall suppressed. Plans had to be submitted for new stalls over four feet high, but no penalties were provided for infringement. Even these watered-down provisions were sufficient to stop the further spread of stalls, but the parliamentary response had ensured that the hundreds of stallholders in the central entertainment district could continue to contribute to the distinctive character of what was fast becoming a trippers' paradise.[58]

Blackpool's stall problem was unique in scale, but it illustrates the pressure for intervention that could be created by responses to a very high level of working-class demand, even in one of the first resorts to make the transition to overall dependence on the working-class market. Blackpool's relatively free and easy attitude to tripper behaviour was a distinct asset, as had been realized in the early 1880s when campaigns against street musicians had been noticeably relaxed; but even here there were limits, and the evident popularity of stalls with trippers was not deemed sufficient recompense for unfair competition, obstruction and loss of amenity. The determined nature of the Corporation's expensive and generally unsuccessful attempt at intervention shows that even the most plebeian areas of the sea front in the pioneer working-class resort could not afford to become too 'common'.

The streets of resorts were difficult enough to control, especially on summer Saturdays, when the crush in even little Barmouth's narrow streets was enough to push its local authority into seeking special traffic regulation powers in 1891.[59] Between the station and their lodgings, or the sea, visitors almost everywhere had to run a gauntlet, contending with a motley crew of touts, hawkers, minstrels, bands, wandering showmen and stallholders. The more popular the resort, the greater the infestation, and though the visiting public at Blackpool or Southend was more tolerant than at Eastbourne or Folkestone, the most urgent and controversial initiatives for regulation came from the resorts with the largest working-class presence. But there was a general validity to *Punch*'s definition of 'Midsummer madness. – Going to the seaside in search of quiet.'[60] In many places, too, the problems of the streets were exacerbated by the even greater difficulty of policing private open spaces and controlling activities on the beach.

Vacant lots and estates awaiting development close to promenades and town centres often generated complaints from neighbours and fastidious visitors in late Victorian times because many landowners or developers were unable to resist the temptation to make an interim profit by letting their land for fairground amusements. The law of nuisance was rarely, if ever, sufficient to cope with such activities, and the powers of local authorities to control temporary structures under the building by-laws were riddled with legal loopholes. Usually these problems were short-term, but where a site was disadvantaged for building by legal or topographical difficulties, fairgrounds could become well-established. Blackpool's controversial Pleasure Beach developed in this way on low-lying land beyond the southern tip of the promenade, and Southend saw bitter controversy over the letting of the Greens along its Marine Parade for fairground purposes. These were copyhold tenements on which the Lord of the Manor owned the soil, subject to general rights of access and enjoyment which successfully inhibited the erection of permanent buildings by his tenants. Gypsies and stallholders claimed the right to operate shooting galleries and other entertainments there, and were encouraged by speculative lessees, with the Lord of the Manor unwilling to intervene. The local authority bought up the Greens and enclosed them between 1884 and 1901, but the last survivor, Pawley's Green, was also the rowdiest, provoking a crescendo of complaint from nearby householders in the mid-1880s. In 1901, indeed, a force of 28 policemen and foreshore inspectors proved insufficient to clear it. The problem was not confined to the Greens: a few years earlier residents had objected so forcefully to a four-acre fairground extension to an existing commercial park (which was intended to encourage the growth of the adjoining building estate) that the Mayor refused to perform the formal opening ceremony.[61]

Fairgrounds on vacant land were most prevalent and long-lived in the more plebeian resorts; but Brighton, Paignton and Southport all had similar problems around the turn of the century.[62] These were essentially localized nuisances, affecting nearby residents by damaging their amenities and driving their visitors away, although Blackpool's Pleasure Beach was said to have lowered the tone of an extensive area of the town's South Shore.[63] Much more serious for a resort as a whole was the colonization of the foreshore by fairground activities, coupled with the other problems of public order and morality which arose when local authorities were unable to control their beaches. This hit directly at a resort's main stock in trade, and it was a common problem in the late nineteenth and early twentieth century.

The growth of unregulated hawking and alfresco entertainment on the beach was already becoming a recognized 'nuisance' in many resorts in the late 1860s and early 1870s, when concern over indecent bathing was also mounting. Resorts all over the country sought by-law powers to regulate their foreshores at this time, as the inadequacies of existing legislation became apparent, and in 1870 an important agreement between the Board of Trade and Redcar Local Board allowed the latter to extend its boundary to cover the beach between high and low water mark, purely for regulatory purposes, with the Board of Trade reserving all of the Crown's rights in the beach and reserving also the right to approve all by-laws.[64] This concern to safeguard Crown prerogatives was shared by the Office of Woods and Forests, which seems to have been less forthcoming than the Board of Trade; and outright purchases of foreshores or foreshore rights were rare until the 1890s, though some authorities were able to take out leases.[65]

The Redcar precedent was widely taken up in the 1870s; but it proved very difficult to frame by-laws which were both effective and acceptable to central government. This was the case even at Great Yarmouth, where Corporation ownership of the foreshore did not prevent the evasion of successive attempts at regulation between the mid-1870s and the mid-1890s.[66] Where other interests had claims on the foreshore which conflicted with those of the Crown or local government, the legal problems were compounded, for individual property rights were carefully safeguarded in this context even when uncertainly defined. New Brighton's Local Board came up against this problem in the late 1880s, after its pretended right to regulate the foreshore (above high water mark in this case) was successfully challenged in the courts by adjoining owners who claimed that their rights extended to this debatable land. The claim was open to dispute, but it was sufficient to free the area from local government controls, and the 'perfect Pandemonium' which ensued drove the Local Board to parliament to seek a remedy in 1890. Despite admitted dangers to life and limb from round-abouts and furious riding, the Local Board had great difficulty in recovering the power to control erections on unenclosed land.[67] Llandudno and Weston-super-Mare suffered similar problems due to manorial claims on parts of the foreshore, and Southend's foreshore rights were described by a judge in 1890 as 'an interesting legal question'. This was a generally applicable phrase.[68]

Administrative and legal remedies for these problems took many years to evolve, for by-laws covering beach activities proved difficult to frame even when the power to enforce them became available. Several resorts shared the experience of Blackpool and Weston-super-Mare, where successive attempts at clearing or controlling the beaches were rebuffed as new loopholes or conflicts of jurisdiction became apparent. Most resorts had to wait until the 1890s for effective powers; and by this time their efforts at strict control or even suppression were running up against the concern of the Local Government Board and Home Office to safeguard the rights of small traders, on the beach as well as in the street.[69] In many cases, indeed, the same people were involved, as their sphere of activity varied according to the state of the tide. By this time, too, a further constraint on beach regulation had developed in the popular resorts: the rich variety of foreshore entertain-ment had become an important attraction in itself, and not just to excursion-ists. By the 1890s, the wheel had turned full circle, and a resort might actually damage itself economically by controlling its beach too strictly. Blackpool discovered this in 1897, when an attempt to clear the beach gave rise to such a chorus of mocking disapproval in the inland press that it was hastily abandoned, and a limited number of ratepayers were allowed to occupy carefully-spaced pitches on a designated stretch of the central beach. Rents were introduced in 1902 to pacify the local shopkeepers, and this form of beach supervision proved both popular and profitable. For 20 years before this, Blackpool, like other popular resorts, had vacillated between tolerance and attempted strictness, with the Corporation uncertain where its duty and interests lay, but by the 1890s the die was cast. By the time the necessary powers were available, the changes they were intended to prevent had already taken place, and the popular resorts were obliged to stop short at moderate measures of regulation.[70]

Attempts to exclude certain activities from the beach, or to regulate them by licensing and the collection of rent, brought seaside local government, representing substantial trading interests, into conflict with a lower class of fishermen and stallholders, generally native to the area, who combined an eagerness to make a profit out of catering for visitors with a deep attachment to their customary right to use the beach for trading purposes. In practice, most beaches had been treated as common land by the locals, except where the owners of the foreshore took steps to preserve their rights to sand and gravel and their control over certain kinds of fishing. But fishermen in the resorts had long proved tenacious of their traditional rights. They had been very difficult to dislodge from the Steine at Brighton, and in 1867 a new sea wall at Bognor led to the arrival at the Board of Trade of a mud-stained petition from the local fishermen, alleging that the wall interfered with 'ancient rights of Bathing, Fishing, Beaching and Boating.'[71] A local clergyman had been the moving spirit behind this unsuccessful initiative, but subsequently the beach trading interests in the popular resorts proved quite capable of petitioning on their own account. At Weston-super-Mare in 1882 the donkey carriage proprietor James Williams began a four-year struggle against the Local Board by-laws thus: 'dear Sir the Weston Peple has allways had full liberty on the shore . . . but now the Commisioners say they have full power over it and make bye laws over it thereby depriving the Poor Peple of using it'. Three years later he was even more direct: Local Board control 'would deprive a large number of us of our daily bread', and he organized a petition against it.[72] This opposition proved unavailing, as the Local Board extended its boundaries to cover the beach below high water, and in 1889 effective new by-laws were introduced. These were also resisted, and the Stark family, who had kept swings on the sands for many years, went to prison rather than pay their fines after refusing to move on.[73] Petitions against foreshore regulation also reached the Board of Trade from Brighton and Southsea, and at Exmouth in 1906 Mrs Bessie Hunt emulated the Starks by going to prison after defying a judge's injunction to cease trading on the beach.[74] The pretensions of private companies were also resisted, as Brighton's fishermen petitioned successfully against a proposed Central Pier in 1884 and 1887, and in 1874 the 'Battle of Southsea' saw petty bourgeois radicals, supported by a large and mainly working-class crowd, demolishing barriers erected by the Pier Company to keep the area between Pier and Assembly Rooms quiet and select. The pattern of conflict identified here by John Field, with 'the local bourgeoisie occasionally trying to make both areas more exclusive, and generally finding themselves frustrated by the assertion of customary use-rights', was repeated in many resorts during the last quarter of the nineteenth century, and it was only during the last decade that the 'local bourgeoisie' and its allies began to get the upper hand.[75]

Even when local government controls became more sophisticated and effective in the 1890s, as improved by-laws and more clear-cut jurisdictions were supervised by local Watch Committees, officials, magistrates and even, in some cases, borough police forces, the numbers and problems involved ensured that regulation could only operate effectively in moderation and working with the grain of demand. By the late nineteenth century, a growing mutual tolerance between 'better-class' and working-class visitors and interests was making this much less difficult in most resorts. This was especially the case where the tripper was well-established, as resort authorities realized the need to curb excesses without angering or alienating the ordinary excursionist, whose contribution to many local economies was visibly growing in importance. Such attitudes (for they were less coherent or articulated than plans or strategies) were encouraged by the reduced social tensions which resulted from the specialization of resorts and parts of resorts

Fig. 24 The Fort at Margate on a quiet day (reproduced from *Black's Guide to Canterbury and the Watering Places of East Kent,* 1915).

which was becoming firmly established by the 1890s. This enabled those who found noise, bustle, frivolity and the company of social inferiors uncongenial, to seek quieter and more select havens, sometimes within the same resort.

In some places, such as Scarborough, topography aided the development of quite elaborate social sub-divisions; even where towns were not so obviously divided by physical features, however, well-defined patterns of social zoning emerged in residential areas, in the use of the beach, and even to some extent in entertainment. At Southend the 'prim respectability' of Cliff Town could be contrasted by 1876 with the old town centre where visitors danced in the streets and consumed beer by the gallon and mussels by the saucer, while by 1901 nearby Westcliff had, in the *Daily Telegraph*'s eyes, at least a 'suggestion of the Leas at Folkestone.'[76] At Margate in the 1880s the Fort attracted 'the more staid and matronly portion of the visitors', while the Jetty was a magnet for 'those who desired to exhibit their wardrobes and indulge in a little innocent "mashing".'[77] At Great Yarmouth, as at Blackpool, the 'masses' congregated in the town centre while those who wanted quiet went to either end of the sea front. Great Yarmouth also contrived to segregate its visitors by time; it was described in 1895 as 'a great place for trippers and 'Arries during August, but a large number of the better class of visitors may be found during the other summer months.'[78] This was an unusual bonus away from the south coast, however, and in most places the segregation of visitors with different tastes and drawn from different classes was achieved largely through geographical diffusion. In some resorts entertainments were also socially segregated, as companies clung to an established 'better-class' clientèle or found it easier to cater for a single class of customer. Each of Blackpool's three piers had well-defined social characteristics of its own by the mid-1890s, and the North Pier with its orchestra and church parade had long been sharply differentiated from the South Jetty (later the Central Pier) which catered for a lower class of visitor. But such divisions of the market were far from universal, and in Blackpool itself the Tower and Winter Gardens were able to accommodate the whole range of visitor tastes at a single admission price by the turn of the century.[79]

In some of the well-established popular resorts, indeed, divisions among the visitors were mattering less by the 1890s, and a common recreational culture was developing at the seaside for the pleasure-loving of all classes. Mainstream middle-class attitudes were relaxing, and working-class behaviour was widely perceived to be improving. Objections to the content of popular entertainment became the preserve of fringe elements associated with Nonconformity, who could no longer be seen to represent a consensus of 'respectable' opinion; and attitudes to Sunday observance began to undergo a similar shift. The changing basis of conflict over 'Lord' George Sanger's Hall-by-the-Sea at Margate is revealing. In 1874, at the beginning of the Sanger régime, a concerted attack was launched at the licensing sessions, as 240 people signed a memorial protesting against the regular Sunday concerts, for admission to which a sixpenny 'refreshment ticket' was required. All the local clergy and ministers featured among the memorialists, who complained that the Sunday band had played sacred music for the wrong motives, and inveighed against blasphemous comic songs and the 'immoral' conversations which were allegedly encouraged by Sanger's 'classical' statues. Sanger had police support and a counter-petition of his own, and kept his licence, but the survival of the whole enterprise had clearly been at risk. Twenty years later a much narrower attack by religious interests on Hall-by-the-Sea's regular licensing extensions was apparently unaccompanied by any petition or memorial, and a local newspaper felt able to dismiss the unsuccessful perpetrators as 'these busy bodies'.[80]

Sunday observance more generally provides a useful touchstone of the prevailing middle-class consensus. We have seen that narrow Sabbatarianism was far from universal among mid-Victorian middle-class visitors; but many resorts were still trying to tighten up in the early 1870s, as Brighton and Blackpool abolished Sunday street-watering, and restrictive by-laws against cabs and even bathing proliferated.[81] Blackpool's attempts to clamp down on Sunday trade and entertainment were directly motivated by the fear of losing 'better-class' custom, especially to the town's strictly-controlled rival Southport; but long before the end of the decade its policy was shifting again, as the composition of the visiting public altered and a well-publicized epidemic knocked Southport out of the reckoning. The Aquarium began to open on Sundays in 1876, and three years later the Winter Gardens opened its doors to Sunday promenaders, in defiance of threats of prosecution. In 1883 the same company began a regular programme of Sunday 'sacred concerts', and in 1887 the new Chief Constable abandoned all attempts to prosecute shopkeepers under the Sunday trading laws after the magistrates had refused to penalize a batch of offenders. By this time one of the local

Fig. 25 Two faces of Blackpool's North Pier: as popular playground on a crowded Easter Sunday, 1911, and as select promenade after church on a quieter Sunday (reproduced from *The North Pier Blackpool 1863–1913*).

newspapers was prepared to accept that Sunday entertainments were 'a growing taste', and that strict Sabbatarians were obsolete, though it urged that the town should be careful not to move too fast at the risk of outpacing changes in consensus morality. In 1896, however, the last bastion crumbled as the Corporation itself, swayed by the changing views of moderate Churchmen, joined the Sabbath-breakers by operating its trams on Sundays. By this time the loss of 'better-class' custom was no longer an effective bogey, and the committed Sabbatarians were isolated by the general awareness that Sunday observance was no longer a paying proposition.[82]

Blackpool was, admittedly, well ahead of most of its rivals in the liberation of Sunday, although Margate's Hall-by-the-Sea and Brighton's Aquarium were prominent among the pioneers of the revival of Sunday entertainment.[83] Rhyl's pier was unusual in introducing Sunday concerts as early as 1885, when the Winter Gardens also began to open on Sunday, in spite of the presence of two clergymen on the Board of Directors. Previous initiatives in 1879 and 1882 had been thwarted by an outcry from the pious, but, as a newspaper correspondent remarked, 'time works wonders'.[84] By 1895, indeed, Sunday entertainment in the form of bands, sacred concerts, promenading and steamer excursions was generally acceptable, though still not uncontroversial, even in the most strait-laced of the high-class south coast resorts.[85] Bournemouth and Southport lagged behind, but even here Sunday concerts were regularly permitted by 1913, when Bournemouth had just acquired Sunday trams, although Southport still forbade trams, taxis, and boats on the Marine Lake, and the municipal fountains were cut off on the Sabbath.[86] Municipal authorities, indeed, were particularly vulnerable to Sabbatarian pressure, and even Southend was still putting clauses forbidding Sunday opening into its leases on the eve of the First World War.[87] Some of the smaller and more sedate resorts no doubt had to exercise more caution than the major centres which have dominated this discussion, but progress towards a 'free Sunday' was far more advanced at the seaside than inland in 1913, as a survey organized by Blackpool's Chief Constable confirmed.[88] The seaside was clearly a liberating agent for middle-class *mores*, and the thawing out of the seaside Sunday in most places by the 1890s is a symptom of a more free-and-easy attitude to holiday enjoyment.

The relaxation of middle-class attitudes was far from complete, of course, especially where sexual overtones were present. Blackpool's Chief Const-able was able to abolish the town's public-house singing-saloons in 1900 on the grounds that they corrupted the young, and a successful campaign against indecent mutoscopes or 'what-the-butler-saw' machines had been conducted a year earlier.[89] Subsequently, however, campaigns for restraints on entertainments and behaviour in Blackpool were channelled almost entirely through the Free Church Council, which was visibly and in-creasingly at odds with mainstream opinion on most issues. In 1907 this organization scored a rare success by forcing the Central Pier's public dancing to move from the pierhead to a safe distance from the promenade, where it would not tempt impressionable visitors. These grounds alone made little impression on the Council, however, and the Free Churchmen were unsuccessful until they emphasized legal and practical rather than moral problems. In any case, they were increasingly out of step with the prevailing (if sometimes grudging) tolerance of a wide range of entertainments which was now exhibited by most religious bodies.[90] By 1913, with Sunday cinemas coming into vogue, complaints about the 'bad taste' of jokes about curates by a sea-front concert party could still be made even in a resort like Margate, but where they would have drawn a concerned and sympathetic response 25 or 30 years earlier, they now fell on stony ground.[91] Much that was unacceptable or controversial in most resorts in 1880 became tolerable to mainstream middle-class public opinion during the 1890s, and was taken as a matter of course by the eve of the First World War.

Commentators on the resorts were also beginning to detect improvements in working-class behaviour at the seaside. Complaints of aggressive mannerisms, drunkenness, dirtiness, spitting and unbecoming forms of dress declined rapidly in frequency and prominence in the late nineteenth century, and excursionists began to receive a greater measure of praise and encouragement. Stray comments suggesting amused tolerance of tripper behaviour can be culled from such resorts as Southend, Great Yarmouth and Ramsgate for the 1860s and 1870s, but a more positive and thorough-going change of attitude first became apparent in the northern resorts in the early 1880s, gathering momentum steadily thereafter. The *Methodist Recorder* in 1883 praised the sobriety and standards of dress of Blackpool's holiday crowds, and commented that the spectacle of 'vast masses of people' enjoying themselves rationally was 'one of the sublimest triumphs of modern civilisation'. In the same year a *Daily Telegraph* correspondent recommended Blackpool as an excellent advertisement for the value of cheap but good-quality entertainment in 'checking visibly the dissipation that springs from idleness and lassitude', and stressed that 'I did not observe a single case of drunkenness or depravity.'[92] Working-class behaviour at several other popular resorts prompted reflections on improving standards of dress, behaviour and rationality in the late nineteenth century, and a Southend guide-book of 1901 praised the 'jollity and laughter' and 'general good fellowship' at the working-class Cockney end of the Marine Parade.[93] Explanations for the perceived improvements in behaviour varied. A Weston-super-Mare newspaper ascribed it to the softening presence of wives and children; the *Daily Telegraph* stressed the availability of rational amusements; credit was also given to rising living standards and the elementary school system. The *Hastings and St Leonards Observer*, in a moment of complacency, thought that excursionists were being 'civilised' by the places they visited into more sober and rational behaviour, though credit was also given to police coercion; and similar comments were made in the Lake District.[94]

The picture is not entirely rosy, however, for the 1890s saw a third phase of tripper penetration which was angrily received in some resorts. Where the working-class presence had grown in importance steadily over the years, resorts with mixed visitor economies had learned to cope with trippers, and working-class visitors in their turn had learned what was expected of them at the seaside. In the 1890s, however, rising real wages enabled a new class of young and unruly excursionists to invade resorts which were unaccustomed to or unprepared for rowdy and drunken behaviour. All along the south coast, complaints proliferated, and they were echoed in North Wales, where drunken Liverpudlians scandalized sedate Llandudno, and even at Minehead, where Bristol trippers were the villains.[95] At Bournemouth the fear was expressed in 1894 that without the introduction of specially-protected select areas and graded admission charges 'the rougher unwashed element will most effectually drive away the more desirable class, the orderly and refined.' Even in Bournemouth, it appears, 'vulgarity' could be seen 'disporting itself, smoking and spitting till one is almost sick.'[96] In this context the strong opposition in remote, respectable Aberystwyth in the same year to proposals for commercial entertainment on quite a large scale, including parks, pavilions, boating lakes, bicycle tracks and refreshment rooms, becomes understandable. Opponents stressed that the town had built its prosperity on the longstay visitor, and argued that the new schemes would need to attract large numbers of excursionists, and change the character of the resort, if they were to pay.[97] This was a sharper dilemma than had been faced by resorts like Blackpool, Rhyl and Cleethorpes in earlier years, because the alternative to middle-class family specialization was visible and disturbing to a resort which had hitherto been insulated by distance from the pressures of working-class demand. Closer to the population centres, however, New Brighton's Local Board was also making a bid to preserve the town's respectability by discouraging excursionist entertainments, with insufficient success to prevent the resort from falling uncomfortably and unsuccessfully between two stools.[98]

Significantly, complaints of rowdyism in the 1890s were associated with trippers who came from the more anonymous and often unskilled working-class environment of London and Liverpool, rather than the northern textile towns and similarly stable working-class communities where whole districts were accustomed to going on holiday together, with neighbours and workmates informally policing each other's behaviour. Here, resorts had been able to adapt, in organization and outlook, to a working-class presence, and working-class visitors on the spree had had time to learn the etiquette of seaside holidaymaking, and to become accustomed to the expectations of local authorities and 'better-class' holidaymakers. But some parts of the country gained this experience earlier and learned their lessons faster than others; and London, in particular, was still sending raw, inexperienced and rowdy day-trippers to relatively select resorts in the 1890s.

By the Edwardian years this last burst of conflict had burned itself out, as even Torquay found itself coming to terms with the tripper, although Teignmouth's Town Clerk was still inveighing in 1905 against 'train-loads of half-drunken people' arriving on day excursions.[99] Most of the larger resorts had found ways of assimilating the working-class visitor, and most of the smaller ones had settled for a sedate holiday style which offered no welcome to those who sought boisterous alternative pleasures. The needs of a complex holiday market had been met by a combination of regulation, coercion, cultural assimilation, specialization and subdivision. Mainstream middle-class and working-class culture had become reconciled in mutual tolerance at those resorts where the classes regularly mingled, and this reflected the more general retreat of the leisure question from a central place in contemporary controversy, although the cinema, especially, was to perpetuate many of the old arguments into the 1930s and beyond.[100] But the Victorian moral and religious conflicts had lost their edge at the seaside, as the old moral certainties no longer imposed themselves on the respectable, while the old economic doubts no longer plagued civic leaders and entrepreneurs. Even in the demanding setting of the seaside resort, the content and control of working-class leisure had become a matter of indifference rather than a cockpit of controversy.[101] The popular resorts, indeed, had long been setting a trend towards a freer approach to the enjoyment of leisure time, and in this as in many other respects they came to exercise an important influence on the nation at large.

9 The seaside and English society

Two duties remain: one explanatory, the other exploratory. We must account for the pace and nature of seaside resort development in this period, and we must examine the relationship between the seaside holiday industry and the wider economy and society.

Explanations must begin on the demand side. Why did the seaside become so universally popular, and how did it contrive to remain fashionable over such a long period? The roots of the answer lie in the peculiar nature of English society, for the seaside holiday long remained an English, or at least a British, phenomenon, and when it was exported overseas the most enthusiastic early response came in the United States.[1] The England of the Industrial Revolution was a remarkably open society, at least on the surface and among the propertied; whatever the limitations on effective social mobility, wealth was capable of buying a good measure of prestige and acceptance even when newly come by, and conspicuous consumption and public display acquired a validity of their own as the fashion cycle spread down the social scale during the eighteenth century. This was above all an emulative society (though this should not blind us to the persistence of deep if selective attachments to tradition at all levels); and the competition for status put pressure from below on established families to express and validate their position by appropriate patterns of consumption, which in turn were copied by aspiring inferiors as best they could. London's West End, the provincial capitals and county towns, and above all the spas all felt the impact of this spiral of conspicuous consumption, and it gave a powerful impetus to the early growth of the seaside resorts, fuelled as it was by royal patronage.[2] As William Hutton remarked in 1788 in precisely this context, 'Wherever the people in high life take the lead, the next class eagerly follow.'[3]

Emulation and social competition were the most important triggers of resort expansion; but they do not explain the channelling of demand into the seaside, or the subsequent consolidation and sustained rapid growth of the holiday industry. Similar explanatory limitations apply to other essential preconditions for the rise of the seaside, such as the spreading increase in disposable wealth and later in real wages, the steady flow of transport improvements (of which the railways were only the most spectacular), and the social, financial and legal innovations which enabled landowners, developers and entrepreneurs to respond quickly and appropriately to rising demand.[4] All this gives us a necessary contextual framework for understanding the seaside, without explaining the nature of the phenomenon itself. It provides the how, but not enough of the why.

The seaside's crucial advantages can be summed up under two headings: accessibility and adaptability. Once the attractions of the seaside had been discovered and publicized, the geography of England and Wales worked strongly in its favour. No major population centre was more than 70 or 80 miles from some point on the coast, although practical journey distances were often significantly longer. This simple geographical fact must be remembered alongside the social and economic explanations for the unique ubiquity and scale of seaside resort development in England during this period.[5] More to the point, however, is the way in which the seaside came to offer something for everyone to an extent which was not shared by the spas and scenic areas which also came into favour during the eighteenth century. The medical properties of seawater provided the first impetus at the highest social levels; but from the beginning, as we have seen, the seaside offered much more than this. It was capable of accommodating the formal institutions of the spa and other leisure centres, and the shoreline (and later the pier) offered opportunities for alfresco promenading which added the medical *rationale* of sea air to the social imperative of public display. But the seaside also offered an escape from formality, as children found their niche on the beach, and more individualistic communicants with Nature, History and landscape could be sure to find objects of interest. As the holiday market broadened during the nineteenth century, the seaside was capacious enough to find room for transplanted versions of popular inland amusements, and innovative enough to provide distinctive variants of its own in a seductive combination of the novel and the familiar. Even within a single resort, the different needs of different classes, cultures, temperaments and age-groups could be catered for; and the endless variety of a very long and indented coastline, some parts of which were much more accessible than others, enabled a multitude of little resorts to pander to more specialized tastes. It was this polymorphous flexibility and adaptability that enabled the seaside to become at once fashionable and popular, and to satisfy the whole range of Victorian and Edwardian tastes and needs.

The success of the seaside thus depended on the existence of a wide variety of resort environments. The necessary diversity came about spontaneously, for individual resorts responded to demand in many different ways according to the pull of location, topography, transport, landownership, social structure, entrepreneurial outlook and local government policy. These influences, acting in often complex and sometimes conflicting interrelationship, and affected in their turn by the timing of initiatives for development, ensured that no two resorts catered for quite the same market in quite the same way, with the result that the endless variety of the English seaside, as set out in an enormous output of popular guide-books, visibly offered satisfaction somewhere to almost everyone.

What were the most important influences on the characteristics of individual resorts? Before the 1840s, the inscrutable vagaries of fashion and medical recommendation bulked disproportionately large, and accessibility from the centres of fashionable society in London or Bath was a major influence on rate of growth. The early starters reaped spectacular benefits from royal and ducal patronage, and where land and capital were available to build on such advantages, a relatively uncomplicated market mechanism enabled growth to proceed apace, with smaller offshoots from the leading resorts appearing to cater for seekers after exclusiveness, privacy or economy.

In the railway age, however, transport and distance from population centres came to have only secondary importance except on the remoter coastlines. The early arrival of a railway could give a resort a head start over actual and potential rivals, admittedly, but communications arteries between population concentrations and coastlines tended to create wide areas of potential development, especially where routes hugged the shore for any distance, without determining the pace and character of that development in any particular place. Resorts close to population centres, and easily accessible from them, had a wider range of potential visiting publics, but the examples of Worthing, Southport and Eastbourne, or on a smaller scale Westgate, Lytham St Annes and Filey, are sufficient to show that they were not foredoomed to specialization in the working-class market.[6] The increasing complexity of holiday demand with the coming of the railways ensured that henceforth the key influences on the development of individual resorts were to be local. At this stage landownership became very important, especially in the newer centres. The existence of a large estate with an interest in promoting and protecting high-class development was a very strong predisposing influence towards a high social tone, especially if other resorts drawing on the same population centres made themselves attractive and accommodating to the tripper and soaked up working-class demand. The residential and trading interests which were attracted by a policy of controlled development tended to reinforce the aims of the landowners, as they created and dominated local government institutions which were designed to perpetuate or enhance the existing 'social tone'. Before the railway age, however, similar local élites and vested interests had appeared spontaneously in response to the prevailing flows of upper- and middle-class demand, even in resorts with fragmented landownership (like Brighton and Worthing) or passive landowners (like Exmouth and Torquay). Moreover, the persisting general importance of the solid middle-class market ensured that such groupings became important in almost all early- and mid-Victorian resorts, whatever their landownership pattern.

In this period, however, the dice were loaded in favour of the spaciousness, uniformity and effective regulation which a town of large estates could offer to the 'better classes'; and sub-divided landholdings made it increasingly likely that developers anxious for a quick profit would permit builders with limited resources and pressing creditors to aim cheaply at the lower levels of the market, producing jerry-built property of no architectural dignity or pretensions. Where a strong presumption in favour of high-class development had not been firmly established at an early stage, resorts with divided landownership found difficulty in competing for the mid-Victorian 'better classes', and were likely to need tripper patronage to stimulate a languishing economy; and there were more opportunities here for caterers for the lower classes to gain a firm foothold. A feedback process might then develop, whereby a benign environment attracted more lower-class visitors, and as their numbers grew in the later nineteenth century the visible demand brought heavier investment at the lower end of the market, culminating in the serried streets of purpose-built lodging-houses and the monster amusement centres of the leading popular resorts. These initiatives in turn drew ever greater crowds, and the excursionist interest could then become powerful enough to affect the composition and policies of local government, channelling still more resources into the working-class season.

Only a handful of resorts, perhaps, and most obviously Blackpool, went all the way along this road; and even at Blackpool there were significant changes of policy in the early twentieth century. But most places took some steps along the journey, and even Bournemouth and Torquay were cultivating relatively plebeian summer seasons by the turn of the century. Eastbourne, indeed, was most unusual even among Cannadine's 'aristocratic' resorts in the extent to which it held itself aloof from the new sources of late Victorian demand. In a few resorts, indeed, the presence of a large estate did not prevent the working-class visitor from gaining the ascendancy by the turn of the century. The clearest cases were Skegness, where the needs of the East Midland working classes were inescapable right from the town's belated origins, and Cleethorpes and Weston-super-Mare where the pressure of demand was too much for large landowners who did not control extensive and strategic areas of the sea-front and town centre.[7] At Weston-super-Mare, especially, the transition was not achieved without conflict; but the same applied to the resorts with divided landownership which went down-market in the later nineteenth century. Where the pressures were particularly strong, resistance from the 'better-class' interest probably had its uses in ensuring an adequate level of regulation and preventing a counter-productive descent into anarchy; but developments at Blackpool suggest that the more substantial caterers for the working-class market were themselves quite capable of defending their interests against untrammelled rowdyism, noise and charlatanry. Only where the forces of 'respectability' and the excursionist interest remained evenly matched, as at New Brighton with its uneasy combination of suburbanites and 'half-holidaymakers', was lasting damage caused by the problems of transition; and with very few exceptions the most successful resorts were able to sustain a mixed visitor economy by offering a variety of satisfactions to several different visiting publics.[8]

Several important resorts, however, from Brighton downwards, managed to preserve a generally elevated social tone despite fragmented landownership; and here above all the rôle of local government was especially important, as it took on many of the regulatory functions and provided the amenities which elsewhere had been the preserve of landed families, building syndicates or estate companies. In every resort, however, the significance of local government increased sharply in the later nineteenth century; and this neglected factor was the most important influence on late Victorian and Edwardian resort development. The social composition, attitudes to expenditure and control, and level of competence of local authorities effectively determined the fortunes of individual resorts in this period, as landowners sold up or retreated into profit-taking, and the needs and problems of the holiday industry demanded an extensive measure of active intervention. It is no coincidence that the most successful resorts of these years, Blackpool and Bournemouth, were especially notable for thrusting and innovative municipal enterprise which was geared up to the needs of the holiday trades.[9]

The seaside resorts remained, of course, absolutely dependent on the regional, national and international economies which generated the incomes of the visitors and wealthy residents who provided their *raison d'être*. Demand at the top end of the resort hierarchy, with a metropolitan and national market, was least vulnerable to economic fluctuations, although more vulnerable to competition, especially as the Continental resorts became more fashionable.[10] Lower down the scale the various regional economies generated differing levels of working-class demand, and the pressures on individual resorts varied considerably in different parts of the country. Where a working-class market developed early, resorts with a regional rather than a national hinterland could be hard hit by localized depressions; and the general depression of 1879, coupled as it was with poor summer weather, hit many resorts hard. But the impact of the trade cycle was declining towards the turn of the century, as the shortfall from people unable to take their usual holiday was made up in the popular resorts by better-off people whose retrenchment took the form of an inexpensive holiday closer to home. Apart from a few hiccups, however, mainly in the 1830s, 1860s and 1880s, what stands out is the remorseless growth of holiday markets and holiday resorts throughout a period in which the normal trading indicators were far from stable.

It would be tempting to argue that the popular resorts increasingly benefited if not from actual depressions, then at least from squeezed margins and falling rates of return in their hinterlands, so long as real wages remained intact. Under such conditions resorts might look particularly attractive as repositories for surplus capital which might otherwise have gone into working-class housing or the modernization of industry. Saul's evidence on house-building offers little help to this argument, emphasizing as it does the importance of local influences and the sluggish nature of developers' responses to changes in the housing market. But several popular resorts did see an abnormally high level of building activity in what was still mainly a middle-class seaside housing market in the early twentieth century, when investment in working-class housing had lost its attractions in some of their industrial hinterlands.[11] Comparisons are affected, moreover, by the generally much larger size and unit cost of seaside housing, and a full study of housing finance would almost certainly confirm a rapid and swelling flow of investment from London and industrial districts into seaside property, which seems to have been attractive whatever the state of the inland economy. There are indications that investment in entertainment *was* to some extent counter-cyclical, however. The troubled 1860s saw much Lancashire capital flowing into pier-building and other resort improvements; the first spate of Aquarium and Winter Gardens promotions came in the mid-1870s, after the great boom of 1870–3 had broken; and the depression of the early 1890s was a peak period for investment in the most capital-hungry of the pleasure palaces.[12] Much more demanding in the long run, however, were the great public works schemes which every resort required: promenades, sea defences, elaborate sewerage schemes designed to reduce pollution, and so on. The income from local rates provided most of the security for these ventures, but the actual capital was raised by individuals (and increasingly companies) in search of a secure investment; and here again the provision of social overhead capital in resorts, as in other kinds of town, competed with other outlets for the employment of the vast accumulation of Victorian savings which needed a safe but lucrative home.[13]

It is very doubtful whether seaside investment had an adverse effect on the productive capacity and rate of return in the late Victorian economy, as Ashworth has suggested.[14] The extent to which capital shortages contributed to lower levels of economic growth is uncertain, and overseas investment is a potentially more plausible and important villain than the seaside. In any case, much of the housing and social overhead capital would have had to be provided somewhere for a growing population; and without the seaside the demand for amusement and consumer spending might well have been met in less healthy and more socially divisive ways. The overall level of investment in the seaside would be very difficult to quantify, and the results of such an exercise would probably be inconclusive. The growing complexities of the nineteenth century do not lend themselves to the emulation of Neale's heroic equation between building investment in eighteenth-century Bath and fixed capital investment in the cotton industry.[15] The rate of return, admittedly, was almost certainly low, especially on risky and highly seasonal speculations like entertainment companies. At the level of the landed estate, Cannadine finds that development at the seaside was disproportionately costly and brought a 'decidedly miserable' return.[16] It is impossible to generalize convincingly about the fortunes of the myriads of smaller landowners, developers and builders lower down the scale, except to suggest that although the rewards (especially for land speculation) might often be greater than was usual inland, the risks were certainly higher. The poor performance of entertainment companies in most resorts has been documented in chapter 7, and the proliferation of seaside branch lines no doubt played its part in the declining economic performance of late Victorian railways, as the false promise of crowded summer seasons and the competitive needs of aspiring resorts built up the pressure for investment whose rationality was highly dubious when viewed in narrow economic terms.

The seaside boom produced its inevitable crop of successful entrepreneurs, but most resorts offered grudging and limited rewards to most investors, and a great deal of capital had to be written off in the high-risk sectors. Nor did the resorts themselves fulfil their crowded seasonal promise of prosperity to the vast majority of those who worked in them, for the fortunes of the small family businesses which predominated at the seaside were fluctuating and usually precarious, and the sharp seasonal fluctuations in most resort economies imposed insecurity and frequent spells of unemployment on wage labourers. Winter in the popular resorts, especially, brought widespread poverty in the midst of residential affluence, or at least comfort. Indeed, the seaside had a much more favourable impact on the living standards of working-class people outside the resorts than within them. The seaside provided an additional, and relatively lucrative, range of hunting-grounds for the seasonally nomadic casual workers and street entertainers of Raphael Samuel's 'Comers and goers';[17] the resorts offered summer employment, often, though not always, well-paid, to urban labourers and domestic servants inland;[18] and their competition for labour may well have pulled up agricultural wages in the vicinity of the larger resorts, while the needs of their visitors certainly stimulated market gardening and intensive cultivation in their immediate surroundings in late Victorian and Edwardian times.[19] Moving up the scale a little, the seaside also provided respectable employment for large numbers of spinsters and widows who needed the income from lodging-house keeping to make ends meet.[20] Most important, however, was the added scope for health, recreation and change of scene which the seaside offered to a rapidly-increasing proportion of the late Victorian and Edwardian working class. This development, like the rise of professional football, the popular press, the music-hall and later the cinema, demonstrates the emergence of an extensive and growing working-class stratum with money to spare for enjoyment, and the logistics of holidaymaking also required a widespread capacity for systematic saving and deferred gratification. Thrift of this specialized and limited kind was not universally acclaimed by middle-class commentators, and it could even be argued that the pressure to participate in the annual rush to the sea might push marginal families into secondary poverty through the irrational diversion of resources into a frivolous and unncessary status symbol. Such a perception would be out of sympathy with the wider needs of closely-confined city-dwellers, and there were many more damaging and less enjoyable ways of sinking into secondary poverty than this.[21] The rise of the working-class seaside holiday is, indeed, the other side of the coin from the grim findings of the turn-of-the-century poverty surveys, and reminds us of the extent of the late Victorian improvement in living standards among the upper and middling strata of an increasingly widely-differentiated working class.

How did the rise of the seaside affect relationships between the classes? Interpretations are complicated by the internal contradictions of the seaside social system, although the patchy, late and limited development of trade unionism and working-class municipal representation in most resorts indicates the disorganized and subordinate position of the local working classes.[22] At the level of the visiting public, the seaside resorts sought to perpetuate the rôle of eighteenth-century Bath, which Professor Neale sees as being to provide a haven of order, decorum and regularity in which the upper levels of society could take refuge from the pressures and disorders of a market-centred society ruled by absolute self-interest.[23] Feelings of security could increasingly be reinforced by the way in which the growth of the larger resorts involved a visible and necessary taming of the natural world in its wildest and most fearsome aspect: the physical expression of a feat of domination and subordination which the cult of the picturesque usually achieved only in the mind.[24] Sir Edmund Gosse expressed outrage at the ultimate results of this trend in a favourite place in the early twentieth century:

A careful municipality has studded the down with rustic seats, and has shut its dangers out with railings, has cut a winding carriage-drive round the curves of the cove down to the shore, and has planted sausage-laurels at intervals in clearings made for that aesthetic purpose. When last I saw the place, thus smartened and secured, with its hair in curl-papers and its feet in patent-leathers, I turned from it in anger and disgust . . . what man could do to make wild beauty ineffectual, tame and empty, has amply been performed at Oddicombe.[25]

As we saw in chapter 8, however, it was not so easy to tame all aspects of seaside society. Sue Farrant has emphasized the importance of the early resorts' 'integrative social role', suggesting that the homogeneity of terraced housing facades helped to promote integration between aristocracy, gentry, professionals and merchants.[26] The same might be argued of the institutions of organized recreation. But Peter Borsay uses similar evidence to point up the importance of leisure towns as centres for social competition as expressed through lifestyles and consumption patterns, and Neale also brings out the inevitability of discord and conflict beneath the polite conventional veneer of resort institutions.[27] Social mixing at the seaside inevitably meant conflict, as established wealth and sophistication encountered unpolished *nouveaux riches*, and the snobbish did battle with the pushing.[28] The arrival of a lower middle-class and working-class presence during the nineteenth century gave an additional dimension to the tensions, demonstrating the limited practical validity of Peter Burke's view that the educated classes were losing their contempt for popular culture by the end of the eighteenth century as they rediscovered it as 'something exotic and therefore interesting'.[29] It took a very long time for élite investigations of popular traditions to become translated into mainstream middle-class tolerance of contemporary working-class recreational behaviour, if this sort of percolation occurred at all. Until the very end of the nineteenth century the seaside brought the classes together more in conflict than in harmony.

By the turn of the century, however, the seaside was coming to be perceived as an influence for social stability. There was widespread praise for improving working-class behaviour at the resorts, some of which was attributed to the civilizing influence of proximity to their 'betters'. More subtly, Darbyshire's *Guide* in 1901 suggested that a visit to Southend had patriotic value in educating 'the finished product of an East End board

Fig. 26 Manx entrepreneurs were particularly keen on the commercial exploitation of scenery, as in this view of Groudle Glen on the island's east coast (reproduced from *A New Pictorial and Descriptive Guide to the Isle of Man*, 1902–3).

Fig. 27 Seaside scenery 'with its hair in curl-papers': Shanklin Chine, Isle of Wight (reproduced from *A Pictorial and Descriptive Guide to the Isle of Wight*, 19th edn).

school' in Britain's naval glories, instilling 'national sentiments and national pride.'[30] But the most important roots of changing working-class attitudes and behaviour surely lay in home, school and workplace. The seaside had long had its uses inland, however, as a focus for counter-attractions, 'rational recreations' and familial pleasures, a genuinely attractive alternative to wakes, fairs, races and drink at local holiday times. But the successful popular resorts soon responded to demand by turning into boisterous, tolerant places, and the dispersal of many Sunday School excursions to quieter venues reflected the perceived immorality and irrationality of much seaside activity. Indeed, we have seen that the seaside evidence brings out the frivolous side of even the mid-Victorian middle classes, setting very narrow limits to the influence of the grim 'respectability' of persistent stereotype. The seaside provided a valuable safety-valve, a legitimized escape from some of the more irksome constraints on everyday behaviour, for the Victorian middle classes as much as for their social inferiors. Just as the evidence for eager holiday-taking undermines easy assumptions about the internalization of a Victorian work ethic, so the behaviour of holiday-makers cuts down to size the tyranny of Victorian respectability, bringing out the extent to which it was a carefully adopted code of public behaviour, reinforced by the fear of sanctions from neighbours, which was rarely accepted into the hearts and minds even of the middle classes.

In addition, of course, the seaside formed one of the new late Victorian items of mass consumption which may have helped to distract the better-off and more articulate of the working classes from class-conscious political activity, although there are plenty of more convincing explanations for what some would argue to be a non-problem. Seaside holidays, too, may have fostered myths of shared prosperity and upward social mobility in ways which marginally strengthened the established order. The seaside, however, also made the gulfs between the classes more visible, in a context of conspicuous consumption, than they might have been in the era of the retreat to suburbia and countryside by merchants and large employers, and even by tradesmen and white-collar workers. As Michael Anderson has pithily pointed out, however, it is very difficult to tell whether the flight to the suburbs exacerbated class tensions by undermining employer paternalism, or reduced their potency by removing the irritating visibility of the enviable lifestyle which employers were able to purchase by their appropriation of surplus value.[31] The same could be said of the flight to the seaside, except that here the enviable lifestyle was still on display to working-class visitors during their brief and crowded visits, despite the growth of seaside social zoning. But it is difficult to tell whether these changes, in themselves, had any deep significance for class relations; and the pleasure-seeking context of a seaside visit was probably in itself sufficient to override any tendency to introspection about the inequalities of the social order, except among those who were already predisposed in that direction. The seaside undoubtedly *expressed* class and cultural differences; the insoluble problem is to show how it *influenced* them.

This book need not end on an inconclusive note, although the attempt to assess the importance of the seaside to the wider economy and society was bound to raise daunting and perhaps unanswerable questions. The reasons for the rise of the seaside holiday town between the mid-eighteenth century and the First World War should now be more fully documented and clearly comprehensible, and the nature of the seaside's influence on lifestyles, attitudes and consumption patterns has been demonstrated. I have also tried to explain the enormous variety of resort experiences which must be encompassed by any attempt to generalize about the seaside at a national level. Despite all the problems of patchy coverage of themes and places in available sources, I hope that this venture beyond the individual case-study or dichotomous comparison will encourage others to study wider groupings and 'families' of English towns over the crucial century and a half which is covered by this book.[32] The need is becoming urgent, as students show increasing bewilderment at the complex variety of experience which the individual case-studies reveal. Further research at the level of the individual town is obviously needed, but the situation also demands some ambitious works of well-informed synthesis, even though many of their conclusions will be tentative and interim in nature. If this book encourages further enterprises of this sort, it will have served an important purpose over and above its contribution to our understanding of the rise of the English seaside holiday town.

List of abbreviations

Note: Places of publication are given only for works published outside the United Kingdom. In abbreviating less frequently cited periodical titles, commonly accepted abbreviations such as *J.* for *Journal*, *Rev.* for *Review* have been used; other abbreviations are listed below.

B.G.	*Blackpool Gazette*
B.S.P.	British Sessional (Parliamentary) Papers
Barrett, 'Seaside resort towns'	J. A. Barrett, 'The seaside resort towns of England and Wales' (Ph.D. thesis, University of London, 1958)
Beale, *Reminiscences*	C. H. Beale, *Reminiscences of a Gentlewoman of the Last Century* (1891)
Br.G.	*Brighton Gazette*
Brookfield, 'Coastal Sussex'	H. Brookfield, 'A regional study of the urban development of coastal Sussex' (Ph.D. thesis, University of London, 1950)
Brown, 'Leisure industries'	B. J. H. Brown, 'A survey of the development of the leisure industries of the Bristol region, with special reference to the seaside resorts' (Ph.D. thesis, University of Bath, 1971)
Cannadine, *Lords and Landlords*	D. Cannadine, *Lords and Landlords: the Aristocracy and the Towns 1774–1967* (1980)
Carey, *Balnea*	G. S. Carey, *The Balnea: or, an Impartial Description of all the Popular Watering-Places in England* (3rd edn, 1801)
Everritt, *Southend*	S. Everritt, *Southend Seaside Holiday* (1980)
Farrant, *Brighton*	S. Farrant, *Georgian Brighton* (1980)
Gilbert, *Brighton*	E. W. Gilbert, *Brighton, Old Ocean's Bauble* (1954, repr. 1976)
Granville, *Spas*	A. B. Granville, *The Spas of England, and Principal Sea-Bathing Places* (1841, repr. 1971)
H.L.R.O.	House of Lords Record Office
Jennings, *Harrogate and Knaresborough*	B. Jennings (ed.), *A History of Harrogate and Knaresborough* (1970)
K.G.	*Keble's Gazette*
Leisure in England, ed. Walton and Walvin	J. K. Walton and J. Walvin (eds), *Leisure in England 1780–1939* (1983)
McIntyre, 'Health and pleasure resorts'	S. McIntyre, 'Towns as health and pleasure resorts' (D.Phil. thesis, University of Oxford, 1974)
May, 'Ilfracombe'	F. B. May, 'The development of Ilfracombe as a resort in the nineteenth century' (M.A. thesis, University of Wales, 1978)
Moncrieff, *Where Shall We Go?*	A. R. H. Moncrieff, *Where Shall We Go?* (1899 edn)
Mr Punch	*Mr Punch at the Seaside* (n.d.)
Neale, *Bath*	R. S. Neale, *Bath: A Social History 1680–1850* (1981)

Oakley, 'Dorset and Somerset'   M. Oakley, 'The holiday industry of Dorset and Somerset' (B.Litt. thesis, University of Oxford, 1964)

Patricians, Power and Politics, ed. Cannadine   D. Cannadine (ed.), *Patricians, Power and Politics in Nineteenth-Century Towns* (1982)

P.C.   *Preston Chronicle*

Perkin, 'Social tone'   H. J. Perkin, 'The "social tone" of Victorian seaside resorts in the north-west', *Northern History*, xi (1976 for 1975), 180–94

Ports and Resorts, ed. Sigsworth   E. M. Sigsworth (ed.), *Ports and Resorts in the Regions* (1980)

P.R.O.   Public Record Office

Pimlott, *Holiday*   J. A. R. Pimlott, *The Englishman's Holiday: a Social History* (1947, repr. 1976)

R.O.   Record Office

S.C.   Select Committee

S.G.   *Scarborough Gazette*

S.S.   *Southend Standard*

S.W.P.   *Seaside Watering-Places*

Stafford, 'Victorian Margate'   F. Stafford, 'Holidaymaking in Victorian Margate, 1870–1900' (M.Phil. thesis, University of Kent, 1979)

Stuart, 'North-east Wales'   A. Stuart, 'The growth and morphology of coastal towns in north-east Wales' (M.A. thesis, University of Wales, 1959)

T.A.   *Thanet Advertiser*

Time to Spare   J. Lowerson and J. Myerscough, *Time to Spare in Victorian England* (1976)

VCH   *Victoria County History*

Walton, 'Blackpool'   J. K. Walton, 'The social development of Blackpool 1788–1914' (Ph.D. thesis, University of Lancaster, 1974)

Walton, 'Demand'   J. K. Walton, 'The demand for working-class seaside holidays in Victorian England', *Economic History Rev.*, 2nd series, xxxiv (1981)

Walton, *Landlady*   J. K. Walton, *The Blackpool Landlady: a Social History* (1978)

Watering Places   *A Guide to all the Watering- and Sea-Bathing Places, by the Editor of the Picture of London* (1803 edn)

Whyman, 'Kentish seaside resorts'   J. Whyman, 'Kentish seaside resorts before 1900' (unpublished paper, 1970)

Whyman, 'Hanoverian watering-place'   J. Whyman, 'A Hanoverian watering-place: Margate before the railway', in *Perspectives in English Urban History*, ed. A. Everitt (1973)

Whyman, 'Aspects of holiday-making'   J. Whyman, 'Aspects of holiday-making and resort development within the Isle of Thanet, with particular reference to Margate, c.1736–c.1840' (D.Phil. thesis, University of Kent, 1980)

Y.I.   *Yarmouth Independent*

Notes

1 INTRODUCTION

1. G. F. A. Best, *Mid-Victorian Britain 1851–75* (1971 edn), 203–7, and E. J. Hobsbawm, *The Age of Capital* (1977 edn), 240–1, provide the best treatments of holidays and resorts in general text-books. At the other extreme are D. Kynaston, *King Labour* (1976), 108–9, who says very little but gets it all wrong, and R. T. Shannon, *The Crisis of Imperialism 1860–1915*, who covers the whole subject in one sentence (p. 203).
2. See below, ch. 3.
3. See below, ch. 4.
4. Walton, 'Blackpool', 122–3.
5. See below, ch. 4.
6. Walton, 'Demand'.
7. J. Myerscough, 'Introduction' in Pimlott, *Holiday*; B. Pimlott, 'Introduction', in J. A. R. Pimlott, *The Englishman's Christmas* (1978); Walvin, *Seaside*.
8. Works of this *genre* run through from the mid-1940s to the present, and are too numerous to list.
9. Barrett, 'Seaside resort towns'.
10. Gilbert, *Brighton*.
11. Esp. H. Gayler, 'The coastal resorts of Essex' (M.A. thesis, University of London, 1966).
12. Cannadine, *Lords and Landlords*; Perkin, 'Social tone', 180–94.
13. These themes are well developed by May, 'Ilfracombe', and Brown, 'Leisure industries' casts his net wider than most. See also the M.A. theses by J. Grass, C. Widdowfield and K. Wilson (all University of Lancaster) cited by Perkin, 'Social tone'.
14. W. Ashworth, 'The late Victorian economy', *Economica*, n.s. XXXIII (1966), 21; O. M. Westall, 'The retreat to Arcadia', in *Windermere in the Nineteenth Century*, ed. O. M. Westall (1976); P. Joyce, *Work, Society and Politics* (1980), 340.
15. S. B. Saul, 'House building in England 1890–1914', *Economic History Rev.*, 2nd ser., XV (1962–3), 120–4; Cannadine, *Lords and Landlords*.
16. R. Roberts, 'The Barnum of Bournemouth' in *Leisure in England*, ed. Walton and Walvin; Walton, 'Blackpool', ch. 4.
17. See below, ch. 8, and for an extreme statement, J. V. N. Soane, 'The general significance of the development of the urban and social structure of Bournemouth, 1840–1940' (Ph.D. thesis, University of Surrey, 1978), 205.
18. For example, G. Crossick (ed.), *The Lower Middle Class in Britain 1870–1914* (1977), and G. Anderson, *Victorian Clerks* (1976).

2 THE DEMAND FOR SEASIDE HOLIDAYS

1. P. Borsay, 'The English urban renaissance 1680–1760', *Social History*, II (1977), 581–603; P. Clark (ed.), *The Early Modern Town* (1976), esp. chs. 9 and 11; P. Clark and P. Slack, *English Towns in Transition 1500–1700* (1976), 54, 68–9, 74–5, 156.
2. Pimlott, *Holiday*, chs. 1–2; McIntyre, 'Health and pleasure resorts'; Neale, *Bath*.
3. See esp. P. Borsay, 'The English urban renaissance' (Ph.D. thesis, University of Lancaster, 1981); also J. H. Plumb, *The Commercialisation of Leisure in Eighteenth-Century England* (1973).
4. See esp. R. G. Wilson, *Gentlemen Merchants* (1971), and N. Rogers, 'Money, land and lineage: the big bourgeoisie of Hanoverian London', *Social History*, IV (1979), 437–54.
5. G. S. Holmes, 'The professions and social change in England 1680–1730', *Procs. British Academy*, LXV (1979), 313–54.

6. E. A. Wrigley, 'A simple model of London's importance in changing English economy and society', *Past and Present*, XXXVII (1967).

7. J. H. Plumb, 'The new world of children in eighteenth-century England', *Past and Present*, LXVII (1975), 64–95; and see above, n. 3.

8. Pimlott, *Holiday*, 31.

9. See esp. W. A. Speck, *Stability and Strife* (1977), ch. 2.

10. Pimlott, *Holiday*, 46–8; Neale, *Bath*, ch. 2.

11. Plumb, *Commercialisation of Leisure*; Neale, *Bath*, ch. 2.

12. Pimlott, *Holiday*, 44–5.

13. *Ibid.*, 100; McIntyre, 'Health and pleasure resorts', 10, 41, 58, 463.

14. Pimlott, *Holiday*, 100–1; Carey, *Balnea*, 39, 46.

15. Pimlott, *Holiday*, 98–104; G. Hart, *A History of Cheltenham* (1965), 187–92.

16. R. V. Lennard (ed.), *Englishmen at Rest and Play* (1931), 61.

17. *Ibid.*, 60; Pimlott, *Holiday*, 33.

18. McIntyre, 'Health and pleasure resorts', 191, 196–7.

19. Jennings, *Harrogate and Knaresborough*, 232, 299; Granville, *Spas*, I: 37; II: 28; T. Marchington, 'The development of Buxton and Matlock since 1800' (M.A. thesis, University of London, 1961), 56–8; Brown, 'Leisure industries', 66–7.

20. Carey, *Balnea*, 177.

21. Pimlott, *Holiday*, 32.

22. Granville, *Spas*, I: 322, 385; II: 71, 115.

23. E. J. Baxter, 'The social life of visitors to Leamington Spa', *Warwicks. History*, III (1975), 17, is critical of Granville, as is Jennings, *Harrogate and Knaresborough*, 299.

24. Jennings, *Harrogate and Knaresborough*, 221; Stuart, 'Northeast Wales', 188; Granville, *Spas*, I: 289. For further eighteenth-century examples see J. Campbell, LL.D., *A Political Survey of Britain*, I (1774), ch. 5.

25. Pimlott, *Holiday*, 25; G. W. Oxley, *Poor Relief in England and Wales 1601–1834* (1974), 67.

26. Granville, *Spas*, I: 294, 299, 402–7.

27. R. W. Malcolmson, *Life and Labour 1700–1780* (1981), 82–107, will help to set this in context.

28. M. Blundell (ed.), *Blundell's Diary and Letter Book 1702–28* (1952), 65–6.

29. H. P. R. Finberg, *Gloucestershire Studies* (1957), 190.

30. P. Whittle, *Marina* (1831), 39; R. Ayton, *A Voyage Round Great Britain*, II (1815), 102; *B.G.*, 22 June 1877.

31. W. J. Lewis, 'Some aspects of the history of Aberystwyth', *Ceredigion*, IV (1960–3), 23.

32. *P.C.*, 9 Aug. 1834; *Lancaster Gaz.*, 5 July 1806, 20 Aug. 1836; F. A. Bailey, *A History of Southport* (1955), 29; W. Hutton, *A Description of Blackpool in 1788* (1944 edn, ed. R. Sharpe France), 18–19, 24.

33. *P.C.*, 20 Aug. 1836.

34. See above, n. 30, and W. Thornber, *The History of Blackpool and its Neighbourhood* (1837).

35. Pimlott, *Holiday*, 50–1.

36. *Ibid.*, 51–2; Whyman, 'Hanoverian watering-place', 139.

37. Pimlott, *Holiday*, 52–4; Gilbert, *Brighton*, 56–62; Whyman, 'Hanoverian watering-place', 146–7.

38. See, for instance, Clark and Slack, *op. cit.*, 109–10.

39. McIntyre, 'Health and pleasure resorts', 308.

40. Gilbert, *Brighton*, 16, 88–90.

41. F. M. L. Thompson, *English Landed Society in the Nineteenth Century* (1971 edn), 25–6, 104–6.

42. Wrigley, *op. cit.*

43. Gilbert, *Brighton*, 91–2; Brookfield, 'Coastal Sussex', 112; Carey, *Balnea*, 63.

44. Whyman, 'Hanoverian watering-place', 156.

45. Carey, *Balnea*, 6–7, 10, 26–8.

46. As at Southend: *Watering Places*, 336.

47. Carey, *Balnea*, 77–90.

48. *Watering Places*, 218–19.

49. Jane Austen, *Sanditon* (Everyman edn, 1978), 14.

50. A. F. J. Brown, *Essex People 1750–1900* (1972), 1, 23–4, 41, 47.

51. *Watering Places*, 262–3; Oakley, 'Dorset and Somerset', 77, 112–13, 270; May, 'Ilfracombe', 5.

52. Lewis, *op. cit.*, 31.

53. Pimlott, *Holiday*, 63.

54. Beale, *Reminiscences*, 150.

55. *Watering Places*, 289.

56. Beale, *Reminiscences*, 156, quoted by Walvin, *Seaside*, 30–1.

57. Carey, *Balnea*, 232.

58. Brown 'Leisure industries', 118, 136–42; J. Money, *Experience and Identity* (1977), *passim*.

59. *Watering Places*, 214; Stuart, 'North-east Wales', 254–7; C. M. L. Bouch and G. P. Jones, *A Short Economic and Social History of the Lake Counties, 1500–1830* (1961), 287; Beale, *Reminiscences*, 152; and for East Anglia, Whyman, 'Aspects of holiday-making', 572.

60. Even Cornwall had Fowey: *Watering Places*, 203*–4*. Cf. Pimlott, *Holiday*, 63.

61. *A New Weymouth Guide* (c. 1800), 25–6; Gilbert, *Brighton*, 64–5, 70.

62. Gilbert, *Brighton*, 76–86; Beale, *Reminiscences*, 62; Pimlott, *Holiday*, 56.

63. Brown, *op. cit.*, 23.

64. Whyman, 'Aspects of holiday-making', 198–9; *The Margate Guide* (1770), 18–19.

65. *The Isle of Wight: A Poem in Three Cantos* (1782), xxv.

66. Austen, *op. cit.*, 44.

67. Pimlott, *Holiday*, 55.

68. *Watering Places*, 202, 233.

69. G. Mingay, *English Landed Society in the Eighteenth Century* (1963), for the case of Sir W. W. Wynn.

70. *Ibid.*, 155.

71. McIntyre, 'Health and pleasure resorts', 407.

72. Plumb, 'The new world of children'; L. Stone, *The Family, Sex and Marriage in England 1500–1800* (1977), 452–68; Pimlott, *Holiday*, 121.

73. McIntyre, 'Health and pleasure resorts', 407.

74. Austen, *op. cit.*, 37.

75. Whyman, 'Kentish seaside resorts', 27.

76. Gilbert, *Brighton*, 92, 109, 152.

77. Whyman, 'Kentish seaside resorts', 29–32.

78. Whyman, 'Hanoverian watering-place', 157, and 'Visitors to Margate in the 1841 census returns', *Local Population Studies*, VIII (1972), 19–39; Walton, 'Blackpool', 232.

79. Whyman, 'Kentish seaside resorts', 8, 12; H. Cunningham, *Leisure in the Industrial Revolution* (1980), 160.

80. A. J. Philip, *A History of Gravesend* (n.d.), 180.

81. Brookfield, 'Coastal Sussex', 140.

82. Whittle, *op. cit.*, 33; W. Thornber, *The History of Blackpool and Its Neighbourhood* (1837), 226; R. P. Craine, 'Douglas: a town's specialisation in tourism' (B.A. dissertation, University of Durham, 1966), 24; Jennings, *Harrogate and Knaresborough*, 299–300.

83. Granville, *Spas*, I: 346–9; Walton, 'Blackpool', 232.

84. Granville, *Spas*, I: 346–7; and in 1857 Nathaniel Hawthorne found its visitors 'principally of the middling-classes': *English Notebooks* (1962 edn), 495.

85. Granville, *Spas*, I: 188.

86. Brown, 'Leisure industries', 142, 313.

87. Granville, *Spas*, I: 269–70, II: 10–16.

88. *Ibid.*, I: 346, II: 447, 583–93.

89. *Ibid.*, II: 472–95, 512–36, 541–2, 598–605.

90. G. S. Duncan, 'Church and society in early Victorian Torquay' (M.A. thesis, University of Exeter, 1972), 32–4; Granville, *Spas*, II: 486.

91. Granville, *Spas*, II: 467–9, 500–3.

92. Brookfield, 'Coastal Sussex', 144–5.

93. Gilbert, *Brighton*, 115–18; Carey, *Balnea*, 3–4.

94. P. S. Bagwell, *The Transport Revolution from 1770* (1974), 41–3.

95. McIntyre, 'Health and pleasure resorts', 436.

96. Brown, 'Leisure industries', 153.

97. Bagwell, *Transport Revolution*, 48–9.

98. Whyman, 'Kentish seaside resorts', 32–3.

99. May, 'Ilfracombe', 48–9; Stuart, 'North-east Wales', 209; Barrett, 'Seaside resort towns', 359–60.

100. F. A. Bailey, *A History of Southport* (1955), 144–6.

101. Gilbert, *Brighton*, 152.

102. Walton, 'Blackpool', 238–63.

103. See below, ch. 3.

104. R. S. Neale, *Class and Ideology in the Nineteenth Century* (1972).

105. Gilbert, *Brighton*, 178, 181; *S.W.P.* (1876), 6, 17, 41–2; *S.G.*, 26 Sept. 1872.

106. Bagwell, *op. cit.*, 108.

107. Whyman, 'Kentish seaside resorts', 32, 37–8; see also several cartoons in *Mr Punch*.

108. Walton, 'Blackpool', 245. Even Criccieth had a 'husband train' in 1895: *S.W.P.* (1895), 391.

109. *S.W.P.* (1876), 89, 128.

110. Bagwell, *op. cit.*, 107.

111. H. J. Perkin, *The Origins of Modern English Society* (1972 edn), 414–15.

112. G. F. A. Best, *Mid-Victorian Britain 1851–75* (1971), 83–5; W. J. Reader, *Professional Men* (1966), 207–11; J. A. Banks, *Prosperity and Parenthood* (1954), 83–4, 92–111.

113. Best, *op. cit.*, 81–3.

114. B.S.P. 1867–8, VIII, S.C. on Bank Holidays, Q. 157–9, 453, 825, 2105.

115. Pimlott, *Holiday*, 154–5.

116. *S.G.*, 8 Aug. 1872.

117. *Y.I.*, 26 May 1860.

118. *S.G.*, 13 June 1872; *B.G.*, 16 Aug. 1878.

119. *Hastings and St Leonards News*, 16 June 1876.

120. Pimlott, *Holiday*, 147–9.

121. G. Crossick, *An Artisan Elite in Victorian Society* (1978), 130–1; G. Anderson, *Victorian Clerks* (1976).

122. Whyman, 'Kentish seaside resorts', 39; L. Gregory, 'The role of sea bathing in the development of Southport' (M.A. thesis, University of Lancaster, 1973); McIntyre, 'Health and pleasure resorts', 238.

123. Bagwell, *op. cit.*, 127.

124. Walton, 'Blackpool', 242–6, 380–7.

125. *Br.G.*, 23 May 1850, 8 Aug. 1850; Lowerson and Myerscough, *Time to Spare*, 31; H. Cunningham, *Leisure in the Industrial Revolution* (1980), 162–3; *S.G.*, 13 June 1850; Brown, 'Leisure industries', 174–5.

126. May, 'Ilfracombe', 323.

127. Walton, 'Blackpool', 283–5.

128. *Preston Guardian*, 18 May 1872, 16 May 1885.

129. *Dudley Herald*, 17 July 1880.

130. *T.A.*, 29 June 1867, 3 Aug. 1867, 4 July 1868.

131. *Hastings and St Leonards News*, 5 July 1867; *T.A.*, 14 March 1868; Stafford, 'Victorian Margate', 94–5.

132. See below, ch. 8.

133. *Fleetwood Chronicle*, 30 Aug. 1845; cf. P. Joyce, *Work, Society and Politics* (1980), 180, 185–7.

134. *Accrington Times*, 23 Aug. 1873; M. Hodgson, 'The working day and the working week in Victorian Britain' (M.Phil. thesis, University of London, 1974), 248.

135. T. J. Matthews, 'Blackpool: the Brighton of the Lancashire and Yorkshire Railway', *Railway Mag.* (1898), Oakley, 'Dorset and Somerset', 119–20.

136. *Sheffield Independent*, 30 Aug. 1873; *Rotherham Advertiser*, 5 July 1873; *S.S.*, 11 Sept. 1874; Stafford, 'Victorian Margate', 95–6.

137. Joyce, *op. cit.*, chs. 5, 8.

138. *Leeds Intelligencer*, 27 June 1846, 11 July 1846.

139. *Bolton Chronicle*, 31 July 1858, 30 July 1870.

140. *Preston Guardian*, 26 May 1866.

141. *Blackburn Standard*, 16 May 1885.

142. Walton, 'Blackpool', 286.

143. *Leeds Intelligencer*, 16 Aug. 1851; *Rotherham Advertiser*, 30 July 1870.

144. Walton, 'Blackpool', 285.

145. MS. diary of C. A. Thorpe, by courtesy of Mr S. J. Westacott.

146. *Manchester Guardian*, 29 July 1854, 5 Aug. 1854.

147. H.L.R.O. (Commons), S.C. on the Blackpool Improvement Bill, 1853, p. 29; *S.G.*, 24 Aug. 1854.

148. Walton, 'Blackpool', 272.

149. B.S.P. 1876, XXX, S.C. on Factories and Workshops, Q. 12451; *Rotherham Advertiser*, 18 June 1870, 14 June 1873.

150. *Hastings and St Leonards News*, 5 July 1867; Lowerson and Myerscough, *Time to Spare*, 31.

151. Culled from statistics occasionally published in local newspapers, especially the *Preston Guardian*.

152. For what follows see Walton, 'Demand'.

153. J. K. Walton, 'Railways and resort development in north-west England, 1830–1914', in *Ports and Resorts*, ed. Sigsworth, 120–37.

154. R. Poole, 'Oldham Wakes', in *Leisure in England*, ed. Walton and Walvin; J. K. Walton and R. Poole, 'The Lancashire Wakes in the nineteenth century', in *Popular Culture in Modern Britain: Persistence and Change*, ed. R. D. Storch (1982).

155. H. Cunningham, *Leisure in the Industrial Revolution* (1980), 60–1, deals perceptively with these issues.

156. H.L.R.O. (Lords), S.C. on the Blackpool Railway Bill, 1884, evidence of B. Walmsley, Q. 614.

157. *Sheffield Independent*, 15–22 July 1899.

158. Walton, *Landlady*, 38–9.

159. *Midland Advertiser*, 30 Aug. 1913; *Walsall Observer*, 23 Aug. 1913.

160. Brown, 'Leisure industries', 196; and cf. G. Stedman Jones, 'Working-class culture and working-class politics in London, 1870–1900: some notes on the remaking of a working class', *J. Social History*, VII (1974), 460–508.

161. Banks, *op. cit.*; A. McLaren, 'Women's work and regulation of family size', *History Workshop*, IV (1977), 70–81.

162. D. C. Marsh, *The Changing Social Structure of England and Wales 1871–1961* (1965), 121–5; G. Anderson, *Victorian Clerks* (1976); G. Crossick (ed.), *The Lower Middle Class in Britain 1870–1914* (1977), 17–20.

163. *Mr Punch*, 101–3, 174–5.

164. L. Davidoff, *The Best Circles* (1973), ch. 2; *Mr Punch*, 130–3, 152.

165. Pimlott, *Holiday*, chs. 11–12.

166. *Mr Punch*, 6.

167. K. Chorley, *Manchester Made Them* (1950), ch. 12.

168. *Mr Punch*, 30.

169. *Torquay Times*, 4 June 1897; Lowerson and Myerscough, *Time to Spare*, 29; Gilbert, *Brighton*, 216–17.

170. Walton, *Landlady*, 149–56; Stafford, 'Victorian Margate', 81–4.

171. Gilbert, *Brighton*, 172.

172. D. S. Young, *The Story of Bournemouth* (1957), 103–5; C. H. Bishop, *Folkestone: The Story of a Town* (1973),

173. M. Hughes, *A London Girl of the 1880s* (1978 edn), 135–41; and see, for example, A. G. Folliott Stokes, *From St Ives to Land's End* (1908), 24–5.

174. T. A. Leonard, *Adventures in Holiday Making* (n.d., c. 1935).

175. Moncrieff, *Where Shall We Go?*, 64–5.

176. *Ibid.*, 42, 65–6; *S.W.P.* (1895), 259–60, 292–3; Ward Lock and Co., *Worthing* (1912–13 edn), 43–4; A. D. King, 'A time for space and a space for time: the social production of the vacation house' in *Buildings and Society*, ed. A. D. King (1980), 193–227.

177. *S.W.P.* (1895), 219–20; R. Burdett Wilson, *Go Great Western: A History of G.W.R. Publicity* (1970); *Walsall Observer*, 23 Aug. 1913.

178. Whyman, 'Kentish seaside resorts', 37; Stafford, 'Victorian Margate', 92 (see above, n. 131). Most of Stafford's figures from visitors' lists are meaningless: see J. K. Walton and P. R. McGloin, 'Holiday resorts and their visitors', *Local Historian*, VIII (1979), 323–31.

179. Pimlott, *Holiday*, 175; Moncrieff, *Where Shall We Go?*, 255.

180. *Mr Punch*, 40–1.

181. But the founders of the new resort of Saltburn took care to provide spa water in the 1860s: J. Leonard, 'Saltburn: the northern Brighton', in *Ports and Resorts*, ed. Sigsworth, 191–200. Sir Henry Drummond Wolff did the same at Boscombe in 1868 (R. Roberts, 'Leasehold estates and municipal enterprise', in *Patricians, Power and Politics*, ed. Cannadine).

182. *Mr Punch*, 54–5; Walton, 'Blackpool', 333.

183. Gilbert, *Brighton*, 181.

184. W. D. Smith, *Stretching their Bodies* (1974), 23; *S.W.P.* (1895), 347–50; Moncrieff, *Where Shall We Go?*, 8; Pimlott, *Holiday*, 182.

185. Moncrieff, *Where Shall We Go?*, 4.

186. *Mr Punch*, 79, 110–16.

187. Stafford, 'Victorian Margate', 58–9.

188. Moncrieff, *Where Shall We Go?*, 2.

3 THE PATTERN OF RESORT
  DEVELOPMENT

1. B.S.P. 1852–3, LXXXV, 464, 632; LXXXVI, 462.
2. *Seaside and Inland ABC Holiday Guide* (1904), 45.
3. A. G. Folliott Stokes, *From St Ives to Land's End* (1908), 30.
4. *S.W.P., passim*; Ward Lock & Co., *Plymouth* (1903–4 edn), x, xxi–xxii, 28–9.
5. B.S.P. 1852–3, LXXXV, p. 655.
6. Moncrieff, *Where Shall We Go?*, 206, an impression confirmed by the census reports.
7. Cf. e.g. May, 'Ilfracombe', *passim*.
8. What follows is based on the 1801 census population figures supported by contemporary comment, especially in Carey, *Balnea*, and *Watering Places*. Cf. Pimlott, *Holiday*, 59–64.
9. J. and S. Farrant, *Aspects of Brighton 1650–1800* (1978), 3–8.
10. Gilbert, *Brighton*, 50–1.
11. Farrant, *Brighton*, 1–3; Gilbert, *Brighton*, 33, 56–63, 83ff.
12. *The Hastings Guide . . . by an Inhabitant* (1797), 41–2, 61–6, 70–1.
13. Eastbourne, Seaford, Rottingdean, Worthing, Littlehampton and Bognor.
14. *Watering Places*, 390–1.
15. Whyman, 'Hanoverian watering-place', esp. 143–5; *The Margate Guide* (1770), 12–15.
16. R. S. Holmes, 'Continuity and change in a mid-Victorian resort: Ramsgate 1851–71' (D.Phil. thesis, University of Kent, 1977), 64, 68–70.
17. Carey, *Balnea*, 33–4; J. Whyman, 'Rise and decline: Dover and Deal in the nineteenth century', *Archaeologica Cantiana*, LXXXIV (1969), 107–37.
18. May, 'Ilfracombe', 2–7, 302–7; *Watering Places*, 193*–199, 352.
19. May, 'Ilfracombe', 2, 5, 24ff., 48–9; Oakley, 'Dorset and Somerset', 77, 241; *Watering Places*, 227, 362–3.
20. McIntyre, 'Health and pleasure resorts', 293–320; *A New Weymouth Guide* (c. 1800), 86–90.
21. *Watering Places*, 160, 237–9, 300–34; Carey, *Balnea*, 91–105.

22. *A New Scarborough Guide* (1808 edn), 62–4; *A New Weymouth Guide*, 50, 86–90; Whyman, 'Kentish seaside resorts', 25.
23. McIntyre, 'Health and pleasure resorts', 180–9; Pimlott, *Holiday*, 63–4.
24. Carey, *Balnea*, 232; *Watering Places*, 340ff.
25. W. J. Lewis, 'Some aspects of the history of Aberystwyth', *Ceredigion*, IV (1960–3), 21; *Watering Places*, 335–7.
26. B.S.P. 1852–3, XXIX, p. xlix. The 11 were Brighton, Ramsgate, Margate, Worthing, Weymouth, Scarborough, Ryde, Cowes, Ilfracombe, Dover and Torquay.
27. These were Bath, Cheltenham, Leamington and Tunbridge Wells.
28. B.S.P. 1852–3, XXIX, p. xlix, Table XXVI.
29. Pimlott, *Holiday*, 97.
30. H. Cunningham, *Leisure in the Industrial Revolution* (1980), 161–2.
31. Calculations from B.S.P. 1852–3, XXIX, p. xlix, Table XXVI.
32. Llandudno is a good example. See N. Hawthorne, *English Notebooks* (1962 edn), 79–80.
33. Excluding Kentish London.
34. Neale, *Bath*, ch. 8.
35. For the north-east, E. L. Blanchard, *Adams's Descriptive Guide to the Watering-Places of England* (1851), 192–202. Population figures for the resort villages themselves are not available.
36. Whyman, 'Kentish seaside resorts', 3–5. Remember that 1841 was a June census.
37. See below, ch. 8.
38. J. K. Walton, 'Railways and resort development in Victorian England: the case of Silloth', *Northern History*, XV (1979), 191–208.
39. *Ibid.* See also J. D. Marshall and J. K. Walton, *The Lake Counties from 1830 to the Mid-Twentieth Century* (1981), 196–201.
40. H.L.R.O. (Commons), S.C. on the Blackpool Railway Bill, 1884, Q. 2160 expresses contemporary perceptions.
41. J. Grass, 'Morecambe: the people's pleasure' (M.A. dissertation, University of Lancaster, 1972), 8–11.

42. B. R. Mitchell, *Abstract of British Historical Statistics* (1962), 24–7.

43. See below, ch. 4.

44. *Torquay Times*, 14 July 1905, 25 Aug. 1905; R. Roberts, 'Leasehold estates and municipal enterprise', in *Patricians, Power and Politics*, ed. Cannadine.

45. Walton, 'Blackpool', ch. 7.

46. C. S. Ward, *Eastern Counties*, Thorough Guides Series (1902 edn), 83.

47. *S.W.P.* (1895), 78.

48. *Isle of Thanet Gaz.*, 17 May 1913.

49. G. W. Wigner, *Sea Side Water* (1878). For the general problems of using visitors' lists, see J. K. Walton and P. R. McGloin, 'Holiday resorts and their visitors', *Local Historian*, XIII (1979), 323–31. For a contemporary view of the quantification problem, see H.L.R.O. (Commons), S.C. on the Margate Extension and Improvement Bill, 1877, evidence of W. D. Pickering, the Mayor of Margate. He said (Q. 8) that the number of visitors at any one time was 'a debateable question which has never been settled; all sorts of calculations have been made from 10,000 up to 60,000; it is a very large number indeed'.

50. Walton, 'Blackpool', 263; H.L.R.O. (Commons), S.C. on the Blackpool Improvement Bill, 1865, Q. 19; Gilbert, *Brighton*, 152; H.L.R.O. (Commons), S.C. on the Blackpool Railway Bill, 1884, Q. 17, 25, 396.

51. Everritt, *Southend*, 24, 122.

52. Wigner, *op. cit.*, 19, 25; Annual Report of the M.O.H., Margate, 1904; *Isle of Thanet Gaz.*, 24 May 1913.

53. P.R.O. MH. 13/162, report on Scarborough cab bye-laws, 20 April 1865; H.L.R.O. (Commons), S.C. on the Scarborough Improvement Bill, 1890, p. 7; H.L.R.O. (Commons) S.C. on the Llandudno Urban District Council Bill, 1897, Q. 3–8; Brown, 'Leisure industries', 197.

54. *Rhyl J.*, 9 Aug. 1913.

55. H.L.R.O. (Commons), S.C. on the Barmouth Local Board Bill, 1890, Q. 31–5; May, 'Ilfracombe', 316–17; Ward Lock & Co., *Newquay* (1910–11 edn), 14.

56. H.L.R.O. (Commons), S.C. on the Great Yarmouth Corporation Bill, 1897, 7–8; Stafford, 'Victorian Margate', 102–5; H.L.R.O. (Commons), S.C. on the Scarborough Improvement Bill (1890), Q. 342.

57. *Grimsby News*, 8 Sept. 1882.

58. H.L.R.O. (Commons), S.C. on the Folkestone Improvement Bill, 1855, evidence of Richard Hart, 94.

4 RESORT SOCIETY: STRUCTURE AND PROBLEMS

1. See J. K. Walton and P. R. McGloin, 'The tourist trade in Victorian lakeland', *Northern History*, XVII (1981), for problems of this nature, and cf. the figures in K. L. Mayoh, 'A comparative study of resorts on the coast of Holderness' (M.A. thesis, University of Hull, 1961), 154 and table 20. Some directories in well-established resorts omitted landladies altogether: *Residential and Trade Directory to Douglas* (1892) and Downsborough's *Guide and Directory of Bexhill-on-Sea* (1888). Some show obvious internal inconsistencies: W. White, *History, Gazetteer and Directory of Norfolk* (1890) lists 98 lodging-house keepers for the small resort of Hunstanton, and only 160 for Great Yarmouth, 154 of whom were men.

2. J. K. Walton and P. R. McGloin, 'Holiday resorts and their visitors', *Local Historian*, XIII (1979), 323–31.

3. M. J. B. Baddeley, *Yorkshire* (part 1), Thorough Guide Series (1908 edn), 93; R. Bush, *The Book of Exmouth* (1978), 75.

4. *S.W.P.* (1895), 14–21; Moncrieff, *Where Shall We Go?*, 197–8; Kelly's *Directory of Northumberland* (1894); *Cumberland Pacquet*, 6 Aug. 1872; *Adair's Maryport Advertiser*, 25 June 1880.

5. T. A. Welton, *England's Recent Progress* (1911), 149–51, shows this for 1880–1900.

6. John Evans, Ll.D., *Recreation for the Young and the Old: An Excursion to*

Brighton (1821), 69; Gilbert, *Brighton*, 248.

7. A. D. M. Phillips and J. Walton, 'The distribution of personal wealth in English towns in the mid-nineteenth century', *Inst. British Geographers*, LXIV (1975), 44.

8. K. Lindley, *Seaside Architecture* (1973), 79.

9. B.S.P. 1833, XXVI. For location factors, see E. Brunner, *Holiday Making and the Holiday Trades* (1945), 25–6.

10. B.S.P. 1844, XXVII, pp. 8–9.

11. B.S.P. 1844, XXVII, pp. 43–349.

12. J. D. Murphy, 'The town and trade of Great Yarmouth' (Ph.D. thesis, University of East Anglia, 1979), 153, 198, 250–3.

13. J. Whyman, 'Visitors to Margate in the 1841 census returns', *Local Population Studies*, VIII (1972), 19–39.

14. Walton, 'Blackpool', 107; May, 'Ilfracombe', 115–17.

15. B.S.P. 1913, lxxviii, pp. 969ff., tables 22A, 22B.

16. For Bournemouth, B.S.P. 1904, CVIII, p. 79. Cf. Cannadine, *Lords and Landlords*, 358–69.

17. Walton, 'Blackpool', ch. 1; H. J. Gayler, 'The coastal resorts of Essex' (M.A. thesis, University of London, 1966).

18. B.S.P. 1844, XXVII; B.S.P. 1913, LXXVIII, LXXIX. The 1841 figures are for 'Servants, domestic', including those in hotels, inns and lodging-houses who are excluded from the figures for 1911, which cover 'Other domestic indoor servants'.

19. For Southend commuters see Everritt, *Southend*, 24, 111, which gives figures suggesting that the main growth came in Edwardian times.

20. B.S.P., county returns for 1901 census, table 35a.

21. See especially Stuart, 'North-east Wales', 306–7; *VCH Sussex*, VI (1) (1980), 38; A. D. King, 'A time for space and a space for time: the social construction of the vacation house', in *Buildings and Society*, ed. A. D. King (1980).

22. McIntyre, 'Health and pleasure resorts', 200; *Watering Places*, 294, 315, 362–3.

23. Walton, *Landlady, passim*.

24. Whyman, 'Aspects of holiday making', 252; *New Scarborough Guide* (1808), 62–4.

25. Whyman, 'Aspects of holiday making', 211.

26. S. Farrant, *Georgian Brighton* (1980), 45–6.

27. Whyman, 'Aspects of holiday making', 268, 270.

28. *New Scarborough Guide* (1808); *New Weymouth Guide* (c. 1800).

29. Farrant, *op. cit.*, 4–5.

30. McIntyre, 'Health and pleasure resorts', 314.

31. Whyman, 'Kentish seaside resorts', 27; Whyman, 'Aspects of holiday making', 233–8.

32. Carey, *Balnea*, 212, 233–4.

33. Bush, *op. cit.*, 44.

34. Carey, *Balnea*, 67.

35. B.S.P. 1904, CVIII, p. 135. David Rubinstein first drew my attention to this phenomenon.

36. Cf. Walton, *Landlady, passim*.

37. B.S.P. 1844, XXVII, pp. 114–349.

38. Murphy, *op. cit.*, 256. Murphy's analysis is made unnecessarily lurid by his confusion of seaside boarding-houses with common lodging-houses.

39. See, for example, *Br.G.*, 26 June 1890: 'There are many who try to represent themselves as private houses, while in fact they are properly speaking boarding houses'.

40. Walton, 'Blackpool', 141.

41. B.S.P. 1913, LXXIX.

42. But we should remember that its lodging-houses were smaller than in the other major resorts: Walton, 'Blackpool', 111–12.

43. Walton, *Landlady*, 213. This was not a universal development, for at Ilfracombe and in the Lake District recruitment was mainly local: May, 'Ilfracombe', 146 and J. D. Marshall, *Old Lakeland* (1971), ch. 11.

44. Mate's *Bournemouth Directory* (1891). Bournemouth's Mayor in 1895 was Merton Russell Cotes, 'the resort's leading hotelier', a 'wealthy businessman from Wolverhampton' who took over the Royal Bath Hotel

when obliged to move to Bournemouth for his health in 1875: R. Roberts, 'Leasehold estates and municipal enterprise', in *Patricians, Power and Politics*, ed. Cannadine.

45. Walton, *Landlady*, ch. 4.
46. Cf. E. Richards, 'Women in the British economy since about 1700: an interpretation', *History*, LXIX (1974), 337–57, a speculative survey which neglects the rôle of women in shopkeeping and accommodation, and takes too little account of the under-recording of female occupations.
47. B.S.P. 1913, LXXIX.
48. Brown's *Popular Guide to the Isle of Man* (n.d.), 70.
49. Barrett's *Directory of Preston and the Fylde* (1901); cf. Stafford, 'Victorian Margate', 124.
50. See below, ch. 7.
51. Lindley, *op. cit.*, 82–7; Gilbert, *Brighton*, 161–3.
52. Lowerson and Myerscough, *Time to Spare*, 29.
53. Lindley, *op. cit.*, 87; Brown's *Isle of Man*, 71; L. J. Bartley, *The Story of Bexhill* (1971), 105–6.
54. Mate's *Bournemouth Directory* (1891).
55. Lowerson and Myerscough, *Time to Spare*, 29; Cannadine, *Lords and Landlords*, 362–4.
56. Walton, *Landlady*, chs. 5–6; May, 'Ilfracombe', 145–7; Mayoh, 'Holderness', 154–6.
57. *Mr Punch*, 12–18, 74–5, 90, 145, 159, 163.
58. M. J. Winstanley, *Life in Kent at the Turn of the Century* (1978), 212–21; Lowerson and Myerscough, *Time to Spare*, 35–6; *Cambrian News*, 23 May 1884.
59. Winstanley, *op. cit.*, 205–31; Walton, 'Blackpool', 108, table 2.3.
60. R. Samuel, 'Comers and goers', in *The Victorian City: Images and Realities*, ed. H. J. Dyos and M. Wolff (1976 edn), I: 123–60.
61. *Mr Punch*, 62–8.
62. B.S.P. 1844, XXVII, pp. 43–349.
63. B.S.P. 1873, LXXI, Part I. It is possible to obtain occupational breakdowns in six 'classes' and 17 'orders' for superintendent registrars' districts in

1871, but it is impossible to disentangle the resorts in the list from their mainly agricultural surroundings for purposes of analysis and comparison.

64. Walton, 'Blackpool', 109; May, 'Ilfracombe', 144.
65. Cf. B.S.P. 1913, LXXVIII, p. 344. For problems and trends nationally, with special reference to actors and actresses, see M. Baker, *The Rise of the Victorian Actor* (1978), 24–5, 83–4, 109–10.
66. B.S.P. 1913, LXXIX.
67. Walton, 'Blackpool', 132–5; H.L.R.O. (Commons), S.C. on the Bournemouth Improvement Bill, 1892, Q. 382, 454–7.
68. Walton, 'Blackpool', 107; Cannadine, *Lords and Landlords*, 362–3; May, 'Ilfracombe', 140.
69. Walton, 'Blackpool', 133; *B.G.*, 16 Jan. 1891, 15 Feb. 1895; R. Tressell, *The Ragged-Trousered Philanthropists* (1965 edn), 370.
70. Walton, 'Blackpool', 135–6.
71. *Ibid.*, 115–16; cf. the uncritical and misleading use made of local directories in Cannadine, *Lords and Landlords*, 358–60, a strange blemish on a generally fine book.
72. Pike's *Brighton and Hove Blue Book* (1888).
73. Walton, 'Blackpool', 113–15.
74. Annual Reports of the M.O.H., Margate, 1905.
75. *B.G.*, 25 Jan. 1898.
76. Gilbert, *Brighton*, 156–7; *VCH Sussex*, VI (1), 95; *Worthing Directory* (1896); C. S. Ward, *Eastern Counties*, Thorough Guides Series (1902 edn), 89–90; Murphy, *op. cit.*, 91, 109–14.
77. B.S.P. 1872, LXVI, Part II, enumerators' notes. The public school at Lancing accounted for half the private school population there: J. R. de S. Honey, *Tom Brown's Universe: the Development of the Victorian Public School* (1977), 51.
78. Bartley, *op. cit.*, 88–90.
79. C. H. Bishop, *Folkestone: The Story of a Town* (1973), 129.
80. B.S.P. 1913, LXXIX; Cannadine, *Lords and Landlords*, 362.
81. B.S.P. 1844, xxvii; B.S.P. 1913, LXXIX.
82. *Torquay Times*, 23 July 1897 (letter from 'A Torquay Tradesman').

83. Evans, *op. cit.*, 38.
84. Calculated from the printed census returns.
85. Cf. V. Karn, *Retiring to the Seaside* (1977), ch. 1.
86. Cf. B.S.P. 1912–13, CXIII, pp. 405–15, and see Welton, *op. cit.*, 43–59, for a full analysis.
87. Specialized areas within resorts displayed some of these characteristics to the point of caricature. Adelaide Ward, Hove, contained three women to every man at the 1911 census (*Brighton Herald*, 12 April 1913), and in 1895 two miles of Hastings' sea-front saw only two or three births per year, a ratio of one per 1,000 population (*Hastings and St Leonards Observer*, 30 March 1895).
88. *Ibid.*, 16–21; R. S. Holmes, 'Continuity and change in a mid-Victorian resort: Ramsgate 1851–71' (D.Phil. thesis, University of Kent, 1977), 246; Welton, *op. cit.*, 9 and *passim*.
89. B.S.P. 1913, LXXVIII, p. 9.
90. Walton, 'Blackpool', 166–72; *S.G.*, 17 Jan. 1861; May, 'Ilfracombe', 128; *Br.G.*, 11 Jan. 1900, 20 Jan. 1900; *Brighton Herald*, 11 Jan. 1913; *Hastings and St Leonards News*, 6 Jan. 1888; *Hastings and St Leonards Observer*, 9 Feb. 1895; Cannadine, *Lords and Landlords*, 370–2.
91. H.L.R.O. (Commons), S.C. on the Southend-on-Sea Corporation Bill, 1895, Q. 164–71; *S.S.*, 9 Aug. 1900; Walton, *Landlady*, 122–8; Winstanley, *op. cit.*, 214; Annual Reports of the MOH, Margate, 1904 and 1910; *Isle of Thanet Gaz.*, 24 May 1913; *Llandudno Register*, 2 May 1913; *Brighton Herald*, 22 March 1913.
92. Walton, *Landlady*, 133–4; *Scarborough Mercury*, 18 April 1913.
93. Tressell, *op. cit.*, 585–6. Cf. Neale, *Bath*, ch. 8.
94. May, 'Ilfracombe', *passim*.
95. Bill Rubinstein kindly supplied this information.
96. *S.S.*, 12 July 1894.

5 PLANNING AND BUILDING: LANDOWNERSHIP AND DEVELOPMENT

1. D. Cannadine, 'Urban development in England and America in the nineteenth century: some comparisons', *Economic History Rev.*, , n.s., XXXIII (1980), 324.
2. Cannadine, *Lords and Landlords*, 412–13.
3. Cf. *ibid.*, 385.
4. Colwyn Bay, Seascale and Silloth are the best examples.
5. Cannadine, *Lords and Landlords*; R. Gurnham, 'The creation of Skegness as a resort town by the ninth earl of Scarbrough', *Lincs. History and Archaeology*, VII (1972); R. E. Pearson, 'Railways in relation to resort development in east Lincolnshire', *East Midlands Geographer*, IV (1968); T. W. Beastall, *A North Country Estate* (1975), 183–200; L. J. Bartley, *The Story of Bexhill* (1971); C. H. Bishop, *Folkestone: The Story of a Town* (1973).
6. See above, tables 3–8. By the later nineteenth century Bournemouth was already divided among several landowning families, whose development policies and attitudes varied considerably: R. Roberts, 'Leasehold Estates and Municipal Enterprise', in *Patricians, Power and Politics*, ed. D. Cannadine (1982).
7. For the pioneer example, see Neale, *Bath*, chs. 4–5.
8. Cf. F. M. L. Thompson, *Hampstead: Building a Borough 1650–1964* (1974), chs. 6–9; and 'Hampstead, 1830–1914', in *Middle Class Housing in Britain*, eds. M. A. Simpson and T. H. Lloyd (1977), 86–113.
9. For a full treatment of topographical influences, see Barrett, 'Seaside resort towns'.
10. M. J. B. Baddeley and C. S. Ward, *North Wales*, Thorough Guides Series (1899), section 1, 26.
11. Abel Heywood and Son, *A Guide to Blackpool and Fleetwood* (n.d., c. 1865), 9; Blackpool Corporation, *West Coast of Lancashire, Fashionable Seaside Resort* (1880), 7–8.

12. Black's *Guide to Yorkshire* (1862), 181; M. J. B. Baddeley, *Yorkshire*, vol. I, Thorough Guides Series (1908), 31.

13. R. S. Holmes, 'Continuity and change in a mid-Victorian resort: Ramsgate 1851–71' (D.Phil. thesis, University of Kent, 1977); Barrett, 'Seaside resort towns'; Bartley, *Bexhill*; *VCH Yorkshire (East Riding)*, II (1974), 33–70.

14. May, 'Ilfracombe', 54, 73, 329.

15. Ward Lock & Co., *Bideford* (1918–19 edn), 27; M. J. B. Baddeley and C. S. Ward, *North Devon and North Cornwall*, Thorough Guides Series (1885), 61.

16. Barrett, 'Seaside resort towns', 70.

17. Thompson, *op. cit.*, 88.

18. See, for example, H.L.R.O. (Commons), S.C. on the Southport Improvement Bill, 19 May 1876, Q. 405ff., about conditions on the 'wrong side of the tracks' at Birkdale.

19. Cannadine, *Lords and Landlords*, 257–60.

20. Walton, *Landlady*, 70–2, 154–6.

21. H.L.R.O. (Commons), S.C. on the Paignton Improvement Bill, 1898, 17–22 and Q. 68–9. For the case of Worthing, where the low-lying east side had larger estates but a lower class of development, see *VCH Sussex*, VI (1), 100, 110.

22. Granville, *Spas*, II: 496–500; N. Wood (ed.), *Health Resorts of the British Islands* (1912), 187.

23. Granville, *Spas*, II: 479–84, 587–91. For Brighton see Gilbert, *Brighton*, ch. 5.

24. May, 'Ilfracombe', 5.

25. Granville, *Spas*, II: 512–36.

26. Wood, *op. cit.*, 152–71, 191–2.

27. *Ibid.*, 141–2.

28. 'Atticus', *Places and Faces* (1875), 129; *B.G.*, 1 Jan. 1897, 27 Feb. 1912, 24 Dec. 1912.

29. Stafford, 'Victorian Margate', 61–2; *Isle of Thanet Gaz.*, 29 Mar. 1913; May, 'Ilfracombe', 350.

30. Gilbert, *Brighton*, 39–43.

31. C. W. Chalklin, *The Provincial Towns of Georgian England* (1974), 64–6 and *passim*; H. J. Dyos, *Victorian Suburb* (1973 edn), 39–40; Neale, *Bath*, ch. 4.

32. J. and S. Farrant, *Aspects of Brighton 1650–1800* (1978), 9, 32, 35, 48–52, 61; Farrant, *Brighton*; Gilbert, *Brighton*, 93.

33. Whyman, 'Aspects of holiday making', 239–44; *New Margate Guide* (1770), 12–15.

34. J. Liddle, 'Estate management and land reform politics', in *Patricians, Power and Politics*, ed. Cannadine; W. Thornber, *The History of Blackpool and its Neighbourhood* (1837), 216.

35. C. Musgrave, *Life in Brighton* (1970), 175–91.

36. Chalklin, *op. cit.*, 74–80; Neale, *Bath*, chs. 4–5.

37. Musgrave, *op. cit.*, 175–86; Gilbert, *Brighton*, 98–101; A. Dale, *Fashionable Brighton* (1967), chs. 3, 5, 9; J. Middleton, *A History of Hove* (1979), 35–8; Farrant, *Brighton*. For the extent of Scutt's obscurity see J. Bateman, *Great Landowners of Great Britain* (1883), 370.

38. A. C. Ellis, *An Historical Survey of Torquay* (1930 edn), 317; P. Russell, *A History of Torquay* (1960), 74–8, 86–90.

39. Liddle, 'Estate management and land reform'; G. Rogers, 'Social and economic change on Lancashire landed estates during the nineteenth century, with special reference to the Clifton Estate, 1832–1916' (Ph.D. thesis, University of Lancaster, 1981). For Exmouth see T. Rammell, *Report to the Board of Health on the Sanitary Condition of Exmouth* (c. 1850), 7–8. R. Bush, *The Book of Exmouth* (1978) and E. R. Delderfield, *Exmouth Milestones* (1948), fly in the face of their own evidence in praising the Rolle estate for the town's early development. Apart from a few grants of land for parks and open spaces, very little was done until the Rolle Estate Act of 1865. Myths of this kind are common in 'aristocratic' resorts.

40. Brown, 'Leisure industries', 121–5.

41. McIntyre, 'Health and pleasure resorts', 379–89; *New Weymouth Guide*, 15.

42. Murphy, *op. cit.*, 250–3; P.R.O. MH. 13/81, W. Lee's memorandum to Board of Health, 26 Oct. 1850. For

similar lack of supervision at
Aberystwyth, see W. J. Lewis, 'Some
aspects of the history of Aberystwyth',
Ceredigion, IV (1960–3), 21; *Cambrian
News*, 15 May 1874.

43. Brown, 'Leisure industries', 126–30,
314; Oakley, 'Dorset and Somerset',
178.

44. Brown, 'Leisure industries', 109–11.

45. Pimlott, *Holiday*, 114–15; Carey,
Balnea, 77–8.

46. H. J. Gayler, 'The coastal resorts of
Essex' (M.A. thesis, University of
London, 1966), 38.

47. J. H. Burrows, *Southend and District*
(1909, repr. 1970), 170–1.

48. D. Neave, 'Transport and the early
development of East Riding resorts', in
Ports and Resorts in the Regions, ed.
Sigsworth, 101–19.

49. Whyman, 'Kentish seaside resorts',
14–21; Granville, *Spas*, II: 10–14; M. J.
Winstanley, 'Conflicting responses to
New Brighton's role as a popular seaside
resort, 1896–1914' (M.A. thesis,
University of Lancaster, 1973).

50. Carey, *Balnea*, 8–9; P. Whittle, *Marina*
(1831), 9–10.

51. E. L. Blanchard, *Adams's Descriptive
Guide to the Watering-Places of
England* (1851), 65–6.

52. Granville, *Spas*, II: 477–80, 495.

53. J. Gloag, *Victorian Taste* (1972 edn),
ch. 4.

54. Holmes, *op. cit.*, 77; Granville, *Spas*,
II: 579.

55. Granville, *Spas*, II: 542–3; cf. Holmes,
'Ramsgate', 80–2.

56. Rogers, *op. cit.*, ch. 6.

57. D. S. Young, *The Story of Bournemouth*
(1957), 36 and ch. 4; R. Roberts,
'Leasehold estates and municipal
enterprise', in *Patricians, Power and
Politics*, ed. Cannadine.

58. Russell, 82–90, 95–7, 101–2.

59. J. H. Sutton, 'Early Fleetwood
1835–47' (M.Litt. thesis, University of
Lancaster, 1968).

60. Bishop, *op. cit.*, 98–102.

61. Cannadine, *Lords and Landlords*,
236–8.

62. Stuart, 'North-east Wales', 225–31; H.
Carter, 'A decision-making approach to
town plan analysis: a case-study of
Llandudno', in *Urban Essays: Studies in
the Geography of Wales*, ed. H. Carter
and W. K. D. Davies (1970), 69–75.

63. Rogers, *op. cit.*; Brown, 'Leisure
industries', 177–80.

64. Liddle, *op. cit.*

65. *Ibid.*

66. Cannadine, *Lords and Landlords*,
ch. 18.

67. Gurnham, *op. cit.*; Pearson, *op. cit.*;
Bartley, *op. cit.*

68. Brown, 'Leisure industries', 194–5.

69. Liddle, *op. cit.* There were also
persistent complaints of jerry-building,
despite the strict requirements officially
laid down by the landowners: see, for
example, *Southport Visiter*, 17 July
1877.

70. G. S. Duncan, 'Church and society in
early Victorian Torquay' (M.A. thesis,
University of Exeter, 1972), 11.

71. B.S.P. 1872, LXVI, Part II, 70; J.V.N.
Soane, 'The general significance of the
development of the urban and social
structure of Bournemouth, 1840–1940'
(Ph.D. thesis, University of Surrey,
1978), 404. Southport's Medical Officer
of Health said in 1876 that at least 500
houses in the town were 'habitually
overcrowded', with a shortage of
cottages pushing up rents to such an
extent that many families were doubling
up. He argued that the building by-laws
required so much space around each
dwelling that cottage property was not
an economic proposition. The
Corporation proposed to provide 40
houses under the Artizans' Dwellings
Act for its own workers to ease the
shortage: H.L.R.O. (Commons), S.C.
on the Southport Improvement Bill,
22 May 1876, Q. 11–19, 41–3, 149. See
also Liddle, *op. cit.*

72. The saga can be followed in P.R.O.
M.H. 13/2.

73. Cf. Russell, *op. cit.*, 131, for the
Mallock family's discouragement of
development at Cockington, and
Rogers, *op. cit.*, for the Clifton family's
restrictive leasing policies, which
retarded development in the 1840s at
Lytham, and their concern to protect

the amenities of Lytham Hall. The
Cliftons long remained ambivalent
about urban development on political
and religious grounds.

74. J. K. Walton, 'Railways and resort
development in Victorian England: the
case of Silloth', *Northern History*, xv
(1979), 191–209.

75. J. D. Marshall, *Old Lakeland* (1971),
ch. 12.

76. K. L. Mayoh, 'Comparative study of
resorts on the coast of Holderness'
(M.A. thesis, University of Hull, 1961),
67–70; Neave, *op. cit.*

77. R. W. Ambler, 'Cleethorpes: the
development of an east coast resort', in
Ports and Resorts, ed. Sigsworth,
179–90.

78. H.L.R.O. (Commons), S.C. on the
Westgate and Birchington Gas and
Water Bill, 1879, evidence of E. F.
Davis; J. Lowerson (ed.), *An
Embryonic Brighton? Victorian and
Edwardian Seaford* (1976 edn), 13ff.;
Oakley, 'Dorset and Somerset', 320–1;
Stuart, 'North-east Wales', 246;
Cambrian News, 28 Aug. 1874, 2 May
1884; *Llandudno Register*, 10 April
1890; C. N. Riches, 'The development
of Felixstowe 1870–1970' (M.Litt.
thesis, University of East Anglia, 1976).

79. A. H. Woolner, 'The economic
geography of the development and
present position of Lowestoft as a port
and holiday resort' (M.Sc. Econ. thesis,
University of London, 1956), 185.

80. *Bridlington Free Press*, 12 July 1873,
1 Aug. 1896; Mayoh, *op. cit.*, 84–8; *S.S.*,
16 July 1880; Walton, 'Blackpool',
80–3.

81. For which see M. J. B. Baddeley and
C. S. Ward, *North Wales*, Thorough
Guides Series (1899), section 1, 160.

82. Barrett, 'Seaside resort towns'; Gayler,
op. cit., 55–62; Moncrieff, *Where Shall
We Go?*, 120–2, for Lowestoft. Peto,
Brassey and Betts developed Southend's
Cliff Town estate while leasing the
London, Tilbury and Southern
Railway: Burrows, *op. cit.*, 195.

83. Gayler, 'Coastal resorts of Essex',
86–91; Stuart, 'North-east Wales', 248;
P. Peers, 'The development of St

Annes-on-the-Sea as a residential town
and watering-place, 1874–1914' (M.A.
thesis, University of Lancaster, 1979);
Rogers, *op. cit.*

84. J. Leonard, 'Saltburn: the northern
Brighton', in *Ports and Resorts*, ed.
Sigsworth, 191–200; *S.W.P.* (1876), 122;
S.W.P. (1895), 104; Oakley, 'Dorset and
Somerset', 264.

85. Ellis, *op. cit.*, 286–7; Russell, *op. cit.*, 90.

86. Cannadine, *Lords and Landlords*, 264–5
and ch. 21; Liddle, *op. cit.*; Roberts, *op.
cit.* At Southport the Corporation had
to lower its sights sharply on its own
estate, putting three houses in 1900 on
plots which had been intended for two
in the early 1880s: *Southport Guardian*,
14 March 1900.

87. Walton, 'Blackpool', 37–40, 79–86; *S.
S.*, 2 June 1876, 16 July 1880,
3 July 1885; Burrows, *op. cit.*, 195, 219;
Gayler, *op. cit.*, 108, 219.

88. Walton, 'Blackpool', ch. 1; H.L.R.O.
(Commons), S.C. on the
Southend-on-Sea Corporation Bill,
1895, evidence of J. H. Burrows and
William Gregson.

89. Walton, *Landlady*, 65–8.

90. Walton, 'Blackpool', 69–76, 79–93.

91. *Y.I.*, 5 March 1890, 17 March 1894.

92. Cannadine, *Lords and Landlords*, 410.

93. Burrows, *op. cit.*, 219.

94. P. J. Aspinall, 'Speculative builders and
the development of Cleethorpes', *Lincs.
History and Archaeology*, xi (1976),
43–52.

95. P. J. Aspinall, *The Evolution of Urban
Tenure Systems in Nineteenth-Century
Cities* (1978), contains much relevant
information.

96. Brown, 'Leisure industries', 321–2.

97. W. F. Pickering, 'The West Brighton
Estate, Hove' (M.A. thesis, University
of Sussex, 1969), 32, 36, 51–8; Gilbert,
Brighton, 172.

6 LOCAL GOVERNMENT AT THE SEASIDE

1. See especially E. P. Hennock, *Fit and
Proper Persons* (1973); M. E. Falkus,
'The development of municipal trading

in the nineteenth century', *Business History*, xix (1977), 134–61; R. Lambert, 'Central and local relations in mid-Victorian England: the Local Government Act Office, 1858–71', *Victorian Studies*, vi (1962–3), 121–50.

2. Brookfield, 'Coastal Sussex', 153.
3. G. T. Clark, *Report to the Board of Health on the Sanitary Condition of Tenby* (1850), 16.
4. Cf. Falkus, 'Municipal trading', for further references.
5. Calculated from B.S.P. 1903, vii, pp. 272ff., Joint S.C. on Municipal Trading, Appendix 1.
6. Similar motives sometimes lay behind railway promotion. For examples of the principle at work, see *K.G.*, reports on debate over the proposed Margate Aquarium, 1874, *passim*; C. Arthur, *A History of the Fylde Waterworks Company, 1861–1911* (1911); J. K. Walton, 'Railways and resort development in Victorian England: the case of Silloth', *Northern History*, xv (1979), 191–209.
7. L. J. Bartley, *The Story of Bexhill* (1971), 33–4; Cannadine, *Lords and Landlords*, especially chs. 18–20.
8. Walton, 'Blackpool', 192.
9. H.L.R.O. (Commons), S.C. on the Llandudno Urban District Council Bill, 1897, 5–9 and evidence of A. Conolly. Cf. also the case of the Raincliff Road Company at Scarborough: *S.G.*, 24 Jan. 1861.
10. Cannadine, *Lords and Landlords*, 348–9.
11. C. H. Bishop, *Folkestone: The Story of a Town* (1973), 119–20.
12. H.L.R.O. (Commons), S.C. on the Llandudno Urban District Council Bill, 1897, 91–2.
13. Lancs. R.O. QEC.2/2, 19 June 1850, 19 Feb. 1851, 20 June 1853, 16 Nov. 1853. For similar arrangements at Lytham, Lancs. R.O. MBLs/2/1, 24 July 1848, and QEC.2/3 for 1865 and 1868; and for Rhyl in 1862, see P.R.O. MH.13/153.
14. Walton, 'Blackpool', 391–2.
15. For the complex evidence on which these generalizations are based, see

especially McIntyre, 'Health and pleasure resorts'; A. Dale, *Brighton Town and Brighton People* (1976); Gilbert, *Brighton*, 38–9; *VCH Sussex*, vi (1), 115; B.S.P. 1835, XXIII, pp. 172, 406–12, XXIV, pp. 1306–15, 1388–95, XXX, pp. 1721–3; *VCH Yorkshire (East Riding)*, iv, 65; May, 'Ilfracombe', ch. 4; and the various Reports to the Board of Health at mid-century on sanitary conditions in resorts.
16. For an introduction to these themes see D. Fraser, *Urban Politics in Victorian England* (1976), especially chs. 4 and 7.
17. Reports to the Board of Health by R. Rawlinson on Southport (p. 8), E. Cresy on Hastings (p. 30) and Margate (pp. 19–21), and W. Lee on Great Yarmouth (pp. 11–12).
18. May, 'Ilfracombe', 156, 171.
19. E. Cresy, *Report to the Board of Health on the Sanitary Condition of Brighton* (1850), 10–19, 30–9.
20. E. Cresy, *Report on Margate* (1850), 9–18, 25ff. For a graphic description of the problems see P.R.O. MH.13/123, William Hart to Board of Health, 7 July 1851.
21. E. Cresy, *Reports on Worthing* (1850), 12, 17, 23–5, and Hastings (1850), 48.
22. B. H. Babbage, *Report on Blackpool* (1851), 25–6.
23. T. W. Rammell, *Report on Littlehampton* (1852), 14–16.
24. Rammell, *Report on Clevedon* (1852), 13–17.
25. Babbage, *Report on Blackpool* (1851), 25–9.
26. G. T. Clark, *Report on Tenby* (1850), 13–14.
27. Cresy, *Report on Hastings* (1850), 27–9.
28. W. Lee, *Report on Great Yarmouth* (1850), 33.
29. Cresy, *Report on Hastings* (1850), 31; Babbage, *Report on Blackpool* (1851), 22.
30. B.S.P. 1835, xxiv, p. 747; May, 'Ilfracombe', 161.
31. Rammell, *Report on Littlehampton* (1852), 13.
32. Rawlinson, *Report on Southport* (1855), 9–11; Lancs. R.O. MBLs/2/1, 11 Dec. 1848, 12 May 1856.

33. Clark, *Report* on Tenby (1850), 15; Rammell, *Report* on Clevedon (1852), 26.

34. Dale, *op. cit.*, 90–2.

35. A. Redford, *The History of Local Government in Manchester* (1939), vols. 1 and 2; B. D. White, *A History of the Corporation of Liverpool* (1951), chs. 4–5, 7–8; Fraser, *op. cit.*, 160–6.

36. Dale, *op. cit.*, *passim.*

37. *Ibid.*, 138–9; McIntyre, 'Health and pleasure resorts', 358; Cresy, *Report* on Hastings (1850), 14, 18–19.

38. For example at Lytham and Fleetwood: Lancs. R.O. MBLs/2/1, MBF/2/1.

39. P. Bailey, *Leisure and Class in Victorian England* (1978), 20–1; R. D. Storch, 'The plague of the blue locusts: police reform and popular resistance in northern England, 1840–57', *International Rev. Social History*, xx (1975), 61–90.

40. B. H. Babbage, *Report* on Blackpool (1851), 39.

41. Lancs. R.O. DDC1/1200/40, 1200/44, 2233/2.

42. May, 'Ilfracombe', 168.

43. *Bridlington Free Press*, 14 Feb. 1863, 21 Feb. 1863, 21 Mar. 1863. Cf. Walton, 'Blackpool', 182–4, and G. Rogers, 'Social and economic change on a Lancashire landed estate during the nineteenth century, with special reference to the Clifton Estate, 1832–1916' (Ph.D. thesis, University of Lancaster, 1981), ch. 6.

44. E. C. Midwinter, *Social Administration in Lancashire 1830–60* (1971), 81. Lambert, *op. cit.*, 123–4, stresses that compulsory powers were seldom invoked even by Chadwick himself.

45. *Blackburn Standard*, 16 Sept. 1846.

46. P.R.O. MH.13/81, Squire to Board of Health, 8 Sept. 1849, 23 July 1850.

47. There was still disquiet in Rhyl about possible interference by 'the London Board' in 1864; P.R.O. MH.13/153, William Hilditch to Local Government Act Office, 3 Feb. 1864.

48. P.R.O. MH.13/162 (Scarborough), especially Dickens' report, 9 June 1859; and see the Great Yarmouth saga in MH.13/81.

49. Walton, 'Blackpool', 185.

50. The 23 per 1,000 had to be maintained as an average for seven years: Midwinter, *op. cit.*, 80–1; Lambert, *op. cit.*, 124.

51. P.R.O. MH.13/181; Lambert, *op. cit.*, 138–42.

52. G. W. Wigner, *Sea Side Water* (1878), 40.

53. Walton, *Landlady*, 24–5; C. Widdowfield, 'The Local Board of Poulton, Bare and Torrisholme and the development of Morecambe, 1852–94' (M.A. thesis, University of Lancaster, 1973), 46–7.

54. P.R.O. MH.13/181, 17 April 1849.

55. P.R.O. MH.13/123, Margate Pier Company to Board of Health, 10 Feb. 1851.

56. P.R.O. MH.13/107. Cf. A. L. Dickens, *Report* on Sandgate (1856), 13–18.

57. The Blackpool of the early 1860s is a good example: Walton, *Landlady*, 18–20, 24–6.

58. Cannadine, *Lords and Landlords*, 296.

59. Walton, 'Silloth', 206–7.

60. *Cambrian News*, 29 May 1874.

61. Wigner, *op. cit.*, 39 and *passim.*

62. *VCH Sussex*, vi (1), 92–5.

63. H.L.R.O. (Commons), S.C. on the Southport Improvement Bill, 16 May 1876, evidence of Walter Smith, Q. 563ff.; 22 May 1876, evidence of Dr H. H. Vernon, Q. 107–11.

64. *VCH Sussex*, VI (1), 116.

65. Midwinter, *op. cit.*, 100–1.

66. Cf. Hennock, *op. cit.*

67. Walton, *Landlady*, 25–6; *Fleetwood Chronicle*, 1 Feb. 1867; P.R.O. MH.13/24, 9 Feb. 1869, 22 March 1871.

68. Dale, *op. cit.*, 217–28; *Br.G.*, 3 Jan. 1850.

69. D. S. Young, *The Story of Bournemouth* (1957), 66–74; R. Roberts, 'The Barnum of Bournemouth', in *Leisure in England*, eds. Walton and Walvin.

70. See below, ch. 8.

71. J. H. Burrows, *Southend and District* (1970 edn); *S.S.*, 7 Aug. 1890.

72. Brown, 'Leisure industries', 184, 187–90.

73. May, 'Ilfracombe', 199–200.

74. H.L.R.O. (Commons), S.C. on the Margate Extension and Improvement Bill, 1877, Q. 70.

75. *S.G.*, 11 Jan. 1872, 21 March 1872; H.L.R.O. (Commons), S.C. on the Scarborough Improvement Bill, 1890, Q. 117–20.

76. Gilbert, *Brighton*, 191; *VCH Yorkshire (East Riding)*, II, 65.

77. A. C. Ellis, *An Historical Survey of Torquay* (1930 edn), 300–1; P. Russell, *A History of Torquay* (1960), 104–5. The new works were inaugurated with fête and firework display, and the whole town was decorated for the occasion.

78. Walton, 'Blackpool', 202.

79. May, 'Ilfracombe', 184–5.

80. H.L.R.O. (Commons), S.C. on the Paignton Improvement Bill, 1898, Q. 163.

81. Burrows, *op. cit.*, 235–6; J. E. Jarratt, *Municipal Recollections: Southport 1900–1930* (1932), 32ff.

82. Walton, 'Blackpool', 205; Everritt, *Southend*, 29; Annual Reports of the MOH, Margate.

83. *Cambrian News*, 23 May 1884; Paignton Improvement Bill, 220–4.

84. *B.G.*, 22 May 1874; Walton, 'Blackpool', 201–5.

85. Annual Reports of the MOH, Margate. For a full account of health provisions in Brighton, see 'London-by-the-Sea', *London* (1895), 429–31.

86. H.L.R.O. (Commons), S.C. on the Bournemouth Improvement Bill, 1892, pp. 12–13, Q. 217, 512–20.

87. Cf. Roberts, 'The Barnum of Bournemouth'.

88. Walton, 'Blackpool', 201; Brown, 'Leisure industries', 187–90, 294; H.L.R.O. (Commons), S.C. on the Rhyl Improvement Commissioners' Bill, 1892, evidence of W. E. Williams: the waterworks purchase followed a sustained agitation by ratepayers eager for an improved supply. For subsequent developments, *Rhyl J.*, 7 May 1898. See also the Exmouth case (below, n. 140).

89. Walton, 'Blackpool', 197; H. Monks, 'Some notes on the municipal gas undertaking, 1852–1949' (typescript in Blackpool Public Library), 4–5, 12.

90. Walton, 'Blackpool', 197–201.

91. *Ibid.*, 209–10; *B.G.*, 3 May 1912; Blackpool Town Hall, Highway Committee minutes, 28 July 1913.

92. *Llandudno Register*, 26 July 1913.

93. Ward Lock and Co., *Torquay* (1915–16 edn), 24.

94. Ward Lock and Co., *Scarborough* (1903–4 edn), 60; *ibid.* (1906–7 edn), 73–4.

95. Margate Improvement Bill, Q. 70 (see above, n. 74).

96. *VCH Yorkshire (East Riding)*, II, 59–60; K. L. Mayoh, 'A comparative study of resorts on the coast of Holderness' (M.A. thesis, University of Hull, 1961), 81–9.

97. Everritt, *Southend*, 31; Burrows, *op. cit.*, 237–8.

98. H.L.R.O. (Commons), S.C. on the Weston-super-Mare Urban District Council Bill, 1896, Q. 33–5; Ward Lock and Co., *Clevedon* (1917 edn), Weston-super-Mare section, 13.

99. See below, ch. 7.

100. Burrows, *op. cit.*, 186–91; *S.S.*, 7 Aug. 1890, 28 June 1900.

101. H.L.R.O. (Commons), S.C. on the Great Yarmouth Corporation Bill, 1897, Q. 253–80; Burrows, *op. cit.*, 190.

102. This list was compiled from scattered evidence in theses, local histories, guide-books and press reports.

103. Great Yarmouth Corporation Bill, 30–2.

104. *Scarborough Mercury*, 27 May 1898; J. V. N. Soane, 'The general significance of the development of the urban and social structure of Bournemouth 1840–1940' (Ph.D. thesis, University of Surrey, 1978), 236.

105. May, 'Ilfracombe', 196–203.

106. H.L.R.O. (Commons), S.C. on the Barmouth Local Board Bill, 1891, Q. 1262.

107. Burrows, *op. cit.*, 238.

108. H.L.R.O. (Commons), S.C. on the Southport Improvement Bill, 19 May 1876, Q. 510; Blackpool Improvement Act, 42–3 Vict. cxcix, Clause lxxxvii.

109. H.L.R.O. (Commons), S.C. on the Bridlington Local Board Bill, 1889, pp. 43–7.

110. *Ibid.*, 20; H.L.R.O. (Commons), S.C. on the Bournemouth Improvement Bill, 1892, Q. 555ff.; *Y.I.*, 17 Nov. 1894.

111. *VCH Yorkshire (East Riding)*, II, 60; Burrows, *op. cit.*; H.L.R.O. (Commons), S.C. on the Weston-super-Mare Urban District Council Bill, 1896, evidence of Dr H. Hamilton; May, 'Ilfracombe', 199, 203; and various contemporary guide-books.

112. H.L.R.O. (Commons), S.C. on the Bournemouth Improvement Bill, 1892, Q. 523–54, 587–626; Roberts, 'The Barnum of Bournemouth'.

113. Young, *op. cit.*, 145–6.

114. Local press, especially *Torquay Times*, 11 July 1913; *Brighton Herald*, 6 Sept. 1913; *Isle of Thanet Gaz.*, 29 March 1913.

115. *Brighton Herald*, 3 May 1913.

116. *Rhyl J.*, 22 Feb. 1913, 17 May 1913, 13 Sept. 1913.

117. *Br.G.*, 19 April 1900.

118. H.L.R.O. (Commons), S.C. on the Great Yarmouth Corporation Bill, 1897, pp. 13–34.

119. H.L.R.O. (Commons), S.C. on the Weston-super-Mare Urban District Council Bill, 1896, especially evidence of Dr W. Smith.

120. *Torquay Times*, 9 July 1897.

121. *Isle of Thanet Gaz.*, 5 April 1913.

122. *Ibid.*, 29 March 1913.

123. For what follows see Walton, 'Blackpool', ch. 7.

124. H.L.R.O. (Commons), S.C. on the Bridlington Local Board Bill, 1889, p. 129.

125. *Ibid.*, 127.

126. In 1898 the Local Government Board reported that no application for such powers had been allowed since 1884, and listed the unsuccessful applicants: H.L.R.O. (Commons), S.C. on the Paignton Improvement Bill, 1898, second day, pp. 138–42.

127. R. H. S. Butterworth, 'Advertising health resorts', *Municipal J.*, 17 Aug. 1912.

128. *Y.I.*, 18 Jan. 1913, 8 March 1913.

129. See above, n. 7.

130. Walton, 'Blackpool', 180.

131. Burrows, *op. cit.*, 229.

132. H.L.R.O. (Commons), S.C. on the Weston-super-Mare Urban District Council Bill, 1896, Q. 492; J. Lowerson (ed.), *An Embryonic Brighton? Victorian and Edwardian Seaford* (1976 edn), 51.

133. Burrows, *op. cit.*, 221–2.

134. But cf. above, n. 88, for similar developments in Rhyl, and *Hornsea Gaz.*, 6 April 1878, 12 Oct. 1878, 10 Feb. 1882, for what seems to have been a sustained campaign over several years, with organized ratepayers appealing to the Local Government Board for intervention.

135. Walton, 'Blackpool', ch. 9, sect. III.

136. Roberts, 'Leasehold estates', in *Patricians, Power and Politics*, ed. Cannadine.

137. Cannadine, *Lords and Landlords*, 356; G. S. Duncan, 'Church and society in early Victorian Torquay' (M.A. thesis, University of Exeter, 1972), 39, 393.

138. May, 'Ilfracombe', 211.

139. K. Wilson, 'Social leaders and public figures in the rise of Morecambe' (M.A. thesis, University of Lancaster, 1972), 10–64.

140. E. R. Delderfield, *Exmouth Milestones* (1948), 136–7, 142, 180–7 (a strangely chequered municipal career, with a lot of new initiatives around the turn of century); 'London-by-the-Sea', *London*, 6 June 1895, 429 (for a lively local authority in which builders and hoteliers counterbalanced the residential interest); Lowerson, *op. cit.*, 48, 51 (farmers and tradesmen showing little initiative); M. J. Winstanley, 'Conflicting responses to New Brighton's role as a popular seaside resort, 1896–1914' (M.A. thesis, University of Lancaster, 1973), chs. 3–4.

141. Russell, *op. cit.*, 146–8; *Torquay Times*, 4 June 1897.

142. Lowerson and Myerscough, *Time to Spare*, 43; J. Travis, 'Lynton: an isolated and exclusive resort', in *Ports and Resorts*, ed. Sigsworth, 152–67; *S.S.*, 18 March 1886; Winstanley, 'New Brighton'; H.L.R.O. (Commons), S.C. on the Weston-super-Mare Urban

District Council Bill, 1896, evidence of
Henry Pethick and Robert Roxburgh
(who favoured expenditure on drainage
improvements and hospitals rather than
holiday amenities); *T.A.*, 9 Aug. 1890.

143. *Bridlington Free Press*, 12 April 1879;
K.G., 15 May 1880; *Cambrian News*,
25 April 1884.

144. Rogers, *op. cit.*, ch. 6.

145. *Hastings and St Leonards News*,
14 April 1876; Walton, 'Blackpool',
ch. 4; *S.S.*, 18 March 1886.

146. Walton, 'Blackpool', ch. 4, sect. V.

147. *S.S.*, 16 July 1880.

148. Cannadine, *Lords and Landlords*,
370–5.

149. Cf. Walton, 'Blackpool', 470.

7 SEASIDE ENTERTAINMENT

1. J. H. Plumb, *The Commercialisation of
Leisure in Eighteenth-Century England*
(1973); P. Borsay, 'The English urban
renaissance 1680–1760', *Social History*,
II (1977), 581–603; H. Cunningham,
Leisure in the Industrial Revolution
(1980), 16–17.

2. See especially Cunningham, *op. cit.*, esp.
chs. 1 and 5; P. Bailey, *Leisure and
Class in Victorian England* (1978),
ch. 7; R. Altick, *The Shows of London*
(1978).

3. For a transatlantic perspective see
R. Lewis, 'Seaside holiday resorts in the
United States and Britain', *Urban
History Yearbook* (1980), 44–52; C. E.
Funnell, *By the Beautiful Sea: the Rise
and High Times of that Great American
Resort, Atlantic City* (New York, 1975);
and with special reference to seaside
fairgrounds and amusement technology,
J. F. Kasson, *Amusing the Million:
Coney Island at the Turn of the Century*
(New York, 1978).

4. Walvin, *Seaside*, chs. 4 and 5; Pimlott,
Holiday, ch. 7; *Mr Punch, passim*.

5. McIntyre, 'Health and pleasure resorts',
194; D. Neave, 'Transport and the early
development of East Riding resorts' (for
spas at Hornsea, Bridlington and
Aldbrough), in *Ports and Resorts*, ed.
Sigsworth, 101–19.

6. Whyman, 'Aspects of holiday-making',
581–3, 622.

7. *Ibid.*, 300, 320, 772–4.

8. McIntyre, 'Health and pleasure resorts',
198–9, 266–7; C. W. Chalklin, *The
Provincial Towns of Georgian England*
(1974), 54.

9. J. and S. Farrant, *Aspects of Brighton
1650–1800* (1978), 8.

10. Whyman, 'Aspects of holiday-making',
198, 239, 274, 279, 292, 335–6;
A. Temple Patterson, *A History of
Southampton 1700–1914*, I (1966),
39–44, 57–60.

11. Whyman, 'Aspects of holiday-making',
163–4; *Watering Places*, 394–5.

12. McIntyre, 'Health and pleasure resorts',
315.

13. Whyman, 'Aspects of holiday-making',
274–84, 303–28; *Watering Places*,
259–65. Two Southampton libraries had
3,000 books each in the 1770s: Temple
Patterson, *op. cit.*, 41–2. Chalklin costs
the Margate theatre at £3,000–3,600;
C. W. Chalklin, 'Capital expenditure
on building for cultural purposes in
provincial England, 1730–1830',
Business History, XXII (1980), 59.

14. Whyman, 'Aspects of holiday-making',
177, 288–9; Pimlott, *Holiday*, 131.

15. Gilbert, *Brighton*, 123–9; J. Middleton,
A History of Hove (1979), 45–7;
C. Musgrave, *Life in Brighton* (1970),
244–5.

16. Chalklin, *op. cit.*, 59.

17. McIntyre, 'Health and pleasure resorts',
308–15; Carey, *Balnea*, 106–8, 125–6.

18. Carey, *Balnea*, 233–4; *Watering Places*,
394–5.

19. *VCH Sussex*, VI (1), 105; Chalklin, *op.
cit.*, 59.

20. Whyman, 'Kentish seaside resorts', 8–9.

21. *Watering Places*, 340–5.

22. Neave, *op. cit.*

23. Brown, 'Leisure industries', 158–64.

24. F. A. Bailey, *A History of Southport*
(1955), 64, 80.

25. Walton, 'Blackpool', 304–5.

26. *Carlisle J.*, 30 July 1836 (I owe this
reference to Mrs June Barnes); Charles
Dickens, 'The lazy tour of two idle
apprentices', in *Christmas Stories* (The
Fireside Dickens, n.d.), 729–30.

27. See especially Whyman, 'Aspects of holiday-making', 273–84; Farrant, *Brighton*, 25–6.

28. Chalklin, *op. cit.*, 57; J. and S. Farrant, *op. cit.*, 8; Whyman, 'Aspects of holiday-making', 335–40.

29. J. and S. Farrant, *op. cit.*, 8. Capital from Lewes, the county town, was of general importance in Brighton's early development.

30. Chalklin, *op. cit.*, 61–3; Whyman, 'Aspects of holiday-making', 351, 356; Gilbert, *Brighton*, 124.

31. Brown, 'Leisure industries', 158; Bailey, *op. cit.*, 80; *Carlisle J.*, 30 July 1836.

32. P. Howell and E. Beazley, *South Wales* (1977), 137–8; *Watering Places*, 351.

33. Cunningham, *op. cit.*, 90.

34. Jane Austen, *Sanditon* (1978 edn), 36–7, 51–2.

35. Cf. Whyman, 'Aspects of holiday-making', *passim*.

36. *Ibid.*, 749; *Watering Places*, 239, 347.

37. K. L. Mayoh, 'A comparative study of resorts on the coast of Holderness' (M.A. thesis, University of Hull, 1961), 24.

38. *VCH Sussex*, VI (1), 105; cf. *New Margate Guide* (1850), 17.

39. Walton, 'Blackpool', 306, 309.

40. *Y.I.*, 25 June 1870; Stafford, 'Victorian Margate', 169, 189–91.

41. *New Margate Guide* (1850), 19–20, 41; *T.A.*, 27 July 1867, 18 July 1868; *K.G.*, 20 Aug. 1898.

42. *Y.I.*, 30 June 1860; *VCH Sussex*, VI (1), 148–9.

43. *S.G.*, 10 Jan. 1861; Farrant, *Brighton*, 22.

44. Pimlott, *Holiday*, 131; Gilbert, *Brighton*, 129.

45. The list of piers and enabling acts in K. Lindley, *Seaside Architecture* (1973), 155–6, which is the basis of comments in Walvin, *Seaside*, 50, 76, omits many piers and in several instances suggests much later opening dates than were actually the case. My own list is built up from newspapers, guide-books and company records. It is an advance on Lindley, but I suspect that it is still not the whole story.

46. Bailey, *op. cit.*, 102.

47. Lindley, *op. cit.*, 36; J. Grass, 'Morecambe, the people's pleasure' (M.A. thesis, University of Lancaster, 1972), 18–19.

48. Bailey, *op. cit.*, 100; Brown, 'Leisure industries', 240–61.

49. Lindley, *op. cit.*, 36; H.L.R.O. (Commons), S.C. on the Weston-super-Mare Urban District Council Bill, 1896, Q. 228.

50. P.R.O. BT.31/805/556c; BT.31/31321/39645; BT.31/1037/1758c; BT.31/1192/2648c; BT.31/0615/2582; Grass, *op. cit.*, 51 (for Morecambe Pier Co., in BT.31/3787); Companies House, File 1636c, Volume 1.

51. P.R.O. BT.31/0615/2582.

52. See further Lindley, *op. cit.*, ch. 2.

53. Gilbert, *Brighton*, 129.

54. *S.W.P.* (1876), 27–9, 36–7, 62, 94–6, 107–8, 112–13.

55. Sir Edmund Gosse, *Father and Son* (Windmill Library edn, 1928), 140–1.

56. May, 'Ilfracombe', 390–1. See also Walvin, *Seaside*, 73–4; Pimlott, *Holiday*, 134–5.

57. S. Baring-Gould, *Devon* (1922 edn), 235; cf. the uncritical presentation of the new resort in R. N. Worth, *Tourist's Guide to North Devon and the Exmoor District* (5th edn, 1890), 60–1. Kingsley shared the fate of Wordsworth and Clement Scott in making a district so famous by his writings that pre-existing pressures for commercial development became irresistible.

58. *S.W.P.* (1876), 31–2.

59. *The Tenby*, 6 Sept. 1873; cf. *Mr Punch*, 108–9.

60. Quoted by May, 'Ilfracombe', 368–9.

61. Gilbert, *Brighton*, 184.

62. Walvin, *Seaside*, 73.

63. Pimlott, *Holiday*, 132–3; Stafford, 'Victorian Margate', 47.

64. Stafford, 'Victorian Margate', 176.

65. *Llandudno Register*, 18 July 1863; *S.S.*, 11 Sept. 1874, 16 Oct. 1874.

66. Lowerson and Myerscough, *Time to Spare*, 80; *Br.G.*, 7 Sept. 1854; *T.A.*, 7 Sept. 1867.

67. *Folkestone Chronicle*, 15 Sept. 1860.

68. E.g. *S.G.*, 25 July 1872, 29 Aug. 1872.

69. *Hastings and St Leonards Gaz.*, 13 Sept. 1856; cf., for a more jaundiced view than local newspapers usually provided, Nathaniel Hawthorne's comments on Southport in 1857: *English Notebooks* (1962 edn), 495–6.

70. *S.W.P.* (1876), 41–2; (1895), 233–6; J. V. N. Soane, 'The general significance of the development of the urban and social structure of Bournemouth, 1840–1940' (Ph.D. thesis, University of Surrey, 1978), 131.

71. H.L.R.O. (Commons), S.C. on the Westgate and Birchington Gas and Water Bill, 1879, Q. 128–30; P. Russell, *A History of Torquay* (1960), 173; Bailey, *op. cit.*, 119–21; Musgrave, *Life in Brighton* (1970), 277–88.

72. *B.G.*, 9 May 1872; *S.G.*, 19 Sept. 1872. See also *Mr Punch*, 144–8.

73. *Silloth Gaz.*, 11 Aug. 1860.

74. D. S. Young, *The Story of Bournemouth* (1957), 103–5; Russell, *op. cit.*, 116–19, 137–40; Bailey, *op. cit.*, 163–75.

75. Pimlott, *Holiday*, ch. 7.

76. See below, ch. 8.

77. See above, n. 2, and Walton, 'Blackpool', 331.

78. Russell, *op. cit.*, 139; Gilbert, *Brighton*, 182; Bailey, *op. cit.*, 142–3; P.R.O. BT.31/1381/3841.

79. The resorts included Ramsgate, Margate, Blackpool, Scarborough, Rhyl, Southport, Tynemouth and Great Yarmouth. There were abortive schemes at New Brighton, Torquay, Bournemouth, Lytham and Margate again.

80. Walton, 'Blackpool', p. 331; Young, *op. cit.*, 94; P.R.O. BT.31/1931/7994; BT.31/1910/7789.

81. P.R.O. BT.31/1781/6728.

82. P.R.O. BT.31/2158/10027.

83. Walton, 'Blackpool', 314–15.

84. Stafford, 'Victorian Margate', 191–6; but *T.A.*, 22 June 1867 suggests that the Hall opened in 1866 rather than 1864.

85. *K.G.*, 30 May 1874, 5 Sept. 1874.

86. *B.G.*, 3 Sept. 1875.

87. Walton, 'Blackpool', 317–18; *B.G.*, 30 May 1879, 1 Aug. 1879, 17 Dec. 1880.

88. *S.G.*, 15 Mar. 1883; *Rhyl J.*, 23 May 1885; Walvin, *Seaside*, 76–7; P.R.O. BT.31/32016/102075; *Br.G.*, 14 April 1900; Stafford, 'Victorian Margate', 197; *Y.I.*, 14 June 1884, 5 July 1884; C. S. Ward, *Eastern Counties*, Thorough Guides Series (1902), 87; P.R.O. BT.31/222/10501; and information from John Liddle.

89. Young, *op. cit.*, 125; P.R.O. BT.31/1910/7789; R. Roberts, 'The Barnum of Bournemouth', in *Leisure in England*, eds. Walton and Walvin.

90. P.R.O. BT.31/8036/57869; *S.G.*, 15 March 1883.

91. Walton, 'Blackpool', 312–14; *B.G.*, 9 Oct. 1874.

92. *K.G.*, 8 May 1880; *S.W.P.* (1876), 124; Brown, 'Leisure industries', 264–5; *Grimsby News*, 30 June 1876.

93. H.L.R.O. (Lords), S.C. on the Blackpool North Pier Bill, 1878, Q. 135.

94. R. C. Riley, *The Growth of Southsea as a Naval Satellite and Victorian Resort*, Portsmouth Papers, XVI (1972), 16; T. W. Beastall, *A North Country Estate* (1975), 195–6; Stuart, 'North-east Wales', 235; Ward Lock and Co., *North Wales: Northern Section* (1907–8 edn), 32.

95. This list is compiled from company records, guide-books, newspapers, local histories and minutes of evidence in H.L.R.O.

96. *Homeland Handbook* for Minehead, Porlock and Dunster (n.d.), 23.

97. Cannadine, *Lords and Landlords*, 276; P.R.O. BT.31/4864/32292.

98. Walton, 'Blackpool', 313; Lindley, *op. cit.*, 35; Musgrave, *op. cit.*, 290–1.

99. P.R.O. BT.31/2212/10419; BT.31/2158/10027; BT.31/2642/14022.

100. P.R.O. BT.31/3188/18528; BT.31/1980/8459; BT.31/1955/8236; BT.31/1643/5678.

101. *B.G.*, 19 May 1876, 28 Nov. 1879.

102. P.R.O. BT.31/5553/38622; BT.31/2489/12788; BT.31/31/2150/9961; BT.31/15648/48861; Companies House, File 33414; Walton, 'Blackpool', 323–5; *Scarborough Mercury*, 12 June 1885, 16 May 1913.

103. Grass, *op. cit.*, ch. 2; T. A. Bawden *et al.*, *The Industrial Archaeology of the Isle of Man* (1972), 112–14.

104. P.R.O. BT.31/5173/34961; BT.31/7711/55090.

105. *Bolton Rev.*, I (1897), 357–8 (Robert Poole kindly supplied this reference).

106. P.R.O. BT.31/17164/79562.

107. Everritt, *Southend*, 33; P.R.O. BT.31/9543/70905.

108. Kasson, *op. cit.*, 34–111.

109. Funnell, *op. cit.*

110. Walton, 'Blackpool', 319–21, 324–6.

111. Mike Winstanley kindly supplied this material.

112. Grass, *op. cit.*, 22–3.

113. See above, ch. 6.

114. Capital shortages, especially in the entertainment industry, were a persistent theme even in major resorts like Margate and Weston-super-Mare: *K.G.*, 16 May 1874; Brown, 'Leisure industries', 183, 202, 300–1.

115. Company records in the P.R.O. BT.31 series provide the main source for the following generalizations.

116. At Margate reactions to an outside company's Aquarium scheme were particularly well-documented in the local press during 1874–5, partly because of the appearance of a locally-sponsored rival.

117. *Cambrian News* during 1894–5.

118. F. K. Pearson, 'The Douglas Head Suspension Bridge', *Manx Museum*, 7, no. 85 (1969), 100–7; Walton, 'Blackpool', 319–22. Ten years earlier the seaside piers boom had encouraged a group of contractors, barristers and 'gentlemen' to set up the Marine Piers Co. Ltd., whose operations at Plymouth, Torquay and Weymouth anticipated the methods used by Standard Contract and Debenture: P.R.O. MT.10/319/H.364/81, and especially MT.10/345/H.195/82. The seaside was clearly a happy hunting-ground for fraudulent promoters, anxious to take advantage of the desperate need for outside initiative in most resorts.

119. Cf. Lowerson and Myerscough, *Time to Spare*, 44–6.

120. Information from Mike Winstanley.

121. *B.G.*, 2 July 1875.

122. D. Reid, 'Popular theatre in Victorian Birmingham', in *Performance and Politics in Popular Drama*, eds. D. Bradby, L. James, B. Sharrat (1980), 65–89; Walton, 'Blackpool', 330; P.R.O. BT.31/8509/61939.

123. Walton, 'Blackpool' 329–32; *B.G.*, 1 May 1903; cf. Funnell, *op. cit.*, for similar developments in Atlantic City.

124. *B.G.*, 12 March 1897, and see below, ch. 8.

125. Cf. Walvin, *Seaside*, 78–9; R. Manning-Saunders, *Seaside England* (1951), 122.

126. Moncrieff, *Where Shall We Go?*, 8.

127. Everritt, *Southend*, 39–40.

128. See esp. S. Yeo, *Religion and Voluntary Organisations in Crisis* (1976).

129. R. Roberts, 'Leasehold estates and municipal enterprise', in *Patricians, Power and Politics*, ed. Cannadine; Russell, *op. cit.*, 146–8 (the transition was particularly controversial here); Moncrieff, *Where Shall We Go?*, 214.

130. *Mr Punch*, 98 (exclamation marks in original).

131. *B.G.*, 26 July 1910, 13 July 1917.

132. Moncrieff, *Where Shall We Go?*, 80–3, 258–9.

133. A. Peaton, *Pictures of East Coast Health Resorts* (n.d.), 67–82.

134. Ward Lock and Co., *North Wales: Northern Section* (1907–8 edn), 45.

135. *Cambrian News*, 7 Sept. 1894.

136. Seed's *Southport and District Directory* (1914), 365; *S.W.P.* (1895), 28–30, 192–3; Moncrieff, *Where Shall We Go?*, 166–7, 172–4.

137. Line Brothers' *Clacton Directory* (1888), advertisement.

138. Pimlott, *Holiday*, 184–5.

139. Cf. Lowerson and Myerscough, *Time to Spare*, 126.

140. *S.W.P.* (1876), 11–12, 24, 37–9, 72–3, 122; Pimlott, *Holiday*, 133.

141. *S.W.P.* (1895), 269, 288–9; Moncrieff, *Where Shall We Go?*, 83–4, 201–2, 219; Lowerson and Myerscough, *Time to Spare*, 126; Peaton, *op. cit.*, advertising appendix; and many local references. In 1904, 116 of the 580 golf courses in

England and Wales listed in *Seaside and Inland ABC Holiday Guide* were at the seaside.

142. Young, *op. cit.*, 137–8.

143. *S.W.P.* (1895), 68, 155–8, 226–9, 257, 263–4, 360–1.

144. *Ibid.*, 32–3.

145. *Ibid.*, 1–2; Moncrieff, *Where Shall We Go?*, 155–6.

146. Moncrieff, *Where Shall We Go?*, 233–4; Walvin, *Seaside*, illustration 23.

147. C. H. Bishop, *Folkestone, the Story of a Town* (1973), 117; J. E. Jarratt, *Municipal Recollections: Southport 1900–1930* (1932), 9–10; Walton, 'Blackpool', 313, 323; and see above, ch. 6.

8 STYLES OF HOLIDAYMAKING: CONFLICT AND RESOLUTION

1. See especially Brown, 'Leisure industries', ch. 7; Perkin, 'Social Tone', 181–94.

2. P. Bailey, *Leisure and Class in Victorian England* (1978); H. Cunningham, *Leisure in the Industrial Revolution* (1980). Both contain good bibliographies.

3. *Preston Guardian*, 4 Feb. 1905. Despite these sentiments, the Preston holidays were extended to a full week in this year.

4. See especially P. Bailey, 'Will the real Bill Banks please stand up?', *J. Social History*, XII (1979), 336–53, and *idem*, '"A mingled mass of perfectly legitimate pleasures": the Victorian middle class and the problem of leisure', *Victorian Studies*, XXI (1977), 7–28.

5. R. D. Storch, 'The plague of the blue locusts', *International Rev. Social History*, XX (1975), 61–90; H. Cunningham, 'The London fairs in the nineteenth century', in *Social Control in Nineteenth Century Britain*, ed. A. P. Donajgrodzki (1977), 163–84; D. Reid, 'Popular culture and the march of progress', and J. K. Walton and R. Poole, 'The Lancashire Wakes in the nineteenth century', in *Popular Culture and Custom in Nineteenth-Century*

England, ed. R. D. Storch (1982); R. Poole, 'Oldham Wakes', in *Leisure in England*, ed. Walton and Walvin.

6. T. R. Tholfsen, *Working-Class Radicalism in Mid-Victorian England* (1976), chs. 3, 5 and 8; D. Vincent, *Bread, Knowledge and Freedom* (1981), chs. 7–8.

7. B. Harrison, *Drink and the Victorians* (1971), ch. 7.

8. B. Harrison, 'Religion and recreation in nineteenth-century England', *Past and Present*, XXXVIII (1967), 98–125; J. Wigley, *The Rise and Fall of the Victorian Sunday* (1980), chs. 8–11.

9. Reid, *op. cit.*; S. Yeo, *Religion and Voluntary Organisations in Crisis* (1976), ch. 6.

10. Bailey, 'Bill Banks'; cf. G. F. A. Best, *Mid-Victorian Britain 1851–75* (1971), 260–3.

11. For lively expositions of these and related themes see especially D. Olsen, *The Growth of Victorian London* (1976); D. Cannadine, 'Victorian cities: how different?', *Social History*, II (1977), 457–82; R. Thorne, 'Places of refreshment in the nineteenth-century city', in *Buildings and Society*, ed. A. D. King (1980), 233 and *passim*.

12. P.R.O. MT.10/319/H.364/81; H.L.R.O. (Commons), S.C. on the Scarborough Improvement Bill, 1890, p. 176; P.R.O. MT.10/83/H.3863/69.

13. P.R.O. MT.10/239/H.3669/77; MT.10/147/H.61/73; MT.10/114/H.920/71; MT.10/443/H.627. Jurisdiction above high-water mark also posed problems if ownership was uncertain: H.L.R.O. (Commons), S.C. on the Llandudno Improvement Bill, 1876, and the Wallasey Local Board Bill, 1890.

14. P.R.O. MH.12/5804, 27 Dec. 1895; Walton, 'Blackpool', 404–8.

15. P.R.O. MT.10/443/H.627.

16. See above, notes 12–13.

17. W. Plomer (ed.), *Kilvert's Diary* (Penguin edn, 1977), 236, 266–7, 310; *K.G.*, 29 Aug. 1874.

18. P.R.O. MH.13/162, 24 Dec. 1866, 16 Feb. 1867.

19. W. Miller, *Our English Shores* (1888),

23–4 and *passim*; *Y.I.*, 19 May 1860; *K.G.*, 19–26 Aug. 1874, 16 June 1880; *S.G.*, 22 Aug. 1850. Mixed bathing in families at Llanfairfechan in 1890 brought responses ranging from sorrow at the 'painful scenes' to ready acceptance of happy faces: *Llandudno Register*, 28 Aug. 1890.

20. *Fleetwood Chronicle*, 14 Aug. 1863, 6 Oct. 1865; Walton, 'Blackpool', 413–22, for a case-study.

21. *S.W.P.* (1876), 42.

22. *S.W.P.* (1895), 123–4; J. Lowerson (ed.), *An Embryonic Brighton? Victorian and Edwardian Seaford* (1976 edn), 42–3.

23. *B.G.*, 3 Aug. 1877.

24. Walton, 'Blackpool', ch. 8.

25. Quoted by Brown, 'Leisure industries', 175. Cf. Gilbert, *Brighton*, 204–6; Lowerson and Myerscough, *Time to Spare*, 31–4.

26. *S.S.*, 4–11 Sept. 1874.

27. *Hastings and St Leonards News*, 16 June 1874; *Mr Punch*, 158–9.

28. *Y.I.*, 26 May 1860.

29. Walton, *Landlady*, ch. 7.

30. J. Travis, 'Lynton: an isolated and exclusive resort', in *Ports and Resorts*, ed. Sigsworth.

31. Oakley, 'Dorset and Somerset', 107; W. Miller, *Our English Shores* (1888), 7.

32. *Hastings and St Leonards News*, 31 May 1867; *T.A.*, 15 June 1867; Lowerson and Myerscough, *Time to Spare*, 33.

33. Walton, 'Blackpool', 382–8.

34. *S.G.*, *passim*, and information from John Liddle.

35. *Br.G.*, 17 Aug. 1854, 9 Aug. 1860; *Hastings and St Leonards Gaz.*, 2 June 1860.

36. See R. S. Holmes, 'Continuity and change in a mid-Victorian resort: Ramsgate 1851–71' (D.Phil. thesis, University of Kent, 1977), 73–6, 183, for emphasis on the limited pace and extent of long-run change, and a denial of Best's assertion that Ramsgate became 'roaringly plebeian' during this period.

37. See above, ch. 2; W. Miller, *Our English Shores* (1888), 54.

38. *S.S.*, 11 Sept. 1874; and see above, ch. 2.

39. Walton, *Landlady*, ch. 7.

40. Cf. especially S. Yeo, *op. cit.*

41. Walton, *Landlady*, ch. 7; Walton, 'Blackpool', ch. 8.

42. Cannadine, 'Victorian cities'; Cannadine, *Lords and Landlords*, 373–5; *Torquay Times*, 4 June 1897; *Bournemouth Visitors' Directory* during 1890 and 30 Aug. 1913 (for trolleybuses).

43. *S.W.P.* (1895), 123–4; G. Rogers, 'Social and economic change on Lancashire landed estates during the nineteenth century, with special reference to the Clifton Estate, 1832–1916' (Ph.D. thesis, University of Lancaster, 1981), ch. 6.

44. Walton, *Landlady*, ch. 7.

45. Cf. Perkin, *op. cit.*

46. See above, ch. 6.

47. *Hastings and St Leonards Observer*, 14 Feb. 1885.

48. *Ibid.*, 11 April 1885, 8 Aug. 1885; W. Miller, *Our English Shores* (1888), 54.

49. Cannadine, *Lords and Landlords*, 354–8.

50. *B.G.*, 18 Aug. 1876, 23 Aug. 1878, 29 Aug. 1884, 26 Aug. 1898.

51. *Bournemouth Visitors' Directory*, 1 Aug. 1894; H.L.R.O. (Commons), S.C. on the Bridlington Local Board Bill, 1889; H.L.R.O. (Commons), S.C. on the Scarborough Improvement Bill, 1890, Q. 50, 266–7; 297; *Hastings and St Leonards Observer*, 2 Aug. 1890; Everritt, *Southend*, 32.

52. Holmes, *op. cit.*, 252–3.

53. Walton, 'Blackpool', 395–6; *K.G.*, 18 July 1874, 14 Aug. 1886; H.L.R.O. (Commons), S.C. on the Llandudno Urban District Council Bill, 1897, pp. 113–15; H.L.R.O. (Commons), S.C. on the Bournemouth Improvement Bill, 1892, Day 4, Q. 454–7; H.L.R.O. (Commons), S.C. on the Bridlington Local Board Bill, 1889, Q. 141–4; *Y.I.*, 8 Sept. 1900; *Weston Mercury*, 21 July 1900; *Llandudno Register*, 8 Aug. 1885; *Rhyl J.*, 18 July 1885.

54. Gilbert, *Brighton*, 195–6; *B.G.*,

4–11 June 1880; Lancs. R.O.,
Blackpool Police Order Book, 1887;
M. J. Winstanley, 'Conflicting
responses to New Brighton's role as a
popular seaside resort' (M.A. thesis,
University of Lancaster, 1973), 23; *Y.I.*,
12 July 1884; Charles Funnell, *By the
Beautiful Sea* (New York, 1975),
95–108; J. F. Kasson, *Amusing the
Million* (New York, 1978), 32–4;
S. Marcus, *The Other Victorians* (1966),
98–100.

55. Walton, *Landlady*, 116–22; *S.S.*,
12 July 1894; *Llandudno Register*,
24 July 1890; *Cambrian News*, 31 July
1874; *Hastings and St Leonards
Observer*, 9 Aug. 1902; *Scarborough
Mercury*, 12 Aug. 1898, 17 March 1905;
H.L.R.O. (Commons), S.C. on the
Barmouth Local Board Bill, 1891,
Q. 1206; *A New Scarborough Guide*
(1808), 10; L. Melville, *Society at
Tunbridge Wells in the Eighteenth
Century – and After* (1912), 78–82,
which includes 'The Touting Song' and
an amusing derivation for the term.

56. Walton, 'Blackpool', 400–2; H.L.R.O.
(Commons), S.C. on the Scarborough
Improvement Bill, 1890, Q. 158–72;
Grimsby News, 18 July 1913; *Southend
Standard*, 5–12 June 1913.

57. W. Kime, *Skeggy! The Story of an East
Coast Town* (1969), 54–6.

58. Walton, 'Blackpool', 396–9.

59. H.L.R.O. (Commons), S.C. on the
Barmouth Local Board Bill, 1891,
Q. 1196.

60. *Mr Punch*, 22.

61. *S.S.*, 10 July to 28 Aug. 1885, 11 March
1886, 17 May 1894, 2 Aug. 1894;
Everritt, *Southend*, 28.

62. H.L.R.O. (Commons), S.C. on the
Brighton Improvement Bill, 1896,
Day 2, Q. 1086–1134; S.C. (Commons)
on the Paignton Improvement Bill,
1898, Q. 68–9; J. E. Jarratt, *Municipal
Recollections: Southport 1900–1930*
(1932), 55.

63. J. K. Walton, 'Residential amenity,
respectable morality and the rise of the
entertainment industry: the case of
Blackpool', *Literature and History*, I
(1975), 72–3.

64. P.R.O. MT.10/114/H.920/71.

65. P.R.O. MT.10/239/H.3669/77.

66. *S.W.P.* (1876), 53; (1895), 79–83; *Y.I.*,
28 Aug. 1880, 2 Aug. 1890; H.L.R.O.
(Commons), S.C. on the Great
Yarmouth Corporation Bill, 1897,
Q. 1062–7.

67. H.L.R.O. (Commons), S.C. on the
Wallasey Local Board Bill, 1890, *passim*.

68. H.L.R.O. (Commons), S.C. on the
Llandudno Improvement Bill, 1876,
passim; P.R.O. MT.10/443/H.627; *S.S.*,
4–11 Sept. 1890.

69. See, for example, H.L.R.O.
(Commons), S.C. on the Great
Yarmouth Corporation Bill, 1897,
p. 31; S.C. on the Paignton
Improvement Bill, 1898, p. 126; and the
extended debate on forecourt stalls in
S.C. on the Blackpool Improvement
Bill, 1901.

70. Walton, 'Blackpool', 404–8.

71. Carey, *Balnea*, 57–8; Gilbert, *Brighton*,
51; P.R.O. MT.10/41/H.2177/67.

72. P.R.O. MT.10/443/H.627.

73. *Weston Mercury*, 13 July 1889.

74. P.R.O. MT.10/223/H.7010/76;
MT.10/740/H.8410; E. R. Delderfield,
Exmouth Milestones (1948), 186.

75. P.R.O. MT.10/474/H.1707; J. Field,
'"When the Riot Act was read": a pub
mural of the battle of Southsea, 1874',
History Workshop J., x (1980), 152–63.
Caroline Forder tells me that 'easement'
is a more appropriate term than
'use-right' in this context.

76. *S.S.*, 1 Sept. 1876; Everritt, *Southend*,
16, 72, 105.

77. *K.G.*, 4 Sept. 1886.

78. *Y.I.*, 12 June 1880, 12 July 1884,
5 April 1890, 17 March 1894; *S.W.P.*
(1895), 79–83.

79. See above, ch. 7, and Walton,
Landlady, ch. 7.

80. *K.G.*, 5 Sept. 1874, 18 Aug. 1894.

81. Walton, 'Blackpool', 415; *Br.G.*,
17 Aug. 1871.

82. Walton, 'Blackpool', 413–20.

83. See above, n. 80, and *B.G.*, 28 March
1879.

84. *Rhyl. J.*, 1 Aug. 1885.

85. *Hastings and St Leonards Observer*,
27 April–10 Aug. 1895.

86. Walton, 'Blackpool', 421.

87. Everritt, *Southend*, 45.

88. Walton, 'Blackpool', 421; cf. Wigley, *op. cit.*, esp. 147–8.

89. Walton, 'Blackpool', 411–13.

90. *Ibid.*, 426–7.

91. *Isle of Thanet Gaz.*, 5 July 1913.

92. Walton, 'Blackpool', 433; *Daily Telegraph*, 20 Aug. 1883; *Burnley Gaz.*, 13 Sept. 1884, quoting *Pall Mall Gaz.*

93. *S.G.*, 12 April 1883; *S.S.*, 5 Aug. 1886, 9 Aug. 1900; Everritt, *Southend*, 114–16; *Weston Mercury*, 27 April 1889; *Y.I.*, 9 June 1900.

94. *Hastings and St Leonards Observer*, 13–20 Apr. 1895; J. D. Marshall and J. K. Walton, *The Lake Counties from 1830 to the Mid-Twentieth Century* (1981), 184.

95. *Hastings and St Leonards News*, 12 Aug. 1892; *Hastings and St Leonards Observer*, 14 Sept. 1895; Oakley, 'Dorset and Somerset', 80; *Torquay Times*, 13 Aug. 1897; *Llandudno Register* from 17 July 1890.

96. *Bournemouth Visitors' Directory*, 1 Aug. 1894.

97. *Cambrian News* from 1 June 1894.

98. Winstanley, *op. cit.*

99. *Torquay Times*, 25 Aug. 1905.

100. J. Richards, 'Cinema-going in Birmingham in the 1930s', in *Leisure in England*, eds. Walton and Walvin.

101. Cf. Wray Vamplew's similar findings about the decline of football crowd violence in the early twentieth century, in his 'Ungentlemanly conduct: the control of soccer-crowd behaviour in England, 1888–1914', in *The Search for Wealth and Stability*, ed. T. C. Smout (1979), 150–2.

9 THE SEASIDE AND ENGLISH SOCIETY

1. J. Myerscough, 'New introduction', in Pimlott, *Holiday* (1976 edn); R. Lewis, 'Seaside holiday resorts in the United States and Britain', *Urban History Yearbook* (1980), 44–52; F. Cribier,

'Les estivants au Touquet', *Annales de Géographie*, LXXIV (1965).

2. H. J. Perkin, *The Origins of Modern English Society* (1971 edn), *passim*; J. H. Plumb, *The Commercialisation of Leisure in Eighteenth-Century England* (1973); P. Borsay, 'The English urban renaissance', *Social History*, II (1977), 581–603; Neale, *Bath*, 169.

3. W. Hutton, *A Description of Blackpool in 1788* (1944 edn), 9.

4. For further thoughts on railway influence see J. K. Walton, 'Railways and resort development in Victorian England: the case of Silloth', *Northern History*, XV (1979), 191–208, and *idem*, 'Railways and resort development in north-west England, 1830–1914', in *Ports and Resorts*, ed. Sigsworth, 120–37. For financial and legal innovations see especially Neale, *Bath*, ch. 4–5.

5. Cf. Lewis, *op. cit.*

6. Cf. Perkin, 'Social tone', 181–94.

7. R. Gurnham, 'The creation of Skegness as a resort town by the 9th earl of Scarbrough', *Lincs. History and Archaeology*, VII (1972); R. W. Ambler, 'Cleethorpes: the development of an east coast resort', in *Ports and Resorts*, ed. Sigsworth, 179–90; Brown, 'Leisure industries', ch. 7.

8. M. J. Winstanley, 'Conflicting responses to New Brighton's role as a popular seaside resort' (M.A. thesis, University of Lancaster, 1973). Landownership at New Brighton seems to have been subdivided to a greater extent than is suggested by Winstanley or by Perkin, 'Social tone'.

9. See especially R. Roberts, 'The Barnum of Bournemouth', and J. K. Walton, 'Municipal government and the holiday industry in Blackpool, 1876–1914', in *Leisure in England*, eds. Walton and Walvin.

10. Roberts, *op. cit.*

11. S. B. Saul, 'House building in England 1890–1914', *Economic History Rev.* 2nd series, XV (1962–3), 119–37; J. Melling (ed.), *Housing, Social Policy and the State* (1980).

12. See above, ch. 7.

13. Some very interesting research could be conducted on this theme, using local government records.

14. W. Ashworth, 'The late Victorian economy', *Economica*, n.s., XXXIII (1966), 21.

15. S. B. Saul, *The Myth of the Great Depression 1873–96* (1969), 40–1; Neale, *Bath*, 47.

16. Cannadine, *Lords and Landlords*, 415.

17. In H. J. Dyos and M. Wolff (eds), *The Victorian City: Images and Realities*, I (1976 edn), 123–60.

18. Walton, 'Blackpool', ch. 3; M. J. Winstanley, *Life in Kent at the Turn of the Century* (1978), ch. 15; and see above, ch. 4.

19. Whyman, 'Aspects of holiday-making', x.

20. Walton, *Landlady*, chs. 4–6.

21. R. Poole, 'Oldham Wakes', in *Leisure in England*, eds. Walton and Walvin; T. Wright, *Some Habits and Customs of the Working Classes* (1967 edn), 128–9.

22. The political precocity of Bath (Neale, *Bath*, chs. 9–10) and Brighton (Gilbert, *Brighton*, 207–8) seems to have been emulated in few other resorts, though Southsea had its radical activities in the 1870s (J. Field, 'When the Riot Act was read', *History Workshop J.*, x (1980), 152–63). The bread-riots in several Devon resorts in 1867 (P. Horn, 'Food riots in Devon, Somerset and Dorset, 1867: HO.45/7992', *Bull. Soc. Study of Labour History*, XLII (1981), 22–5)

provide a more plausible indicator of the state of plebeian consciousness in most seaside resorts; and most of the political activists elsewhere were probably petty tradesmen rather than genuine working-class representatives. Tressell's jaundiced view of Hastings building workers in *The Ragged-Trousered Philanthropists* carries a conviction which overrides the counter-productive aspects of his didactic intentions.

23. Neale, *Bath*, 225.

24. Cf. C. E. Funnell, *By the Beautiful Sea* (New York, 1975), for interesting if not always convincing elaborations on this theme.

25. Sir Edmund Gosse, *Father and Son* (Windmill Library edn, 1928), 101–2.

26. Farrant, *Brighton*, 3.

27. Borsay, *op. cit.*; Neale, *Bath*, 37–8.

28. *Mr Punch*, 152 and *passim*, brings out some of the tensions nicely.

29. P. Burke, *Popular Culture in Early Modern Europe* (1978), 286.

30. Everritt, *Southend*, 112.

31. M. Anderson, 'Smelser revisited', *Social History*, I (1976), 334, n. 59.

32. D. Fraser, *Urban Politics in Victorian England*, J. H. Treble, *Urban Poverty in Britain 1830–1914* (1978), and P. Joyce, *Work, Society and Politics: the Factory North of England 1860–90* (1980), are encouraging pointers towards the closely-related development of thematic studies across a range of urban experiences.

Index

artisans, skilled workers, 2, 10–11, 18–19, 25–6, 34–5, 38, 180

Working Men's Clubs, 29

Worthing, 12, 18, 49, 53–4, 56, 59–62, 65–8, 77, 81, 86, 96–7, 99–100, 109, 125, 132, 134, 140–1, 160, 162–3, 174, 218, 239 n.21

Yarmouth (Isle of Wight), 56, 65–6, 68

York, 8, 51

Yorkshire, 51, 59, 64, 67–8, 73, 81, 150, 197
East Riding, 19
North Riding, 40, 185
West Riding, 8–9, 15, 19, 28–30, 34–5, 59, 63, 178–9

zoning, social, 70, 105–6, 108–9, 117–20, 122, 124–5, 186, 190, 198, 200, 202, 208–10, 214, 225